TRIALS AND TRIUMPHS

FRONTISPIECE.
Over main entrance of Huntly Castle,
by Fenton Wyness.

TRIALS
AND
TRIUMPHS

*The Gordons of Huntly in
Sixteenth-Century Scotland*

ANNE L. FORBES

To my husband
for all his patient support

First published in Great Britain in 2012 by
John Donald, an imprint of Birlinn Ltd

West Newington House
10 Newington Road
Edinburgh
EH9 1QS

www.birlinn.co.uk

ISBN: 978 1 906566 52 4

The publishers gratefully acknowledge the support of the House of Gordon UK,
the House of Gordon USA, and the Strathmartine Trust
towards the publication of this book

British Library Cataloguing-in-Publication Data
A catalogue record for this book is available on request from the British Library

Typeset by Hewer Text UK Ltd, Edinburgh
Printed and bound in Britain by Bell & Bain Ltd, Glasgow

CONTENTS

Appendices

Foreword

GRANVILLE, 13TH MARQUIS OF HUNTLY

The first credible mention of the Gordons falls somewhere in the twelfth century. We learn from hazy and obscure records that we were playing a part in the affairs of the nation at that time – now some nine hundred years ago.

I am not an historian but I would suggest that two factors sustained us over the centuries – courage and perspicacity. From positions of enormous strength and influence we suffered national disgrace on more than one occasion but, variously, discovered the elusive formulae for restoring our fortunes.

In the early years, family survival will have called for adherence to the crown and heroism on the battlefield. More recently it will have surrounded managing issues of fiscal and social consequence, but a constant running in the blood will have been a flair for diplomacy and a gift for settling conflict.

Anne Forbes has chosen to write about perhaps the most romantic and tragic time in our long history. I am grateful to her for adding to our understanding of this most extraordinary period in this authoritative and absorbing work.

Aboyne Castle

Acknowledgements

I wish to thank the following people:

First, my husband, for his patience in putting up with the many hours, weeks and years of my preoccupation with the project, and for his critical help with the prose. Alexander Forbes of Druminnor Castle, an amateur historian who, at the early stages of my research, was incredibly generous with his singularly wide and detailed knowledge. This help from my husband and from Alex is all the more commendable in view of the Gordons' historical role as traditional enemies of the Forbeses!

Charles Jordan and Anthony Atha for their help on publishing matters; the members of the Huntly Writers Group, who were an invaluable sounding board and a great source of encouragement throughout, especially Maureen Ross (its Convenor) and Phyllis Goodhall, who both proofread the text; Barry Robertson, author of *Lordship and Power in the North of Scotland: The Noble House of Huntly 1603–1690* (2011) for generously sharing with me the benefit of his recent experience in bringing such a book to publication.

The trustees of the House of Gordon UK, the House of Gordon USA, and the Strathmartine Trust, for their generous contributions towards the book's publication.

The University of Aberdeen's Queen Mother Library (now the new University of Aberdeen Library) and its Special Collections Centre, where I consulted their excellent resources for most of my research.

Charles Burnett, Ross Herald Extraordinary, for much help on the subject of heraldry; Thomas Brotchard for transcribing John, Master of Forbes's divorce plea against Margaret Gordon; Alaistair Roberts, Michael Morrison and Fr Barnett SJ, for their help and encouragement regarding the chapter on the Jesuit James Gordon; Fiona Hill for her kind contribution towards the cover design. Finally, Mairi Sutherland of Birlinn, who has been at once professional, personal and encouraging throughout, as was the copy editor, Jacqueline Young.

ALF

List of Illustrations

Front Cover: 'The Palace of Strathbogie at the height of its glory', by Fenton Wyness

Illustration Acknowledgements

The illustrations listed below are reproduced by kind permission of the following organisations:

Diomedia: 10
The Heraldry Society of Scotland: 33
Lord Strathnaver, Dunrobin Castle: 28, 29
The Lyon Office: 34
The National Portrait Gallery, London: 6, 19, 22, 25
Private Collections: 9, 32
The Trustees of the Scottish National Gallery: 15
The Trustees of the National Library of Scotland: 1, 2, 3, 4, 7, 8, 14, 18
The Trustees of the Scottish National Portrait Gallery: 5, 16, 20, 21, 23, 24, 26, 27, 30, 31, 32
The University of Aberdeen: 13

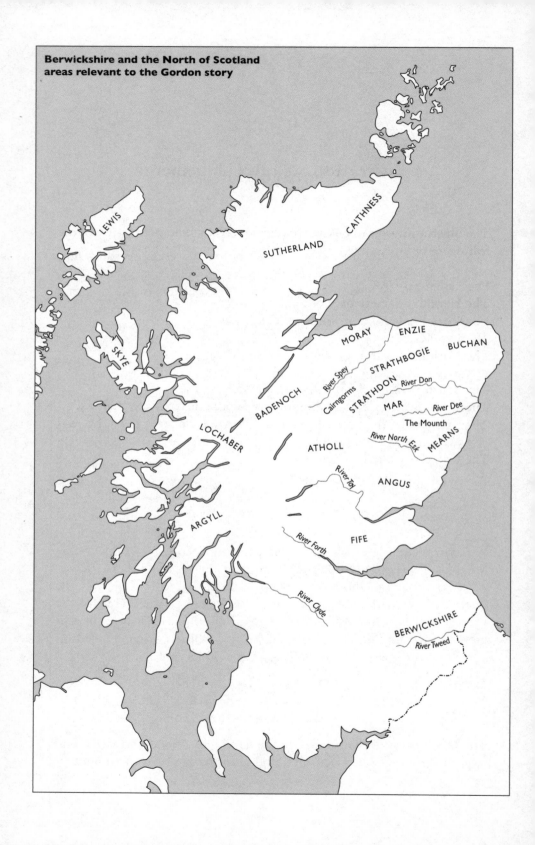

Berwickshire and the North of Scotland areas relevant to the Gordon story

LEWIS

SUTHERLAND

CAITHNESS

SKYE

MORAY

ENZIE

BUCHAN

River Spey

STRATHBOGIE

Cairngorms

STRATHDON

River Don

BADENOCH

STRATHDON

MAR

River Dee

LOCHABER

The Mounth

River North Esk

MEARNS

ATHOLL

River Tay

ANGUS

ARGYLL

River Forth

FIFE

River Clyde

BERWICKSHIRE

River Tweed

Introduction

THE RISE OF THE GORDONS

What follows is the story of a family – an immensely powerful family living through turbulent and still largely feudal times in sixteenth-century Scotland. The earls of Huntly were involved in most significant events of the time, and were often leading players. No other family's activities and aspirations had such an impact on Scottish politics, especially on the question of religion, and consequently at times they affected the politics of England, France and Spain. The Gordons reached their zenith of power in the person of the 4th Earl of Huntly, and here we see the history of the period through the parallel biographies of four of his sons and two of his daughters.

But first, we should look at the background they shared. Their family's main power base was Huntly Castle, which was often still called Strathbogie Castle, its original name. As they grew up, the children would have been told how the Gordons had long enjoyed a position of unchallenged supremacy in the north and nationally. But how did their family rise to such a position? No doubt they were told the story of their family's ascent.

An Italian monk at Pluscarden wrote an early history of the Gordons, which was used later as a historical source, although it is not totally reliable.[1] There is a town called Gourdon in Quercy in southern France, where a Viscount Gourdon lived who, paradoxically (in light of the history of the Catholic Scottish Gordons), made a safe retreat for the Protestants, under Henry of Navarre, during the French wars of religion.[2] There does not seem to be any proof that the original Gordons came over from France with William the Conqueror.

Earliest Mention of the Gordons in Scotland in the Time of William 'the Lion'

The first mention of Gordons holding land in Scotland was in the late twelfth century, in Berwickshire, and granting lands to the monks of

Kelso and the nuns of Coldstream. They had settled in the village and estates called Gordon, and gradually expanded to include the neighbouring barony of Huntly on their western border.[3] For the next two centuries Gordons carried out their responsibilities in the turbulent border region of Berwickshire as minor magnates. Successive generations are seen signing charters confirming lands to the nearby abbeys.

There is a family legend that a Gordon killed a boar that had destroyed and wasted the whole of the Merse in Berwickshire, and accordingly King Malcolm Canmore gave him the lands of Huntly and bestowed on the family the arms with three yellow boar heads, set in a blue field. However, the boar heads were first used by the Swintons, who also had a Berwickshire base, in the 1270s, and they were not employed by the Gordons (and several other families in the area) until much later. The Swintons trace their ancestors to tenth-century earls of Northumberland and, originally, the royal family of Northumbria (Beornicia). The Gordons may have been a cadet branch of that family. There was also a related branch of Gordons in Galloway, who became viscounts of Kenmure, but their name died out in the nineteenth century.[4]

The first Gordon of importance in this story is the Sir Adam Gordon of Berwickshire, who is first on record as having sworn fealty to Edward 1st at Elgin on 28 July 1296. He was one of ten commissioners elected at the General Council of the Scottish nation at Perth, invested with full parliamentary powers for the settlement of Scotland under the English king. In 1311 he was sent with the Earl of Athol and others by Edward II to make a truce with Scotland.[5]

Adam Gordon of Berwickshire Granted Land in Strathbogie by Robert I, c.1320

The big break for the Gordons of Berwickshire came as a result of changing loyalties during the Wars of Independence and Robert the Bruce's struggle to be accepted as King of Scotland. Adam Gordon of Huntly in Berwickshire, who had been on the English side for seventeen years, changed sides on the eve of Bannockburn to become a trusted supporter of Bruce. In 1320 Bruce granted him the lands of Strathbogie. It became available because the 10th Earl of Athol, David of Strathbogie, hereditary Constable of Scotland, had made the tactical error of turning against Bruce after he had murdered Red Comyn, Athol's father-in-law. Unfortunately for him, it was just before Bruce's greatest triumph at Bannockburn. Athol disappeared into England, where he was confirmed in the estate of Chilham in Kent, previously held by his family as a result of marriage to a daughter of King John.[6]

Adam Gordon may have been granted the barony of Strathbogie specifically for his role at that time of taking the famous document known as the Declaration of Arbroath to the Pope. It was signed by the major barons asking him to accept Bruce as the rightful King of an independent Scotland and to warn off the English.

However, the Gordons did not move north until over fifty years later, after the last of the Athol line had died out, when Adam Gordon's great-grandson, Sir John de Gordon, was re-granted the land by Robert II in 1376.[7] This was the year the Gordons arrived in the north to make Strathbogie the centre of their power base. It is thought that it was John de Gordon who built the tower house, the base of which can still be seen at Huntly Castle, with its immensely thick walls.

The move was a turning point in the family's fortunes. The extent of Gordon lands in the north expanded greatly over the next two centuries, particularly as a result of strategic marriages and their close relationship with successive monarchs, as will be seen below.

At first, in the late fourteenth century, the Gordon family married locally, within their own social group – as, for example, Sir John Gordon's union with Elizabeth Cruikshank of Aswanley. He was never legally married to her, but she bore him two sons, the controversial Jock and Tam (John of Essie, or Scardargue; and Tam o'Riven, or Thomas of Ruthven – now part of Cairnie). The two may have been the offspring of a handfast union, which in the Highlands would not have been considered illegitimate. Jock married Elizabeth, the daughter of Robert Maitland of Netherdale. Their offspring were the ancestors of the Gordons of Pitlurg, Lesmoir, Craig, Haddo and Buckie. Tam married, first, the sister of Sir Thomas Hay of Enzie, second, the daughter of Innes of Invermarkie, and third, the daughter of Chisholm of Strathglass. From them came many of the cadet branches of the Gordon family, as Thomas had sixteen sons (see Genealogy II, Chart 1).[8] However, Jock and Tam were dismissed as illegitimate.

Perhaps this was because their father's brother, who succeeded him, another Sir Adam Gordon, had made a much grander marriage to Elizabeth Keith of Aboyne, the daughter of Sir William Keith, Marischal of Scotland. Her mother was Margaret Fraser, who was heir to her uncle, Lord Fraser of Touch in Stirlingshire. His estate included not only the lands of Touch, but also the lordship of Aboyne, including Glentanner, and the Lordship and baronies of Cluny, with Midmar

and Tough in Aberdeenshire. This was the lion's share of the great
Deeside fief that had been granted by King Robert I to his sister and
her husband, Sir Alexander Fraser of Touch, who was his chamberlain.[9] It was through this marriage that the Gordons eventually gained
these extensive Fraser lands. However, Adam was killed in royal
service at the battle of Homildon in 1402, when the Scots were heavily
defeated by the English in Northumberland. Adam and Elizabeth's
offspring was a son named John (of whom little is known), who died
in 1407–8, and a daughter, Elizabeth, who succeeded him.[10]

Elizabeth Gordon Marries Alexander de Seton during the Reign of James I

The Regent Albany, who was Governor during the time that King
James I was retained in England, arranged another extremely significant marriage for the Gordons. This was for the heiress, Elizabeth
Gordon, to marry his trusted supporter, Alexander de Seton, younger
son of Sir William Seton, one of the most aristocratic and distinguished
families in Lothian.[11] On his marriage to Elizabeth, Alexander Seton
was confirmed in the Gordon lands in both Berwickshire and Strathbogie. This marriage was significant because it was he who ensured that
the vast Fraser properties passed to his mother-in-law, Elizabeth Keith.
However, it was not until the next generation, in 1437, that the son of
Alexander Seton and Elizabeth Gordon, Alexander Seton II, finally
obtained the Fraser inheritance, after the death of his grandmother,
Elizabeth Keith, and a long legal battle with her family.

Alexander Seton II Gains the Fraser and Tullybothwell Inheritance and is Created 1st Earl of Huntly in 1445 by James II

Through his first marriage to Egidia Hay, the Tullybothwell heiress (in
1426/7), Alexander Seton II gained the lordship of Enzie and the neighbouring Forest of Boyne in Banffshire, the baronies of Tullybothwell (now
Tullibole) in Perthshire, Kinmundy in Buchan, and Panbride in Angus.

Now that Alexander Seton II was such a landowner of note and thus
able to command so many men to his service, James II created him 1st
Earl of Huntly in 1445.[12] As befitted an earl, he built the great hall, or
'palace', across the courtyard from the original tower house at Strathbogie Castle.

Alexander Seton II, 1st Earl of Huntly, was the closest friend of James II and his most successful supporter in his claim to the earldom of Mar against that of Lord Erskine, and in the destruction of the rebellious Black Douglases in 1452. Huntly was rewarded for his support with grants of large sections of their earldoms – Kildrummy and Kindrochit in Mar, and Elgin and Darnaway in Moray – though not the earldoms themselves, which were now reserved for members of the royal family. James II also granted Huntly the old Comyn lordship of Badenoch (which included the Cairngorms) and Lochaber,[13] possibly because he had lent the King money.[14] This enormously expanded the area of his control westwards, right to the coast. Seton changed the family name to Gordon in 1458. He was present when the King was killed by the bursting of his own cannon in 1460.

The 1st Earl of Huntly's second wife was Elizabeth Crichton, daughter of Lord Crichton, who was Chancellor of Scotland. George, the first offspring of this marriage, inherited the earldom of Huntly. Their second son became Dean of Caithness and had several natural sons, including George Gordon of Beldorney, ancestor of the Gordons of Wardhouse; and a daughter, Elizabeth, who married Alexander Ogilvie of Deskford and Findlater.[15]

George Gordon, 2nd Earl of Huntly, Lieutenant of the North, Judiciar and Chancellor for James III

This vast Gordon inheritance was divided in two. The eldest son by the 1st Earl's marriage, to Egidia Hay, was also an Alexander Seton. He inherited his mother's baronies of Tullybothwell in Perthshire, Kinmundy in Buchan, and Panbride in Angus, as well as his father's Fraser lands of Touch in Stirlingshire, becoming the founder of the Setons of Touch. By agreement with his half-brother, George, Alexander Seton III was also granted the Berwickshire lands of Gordon, Huntly and Fogo and, in return, he granted George the forests of Enzie and Boyne from his own inheritance.[16] Enzie is significant, because the adjoining Bog of Gight (Fochabers) became the second most important Gordon base.

George, unlike his half brother, Alexander Seton III, adopted the Gordon as opposed to the Seton name. He succeeded to the earldom as the 2nd Earl of Huntly, and inherited the rest of his father's vast land holdings in the north. He married three times: first to Elizabeth Dunbar, widow of the Earl of Moray and 1st Countess of Moray in her own right – this looked like a good match with regard to the richly fertile lands of Moray, where his father had already gained a toehold with its caput of Darnaway and Elgin, but the marriage soon ended in divorce. Second, he married into royalty via a sister of James II, Annabella Stewart, whose forty-year engagement to the Duke of Savoy had been called off; that, too, ended in divorce (in 1471). Third, he married Elizabeth Hay, daughter of the 1st Earl of Errol. The Hays of Slains were of Norman origin and had been rewarded for their loyalty to Bruce with the earldom of Errol and the hereditary office of Lord High Constable of Scotland.[17] This marriage brought about an important family alliance between two rivals for power in the north-east.

James III appointed the 2nd Earl of Huntly Keeper of the castles of Kildrummy, Kindrochat and Inverness[18] and, in 1476, made him his Lieutenant of the North.[19] This office meant that the King depended on him to act as his representative, or deputy, a royal viceroy, keeping order in the north, including all of the Highlands and central regions. This would be for a given period, which was set out in the document appointing him. The office was particularly useful to the King if he was otherwise occupied – for example, if Scotland was at war with England. In addition to this, in 1488, the 2nd Earl was appointed Judiciar north of the Forth, along with the Earl of Crawford. Then, in 1497, to crown it all, he was appointed Chancellor of Scotland.[20] By the time that the 2nd Earl died, in 1501, the Gordons were clearly very much a power in the land,[21] with a giant patchwork of Gordon holdings across the whole of northern Scotland. Thus the 2nd Earl of Huntly had become the supreme unchallenged power in the north.

Alexander Gordon, 3rd Earl of Huntly, Lieutenant of the North for James IV

The 2nd Earl's son, Alexander Gordon, 3rd Earl of Huntly, was in great favour with King James IV, who often visited his castle of Strath-bogie. Huntly's half-sister, Margaret, known as 'the White Rose of Scotland', was married in Huntly Castle to Perkin Warbeck, who claimed to be the Duke of York, one of the princes murdered in the Tower of London. James IV had supported his claim to the English throne, which ended in failure.

Huntly was Keeper of the King's castles of Inverness and Aberdeen, and was now made hereditary sheriff of Inverness. He showed himself to be the King's most reliable general and was the obvious candidate to help him bring order to the Highlands and Islands, as his Lieutenant north of the Forth. Royal reward resulted in increased land holdings in the counties of Aberdeen, Banff, Perth and Berwick.[22] Alexander, 3rd Earl of Huntly, was witness to the contract for the King's marriage to Margaret Tudor, sister of Henry VIII, with its new treaty of 'perpetual peace' between the two countries. However, when England and France went to war, Scotland's 'auld alliance' with the latter proved the stronger.[23] Scotland invaded England and, at the battle of Flodden on 9 September 1513, it was the 3rd Earl of Huntly, as commander of a battalion, who alone vainly called the reserve to aid the King as he was hacked down amongst his troops. Ten thousand Scots died that day, and Huntly was the only earl who managed to gallop away with his life. The following earls all died in that battle: Montrose, Crawford, Argyll, Lennox, Glencairn, Caithness, Cassillis, Bothwell, Erroll, Athol and Rothes.[24] With the King dead, Huntly was appointed, in 1517–18, one of the Vice Regents and Lieutenant of all Scotland (except within Argyll's bounds).[25]

The 3rd Earl's younger brother, Adam Gordon, Lord of Aboyne, married the Countess of Sutherland, and by right of her became 10th Earl of Sutherland in 1515, after a protracted law case about the alleged insanity of her brother, the 9th Earl, and struggles with her illegitimate half-brother. Thus began the line of Gordon earls of Sutherland and the spread of Gordon influence even further north.

The 3rd Earl of Huntly negotiated a marriage between his eldest son, John Gordon, and Margaret Stewart, a natural daughter of King James IV and Margaret Drummond. John died seven years before his father, in 1517, but he had at least sired three sons, the eldest of which was George, who became the 4th Earl of Huntly. The second son, also an Alexander like his grandfather, became the Bishop of Galloway, titular Archbishop of Athens (the only bishop to join the reformers), and played a notable role in national affairs.

George Gordon, 4th Earl of Huntly, Lieutenant of the North, Chancellor for James V, the Regent Mary of Guise, and Mary Queen of Scots; Gained Lands in the Earldom of Mar and Moray, and Church Lands

George Gordon, 4th Earl of Huntly, was born in 1514 and was three years old when his father died. He succeeded his grandfather Alexander Gordon in 1524, when he was only ten years old. He was brought up at court, as ward of Margaret Tudor, widow of his grandfather, James IV. He was to wait on the young King James V, who was only two years older than him and also fatherless. They became boon companions. It was said that Huntly was 'a youth of so lovely a countenance and carriage, so quick and witty in jests and discourse that King James could hardly ever want him from his presence and conversation'.[26] In fact, the childhood bond between them created a trust and affection that James had for no other of his nobles.

In 1535, when Huntly was twenty-one, he was on the Privy Council, and King James V left him as one of several governors when he went to France to marry his first wife, Princess Madeleine. Trust and favour flowed together.[27] In 1529, Huntly was awarded the lordship of Braemar, Strathdee and Cromar – all lands in the temporarily defunct earldom of Mar, held by the Crown – along with the forest of Cluny.[28] James, in turn, borrowed 2,000 merks from his friend when the royal coffers ran dry.[29] George managed, with difficulty, to gain from his mother, Margaret Stewart, the forests of Enzie and Boyne (which had come to the family through the 1st Earl's marriage to Egidia Hay) together with the tower of Bog of Gight (Fochabers) in exchange for the life rent. This soon became the family's second most important base. He sold the Forest of Boyne to Ogilvie of Findlater.[30]

The 4th Earl distinguished himself as chief military commander in a victory against the English in the battle of Hadden Rig in August 1542. After the death of James V in November that same year, following the disastrous battle of Solway Moss, the 4th Earl became a member of the Council of Government for the infant Mary Queen of Scots.

Apart from all the lands he already had, the 4th Earl gained considerably from being given overlordship of Church lands. Cardinal Beaton, who was made Chancellor in 1543, granted him the lordship of Keig and Monymusk (from his Archbishopric of St Andrew's lands) and the lordship of Tarves (from his Abbey of Arbroath lands, of which he was Commendator).

Huntly's uncle, William Gordon, Bishop of Aberdeen, appointed him hereditary Baillie of the Bishopric of Aberdeen lands. This gave Huntly full power over all the property – not only the estates, but also the rights to enormous income from lands all over the bishopric, including the parishes of Old Machar; Clatt and Tullynessle; Birse; Oyne and Rayne; the baronies of Fetternear, Lethenty and Fingask; and Daviot. Previously, the lands had been let to farming tenants on nineteen-year terms, many of which had been renewed every nineteen years to the same family, such as the Forbeses, for centuries. These were called 'kindly tenancies'.

Instead of this arrangment, Huntly feued the lands hereditarily in return for a large capital sum. The new 'feuars' were aristocrats, mostly cadet Gordons, who could afford the investment needed. For example, part of Oyne and Rayne went to the Gordons of Newton and West-hall; the parish of Birse to Gordon of Cluny, and part of Tullynessle to Gordons of Terspersie, Knokespok, Tillyangus, Auchmenzie, Towie-Clatt, Tailzeauch and Auchlinn. Huntly tenanted Fetternear to Leslie of Balquhain, with the bishop's palace, along with some of Clatt and Tullynessle, and some of that to Lord Forbes. Some parishes were tenanted to various 'goodmen',[31] such as Lethenty and Fingask to the long-term resident Forbes of Pitsligo, and other parishes to Leslie of Warthall, Elphinstone of Glack, and Cruikshank of Tullymorgan.

The old farming tenants, such as the Forbeses, had by and large simply become nineteen-year farming tenants of the new 'feuars', or they were replaced by loyal Gordon supporters. This caused much resentment on the part of the Forbeses, and was a root cause of the long-running feud between the two families.

James V's widow, Mary of Guise, granted the 4th Earl of Huntly Braemar, hereditarily, which gave him and his heirs control of the whole of the upper Dee valley.[32] After Cardinal Beaton's assassination in 1546, the 4th Earl became Chancellor, as his great-grandfather, the 2nd Earl and his grandfather, the 3rd Earl, had been.

The 4th Earl favoured the marriage of the infant Queen Mary not to England's Prince Edward, but to the French Dauphin. In 1548, after Henry VIII's 'rough wooing' invasion of Scotland, the Privy Council sent young Mary to France, as a security measure. Huntly supported Mary of Guise in becoming Regent over the Governor, the Earl of Arran, who was made Duke of Chatelherault by the French king, as compensation.

In 1549, Mary of Guise, now Regent, gave Huntly the lands and administration of the earldoms of Mar and the much coveted earldom of Moray, for himself and his heirs. This was in reward for his faithful services to herself and to her deceased husband, James V, for adminis-tering justice and keeping the peace in the country while the King was away in France, as well as for defending the realm against the English, and for his support of her daughter's marriage to the Dauphin.[33] He was also made Sheriff of Elgin and Forres.[34]

The revenues of these lands, along with his post of Sheriff of Inver-ness and Aberdeen, added considerably to his wealth. In the autumn of 1550, he accompanied Mary of Guise when she went to France to visit her eight-year-old daughter, Mary Queen of Scots and prospective

wife of the French Dauphin. It was said that they took part in many
games and pastimes at the chateau of Blois.[35] There the French King
made Huntly and other Scots nobles, including the Earl of Sutherland,
Knights of the Honourable Order of St Michael, which was the first
order at that time in France. It had been bestowed on the Duke of
Chatelherault five years previously.

As a result of their massive land holdings, the Gordons had control
of an extensive following, which was most important in terms of pres-
tige in their locality. Over 150 families of the Gordon name were
established in the counties of Aberdeen and Banff. Not all were blood
kin or old feudal retainers, but had acquired the connection as a result
of alliances with local lairds round the nucleus of a powerful and
united clan group. As was common in the Scottish clans, many adopted
the name in order to demonstrate a spurious affinity and so elicit kin
protection in an area where the King was rarely present but the chief
frequently was.[36] Gordons attached other lesser people by bonds of
loyalty or manrent. Between 1440 and 1610 fifty-two non-Gordon
families were associated with the Gordons by blood or bond, which
gave the Gordons of Huntly a massive advantage in their dealings with
others, like the Forbeses and the Macintoshes, who were often associated with the Gordons by blood or bond.[37]

While the children of the 4th Earl of Huntly, who are the subjects of
this book, were growing up in the 1550s, they would have witnessed
the extensive modernisation of the palace block, built by the 1st Earl
of Huntly a hundred years earlier across the courtyard from the original tower house. They would have seen two storeys being added over
the great hall, making it much taller, and wings being added to the
north and east. This greatly increased the residential accommodation
and was more appropriate for their father, who was by far the most
important magnate in the north, with control over a vast expanse of
land stretching from Banffshire, through rural Aberdeenshire, to the
highland vastnesses of Badenoch and Lochaber to the west coast, and
northwards up through Moray to Sutherland. Apart from his palace of
Huntly, he had a string of other castles – in Bog of Gight (Fochabers),
Aboyne, Glenlivet and Badenoch – as well as houses in Elgin, Aberdeen and the Canongate in Edinburgh. Not only was their father
Sheriff of Aberdeen, Elgin, Forres and Inverness, but he held the
castles of Aberdeen and Inverness for the Crown and was Lieutenant
of the North, acting as the monarch's viceroy, adding enormously to
his area of control. As a result, the children would know that he could

command allegiance of a very large number of clan members and associated followers.

They would also be well aware that their father was closely connected to the Crown through his mother, Margaret Stewart, natural daughter of James IV, who had often stayed at Huntly Castle. He had grown up at Court as boon companion of the young King James V. Their father was, in fact, not only Chancellor, but also the second most important man in the whole of Scotland after the Duke of Chatelherault, heir apparent.

Thus it can be seen that the rise of Gordon power and wealth rose from a timely change of sides, then useful services to Robert the Bruce, followed by strategic marriages to heiresses, which greatly expanded their land holdings, as did the effort of Alexander Seton through the inheritance of his mother-in-law. Successive generations of Gordon earls had close personal relationships with their monarchs, and the expanse of their lands made them useful in terms of the number of men they could call to their service. They were therefore created earls and given office, then rewarded for service and loyalty with further lands and responsibilities. Religious affiliation and family connections led to the acquisition of Church lands. Through parcelling out parishes and baronies to cadet Gordons, as well as to Leslies and Forbeses, they expanded the number of men who owed them allegiance and rental income. All of this increased Gordon status and wealth, which reached its zenith in the person of George Gordon, 4th Earl of Huntly.

Now, on to the stories of his offspring: John, through whom Gordon control extended further to much of the Banffshire coast and the Cabrach, which joined up the Strathbogie and Strathavon lands; George, whose life was tied up so closely with that of Mary Queen of Scots; Adam, who fought for her in the north; Catholic Margaret and her two Forbes sons, who abandoned Scotland for a contemplative life in the Low Countries; Jean, an example of what women could achieve; and, finally, James the banned Jesuit.

I

John Gordon – Trials

On 26 March 1530, George Gordon, 4th Earl of Huntly married Elizabeth Keith, sister of William, 4th Earl Marischal. She and George had nine sons and three daughters. This is the story of four of their sons and two of their daughters, all chosen because of their particularly interesting lives and the light they shed on their time.

While they were growing up, their home of Huntly Castle was being greatly extended, with added height and two new wings, as befitted someone of such importance in the land as their father. The castle was sumptuously furnished, and was even thought to shame the royal palaces. The modern part had beds furnished with silk, velvet and gold-embroidered coverings, and had yellow, crimson, blue, green and violet curtains. People not only slept in the bedchamber but ate and talked there too, so they had tables (known as boards) covered with velvet 'board cloths' trimmed to match the beds. In the hall, Huntly met his guests like a king, enthroned on a seat surmounted by a cloth of state in crimson satin embroidered with gold. A cloth of state is a rich textile arranged as a canopy or backdrop behind a throne or dais. For seating others, there were benches and many coloured velvet cushions. There were hangings on the walls, one of gilt leather and another a fine Flemish tapestry in five pieces 'maid in the figures of birdis and greit leiffis of treiss'.[1]

The first story is about John, the third son, because it concerns events that were chronologically the earliest, and because he was the first to die. He was described as 'a bold cavalier' and 'the handsomest man in Scotland'.[2]

The significant happening in John's life concerned Alexander Ogilvie of Findlater and Deskford, Alexander's second wife Elizabeth Gordon, and James Ogilvie of Cardell, his son by his first wife. Elizabeth Gordon was related to the Gordons of Huntly: George Gordon of Beldorney was her brother. Their father, the Gordon Dean of Caithness, was the son of the 1st Earl of Huntly. The Ogilvies were frequent visitors to Huntly Castle, as they were 'on terms of close amity with the Huntly family'.[3]

Elizabeth Gordon 'caused her husband to have a hostile attitude towards his son', telling him that her stepson, James Ogilvie, had 'solicited her to dishonesty, not only with himself but also other men' and had planned 'to put his father in a dark house and keep him awake till he became starke madde, then to take possession of his land and house'.[4]

It appears that Alexander Ogilvie was beholden to John's father, the Earl of Huntly, for 'alleged reasons of favour shown him', and Ogilvie had developed an affection for young John, who could not have been more than about thirteen at the most. On 20 July 1545, a contract was drawn up between old Ogilvie and John's father, the 4th Earl of Huntly, by which young John would, in future, bear the name and arms of Ogilvie and be granted the lands and baronies of Findlater, Deskford, Keithmore and Auchindoun, with their castles, mills, fishings and forests, belonging to him, in Banffshire and Aberdeenshire. This was on condition that 'in all time coming, he bore the name and arms of Ogilvie', but reserving his own and his wife's life rent.[5] John was also to 'render certain services to him'. It is not clear what these were. As a result, John must have henceforth taken the name of Ogilvie, because there is a charter of Ogilvie lands for his benefit dated ten months later, in which he is named as 'John Ogilvie, formerly Gordon, laird of fee of Ogilvie of Fynlettir, 3rd son of George Earl of Huntly'.[6] 'Laird of fee' means that he was the heir of Ogilvie of Findlater.

The charter shows the enormous extent of Alexander Ogilvie's hostility towards his own son, because it states that if John died without issue, the title and barony would pass not to his own or to the wider family of Ogilvies, but instead to several of John's younger brothers; and not until failing them would the lands pass back to other branches of the Ogilvie clan. Thus Alexander's own Ogilvie blood line, through his only son and heirs, were completely cut out of the inheritance.

The question here is whether the powerful and influential Earl of Huntly manipulated old Ogilvie, who seems to have been beholden to him – perhaps financially? Did John's father manipulate John to use his attractiveness, even at this young age, for Gordon gain? Acquiring Findlater and Auchindoun estates was to huge advantage for the Gordons, because it joined up the Gordon Strathbogie and Strathavon lands, giving them vast swathes of undivided territory and more of

Banffshire, including the constabulary of Cullen, so they would effectively control that county.[7]

John was the third son, and he gained enormous personal advantage from this contract. He obtained a new title and large estates from which to draw income, though the rents would still be in the hands of Alexander and Elizabeth.

On 10 September 1547, Huntly was away fighting the English, in his gilt and enamelled armour, for James V at the battle of Pinkie. However, he was captured and imprisoned in England for more than a year as surety for his fellow prisoners. He asked permission for his wife and children to visit him, but he was told that wasn't possible until the war was over. However, he was brought north to Morpeth, which was only twenty-four miles from the Scottish border, with the understanding that he would go back to Scotland to further the cause of the marriage of the infant Mary to Henry VIII's only son, Prince Edward. His wife and sons were to take his place, to guarantee his return. However, he managed to dupe the guards during a game of cards and escaped with the help of George Kerr of Heton, who had brought two fast horses.[8] He received a warm welcome from one and all when he arrived in Edinburgh on Christmas Eve, and the Regent, Mary of Guise, restored him as her Chancellor. After he accompanied her to France in 1550, to visit her eight-year-old daughter Mary, most of the party landed at Portsmouth and travelled back to Scotland through England. But Huntly took another route, because he feared capture as a result of the subterfuge involved in his escape from Morpeth.[9]

At first, the disinherited James Ogilvie could do nothing during his father's lifetime but remain a passive spectator of events. However, he received the full sympathy of his neighbours and clan. In 1552, Mary of Guise, who was said to love justice, agreed that he had been 'evill done to' by his father and she 'was movit of zeile and pitie to his help'. This gave James Ogilvie an opportunity to attempt to recover possession of his father's estate.[10] Mary persuaded James, John Gordon, and John's father, the 4th Earl of Huntly, to submit the issue to the arbitration of judges. If the result was discord, the case was to be decided by herself.

This is evidently what happened, because in the end the whole controversy was referred back to her. She ordered John to transfer all of his right and title to the grieved James Ogilvie, and to assign the ward of the property to him. This was registered as a decree of the Lords of Council, and was even ratified by John 'after his perfect age' (twenty-one). He was commanded to fulfil the decree, but disobeyed.[11] Here we have the first of his many acts of defiance against the Crown. However, was it fair of the Regent to try to reverse a contract by which a man had made his own decision on who should inherit? Was that his right? Or should a property automatically go to an eldest son, whatever his father thought of him? Could we say that the Regent, Mary of Guise, was to blame for the consequences of trying to force John to give up title and lands freely bequeathed to him?

In 1553, John's eldest brother Alexander, heir to the Huntly earldom and the vast areas of Gordon control, tragically died, not long after his prestigious marriage to the eldest daughter of the Duke of Chatelherault, heir presumptive to the Scottish throne.[12] Brother George became the new heir to the Huntly earldom, followed by John.

In July of the following year, 1554, old Alexander Ogilvie died. John, who was continuing to disobey the Regent's order, promptly married Alexander's widow, Elizabeth. Was it a genuine marriage or a 'pretendit marriage', as described by John Knox later, contracted just to take over the lands, whose rents Elizabeth held for her lifetime? It looks as if this was the case, because after only a month of marriage to Elizabeth, the handsome John 'casteth his fantasie unto another, but could not leave her as he would lose the inheritance'. Randolph, the English ambassador, writing later to William Cecil, Queen Elizabeth's Chief Secretary of State, said that John 'could not secure from her for him all the lands he wanted, so he both discarded her as a mistress and disowned her as his wife, and shut her up in a close chamber' in the impregnable Findlater Castle on the coast – 'where she yet remaynethe', said Randolph 'and for her deliverance there is much controversy in the country and one of the chief causes for his enterprising is his fear to be forced to put her to liberty and forego the land while she lives'.[13] It is ironic that Elizabeth Gordon's fate was the same as the one she had accused her stepson of threatening for his father. It is from Randolph, in his letters to Cecil, that we get the most vivid accounts of the dramatic events in John's life.

Meanwhile, the family had a brief crisis when their father was temporarily out of favour with the Regent for failing to subdue a rebellion raised by Ronald Moydart in the west. He was removed as her Chancellor and, in 1555, kept in Edinburgh Castle for a while. Eventually he agreed to pay the Regent large sums of money, renouncing all the tacks (leases of land[14]) that he had of the earldom of Moray, Rothes and Orkney and returning them to her.[15] With this concession and the intervention of his friends, he regained his freedom and was restored to his former positions and responsibilities.

Was John part of the reception held for the Queen–Regent at Huntly Castle, the following year, 1556, or was he skulking in the background? One thousand men formed the guard of honour at this event, and she was treated to entertainment after entertainment, interspersed with games and other amusements. She was amazed at the castle's opulence and the Earl's lavish hospitality. After staying some time, she offered to leave in order to spare Huntly further straining his resources. Did John hear his father assuring her that the display was well within his means, as fresh supplies came in from all parts of his estates every day? Did he accompany his father when he took the French ambassador, d'Oysel, on a tour of his cellars and storehouses, full of provisions of all kinds, including much grain and venison? And did he, perhaps, overhear the ambassador remarking to the Regent that Huntly needed his wings clipped, as his power so far exceeded that of his equals that he might become too arrogant for so small a kingdom, and thus make even a monarch apprehensive?[16]

Mary had not forgotten the issue of the Ogilvie inheritance, especially as James Ogilvie was one of her faithful supporters. In May of that year she issued a compromise decree-arbitral, by which John would keep a liberal portion of the barony but would have to give up the rest to James. John again defied her. The Gordons were unwilling to lose any of the barony and James Ogilvie was determined to recover it all, so neither side would abide by the ruling.[17]

Despite this defiance, John saw the Regent make his father Lieutenant General of the Kingdom in 1557.[18] The following year, there were two important marriages in the family: his now eldest brother, George, married the third daughter of the Duke of Chatelherault; and his younger sister Margaret married John, Master of Forbes.

The family had to face the unsettling religious and nationalist revolutions taking place at the time, which were bringing in the new, Reformed faith of John Calvin and driving out the French brought to Scotland by the Regent. At first John's father supported Mary of Guise and was one of her negotiators with the Lords of the Congregation, who were the leaders of the Protestant Revolution. However, the evidence of French domination was an affront to national sentiment, and Huntly found himself being sidelined by the Regent's French advisers, particularly her Vice Chancellor, de Robay.[19] During 1560, as events favoured the Reformers, he began to sit on the fence. In April that year, when the Lords of the Congregation were sure of English help, and after much hesitation, he finally signed the Band of Leith. This was 'a fresh bond' drawn up at the end of April and the beginning of May, and signed by those committed to 'the reformation of religion and the end of French domination, but proferring future obedience to the lawful sovereigns.' It 'was signed by about a dozen peers, some sons of peers, and about thirty lairds'.[20] 'Among the signatories was Huntly, who had previously been 'hesitant'.[21] He excused the cause of his tardiness as being the extreme conservatism of his people in the north. His ability to look after his own interests caused the English ambassador, Randolph, to say that 'no man would trust him in word or deed'. No doubt this view of him originated in the ruse he had employed for his escape from Morpeth. Mary of Guise died in Edinburgh Castle on 11 June 1560.

Meanwhile, her daughter, Mary Queen of Scots, also lost her young husband, Francis II. She was no longer welcome in France, especially by her mother-in-law, the dowager, Catherine de Medici. She prepared to return to her other kingdom of Scotland. However, she had a mandate from her powerful Guise uncles to regard this as merely a stepping stone to the more desirable throne of England.

Huntly and his wife turned Huntly Castle into a Catholic stronghold, a repository for church treasures from St Machar's Cathedral in Old Aberdeen, brought there for safety lest they fall into the Reformers' clutches. There were gold and silver vessels, statues, candlesticks, altar cloths and vestments. The silver plate alone weighed more than 140 pounds. Among the treasures was the silken tent which Robert the Bruce had captured from the English King, Edward II, and given to St Machar's.

The Lords of the Congregation thought that the 4th Earl had been bought off with a share of the monastic lands but, by the end of 1560, it was said that he had reinstituted the mass in the north.[22] He determined to be a leader in a great contest for a return to the old faith. He sent an envoy, the Bishop of Ross, John Leslie, to France to suggest that Mary land at Aberdeen. There Huntly, and no doubt his sons, would meet her with a large force to begin the return of Scotland to the Catholic fold under its Catholic queen. It was rumoured that Huntly had informed Mary that he could easily reinstitute the mass in three counties.

However, it seems that Mary's Protestant half-brother, Lord James Stewart, may have heard about the Earl's plot while he was visiting his sister in France.[23] As leader of the Lords of the Congregation, the current rulers of the country, he was the obvious choice to be her principal adviser. He had the support of the reformed church, the aristocracy and the towns, as well as the trust of Queen Elizabeth, whom Mary wished above all else to impress if she was to be named as her heir. For Mary, and her Guise relatives in France, this was to be the chief aim of her reign.

Queen Mary's Arrival in Scotland

A new era began in Scotland in 1560. First, the government (which Huntly did not attend) passed the revolutionary Treaty of Edinburgh, which ratified the Reformed Confession of Faith, abolished the jurisdiction of the Pope in Scotland, and made the saying of mass and attendance a serious offence. Then, on 20 August, the young Catholic Queen, who had refused to ratify the Confession of Faith, arrived from France.

John Gordon must have been in favour with the Queen at the start of 1562 – that fateful year for himself and his family – because in February she knighted him, along with nine others. His official title now was Sir John Ogilvie of Deskford,[24] which acknowledges his hold of at least that part of the Ogilvie barony. The event was part of the celebrations for the marriage of her half-brother, James Stewart, to John's first cousin, Agnes Keith, whom Stewart had been courting for some time. She was the daughter of John's uncle William, 4th Earl Marischal, brother of John's mother, Elizabeth Keith, the Countess of Huntly. Like her, Moray's new wife was a forceful and shrewd lady. The marriage was a family affair, so John must have been there, along with the rest of the nobility in St Giles', where the Protestant marriage was performed by John Knox. If the Catholics among them were offended, they must at least have joined in the banquet at the Palace of Holyroodhouse attended by Queen Mary, and the general festivities that followed, which probably involved jousting and horse racing, as well as the sending of fire balls.

The day before the wedding, the Queen, as a wedding present, secretly conferred on Lord James the title and possession of the earldom of Moray, which was held by John's father and was extremely important to him. For the moment, he was ennobled as Earl of Mar until the gift of the Moray earldom could be made effectual by the actual transfer of the estates from the retentive grasp of Huntly, who was not expected to peacefully surrender them.[25] James Stewart was already entitled Commendator of St Andrew's. Although he was still Chancellor, John's father was now being sidelined again, this time by the partnership of Lord James and Maitland of Lethington, who was Mary's secretary. Mary relied on their counsel in all she did.

John must have been much at Court because, in April, the Duke of Chatelherault's eldest son, the Earl of Arran, who had been a contender for Mary's hand, collapsed and 'went off his head' because, it was said, of a passionate love of Mary and jealousy of John, thinking that 'she paid more attention to John than to himself'.

That spring John was again challenged in his possession of the Ogilvie title and baronies by the still grieved James Ogilvie. He was a master of Queen Mary's household in France and, now back in Scotland, was beginning a serious effort to regain his estates by legal means in the Court of Session. At the end of June, two days before the case was to come to court, John met James Ogilvie's cousin and clan chief, Lord James Ogilvie of Airlie, in the streets of Edinburgh. They got into a serious fight – no doubt over the wrongs done to his disinherited cousin, and John's refusal to compromise. Many blows were given and taken 'and many were hurt', according to John's nephew, Robert Gordon of Gordonstoun, writing about it later.[26] During the fight John wounded Lord James Ogilvie so badly that he lost his right arm, and nearly his life.[27] He recovered, but the incident brought the Queen's attention to the wrong done to James Ogilvie by her new knight, Sir John Ogilvie of Deskford. John was apprehended by the magistrates in Edinburgh. Lord James Stewart hastened from Stirling to take advantage of the situation, and directed that John be put under pressure while he awaited trial. But Scottish prisons were 'ever notorious for their unretentiveness of prisoners of his rank',[28] and John's 'volatile temper could not long endure the incarceration of prison'.[29] After twenty days, he escaped and fled north to the safety of his father's domain.[30] It was rumoured that he had escaped at his father's instigation, as he was making preparations for the Queen coming north.[31] John refused to surrender himself.

Mary had very much hoped that she would be able to meet Queen Elizabeth, despite Huntly's opposition – he favoured Scotland's French alliance rather than English. Maitland of Lethington had returned from England, triumphant that a meeting between the two queens had been agreed. Disappointingly for Mary, Elizabeth now cancelled it because of a crisis concerning the Huguenots in France, who needed English help.

However, Mary could now fulfil her other desire, to make a

northern progress. She set off from the Palace of Holyroodhouse in August 1562. Lord James, now Earl of Mar, her secretary Maitland of Lethington, and the English ambassador Randolph accompanied her, as well as the disinherited James Ogilvie of Cardell, as master of her household. Her main purpose was to reduce Huntly and his son to obedience and put Lord James in possession of the earldom of Moray.[32]

The royal party progressed north via Stirling, Coupar Angus, Perth and Glamis. While Mary was en route, she received a message from the Pope and her Guise uncles reiterating that her best course of action for restoring the old religion was to 'entertain well Huntly, as the man of greatest power in Scotland, with a fallacious hope of marriage between his son and her'. What is more, they indicated that money would be available but, as a prelude, she should 'cut off' those reckoned the greatest enemies of the Catholic faith, especially Lord James. Mary foolishly showed the letters to Lord James, to demonstrate her good faith, because she feared that he might have heard about the contents from other sources.[33] It must then have been a simple matter for him to work on her credulity and make her believe that Huntly and his son John had traitorous designs on both himself and her.[34] This was probably the main source of all that befell Huntly and his family in the days ahead. Mary exploited the situation by asking the Pope for money to 'sustain her pomp and prodigality'.[35]

The Queen in the North-East

John received a message from the Queen ordering him to appear before the Justice and his deputies in the Aberdeen Tolbooth by the last day of August, to answer for the 'mutilation of my lord Ogilvie'.[36]

When Mary and her entourage arrived in Aberdeen, on 27 August 1562, Randolph and Maitland of Lethington had to share the same bed in Old Aberdeen, because of a shortage of sleeping places.[37] She paid a visit to the university which, as Randolph reported to Cecil, had one college in 'Olde Aberdine' with about sixteen scholars. She then held court in the Bishop's Palace. Although Huntly was still her Chancellor and much else besides, she refused to see him. He was definitely out of favour, something that was noticed by Randolph, who sent frequent reports back to Cecil in England. Huntly was under a cloud, not only because of his son John's refusal to give himself up, but also because he had opposed Queen Mary's pro-English stance and her attempts to meet Queen Elizabeth. He had also made complaints that she had done nothing to ease the life of Catholics in the country. Randolph reported that she 'has had a long time to mislike Huntly and his doings in the country, his extortions being so great and disobedience such as no longer to be borne'.[38]

John's redoubtable and outspoken mother, Elizabeth Keith, arrived with a great entourage in order to beg the Queen to overlook her son's misdemeanours, blaming his youthfulness. Mary replied that her authority had been impaired and, unless John submitted himself to await her judgment, he could not be reconciled with her.[39] She also refused the Countess's pleas to honour them with a visit to Huntly Castle, where massive preparations had been made to receive her.

On 31 August John arrived in Aberdeen, but he was accompanied by 1,000 followers instead of the 100 that were permitted. However, he was ready to present himself before the Queen at a court of justice in the Tolbooth. The record refers to him as 'Sir John Gordoun of Deskford, Knight', saying that 'he compeared in the Court on the charge of contempt and disobedience, committed in breaking the Queen's ward – nominal imprisonment – and leaving Edinburgh's Tolbooth, where he was warded for the cruell onsetting of James Lord Ogilvie, and mutilating him of his rycht arme, and utheris crymes'.[40]

He was ordered to be conveyed by the Deputy Sheriff to the Provost of Aberdeen's lodging, and there to remain 'under pain of rebellion and horning, pending her instructions on where he was to be warded until she could pass judgment on him'.[41] To be 'horned' meant that he would be declared an outlaw by three blows of the horn at the market crosses in the main towns of the country. On 1 September 'ane officer of armes' arrived with the Queen's instructions that, before a pardon could be contemplated, he must return to Stirling Castle within seven days, on pain of treason, but, even then, pardon was not certain. Here he had plenty of warning of the consequences of defiance.

When Mary came within sight of Huntly Castle she turned away, not even taking advantage of the chapel with its vestments all set out and prepared for her to hear mass. Such public snubbing of her Chancellor, by far the most important man in the north, must have been humiliating for the whole family. Instead, she chose to go via Balvenie to Inverness.[42] However, Maitland of Lethington and Randolph were both accommodated in Huntly Castle. Randolph reported to Cecil that the Queen would not go to Huntly's house 'though it be within three miles of her way, and the fayer best furnished of any house I have seen in this country, his cher is marvellous great'. Interestingly, he also noted that Huntly's mind was 'such as it appeared to us, as ought to be in any subject to his sovereign'.⁴³ The Queen also stayed at Balquhain, home of William Leslie, one of Huntly's friends, and at the Rothiemay, home of Lord Saltoun. She then went on to Elgin, described by Randolph as 'a fair and famous market town'. This was followed by two days at Kinloss Abbey.⁴⁴

Meanwhile, John escaped for a second time, taking the risk of being accused of treason and being put to the horn. He was obviously more fearful of being incarcerated in the mighty Stirling Castle, especially as it was in the charge of Lord James' uncle, Lord Erskine. Instead, John followed Mary's progress north like a stalker, with 'certain other inobedient people', a thousand of them, lurking in the woods. She was enraged at his defiance, realising what a bad example it was setting. Added to that, she was also being told 'of the many grievous complaints of the poor people of this country, oppressed by them in the past, and fearing the like to be done in the future'.⁴⁵

Randolph reported to Cecil that there was 'malicious gossip abroad as to the relations between Ogilvie's father and his son'. He also declared: 'The true origin of the evil was the infatuation of the step-mother for John Gordon, her second husband'.⁴⁶ It was at this point that those accompanying Mary became convinced that John was following the Queen with the intention of abducting her, being confident of his powers of physical attraction to bring about a marriage between the Queen and himself.⁴⁷ There were real fears of a Catholic coup and the intention of getting rid of Mary's Protestant chief advisers, Lord James Stewart – now Earl of Mar – Maitland of Lethington and the Earl of Morton. Randolph complained that the journey was 'cumbersome, paynefull and mervileus longe, the wether extreame fowle and cold, victuals merveleus dere and the corne that is never like to come to rypenes'.⁴⁸

On 9 September, Mary and her entourage arrived at Darnaway, 'a castle of the kings, celebrated, and of great renown'.⁴⁹ 'Very ruinous', complained Randolph, except for the hall (begun in about 1450), which he described as 'fair and large, able to house one thousand armed men'.⁵⁰ There, at last, the Queen publicly announced that Lord James had been granted the earldom of Moray, rather than that of Mar, which he had resigned following complaints from his uncle, Lord Erskine, Keeper of Stirling Castle, who considered it rightfully his. The title had probably always been meant as an interim award, lending Lord James status until his Moray earldom could be made public.

Giving the earldom of Moray to Lord James added insult to injury for Huntly, and was the real source of his resentment. He had been administering the earldom, held in feu, since 1549. It had been granted by Mary of Guise for 'service to Mary's father (James V) in peace and war, for maintaining peace throughout Scotland as Regent and Lieutenant General while the King was in France and, since then for service to the Queen and Regent in defending the kingdom against the English, and as Lieutenant of the North, administering justice firmly and maintaining the royal authority there'.[51]

It is clear how much Huntly stood to lose, if you read the actual words of the grant:

> To George, Earl of Huntly, Lord Gordon and Badynauch, Chancellor and Lieutenant of the North and Knight of the order of St. Michael and his heirs, he was granted the lands and earldom of Moray with its appendices, the burgh rents and customs of Elgin and Forres, the castle of Darnaway with its forest and park and all other castles, towers and fortalices, the fishings of the Spey, Slewpule, Lossie and Findhorn, the customs of those waters, with the tenances, advocation of churches, chapels and hospitals in the shire of Elgin and Forres, the office of sheriff of said shire with its fees, the lands and lordship of Abernethy with the castle etc., advocation of the prebend and rectory of Duthell, the lands and barony of Pettye, Brachlie and Stratherne with the castle of Hallhill, the mains etc all incorporated in the free earldom and barony of Moray, caput Darnaway, to be held with privilege of free forest where there are woods.[52]

All this had made Huntly more omnipotent in the north and, with his offices of Chancellor and Lieutenant, by far the most powerful man in the country. He had not actually been made Earl of Moray, as he was Earl of Huntly, but it was a permanent grant and, what is more, it was hereditary. Mary of Guise had removed it at one point – probably part of her attempt to clip his wings, as advocated by her Ambassador – but he had held it sporadically. It was a very major loss for Huntly and his heirs.

Randolph said 'men hope that Murray will do much good in the country. His power of men is great'. He added: 'His pleasant place has been under Huntly's government and being given away from him, he has lost great commonality and profit, making him more offended.'[53] This is a perceptive view of the situation, and clearly reveals the source of Huntly's antagonism towards Moray and his towering ambition.

Randolph now reported that Huntly's aim was to cut off Moray and Maitland 'whose credit, he thinks, so great with her [Mary] that he could not prevail in anything he aspired to, or to have had a pension of some abbey that he might be better able to attend Court and bare charges in her service'. Huntly was obviously concerned about the loss to his finances and the need for compensation, such as the benefice of an abbey, to help him finance future appearances at Court.

At Darnaway, the Queen held a meeting of her Privy Council.[54] The events concerning John Gordon were meticulously gone over, from why he was imprisoned in Edinburgh – his wounding of Lord James Ogilvie – to how he had contemptuously disobeyed orders and therefore incurred the charge of treason, as well as his actions in assembling other disobedient people, endangering the peace of the country. He set a very bad example. He should not be allowed to hold fortified houses or fortresses, and so the Gordons must return the castles of Findlater and Auchindoun to the Crown.[55]

Mary sent heralds and messengers to seek John out and

in her Hienes's name and authority command and charge the said John Gordoun and Lady Finlater, his pretendit spouse, to deliver the houses and fortresses of Findlater and Auchindoun and other of them to her Grace's officer. The executor of this charge to whom she charges the commission, to remove them, their servants and all others, so they may be visited at the Queen's pleasure within twenty-four hours after they be charged, under pane of treason and the process of forfeiture shall be led against them according to the Acts of Parliament, law and practice of this realm.[56]

It is not only John who must return the castles or be forfeited – it is now 'they'. This was even more serious. The process of forfeiture meant that all of a person's property, land and cash were confiscated by the Crown. In the worst cases, individuals might also forfeit their liberty, and even their lives.

The Queen reached Inverness on 11 September. The royal castle was held by Alexander Gordon of Bothrom, who was officially under the command of Huntly's eldest son George, Lord Gordon, although he was not present. Despite the Queen's herald ordering Alexander to surrender the castle he refused, because he had not received such an order from Lord Gordon.[57] As a result, the Queen had the indignity of spending the night in private lodgings in Bridge Street. Next day, permission arrived from Huntly for Alexander to open the gates. However, he, as keeper of the castle, and the whole garrison, were condemned to death for treason. At the last minute the men of the garrison were reprieved, but Alexander was hanged over the battlements and his severed head exhibited on the town bridge as an example to all.[58] He was given no chance to defend himself at a trial.

The Queen and her entourage spent five days in Inverness. All this time Huntly was excusing his own part in the behaviour of his son, and 'would have it thought that it came rather through the youth and evil behaviour of his sons than his will', but the Queen remained 'highly offended by him'.[59] John's elder brother George, Lord Gordon, arrived in Inverness with many friends, but the friends began abandoning the Gordons 'when they understood their purpose', and came to Queen Mary's side. What was their purpose?

Randolph gathered that Huntly's anger was wholly directed at those whose influence was so strong with the Queen: that is, Moray and Lethington. It was thought that Huntly planned to waylay the Queen, because 'he took it ill his son was commanded to prison, the captain of Inverness hanged, and others imprisoned'.[60] Rumours went round that 'if he intends anything, it will be on her Grace passing the Spey, which she does next Sunday, 20th September'.[61] This crossing was to be near the Gordon second most important base at Bog of Gight (now Fochabers).

Mary now sent for experienced soldiers, including the renowned Kirkcaldy of Grange, Cockburn of Ormiston, and 120 harquebusiers, with some cannon.[62] They were to be brought to Aberdeen from Stirling, Fife and Angus in the Mearns by 5 October, and to be ready to remain with her for twenty days.[63] Was all this just to defend her, or was more serious action being prepared for?

Meanwhile, scouts were sent out to check the surrounding countryside. Some came back saying they had seen about 1,000 men lurking in the woods, and others returned saying they had seen no one. About 2,000 of 'those they caule har Hylande men' came to join the Queen. It was said that Huntly had committed men to his son, and it was excitedly reported that 'there could have been a big battle in front of the Queen and her ladies'. 'At Aberdeen she will take advice and teach them how to welcome their prince in time to come.'[64]

Mary obviously found the situation and these many Highlanders coming to her aid extremely stimulating, as Randolph reported that he 'never saw her merrier, never dismayed, nor never thought that stomache to be in her that I find'.[65] In fact, she said she regretted that she was not a man, so that she could know 'what it was like to lie all night in the fields, and to walk on the causeway with a jack and knapsack, a Glasgow buckler and a broadsword'.[66] She was certainly a feisty lady.

The Return Journey

On 15 September Mary and her entourage set out from Inverness, accompanied by 3,000 men, to return to Aberdeen. They stopped for the night at Kilvarock, again at Darnaway, and at the Bishop of Moray's palace of Spynie beside Spynie Loch outside Elgin. She safely recrossed the Spey at Fochabers without incident.[67] She sent a trumpeter to John Gordon's Findlater Castle stronghold on the coast, near Cullen, to demand its surrender, but there was no response. Without cannon the party could not enforce the order, so they left, proceeding to Aberdeen via Banff Castle and Gight, home of a Gordon.[68]

On 22 September, Mary arrived in Aberdeen to 'a rapturous welcome'. The following day she made her public entry into the new town. She was presented with 'a cup of silver in double gilt, well wrought with five hundred crowns in it. Wine, coal and wax candles were also delivered'.[69] She was entertained with plays and spectacles, and expressed a determination to stay at least forty days, to 'put the country in quiet'.[70] She announced that Huntly must either submit himself or deliver his disobedient son 'in whose name all these problems have been wrought', Randolph claimed 'or she would utterly use all force against him for subverting of his line for ever'.[71] She also sent a message to Huntly to surrender his own cannon, kept in the basement of Huntly Castle.[72]

The future prospects were looking serious for John and his father. Huntly was unsure what to do. He sent his eldest son, George, south to consult his father-in-law, the Duke of Chatelherault. John Knox maintained that George was trying to raise rebellion in the south with the help of the notorious James Hepburn, Earl of Bothwell, who had himself recently escaped from his imprisonment in Edinburgh Castle. Earlier, he had intercepted money sent by England to the Lords of the

Congregation, and had also been suspected of plotting to abduct the Queen.[73]

The Queen's messenger, Captain Hay, arrived at Huntly Castle to demand Huntly's assurance that his son would deliver Findlater and Auchindoun castles, and that the cannon kept in the cellar would be dismantled and carried four miles from the castle, to an appointed place. Huntly was effusive in his protestations of loyalty, offering not only his body, but his goods. He even offered to besiege Findlater and Auchindoun himself, if the Queen so commanded him, or to join Mary's force, if he could bring his own men. He again insisted that he was not a party to his son's transgressions, complaining that 'it was strange to be so hardly dealt with' for his son's offences, to which he was 'never privy or could correct'. He said that the cannon could not be moved in time to assist the Queen. 'These and like words, mingled with many tears and sobs, he desired to be reported to his dear mistress from her most obedient servant'.

The Countess of Huntly took Hay to see the castle chapel 'all ornaments and mass robes ready lying upon the altar with cross and candles standing upon it'. She said: 'God, whom I believe in, wyll, I am sure, preserve us and lette our treue meanings arter be knowne'. She assured Hay that her 'husband was ever obedient under her (Mary) and so wyll dye her faythfull subject', and added that he should 'tell her, if he had forsaken the true faith, like her other ministers, he would not have been set upon in this way'.

All of this was reported to the Queen, at length, in front of her Privy Council in Aberdeen. However, her response was that 'she knew their conceits and believes not a word of it'.[74] Mary was clearly unmoved, and joked about the matter in front of her Council. Huntly became the butt of much merriment at Court.[75] Lethington wrote a letter to Cecil saying that Huntly would plead not guilty, and apparently blaming what had come about on the youth and folly of his children. 'If any fault be his, it may be thought to have proceeded from too great simplicity, rather than any craft or malice, especially by so many as have had experience how playnely, sincerely and uprightly he has been allwayes accustomed to deal'.[76] Is this a sympathetic view of Huntly on Lethington's part, or is it sarcasm? The reference to 'too great simplicity', rather than 'craft or malice', suggest the former.

The Countess of Huntly arrived in Aberdeen to deliver her profuse apologies for her son's behaviour, but Mary refused to see her. The younger brother of Sir Thomas Kerr of Fernihurst, Huntly's chief counsellor, arrived with the keys of Auchindoun and Findlater castles, brought as a sign of Huntly's obedience. Mary refused to receive them 'off a stable lad', as she described him. He was put in ward. He excused his master, and 'burdens John Gordon as the author of the whole event', yet he agreed that Huntly 'is certainly in his father's company and does nothing without his advice'.[77] Mary declared that she had 'other means of opening doors', and she was now determined to apprehend Huntly as 'the chief deviser of the mischief'.[78] Clearly, Mary's opinion was that Huntly was manipulating his son, rather than believing his protestations that John was to blame.

Outlaws

Huntly was now afraid of being captured and took to sleeping every night under a different roof, but he spent the daytime at Strathbogie.[79] Kirkcaldy of Grange left Aberdeen with twelve men to surprise Huntly, and to check whether or not Sir John was received at his home. If he was found there, the house was to be secured until reinforcements came. On arrival, Kirkcaldy spoke to a gateman, and sent a horse around to prevent escape. However, a watchman in the tower spotted the approaching reinforcements led by Lord John Cowdingham, almost a mile away, and alerted Huntly, who was enjoying his midday meal.[80] John Gordon was not there, but the incident gave the Earl 'such alarome' that he abandoned his half eaten meal and escaped over a low wall at the back, without his boots or sword, to a waiting horse. He escaped his pursuers because, unlike their mounts, his horse was fresh. Lady Huntly welcomed the emissaries 'with such cher as she could',[81] and they discovered that Huntly had taken the precaution of stripping the castle bare, apart from the chapel, which was still in readiness for the Queen. He was obviously expecting an assault of some kind.

On 11 October, Captain Alexander Stewart was sent with 120 men to besiege Findlater Castle. During the night John Gordon came to Cullen, where the soldiers were lodged, with a detachment of about 150 men. He attacked the captain in bed, and fifty-six of the harquebusiers, who were newly arrived in the north. During the skirmish, some of the soldiers were killed and others were released.

When the Queen heard about this, she was incensed and said that all hope of reconciliation was gone. Total submission was required. Huntly was ordered to present himself with his son John within a week, or face being outlawed under pain of rebellion.[82] However, Huntly refused to submit in front of those he regarded as his enemies in Aberdeen – presumably principally Moray. Instead, he offered himself for trial by his peers in parliament. Meanwhile, Thomas Kerr and his young brother admitted under torture that they knew of a plan that had been hatched on three different occasions to kill Moray and Maitland of Lethington. Letters were found purporting to prove that John Gordon's actions were instigated by his father.[83]

On 15 October there was a Privy Council meeting in Aberdeen, attended by the earls of Argyll, Morton and Mar, and William, Earl Marischal, Huntly's brother-in-law. It 'concluded and ordered by the Queen's Majesty, with advice of the lords of her Secret Council, that if Huntly compare not before her the 16th day of October [the following day] to answer to such things as are laid to his charge, conforming to the letters, he be put to the horne for his contemptioun'. Further 'that his houses, strengths and friends be taken from him and other gentlemen of the country . . . He was to compare before the Queen's Majesty and Council with all speed and order . . . for obedience to be made to the Queen's Majesty and quietness of the country'.[84]

As Huntly and John did not appear as stipulated on the following day, they were formally put to the horn by order of the Privy Council. Royal messengers were dispatched throughout the kingdom to denounce the renegades as rebels. The news was announced with three blasts of the horn at the market crosses of Edinburgh, Linlithgow, Stirling and Glasgow. Summonses were sent to Stirling, Glasgow, Hamilton and Paisley charging John's older brother George, Lord Gordon, to surrender to Queen Mary in Aberdeen. A general round-up of dissident Gordons was ordered.[85]

Huntly retired to the wilds of Badenoch (the area around the Cairngorms) and strengthened himself there 'whither it is thought to be impossible to bring men or artillery in winter'. He hoped the Queen would weary of the country as winter approached, but she resolved not to depart until the matter was resolved. Randolph wrote to report the incident in Cullen. He also mentioned that George, Lord Gordon, was with the Duke of Chatelherault, his father-in-law 'either to persuade him to join a rebellion or to remain, as if innocent'.[86]

Lady Huntly made her third attempt at an audience with the Queen. When she was within two miles of Aberdeen, she was met by Leslie, who had been sent by Moray. Much to her fury, he commanded that she return to Strathbogie. She was at the end of her tether, not

knowing where to turn next, and believing that there was no safety
in either surrender or resistance.[87] Thus, she consulted her 'tame
witches', or fortune-telling oracles.[88] They told her that her husband
would lie in the Tolbooth without a wound in his body. She foolishly
took this as a sign that their only option was to take the initiative and
attack. She persuaded her husband to return from the fastnesses of
Badenoch and take positive action. If they won, they might be able to
rescue the Queen from her 'evil councillors'. After all, de Gouda, the
papal legate, had complained in a long letter to his superiors that
Scotland was in a bad way, as the Queen had no Catholic advisers.
Lord James was the main problem, he said. Catholic advisers in
Europe and visitors were almost unanimous in their view that Lord
James was chiefly responsible for conditions in Scotland. He was
their bête noir. Get rid of him, they advised, and the old religion
might be able to win out. Catholic Europe would support their action
and hope they would succeed. If they did, it might be possible for
John Gordon's good looks and charm to win him the Queen's hand
in marriage, once his 'pretendit marriage' to Elizabeth Gordon of
Findlater was annulled.

The Battle of Corrichie

On 27 October 1562 John and his brother Adam accompanied their
father, with 800 Gordons and followers, marching towards Aberdeen
'in warlike manner'. Calderwood reported that Huntly's purpose was
'to take the Queen, hoping to appease her with flattery, officious service and marriage of his son, and fully resolved to cut off Moray'.[89]
Because letters from the Earl of Sutherland and William Leslie had
been intercepted, Huntly's plans were revealed to Moray. Leslie
confessed and was pardoned.

   The same day, an important Privy Council meeting was held in
Aberdeen, attended by Moray, Errol, Athol, Morton, Mar and William,
Earl Marischal, during which it was reported that Huntly was advancing towards Aberdeen to 'pursue our sovereign lady's person'. She was
to resist, with 'her true liegis' going out to meet him. Not only was
Mary's person threatened, but so was the whole Protestant Revolution, along with the lives of her chief ministers. Precautionary
arrangements were made, in case any of those involved in the enterprise were killed or wounded, on behalf of their families and heirs. The
Council decided to call to their aid the local nobility who were at odds

with Huntly, to ask their advice on resisting the conspirators. These were the Lords Errol, Forbes, Saltoun and Leslie of Balquhain, and 'others of the country folk'. After deliberation, these offered to go forward with their kin, to apprehend Huntly, his children and others. They said that they were prepared to put their lives at stake. The Queen and her council ordered them to go ahead.

The Privy Council records note that the Queen committed full power to her

> dearest brother James, Earl of Murray, with others of her Secret Council and noblemen to pass forward with kin, friends and servants to the place where Huntly shall happen to be on the following day, 28 October, and to take with them her banner, to resist and, if necessary, pursue for apprehending, to take them to the law for their treasonable coming in plane battle and other treasonable crimes committed by them before, and if resist, pursue to death; if flee to houses of strength, to lay assage to the samyn and to raise fire for taking the said houses, as if under the great seal.[90]

All of this was to be recorded 'ad perpetuam'. This is an interesting comment to add at the end of the document. It is possible that Moray aimed to ensure, by this commission, that he would be absolved from any charge in the future of levying war on his own behalf.[91]

The day of 28 October 1562 was a momentous one for John, his father, brothers and Gordon followers. Huntly led about 800 men, including the Gordons of Beldorney, Cairnborrow, Tillyangus, Strathdoun and Sutherland, who were ready to liberate the Queen from 'her evil councillors'. They marched via Keig and Loch Skene to the Hill of Fare, about twelve miles from Aberdeen.[92] They were joined by Irvine of Drum and Abercrombie of Pitmedden, and even a Forbes laird. The Duke of Chatelherault sent a message to say that he would take no part.[93] The men camped a short distance west of Garlogie, in an area still called Gordon's Moss. That night Huntly made a rather pathetic little prayer: he vowed that, although he had been a bloodthirsty man and the cause of the death of many an innocent man, if God would grant him victory now, he would serve him all his life.

Marching eagerly out of Aberdeen before ten o'clock in the morning were those who had been freed from their feudal obedience to the earl, promising to fight without any help from others. They had been ordered to harass the Gordons and hinder their retreat. However, when they drew near their objective, they waited for Moray to arrive.[94] He had been ordered to lead the force of 2,000, but he was merely to 'behold the battle'.[95] Morton and Athol each commanded a division. They arrived in the early afternoon.

Maitland of Lethington said a prayer before the Queen's force: 'Judge thou, O Lord, this day betwixt us and the Earl of Huntly. If ever we have sought unjustlie his or their destruction and blood, let us fall on the edge of the sword.'[96] Does this suggest, perhaps, that Lethington was a little unsure of the rightness of their cause?

It is thought that, when Huntly realised what was coming towards him, he meant to pull out at daybreak, but that he overslept until ten o'clock.[97] It is surprising that none of his sons came to wake him. As he was being helped into his armour, he seems to have been in a state of confusion, as 'speech failed him and he could not do anything right, by reason of his corpulence'. Perhaps he had had a small stroke in the night. Meanwhile, there had been desertions from his side 'of whom diverse stole away two nights before',[98] so that his forces were reduced from 800 to nearer 500.

Nevertheless, when he saw who was approaching, and realised that most of them were people he regarded as friends, he considered that he had a chance. He said that he feared not 'the large company, but those on the hill' – who were, presumably, the Queen's force under her banner, led by Moray. However: 'Our friends are honest men,' Huntly assured his troops. 'Let us encounter the rest ... We are sufficient, if God be with us.'[99]

When the local levies under Errol, Forbes and Leslie of Balquhain saw the Queen's forces under Moray, Morton and Lethington approaching on foot, they charged towards the advancing Gordons. But, before they came within shot, they fastened heather to their steel bonnets[100] as a sign that they were friends, and scattered in all directions, throwing aside their weapons as they ran. It is suggested that they ran deliberately into the massed ranks of Lothian pikemen coming up behind, in order to sow confusion and break up their ranks. Randolph suspected treachery, and hinted that this precipitate flight had been pre-arranged. 'No doubt there is treason,' said Lethington. 'Let us level our spears to the foremost and let them not come among us.'[101]

They marched forward in order, led by William Douglas, laird of Kemnay. The Gordons advanced at speed but were driven back by Lethington and his company. Musket fire from Moray's main force, approaching up the valley from the south, forced the Gordons back towards the head of the valley. Moray's guns raked the hillside and snipers harried higher summits with their shot. Huntly's men were forced ever lower off the heights by the harquebus shot into a corner of the valley of mossy ground between the hill and marshland. It became a rout. The Gordons were finally brought to bay, floundering in a bog at the head of the Howe of Corrichie.[102] In the space of an hour the battle was over. By four o'clock that afternoon, 120 of Huntly's men were dead and a similar number captured.[103] On the royal side there were none dead, only wounded. All reports agree that the local levies fought badly, if at all. However, John Knox reported that some of Huntly's erstwhile 'friends' returned, but 'gave no strokes' until they saw that his men were driven back. Then they struck, committing 'almost all the slaughter that day, to clear themselves of suspicion'.[104]

John Gordon was captured, along with his father, his brother Adam, and other Gordons. The humiliated Earl of Huntly was mounted on a horse to take him to the Queen. He suddenly keeled over and fell to the ground, stone dead. Legend has it that, on his defeat, Huntly shouted out the name 'Corrichie' three times, as it had been foretold that one day he would die at 'Corrichie'. He had taken it to mean Crichie, near Inverurie, which he had consequently always avoided. A supply horse, with a pair of fish baskets on its back, was brought, and Huntly's body was thrown ignominiously over it for the journey to the Tolbooth in Aberdeen. What a stir it must have caused, the news rippling through the surrounding countryside. John and Adam were also taken to the Tolbooth, along with other captured Gordons. A tailor was paid £350 for clothing, food and drink for them.[105]

Word reached the Queen at six that evening. Moray sent a message that she should 'convene with them to give thanks to God for such a notable deliverance'. However, it was noted that she 'glowmed at the messenger and would scarce speak a good word or look with a cheerful countenance to any she knew favoured Moray'.[106]

The redoubtable Lady Forbes, wife of Lord Forbes, observed Huntly's corpse lying on the cold stone floor clad in a doublet of canvas and a pair of Scottish grey hose.[107] She famously exclaimed: 'What stability shall we judge to be in this world! There lyeth he, that yesterday in the morning was holden the wisest, richest and man of greatest power in Scotland!'

When the Countess of Huntly heard the terrible news of her

husband's death, she blamed her chief witch, Jonet, for saying that he would lie in the Tolbooth without a wound in his body. Jonet defended herself stoutly, affirming that she gave a true response, but not the whole truth 'for she knew he would be dead'.

Randolph was already writing his report to Cecil late that night.[108] Interestingly, he said that John confessed all, and 'lays fault on his father, as he did do nothing but by his commandment'. Did he hope to save himself by blaming his dead father, or was it true? Calderwood reported that John 'the author of all these troubles', made full confessions about the 'many things devised by himself, his father and his brothers', and that letters were found in their pockets revealing communications between them, the Earl of Sutherland, and others. The Queen was disillusioned to find that the Earl of Sutherland, whom she had had in her company and trusted, was 'one of the contrivers of the whole mischief'.[109] He was not held with the others, as he had managed to escape to the Continent.

Thomas Kerr, Huntly's chief counsellor, also revealed what he knew, which was that Moray and some others, including the earls of Morton and Lethington, and the Justice Clerk, were to have been slain at Strathbogie and the Queen taken. Also, he and his company would have 'burned the Queen and as many as were in the house'. What one does not know is how much these confessions were the result of torture, which would nowadays mean they would be discounted as totally 'unsafe'.

Knox reported that the battle of Corrichie ensured the triumph of Moray and the ruin of Huntly.[110] Chalmers and other writers assert this was Moray's chief object in inducing the Queen to undertake the journey. So was it all Moray's doing?

Five of the leading Gordon accomplices were hanged. John was spared death by hanging, because of his high rank. The Queen was compelled to witness his execution, in order to give a lie to stories that she had encouraged him. She was extremely reluctant, as she had a horror of bloodshed. John Gordon was executed on 2 November, on Heading Hill, Aberdeen. He cried out that her presence solaced him, as he was about to suffer for love of her. The execution was clumsy, causing the Queen to break down completely; she had to be carried out, and was ill for several days afterwards.[111] Little did she know that she would endure the same horrifically messed-up execution a quarter of a century later. Rumours went round that she must have 'loved Sir John passionately'.[112] John's nephew, Robert Gordon of Gordonstoun, wrote later that the Queen 'intended to marry Sir John', which seems unlikely. He describes his uncle John as 'a comely gentleman, very personable and of good expectation, whom she loved entirely'. He goes on to say that the marriage had been intended by the Cardinal of Guise and the rest of the Queen's uncles 'so that the Roman religion might be maintained and preserved in Scotland by reason of the Earl of Huntly's power and force, chiefly in the northern parts of the kingdom'. He adds: 'Moray did cross the marriage in all his might and slight.' John lies buried in the crypt of St Nicholas, the town kirk of new Aberdeen.[113]

Findlater Castle surrendered and was handed back to the Ogilvies. At the Gordon trial the following year, the Queen granted a royal charter to James Ogilvie of Cardell. These included 'the lands and barony of Ogilvy, the Land and barony of Auchindoun and Keythmoir, the lands of Knokdurne in the forests of Boyne held of Huntly and forfeited to the Queen'.[114] The Queen commanded Ogilvie to pass the lands of Strathnairn and Cardell to Moray. This was his reward.[115] It also made sense, however, because these lands were within his new earldom of Moray. What became of John's widow, Elizabeth Gordon of Findlater? She was arguably the cause of all the trouble, her first husband's Will stating that it was she who should hold the rents during her lifetime. She lived on until 1606 and is buried with him, Alexander Ogilvie of Deskford and Findlater, in a grand, ornate tomb in St Mary's Kirk of Old Cullen.

Conclusion

Many writers consider John Gordon the cause of his family's conflict with Mary Queen of Scots, resulting in the battle of Corrichie on 28 October 1562, and the family's subsequent downfall. However, some contemporary sources and later writers blame other characters involved in the story: his father, for example, for planning a Catholic coup and manipulating John to bring it about, or directing John's actions merely for Gordon gain. There is the Queen herself. Did she come north because she wanted to ensure her most important Catholic nobleman's destruction, in order to win favour with Queen Elizabeth and prove herself a suitable candidate to inherit her throne? Then there is Mary's illegitimate half-brother, James Stewart, who became Earl of Moray and might have intended to supplant John's father as the power in the north. There are other minor players who could be blamed: for example, John's lover, later his wife, Elizabeth Gordon, for starting off the whole chain of events; and her husband, Alexander Ogilvie of Deskford and Findlater, for listening to her and disinheriting his own son, James Ogilvie of Cardell, by a previous marriage. Perhaps Mary's mother, the Regent, Mary of Guise, should also take some blame for trying to reverse the disinheritance issue. Finally, there is John's mother, the Countess of Huntly, who persuaded her husband to confront the Queen's forces as a result of a witch's prophesy.

So was John Gordon to blame for his own death, as well as his father's and all of the 120 men killed on the field of Corrichie, leading to the downfall of his family and their principal supporters? Before answering this question, the other possibilities will be considered in turn.

Elizabeth Gordon, Alexander Ogilvy's Second Wife

She began the whole saga by telling her husband evil stories about her stepson, James Ogilvie of Cardell, bringing about his disinheritance in John's favour. If the stories she told were true, she is innocent; but if not, she is a liar.

Alexander Ogilvie of Deskford and Findlater

Ogilvie obviously believed the stories about his son – so much so that his anger led him to disinherit the boy. Who could blame him? As the distinguished late sixteenth-century lawyer, Thomas Craig of Riccarton, said: 'The most violent hatred of which human nature is capable occurs between brothers and sometimes even between father and son.'[116] This is obviously the case here, and both his and his wife's actions set in train the events that culminated in the downfall of the Gordons.

James Ogilvie of Cardell had the law of primogeniture on his side, by which inheritance would automatically go to the eldest surviving son. This law was reinforced in the late sixteenth century with the practice of entailing lands.[117] In other words, landed estates were to be settled on persons successively, so that they could not be bequeathed at pleasure. Thus, James could have argued that, whatever provision was made by the parents, they had to be made within the law of primogeniture, or with the heir's consent.[118] Therefore, he was right to try to regain his lost inheritance. In this, he was clearly supported by the Regent, Mary of Guise, as well as his friends, neighbours and clan. He should therefore be absolved of blame.

The Regent, Mary of Guise

The Regent was well known for her passion for justice. She obviously believed in the law of primogeniture, and that James Ogilvie had been wronged. This is shown by her ruling that John should relinquish his entire inheritance and, later, following his defiance, her proposition that they share it. She could be accused of not enforcing her ruling on either occasion, which would have avoided all of the later trouble. However, there was no power in the land capable of enforcing an obnoxious statute against the will of someone who was supreme at home and in most of the north, as was John's father.[119] She would have been powerless unless supported by Huntly, as John's feudal lord, especially in a place that was so far from the capital, which effectively made the law a dead letter. Thus she should be exonerated.

The Countess of Huntly

John's mother tried to placate the Queen on behalf of her son several times. She had also managed to get the keys of Findlater and Auchindoun to Mary but, sadly, such gestures came too late. She was evidently an ardent Catholic, as she showed her chapel to Captain Hay, the Queen's messenger, all set out with its vestments ready for the Queen to use for mass, illegal for anyone but the Queen. She must have gone along with the Pope's idea that the current Protestant cabal led by Lord James, Lethington and Morton should be confronted and defeated for the sake of Mother Church. So perhaps it is the Pope and the Catholic princes whom we should blame for encouraging such an action.

The Countess can certainly take some blame for taking the word of soothsayers, encouraging her husband to collect his forces to confront those of the Queen, and advancing threateningly on Aberdeen. This was obviously a treasonable act; so, if it failed, disaster was bound to follow. For an intelligent woman, she acted very unwisely and put the lives of her loved ones at serious risk, especially as she had been warned that her husband would lie in the Tolbooth that night – a prediction that did not suggest the success of the enterprise.

George Gordon, 4th Earl of Huntly

The main defence of John's father, 4th Earl of Huntly, comes from the unlikely source of Lethington. He praised Huntly's personal loyalty to the Queen in letters to Cecil after staying in Huntly Castle, and from Aberdeen a few days before Huntly's death, stating that his attitude could not be faulted and praising his 'upright dealings with all men'.[120] He also suggested that the whole affair might have arisen due to simple misunderstanding. John's mother, the Countess, clearly believed that her husband was being persecuted because of his religion, and that if he had been prepared to 'renounce Catholicism, despoil the church and act consistently with the Lords of the Congregation, his supremacy in the north would, in all probability, have been allowed to remain unquestioned'.[121] Huntly's refusal to submit himself to trial by those he considered his enemies in Aberdeen obviously refers, in the main, to Moray. The two men were rivals for the Queen's ear and Huntly had lost out, despite still being Chancellor. The biggest blow was to lose control of lands to his enemy, first the earldom of Mar, and then Moray in his backyard. Desperation may have led him to succumb to pressure from the Pope and the Catholic princes to attempt an overthrow of Moray and to 'rescue' the Queen from his influence. It is also very possible that he was 'worried into rebellion by Moray'.[122] Interestingly, his own defence was that he could not be held responsible for his son's actions, even offering to besiege Findlater and Auchindoun himself, on behalf of the Queen, if he could do so with his own men, and force John to surrender them.

Against all of that, Huntly must stand guilty, as Chancellor and Lieutenant of the North, and with all his power, of not enforcing the Regent's orders on his son; not making sure that Inverness Castle opened its doors to the Queen; and, above all, of advancing on Aberdeen in 'warlike manner', endangering Mary and her ministers. This was all made clear at his posthumous trial.

Mary Queen of Scots

The Queen could not let John get away with his blatant disobedience and defiance towards both her mother and herself. She also had good reason to act decisively after the humiliation of being refused entry to the royal castle of Inverness, and then Findlater. For the former, she could blame the eldest son, George Gordon, who been given responsibility for the castle as a wedding gift from his father. It is not surprising that she was indignant with the defiant John: he had escaped prison in Edinburgh; refused her instructions to ward himself in Stirling pending her judgment on him; and come to Aberdeen with far more men than was allowed. He and his thousand men were also stalking her progress to Inverness, alarming everyone, and he had refused to give up his castles of Findlater and Auchindoun. Additionally, he had killed some of the soldiers and stolen their armaments; and, above all the Gordons led by Huntly, came towards Aberdeen prepared to fight her royal forces. She did not need rumours of threats to herself or her ministers – though that no doubt, encouraged action. Huntly had been given plenty of opportunity to bring his son to order, and Mary had to act decisively. Impressing Elizabeth did not need to come into it: not to act would have resulted in anarchy. However, her reported reaction to hearing about the outcome of the battle of Corrichie suggests that it gave her no joy to hear of the deaths of Huntly and so many of his Gordon followers. She was devastated by John's gruesome execution. How ironic it was that she would suffer the same fate in future.

However, she could accept some blame for the disastrous outcome of the whole affair, first in provoking Huntly by sidelining him in favour of her half-brother Lord James and Lethington, but mostly by offering Lord James the earldom of Moray. He had no family history in, nor connections with, the area. However, it had been in the hands of a previous royal bastard. Then she did not take up Huntly's offer to besiege his son's castles with his own men and bring him to justice. A little more patience might have restored order and prevented the deaths of many. She obviously did not trust Huntly enough to allow him to besiege his own son's castles. Later she presided over the court in Edinburgh that saw what looked like the downfall of the House of Huntly and its followers. Were such extreme measures really necessary to restore order and avoid anarchy? Surely the family had suffered enough. However, it was all in the interests of another major character in the story, Lord James Stewart.

Lord James Stewart, Earl of Moray

The Queen chose to put her trust in Moray's guidance and advice rather than in her Chancellor, Huntly. When faced with John Gordon's defiance, his father's failure to bring him to justice, and then the Gordon refusal to allow a queen entry to a royal castle, James Stewart must surely have had to advise strong action. This was the start of a new regime, when discipline over unruly nobles would have to be established. There was also the letter from Mary's uncles, which she was unwise enough to show him, that revealed the possibility of Catholic plots to assassinate himself and Lethington, and to bring about a marriage between herself and John Gordon. This was helpful information to him, and would obviously make the Queen's party wary on their journey in the north – all the more so with John lurking in woods on their journey to Inverness, and Huntly and his son entering Aberdeen with large numbers of men.

It would have been Moray's job to ensure the Queen's safety, so it is not surprising that the party felt the need to send for more men and arms. It is interesting that Mary's commission to send troops out to meet Huntly under her royal banner, led by Moray, was so clearly recorded in detail 'for perpetuity', as if to ensure that he was not to be blamed for instigating it. Moray must have realised that everyone would know how much he stood to gain by the destruction of the Gordon earldom, and this gives rise to the suspicion that he might well have exploited the rumours and quietly encouraged the Queen to go north. Huntly was his rival for power, both in the Privy Council and in the north-east. Although moderate in his religious views, Moray was a reformer and a leader of the Lords of the Congregation. He might well have thought that it was his religious duty to establish a Protestant presence in the north-east, in order to spread the influence of the Reformation and counteract the conservative Catholic influence of Huntly and his followers. He may have encouraged the Queen's journey north in order to force the issue of the takeover of his long-coveted earldom of the Moray estates. John's misdemeanours were a perfect pretext for taking action. With his sophistry and towering ambition, Moray may have helped enflame any prejudices a gullible Queen may have already held, particularly the idea that Huntly had traitorous designs to marry her to his son John. The more violent the course of action, the better – and so more troops and arms were sent for. Moray must have been delighted with the outcome of the battle. The trial merely finished off the job.

However, all of this is speculation. Although Mary took the initiative for her northern progress, we can only surmise that it is extremely likely that Moray had a part in her decision, giving Huntly no other option but to rebel, leading to his downfall. It is interesting to note that when Moray himself was sidelined by Lord Darnley following Mary's marriage, it was he who led a traitorous rebellion against her.

John Gordon

Finally John, as the author of his own death and his family's disaster, must be faced. It is possible that his undisciplined behaviour was the result of his father's absence for long periods of time. A modern study of father/son relationships reveals that men in a sample of those who had been most disruptive, or who had truanted or offended often, had fathers who were frequently absent for long periods. Males want close relationships with their fathers, and if they can achieve one, it contributes to keeping them out of trouble.[123] It might be that John did not enjoy such a meaningful relationship.[124]

His strongest defence must be that he had gained legal charter to the Ogilvie title and lands, freely given by Alexander Ogilvie. Although the feudal law of primogeniture decreed that an inheritance should go to the eldest son, in the event, and whatever the law said, it was the wishes of the parents that determined what actually happened.[125] This obviously applied to Alexander Ogilvie in 1545. However, as has already been mentioned, by the late sixteenth century, the law of primogeniture had been reinforced by the increasingly common practice of entailing lands so that an inheritance could not be bequeathed at pleasure.[126] As a third son, therefore, John would have to fend for himself where entitlement to land and income were concerned. This is plainly what he was determined to do by holding onto the lands through his so-called 'pretendit' marriage to Elizabeth Gordon. The Reformation reduced the chance of a lucrative career, through benefices, for younger sons in the Church. And, with the disappearance of the old Church, so went the traditional alliance with France – that haven for the Scots soldier of fortune abroad.[127] The violence of his fight against Lord James Ogilvie of Airlie in the streets of Edinburgh might have been caused by desperation about his future options if he let go of his inheritance.

John's main defence when he was taken prisoner after the battle of Corrichie was that everything he had done had been at his father's direction. It is possible that Huntly encouraged him to hold onto his lands, as they were of such huge benefit to the Gordons. They joined up their lands of Strathbogie and Strathavon, and extended them to the Banffshire coast. Huntly may well have encouraged his son to escape Moray's clutches in Edinburgh, and to return to his protection in the north. He might have persuaded him not to risk warding himself in Stirling Castle. If Mary had accepted his invitation to stay at Huntly Castle, he could have argued his son's case.

There is also the religious element in John's defence. He may have seen himself as a romantic champion of the Catholic faith and of the Queen personally, whom he regarded as a helpless prisoner of the Protestant faction, as encouraged by Catholic forces abroad. It may have been a common belief of the north-east Catholics but, unlike

them, he was willing to risk his neck by plotting to abduct the Queen
with the aid of his Gordon kinsmen. His mind was confused further by
an adolescent infatuation for the Queen, whom he apparently expected
to marry once the rescue had been achieved.

However, John is clearly guilty of acts of blatant disobedience to
royal commands and putting himself in the wrong where Mary was
concerned, by defiantly escaping prison twice instead of facing justice.
His arrival in Aberdeen with 1,000 followers, instead of the 100
allowed, was aggressive and provocative. Having been threatened with
treason if he did not take himself off to Stirling Castle, he still escaped.
Then, refusing to open up Findlater Castle, as ordered by the Queen's
royal messenger, was asking for trouble. Attacking her soldiers, who
were intending to besiege it, and stealing their harquebuses, shows that
he was spoiling for a fight. He had no respect for the Queen, or for
royal authority. By stalking her with his thousand followers, he obviously created fear in her, and provided a threat.

John was deluded if he truly thought that, as a third son, he had a
chance of becoming the royal spouse of someone who had once been
Queen of France. This was a preposterous ambition for a younger son,
especially as he was already married. He was not a fit consort for a
princess 'at whose feet half the crowned heads of Europe were
sighing'.[128]

We can certainly blame John for his actions that led to his own and
his family's woes. His father could not control him, even if he had
wanted to, leaving his family few options but to attempt a Catholic
coup through confrontation and battle. The best they could hope for
was a miracle. This they did not get.

It was a sad end to the story for the Gordons of Huntly, especially
as they owed much of their eminence to loyalty and service to the
Crown through successive generations. Had it not been for the
combined actions of themselves and the other characters in this story,
John and his father, might have survived and become pillars of strength
for Queen Mary – as John's brothers, George and Adam, were to prove
in the time of Mary's greatest need.

2

George Gordon – Ambivalent?

DRAMAS IN THE LIFE OF MARY QUEEN OF SCOTS

PART I

Childhood

George Gordon, who became the 5th Earl of Huntly, grew up as the second son of the 4th Earl of Huntly until a tragedy changed his life for ever. It was not the first tragedy in his life. He lived in turbulent times, and might not even have survived as long as he did. He was more closely tied up with the life of Mary Queen of Scots than all the rest of his family and most of the other nobles, except for the Earl of Bothwell. The question to ask about George is: was he ambivalent in his support for Mary?

It is thought that George was born about 1535. His father, George Gordon, 4th Earl of Huntly, had married Elizabeth Keith, sister of William, 4th Earl Marischal in February that year. When his father's cousin, and erstwhile playmate, James V went to France for six months to marry Princess Madeleine, his first wife, he left Scotland in Huntly's charge. He must have been a good custodian, as there were reportedly 'no tumults or disorders' during this time. However, the religious reformist zeal coming from the Continent was rumbling in Scotland and beginning to affect his family. George, the 4th Earl, was asked by Cardinal Beaton to assist with an inquisition aimed at detecting and punishing heretics.

However, little George would have known nothing of such struggles. By the age of seven, he would have been more aware of the fact that his father was considered a hero for leading Scottish forces to victory against the English at the battle of Hadden Rig. Maybe young George would have sensed anxiety in his parents when his father fell out of favour with the King and was sidelined. This came about because he had opposed the King's wish to invade England after Henry VIII had claimed suzerainty over Scotland and sent another army across the border. James V's subsequent invasion led to the disastrous defeat of the Scottish force at the battle of Solway Moss, where so many nobles were slain. This was shortly followed by the death of the devastated King only days after hearing of the birth of a daughter, Mary, on 8 December 1542, to Mary of Guise, his second wife, whom he had married after Madeleine died.

George's father was immediately put on the Council of Regency. In 1546, at the age of eleven, young George might have become aware of the religious arguments heating up close to home: his uncle, William Keith, 4th Earl Marischal, publicly supported the Scottish reformer George Wishart, who was burnt at the stake that year in St Andrews for his Reformist teachings. After the powerful Cardinal Beaton was murdered in revenge for this act, George's father was made Chancellor in his place. He was now the second most important man in Scotland after the Governor, James Hamilton, the Earl of Arran.

The following year, when George was about twelve, he would have been well aware of his father going to fight the English forces at the battle of Pinkie, resplendent in his gilt and enamelled armour; but he must also have been dismayed to hear that his father had been captured and taken to London. Permission was refused for his wife and family to visit him, but his English captors agreed that he could be released if he returned to Scotland for two-and-a-half months on condition that he sent his wife, his three eldest sons – Alexander, George and John – as well as his uncle, Alexander Gordon, as surety that he would return at the appointed time. The deal was that the 4th Earl would encourage a match between young Mary and Henry VIII's only son, Prince Edward. What a triumph for Huntly, who favoured a French marriage for Mary, when he managed to avoid having to fulfil these conditions by escaping from his captors at Morpeth, crossing the Tweed on Christmas Eve. He was welcomed royally by the Queen Mother, Mary of Guise, the Council and his family, including George. The following year, six-year-old Mary was sent to France for security, as a prospective bride for Francis, the young Dauphin.

In 1550, George was aged about fifteen. It was a year of honours for his father because he and his cousin John, Earl of Sutherland, accompanied Mary of Guise to France, in a fleet of galleys, when she went to visit her little daughter, Mary. They were royally entertained by the French King, Henry II, who made Huntly and others of Mary's entourage members of the Honourable Order of St Michael, the first order in France at the time. A plot was hatched by Mary of Guise that she should take over from Arran, the Governor, the business of running Scotland. Henry II advised her that if she did this, she should do it quietly, without fuss. Huntly supported her in her bid to become Regent, and succeeded in gaining Arran's agreement. As a result of his compliance, Arran was given the French Dukedom of Chatelherault. It was at this time that the Queen Regent confirmed on George's father the lucrative earldom of Moray for his faithful services to herself and her deceased husband, James V. He was also made Sheriff of Elgin and Forres.[1] George would have been well aware of his father's increasing power and wealth at this time.

During George's middle and late teens in the 1550s he would have enjoyed seeing his home of Huntly Castle being rebuilt with two further floors, and a grand new extension to the old part. His father had been inspired by his time in France to build a Renaissance 'palace'. This was the fourth stage in the castle's story. This new, modern part was much more convenient for comfortable living, and the 4th Earl of Athol was doing much the same at Balvenie – although, lacking Huntly's wealth, in not nearly so grand a fashion. Mary of Guise was also greatly enhancing her chambers in Stirling Castle, suitable for her role as Queen Regent.

George, his elder brother Alexander, and his younger brothers and sisters must have been present and on their best behaviour when his parents entertained the Queen Regent, the Duke of Chatelherault and their retinue in the new grandeur of Huntly Castle. Perhaps he noticed how obsequiously and dutifully his father behaved towards her.

Family Marriages

Tragedy hit the family with the death of George's eldest sister, Elizabeth, shortly after her marriage to John Stewart, 4th Earl of Athol, of Balvenie Castle. Even worse for George was the death in 1552 of his older brother, Alexander. Ironically, this also occurred shortly after his own marriage to the Duke of Chatelherault's eldest daughter. Both marriages were without issue. The last had been a perfect match for uniting the two most powerful families in Scotland. George was now the heir to the earldom of Huntly and much else besides.

Over the next ten years, George was involved in several significant family marriages, one of which was his own. In 1554, he saw his next brother, John, aged about eighteen, marry their much older relative Elizabeth Gordon, the widow of Alexander Ogilvie of Findlater and Deskford. No doubt he knew well the drama of how, nine years earlier, Alexander Ogilvie had fallen out with his own son by his first marriage, James Ogilvie of Cardell, and in 1545 had instead granted his name, titles and lands to John.

George must also have been well aware that James Ogilvie had won the support of the Queen Regent, Mary of Guise, in attempting to win back his inheritance. It became a battle of wills. We are not told what George's reaction was but, being the Huntly heir, he probably hoped that John would succeed in holding onto the Ogilvie lands, because Auchindoun and Keithmore connected the Gordon lands of Strathbogie and Strathavon so conveniently, and the Findlater lands gave useful access to the Banffshire sea coast. The Regent failed to persuade John, who was probably backed by his powerful father, to give up the inheritance. The family obviously thought John had the right to keep the inheritance, as the contract had been formally ratified. In any case, when Alexander Ogilvie died in 1554, John promptly married his widow, who had the right to the rents for the rest of her lifetime. No doubt they all thought the matter was now settled.

The following year, when George was about twenty, he had the shock of seeing his father briefly locked up in Edinburgh Castle for failing to subdue a rebellion by Ronald Moydart in the west. His power and income was much reduced when the Regent also took away the earldom of Moray, and other titles and administrations he had acquired, such as the earldoms of Mar, Orkney and Shetland. However, George must have been as relieved as his father when the relationship with the Regent was restored, along with his positions of power and wealth. After all, George was now heir to it all.

However, John's non-compliance with the attempts by Mary of Guise to solve the problem between James Ogilvie and himself, dividing the inheritance between the two of them, must have caused a rift between the Ogilvies and Gordons, who had previously been close, especially after John subsequently rejected Elizabeth, later referred to as his 'pretendit wife'. He did not divorce her, because if he did so, he would lose the financial benefits of the baronies. Instead, it was rumoured that he kept her locked up in Findlater Castle. We are not told what George thought about all of this, nor whether John confided in him or his father.

The year 1558 was a very important one for George and the whole family. First came his own marriage to Anna Hamilton, 3rd daughter of the Duke of Chatelherault, at their grand mansion in Hamilton. This marriage brought these two important families together again after the sad death six years previously of his older brother Alexander, who had been married to Anna's elder sister.

In November the same year, his fourteen-year-old sister Margaret married John, Master of Forbes, aged seventeen. A contract had been drawn up for this marriage in 1547, when Margaret was only four and John was six. It was to be an unhappy match for her, and it did not heal the feud between the two families. The Forbeses had embraced the new Reformed faith, and Margaret remained a Catholic

In 1559 seventeen-year-old Queen Mary became Queen of France as well as Queen of Scotland when her husband became King Francis II on the death of his father. By this time the Scottish Reformation was in full swing. George's father, who supported Mary of Guise, was one of her negotiators with the Lords of the Congregation. In April 1560, he eventually, and reluctantly, agreed to sign the Reformist Band of Leith (see Chapter 1). Parliament then ratified the Confession of Faith, which abolished the jurisdiction of the Pope and made the attendance at mass a punishable offence. George's family remained Catholic, so this must have been a shock. It was a step too far for his father, who did not attend the next meeting of the Privy Council, citing a sore leg as his excuse.

Queen Mary's illegitimate half-brother, Lord James Stewart, came up to the northern shires to reform the churches. He reportedly saw and envied the jurisdiction and personal influence of Huntly, and resolved to wrest it from him.[2] He would soon have his chance.

Events began to favour the reforming Lords of the Congregation. However, the situation changed dramatically on 5 December when Queen Mary's young husband, Francis II, suddenly died. Her mother-in-law, Catherine de Medici, who wielded great power as Queen Dowager and Regent, did not want a rival Queen Dowager in the palace. It was clear that Mary, as Queen of Scotland, had to return to her own country.

It had been hoped that her arrival would be a new opportunity for those who opposed the Reformist religious settlement, which Mary had refused to ratify. If it is true that George's father offered a military force if Mary landed in Aberdeen, then George, his 25-year-old eldest son, would have been an important part of it, along with all the other Gordons and their followers. That she chose instead to land at Leith and put herself in the hands of her half-brother instead of her Chancellor, Huntly, was bad news for the family.

Queen Mary's Return, 19 August 1561

Although he was still Chancellor when Mary arrived in Scotland, Huntly felt himself again being pushed aside, this time by Lord James Stewart and Mary's capable secretary, Maitland of Lethington. However, all of George's family must have attended the grand wedding of Stewart to their cousin Agnes Keith. Despite the dispute between his brother John and James Ogilvie, who was Master of the Queen's Bedchamber, George witnessed John being knighted during the wedding celebrations, becoming Sir John Ogilvie of Deskford. Little did they know that the young Queen's wedding present for Lord James was the earldom of Moray, as this was to remain secret until a suitable moment arrived for it to be revealed. Publicly, he was made Earl of Mar, but this apparently offended his uncle, John Erskine, who believed that the earldom should rightfully be his.

For George and his wider family, 1562 was an annus horribilus, thanks to John, who had fought with the Ogilvies in the streets of Edinburgh and whose case was shortly to come up in court. The Ogilvies were still challenging John's right to inherit from James Ogilvie of Cardell, who by now was a grandfather. John wounded the young clan chief, Lord James Ogilvie of Airlie, so badly that he lost his right arm and was at one time near death. John was imprisoned in the Tolbooth and Lord James, now Earl of Mar, rushed down from Stirling to ensure that John's imprisonment was as stringent as possible, with twelve men to guard him. Despite this, John managed to escape and fled north to the protection of their father.

This put the family in an awkward situation, especially when John refused to give himself up and Mary, with Lord James Stewart, decided to make a royal progress to the north, with James Ogilvie of Cardell in her entourage. James Stewart must have sensed this as the ideal opportunity to wrest the earldom of Moray from the Gordons.

George must have been in Aberdeen ready to welcome the Queen, and involved in the family's preparations to receive her at Huntly Castle. He, too, would have felt humiliated when she refused to see his father, even though Huntly was still her Chancellor and by far the most important man in the north. More publicly humiliating was her refusal to stay at Huntly Castle, although she passed within three or four miles of it.

News must soon have arrived that Lord James had been publicly granted the earldom of Moray when he had entertained the Queen at Darnaway, caput of Moray, previously in the charge of his father. George knew how much Moray meant to his father, because of the power, status and wealth it gave him.

George had been made Keeper of Inverness Castle four years previously, as a wedding present from his father, who was Sheriff of Inverness. It seems that neither he nor his father could have expected the Queen to stay in Inverness Castle, because they had not thought to prepare for her visit. This is surprising, considering the castle was held for her as a royal residence. Perhaps, also, George was distracted by Anna's pregnancy with their first child. Father and son would have been shocked to hear that the warden, Alexander Gordon, had refused the Queen entrance, not having received permission from them. What is more, Mary had to endure the indignity of staying in high street lodgings. No wonder she was incensed. Moray immediately embarked on a siege, until George's father sent the keys to him. Alexander Gordon was immediately executed, without any form of trial, and his head put on the castle battlements.

Meanwhile, some of Huntly's erstwhile supporters, who had also gathered in Inverness, were joining up with the many Highlanders rallying to Mary's defence because of rumours that his father wanted to kidnap the Queen and marry her to John. It appears that George also arrived in Inverness with a group of friends, but they soon deserted him when they saw which way the wind was blowing. Of course George was now in deep trouble, like his father and brother. He decided that he must go south to seek advice from his father-in-law, the Duke of Chatelheraut, on how to get out of the impasse. John Knox suggested that George actually travelled south to raise a rebellion with the Earl of Bothwell, who also regarded Lord James Stewart as an enemy.

George must have been in despair, especially when he learned that John had made things worse by refusing to surrender the keys of Findlater and Auchindoun castles, in addition to his men killing some of the Queen's men, taking their captain prisoner and stealing some of their armaments. What is more, his father was driven to escaping over a back wall of Huntly Castle to escape Kirkcaldy of Grange and his advancing men-at-arms. What an indignity for the erstwhile 'Cock of the North'.

Even worse, his father and brother were both publicly outlawed. They felt so driven into a corner that they were now collecting an army to attempt a coup, in the hope of 'cutting off' Lord James, now officially Earl of Moray, and removing what they considered his malign influence on the Queen. George's father-in-law, the Duke of Chatelherault, sent a message that he would not be involved, and George remained in the south. Moray transferred the Great Seal, which had been held by Huntly as Chancellor, to his friend the formidable Earl of Morton, who was now made Chancellor in Huntly's place.[3]

It must have been unbearable news for George to hear that his father had died on the field of battle at Corrichie, probably of a heart attack; and that the errant John had been messily executed, watched by the Queen. Young Adam was, at least, spared, but the Duke of Chatelherault received instructions to arrest George. At first he was warded in his own house of Kinnert, while his father's body was brought by boat from Aberdeen to the vault of Holyrood Chapel, then taken to the monastery of the Blackfriars.

George had the support of his father-in-law, who went up to Dundee to meet the Queen on her way south. He pleaded for George on the grounds that he had not been involved in the battle of Corrichie. She responded that his fate depended on the decision of parliament.[4] The duke returned south and, as instructed, took George to Moray, who warded him in Edinburgh Castle on 28 November, where he remained over the winter until his trial in February 1563.

His mother Elizabeth, Countess of Huntly, came south with his father's cousin, John Gordon, 11th Earl of Sutherland, to plead for their two families, but she gained no encouraging news. It would have been painful for George to hear about Huntly Castle being looted and its valuables, such as the Flemish tapestries, carted away to Darnaway, or to Edinburgh for the Queen's use. Now that his father was gone, George was heir to all he had held. However, he had to await his fate, which was to be decided at the forthcoming trial. Maitland of Lethington, Mary's secretary, travelling back to Edinburgh with her, obviously believed that Huntly had harboured evil intentions against Moray and himself, and even against the Queen. He wrote in a letter: 'I am sorry that the soil of my native country did ever produce so unnatural a subject as the Earl of Huntley', who apparently wanted to act against 'a princess so gentle, and benign' as Mary.[5] Little did he realise that he would soon be doing the same himself.

Mary and Moray, and those of influence around them, must also have been distracted by Scotland being pulled between two sides in the war that had broken out between England and France.[6] Moray began acting like a dictator, urged on by Queen Elizabeth, her Secretary of State, William Cecil, the Reformed Church, and even the populace. George must have been concerned for his family when he heard from prison of violent measures being instigated against the Catholic Church, with priests being taken and convicted for saying mass in secret houses and woods.[7]

On 8 February 1563, George was convicted, forfeited and sentenced to execution, to be drawn and quartered at his 'sovereign's pleasure'. Fortunately for him, however, Mary exercised her prerogative, deferring the execution and commuting it to ward in Dunbar Castle, under the governor, Sir Simon Preston of Craigmillar. Moray, with his ambitions in the north-east, must have been frustrated at this decision. Although John Knox said in his writings that it was Moray who had appealed for George's life, this seems unlikely. George's nephew, Robert Gordon of Gordonstoun, reported later that 'Moray continually and eagerly persuaded the Queen to take his life'.[8] However, he had another opportunity to see the family destroyed the following May.

George was brought to the front of the Three Estates in the Tolbooth in Edinburgh on 28 May 1563. Mary Queen of Scots arrived, with great pomp, for the public trial, which was to take place in the presence of the entire parliament. George had the humiliating and heartbreaking experience of seeing his father's embalmed body, propped upright in its coffin, being condemned as a traitor. The deceased earl was accused of coming with 'a great number of men of war from the land of Strathbogie towards Aberdeen', and for the 'treasonable battle against the said lieutenant (the Earl of Moray), having her commission and banner displayed'. Huntly's armourial bearings were formally struck from the Herald's roll, and his escutcheon (shield bearing his coat of arms) was 'torn to pieces in front of the people'. (If a person was declared a traitor in the sixteenth and seventeenth centuries it was common practice for a painting on paper of their coat of arms to be hung upside down on the Mercat Cross of Edinburgh; then, after a specific period, a Herald would pull the Arms down and tear up the piece of paper. Any record of the Arms held by the Lord Lyon King of Arms would be defaced or destroyed.[9]) All of the Gordons who had supported Huntly had their lands forfeited, including his brothers and two sisters, and George Gordon of Beldorney, John Gordon of Cairnborrow, James Gordon of Tillyangus, and John Gordon, 11th Earl of Sutherland. Forfeiture meant losing their titles, property, movable goods and income, all confiscated by the Crown. His father's 'dignity, name and memory was to be extinct and his arms cancelled, deleted and put from the book of arms, and his posterity to be unable to hold honourable title and dignity within this realm'.[10] There was to be no more Cock of the North for the Gordons.

It must have been galling for George to witness Lord James Stewart's satisfaction at gaining full title to the earldom of Moray, and acquiring the Castle of Inverness and becoming its sherriff, which extended his jurisdiction over Ross. James Ogilvie of Cardell at last gained Findlater and Deskford, but he bequeathed or sold some of it to Moray, including Cardell in Strathnairn, probably as a token of thanks for Moray's efforts on his behalf.[11]

George was condemned to continue his imprisonment in Dunbar Castle under Sir Simon Preston. Not long after the trial, George narrowly escaped death. Sir Simon received an order, signed by the Queen, to execute him immediately, but George was convinced that it must be false and pleaded with him to confirm it at once with the Queen. Preston rode to Holyrood, arriving late at night, and managed to persuade the guards about the urgency of his mission. He reported to the Queen that he had carried out her order to execute George Gordon, but she broke down in tears and denied sending such an order. It must have been done by her evil brother, she said. She then insisted that Preston must never harm George Gordon unless he heard the order from her own mouth.[12] Although his life was saved, George must have despaired when he contemplated the prospects of his ever getting out of the Dunbar stronghold and being able to resume normal life as long as Moray held sway over Mary. However, he did not know what lay round the corner.

Restored to Favour

George was well into his third year of ward in Dunbar Castle when everything changed, thanks to Mary's choice of a second husband, Lord Darnley. Now it was Moray's turn to feel sidelined. Darnley had offended everyone, with his arrogant manner and secret plotting with Rome. Moray, who in 1562 had so strongly condemned George's father and his brothers for treason, now committed treason himself and led a rebellion against the Queen. Most of the nobles who had been closest to her joined him, including George's father-in-law and Maitland of Lethington. The rebellion was also supported by England, as Queen Elizabeth did not approve of the Darnley match, which had been arranged without her consent. She gave George's cousin Agnes, Countess of Moray, 3,000 crowns to take to her husband in support of his rebellion.[13]

As a result of losing so many people that she had relied on, Mary desperately needed to strengthen her own power base. Who better to call to her side than one who considered Moray his enemy – George Gordon? As a result, on 3 August 1565, George received the good news that he was released from ward. He was brought to Court and had his father's titles and honours unofficially restored.[14] It was now Moray who was summoned on pain of treason. On 25 August a proclamation was made at the market cross in Edinburgh that George had been restored to the lordship of Gordon.[15] He was now able to ride with Mary, pursuing the rebels on what became known as 'The Chaseabout Raid', from Edinburgh to Ayr and back to Edinburgh, and then to Dumfries. The rebels received little support and fled across the border to England.

In the autumn, James Hepburn, Earl of Bothwell, also came on the scene, having been recalled from exile in Europe by Mary. In October, he and George were appointed to the Privy Council, and George was officially entitled the 5th Earl of Huntly. On 1 December both men had the satisfaction of being present when the Privy Council declared their enemy, the Earl of Moray, guilty of treason.[16] The Duke of Chatelherault now had a change of heart and wrote to Mary from England begging forgiveness. He received it, but was ordered to retire to France.[17]

George's mother, the Dowager Countess of Huntly, and his sister Jean, were brought to Court. The countess became a much-valued confidante of the Queen. Jean, who was twenty, was of marriageable age, and Mary proposed that she would be a good match for Bothwell. He was described by one of Queen Elizabeth's secretaries of state, Sir William Walsingham, as a 'glorious, rash and hazardous young man'.[18] The marriage contract was signed by Queen Mary, George and his mother, whose hand was guided by her brother-in-law, Alexander Gordon, the reformed Bishop of Galloway. It was also signed by the bride and groom, Jean and Bothwell. The portraits of the bridal pair were painted in miniature. George must have attended the very grand wedding. The banquet was graced by the presence of the Queen and her husband, now referred to as the King. There were five days of celebrations, including tournaments with jousting. No doubt George and his wife visited the couple when they set up home in Crichton Castle, south-east of Edinburgh, in Midlothian.

Mary had previously succeeded in drawing many of the Protestant nobles to her side because of her reassurances not to change the status quo, but now, because of the rebellion, she appealed on religious grounds to Philip II of Spain for aid. William Chisholm, the Bishop of Dunblane, went to Rome to ask for men and money on her behalf, and professed that she had the intention of doing something in Parliament for 'the auld religion'.[19]

In March the following year, 1566, George had the honour of being appointed to his father's old position as Lord High Chancellor,[20] which was now almost hereditary in the family. Mary came to the opening of Parliament in a glittering silver head-dress. George bore the crown, and Bothwell the sceptre. Lord Darnley did not attend: he was in a sulk because Parliament refused to grant him his greatest wish, the Crown Matrimonial, meaning that he would inherit the throne if Mary predeceased him.[21] Parliament was put under considerable pressure by Mary to draw up a bill of attainder against Moray, which would have resulted in his lands being forfeited. George and his family must have looked forward to the day when the earldom of Moray might be reclaimed. The bill was to come before Parliament on Tuesday 12 March.

The Murder of Riccio

One of the complaints of the rebels, including Moray, Maitland of Lethington, Morton, Ruthven and Lindsay, was that Mary was 'leaving the wholesome advice and counsel of her nobles and barons and following, instead, that of such men, strangers, as have neither judgment nor experience of the ancient laws of governance of this realm and were of base degree and seeking nothing but their own commodities'.[22] It was true that the only peers she now had by her side were George, Bothwell, Athol, and Darnley's father, the Earl of Lennox. George, suddenly elevated to the position of Chancellor, must have had little experience of the affairs of state, having been locked up in Dunbar Castle for the previous few years, while Bothwell had been in exile. The concessions agreed with the Lords of the Congregation in 1560 forbade the appointment of foreigners to office, and yet now there was much activity at Court by foreigners – such as David Riccio, an Italian.[23] He had come to Scotland with the Savoy ambassador and was employed by Mary as a singer, and latterly as her French Secretary.

With the imminent threat that their estates might be forfeited by Parliament, the rebel lords now resorted to desperate measures. This was a plot to murder Riccio, who they considered had too much influence, behaved haughtily, and always argued against them. Even at that early stage, they had plans to dethrone Mary, send her to Stirling Castle,[24] and then set up Protestant rule.

Because Mary was foolish enough to play cards with Riccio late at night, even locking the door of the little room they were in, it was easy enough for the plotters to build on Darnley's natural jealousy and get his co-operation. In exchange, they promised to help him gain the Crown Matrimonial.

George and Bothwell both had apartments in the Palace of Holyroodhouse. They and two of her other close associates, the lords Fleming and Livingstone, were also, it seems, intended victims of the planned coup on 9 March 1566.[25] George and Bothwell must either have heard what was going on or were told about the shocking murder of Riccio, who was stabbed many times on the stairwell, having been dragged screaming from where he clung to Mary's skirts. George and Bothwell came rushing into the inner court, intending to make a rescue, but they were stopped by Morton, who ordered them to return to their chambers or else worse would happen.[26] Fearing for their lives, they immediately obeyed. However, they managed to escape by breaking a window, letting themselves down with cords, eluding the guards and jumping over a wall at the back into grounds where lions and other wild animals were kept.[27] They travelled on foot to Edmonstone, on the south-eastern outskirts of the city, fearing to enter Edinburgh, and went on to Jean and Bothwell's home of Crichton Castle, where they concocted a plan to rescue Mary with ropes and chairs. This was standard practice for getting people out of burning buildings.

Meanwhile, Darnley had fulfilled his part of the bargain with the plotters by taking over regal power, dissolving parliament, and ordering the Three Estates to leave Edinburgh within three hours on pain of treason. He allowed no one to leave the Palace of Holyroodhouse, and all Catholics were forbidden to leave their houses.

George's mother was full of ideas for Mary's escape, including smuggling in a rope concealed between plates. However, the rebels ordered her to leave. The Countess managed to smuggle a note from Mary to Bothwell and George, asking them to meet her at Lord Seton's home, Seton House, on the Forth.

Mary had managed to keep her head, and calmly succeeded in winning the feckless Darnley to her side. She persuaded him to reveal the whole plot to her, and convinced him that his life would also be in danger from his fellow plotters. She thus won his co-operation for a joint escape. Meanwhile, Moray had arrived back in Edinburgh and attempted to negotiate a pardon for the rebels with Mary. She cleverly managed to avoid signing the paper by feigning faintness, due to her pregnancy, and the need to rest. She assured him she would sign next morning.

No doubt George and Bothwell would have been surprised to see Darnley accompanying Mary when she arrived at Seton. The pair had escaped with the help of a serving maid and the Captain of the Guard. Darnley thoughtlessly urged the pregnant Mary to ride ever faster through the night from Seton to the impregnable castle of Dunbar, where George had so recently been warded. They were joined there by Athol and the lords Seton and Fleming.[28] About 4,000 citizens came to their support and five days later, on 18 March, they rode back into Edinburgh.[29] All those who had boasted about taking part in Riccio's murder fled, or denied their complicity, including John Knox, who had previously praised the deed.

The plotters took their revenge on Darnley for betraying them to Mary by sending her a bond – the 'pre-murder bond' – by which the signatories committed themselves to getting rid of Riccio and which proved his complicity in the murder.[30] As a result, her relationship with him was doomed. She believed to the end of her life that he had also meant to kill her and their unborn child. It was noticed from then on how little she regarded him. Instead, she depended on Bothwell as her most resourceful and trustworthy follower. It was said that nothing of importance was now done without him. The Privy Council met on 19 March and summoned Morton, Ruthven, Lindsay and more than sixty others to appear within six days, but as they had already crossed the border into England they were banished indefinitely. Even though Moray had not been involved in the actual murder, George and Bothwell tried to persuade the Queen to imprison him, because they believed there was a danger that he might attempt to usurp her authority and bring back the banished lords.[31] However, she now split the opposition by pardoning the Chaseabout rebels, including Moray and Athol, but not Riccio's murderers.

On 21 April 1566, George, in his new position of authority as Chancellor, had the satisfaction of being able to arrange for the body of his father, the 4th Earl of Huntly, to be transported north to Strathbogie. There, at last, he could receive an honourable burial in the family vault at Elgin Cathedral, three-and-a-half years after his death on the field at Corrichie.

Reconciliation?

As the birth of her first child approached, Mary decided to bring Moray and Argyll back onto her council, contrary to the wishes of George, Bothwell and Athol. She attempted to bring about reconciliation between her nobles by summoning them to a feast in Edinburgh Castle. George regarded it as merely a temporary truce, because he blamed Moray for the death of his father and the attempted ruin of his family.[32] He would not have been pleased to hear that Mary now decreed that Moray's heirs should also succeed to the earldom of Moray. However, the antagonists formed the core of her Council for almost a year,[33] and it marked the beginning of a new close friendship between George and Archibald Campbell, 5th Earl of Argyll.

On 3 May 1566, George was one of those who signed the marriage contract between Alexander Ogilvie of Boyne and Mary Beaton, one of the Queen's four 'Mary' companions since her childhood days in France.[34] Perhaps George knew that Alexander had been his sister Jean's one-time suitor and first love, and it must have been a poignant time for her, especially as she had discovered that her husband, Bothwell, had started a liaison with her own serving maid, Bessie Crawford.

Mary made a new Will before her confinement. She made George, his mother, and his wife Anna beneficiaries with legacies, showing how fond of them she was.[35] She moved into Edinburgh Castle for the birth. The earls of Moray, Argyll, Athol and Mar joined her there, while George and Bothwell resided in town. On 19 June 1566, the country heard the joyful news that Mary had safely given birth to a son and heir. She sent messages to the King of France and the Duke of Savoy, asking them to be godfathers, and to Queen Elizabeth of England to be his godmother.

Meanwhile, George must have been aware that his sister Jean was humiliated by her husband's infidelities. However, Bothwell, whose family were the Hepburns of Hailes, attempted to mollify her by giving her life rent for his castle and lands of Nether Hailes.[36] It seemed to work for a while, as they were described as living amicably together.

George had been formally restored to the earldom of Huntly by proclamation, with all the lands and dignities that formally belonged to his father,[37] but it was still to be ratified by Parliament. Was that why he now professed to be an adherent of the Reformed faith – probably influenced by Bothwell – and refused to attend mass in the Queen's chapel?[38]

The Murder of Darnley

Although there was much celebration that Mary now had a son and heir, George and the other nobles were well aware of the serious deterioration in the relationship between Mary and her husband. She was so unhappy that she expressed a wish to die and suffered a nervous breakdown. On 20 November 1566, she went to Craigmillar Castle, on the outskirts of Edinburgh, to convalesce for two weeks. Her nobles, including George, Moray, Argyll and Maitland of Lethington, collected around her in what became known as the notorious Craigmillar Conference. Their aim was to attempt to resolve the problem. Darnley was clearly a disaster for them and the country, as well as the Queen.

However, they had a double agenda. Mainly, they wanted the Queen to pardon the exiled rebels in exchange for promising to find a solution to the problem of her husband. They revealed that Riccio was slain because Morton, Lindsay and Ruthven had wanted to save Moray from being forfeited by Parliament.

Mary was afraid to agree to a divorce in case it made her son illegitimate. Ironically, in view of what happened later, she insisted that 'Ye do nothing whereto any spot may be laid to my honour or conscience and, therefore, I pray ye rather let the matter be in the state which is abiding, till God of his goodness put remit thereto, that ye believing to do me service, may possibly turn to my hurt and displeasure.'[39] Mary was in a state of deep depression and expressed a longing to die or, at least, retire to France. However, in her weakened state, she was too trusting of Maitland's assurances that she would 'see nothing but good and approved by Parliament'.[40] He reminded her of Darnley's many offences towards her. If she would pardon the rebels, he said, they would find means to make divorce possible, for the good of herself and the realm, before he did her further evil. She said she would agree under two conditions: it must be lawful, and it must not prejudice her son. Led by Maitland, the erstwhile rebels promised to find a solution that would not harm her good name, or the legitimacy of her son.

Disastrously, she put her faith in her ministers and agreed to pardon the three main conspirators and seventy-four others. They drew up a bond known as the Craigmillar Bond for the feckless Darnley's elimination. Murder was not mentioned, but they agreed that 'such a young fool and proud tyrant should not reign or bear rule over them; he should be put off by one way or another'. The die was cast.

They got George's agreement by promising to support the official restoration of his estates and offices in Parliament, to be friends, and to persuade the Earl of Morton to agree the same. However, George added that he would only agree if whatever was done would please Mary. As was his wont, Moray skilfully avoided signing his name to the bond, but promised to 'look through his fingers'.[41]

Prince James was baptised in the Chapel Royal at Stirling Castle, according to Catholic rites, by John Hamilton, the Archbishop of St Andrews, but without the presence of his father. Aware of the hostility of nobles towards him, and probably fearing for his safety, Darnley kept saying that he was about to go abroad. George, in his new guise as a member of the Reformed Church, stood with Bothwell at the chapel door to receive the ambassadors, accompanied by the Duke of Bedford. Baby James was carried from his room by the French ambassador, who acted for the Duke of Savoy. Lady Argyll acted as proxy godmother for Queen Elizabeth, and afterwards was criticised for taking part in the mass, during which she had held Prince James in her arms. It was a grand affair. At 5 p.m. they all passed from the Chapel Royal to the grandeur of the Great Hall for supper, with the nobles standing on each side of the route, holding flaming torches. In the Great Hall, decorated with its fine tapestries, Mary sat at the middle of the long table, with the French ambassador on her right and the English ambassador on her left. George, Moray and Bothwell were all in attendance. Later, there was dancing.[42]

Mary made gifts and concessions to the Reformed Church, and assigned ecclesiastical properties in the burghs to the town councils. On Christmas Eve, she made the fatal mistake of pardoning the Riccio murderers, the men Darnley most feared, because he had betrayed them. To add to Darnley's troubles, he was now sick, probably with syphilis. He returned to his father's house in Glasgow, where he felt safer, in the centre of his family's Lennox influence. He wrote letters to the Pope and Philip II expressing devotion to the mass, possibly considering posing as an alternative to Mary as champion of the Catholic faith.[43]

His wife feared that she might be pregnant again, so she needed at least the appearance of a reconciliation with Darnley, as the child could not have been his. Mary and Darnley had been estranged at least since James' christening the previous December. On 20 January 1567, George and Bothwell accompanied her for part of the way when she went to visit Darnley in Glasgow. She was gentle with her husband, and persuaded him to come back to Edinburgh. It was decided that it would be healthier for him to recuperate in the old provost's lodge at Kirk o'Field until he recovered, rather than in the low-lying Palace of Holyroodhouse. He regretfully agreed to this plan, after Mary promised to renew conjugal relations, and was conveyed there. George and Bothwell visited him on that fateful night of 9 February 1567. Mary spent the evening with him, but then went off to attend the wedding celebrations of a favourite courtier.

In the early hours of the following day, George was awoken in his room in Holyroodhouse to be told the shocking news about an explosion, and the finding of Darnley's body in the grounds of Kirk o'Field. He immediately rushed to Bothwell's room and, together, they went to inform the Queen.[44] Once again, Mary could have been a victim, or she could at least have been blamed for the murder, along with Bothwell.

The Consequences of Darnley's Murder

Darnley was buried quietly at Holyroodhouse, beside Mary's father, James V. Mary was in such a state of nervous collapse that her doctors urged a change of air, so two days later she went to Seton House for three days. George and Bothwell were left in charge of baby James. When she returned to Edinburgh, she commissioned them to take him to Stirling and into the care of John Erskine, Earl of Mar, who consequently had to give up his charge of Edinburgh Castle, much to the regret of the people of Edinburgh.

Instead, Bothwell was now given charge of the castle and town as Provost. This was particularly provocative, because he was commonly believed to be guilty of Darnley's murder. On 28 March 1567 the Privy Council ordered that he be put on trial. As a result of pressure from Darnley's father, the Earl of Lennox, Queen Elizabeth and her French relatives, Mary agreed. Parliament issued a proclamation summoning all of the Estates to Edinburgh for the trial to begin on 12 April. Moray left Edinburgh on 7 April, just five days before the trial was due to begin. He had obtained a pass to go through England on his way to Flanders or France.[45]

The trial was a farce, because no one had the courage to accuse

Bothwell while 'such a dangerous and unprincipled man was clearly paramount at Court' and had command of the castle, town and the port of Leith', as well as so many officers around him. Lennox begged for a delay in the trial so that he could assemble supporters. He set off from Glasgow with a large party, but was stopped en route and told he could only bring six of them. He decided to turn back. England's new ambassador, Sir William Drury, arrived in Edinburgh from Berwick on the day of the trial with a strongly worded letter from Elizabeth supporting Lennox's plea to delay the trial. However, he was not able to gain access to Mary, because she made excuses not see him.[46] He reported that he found Edinburgh packed with 4,000 of Bothwell's followers, and 200 harquebusier guards. The trial was not delayed even though Lennox, the chief accuser, was not present. Bothwell was declared innocent, although it was 'heavily murmured that he was guilty thereof'.[47] Many of those who cleared him, including George, had themselves signed the Craigmillar Bond in an attempt to free Mary of Darnley.

Bothwell's Marriage to the Queen

Now that Bothwell was officially cleared of the murder, he immediately set about marrying the Queen, despite the fact that he was already married to George's sister Jean. On 27 April, he invited George and twenty-seven of the other lords and prelates, who were in Edinburgh for the Parliament, to a lavish feast at the Ainslie Tavern. Following 'a liberal flow of alcohol', a document was produced by Bothwell and passed around for all to sign. It expressed support for a plan that he should marry Mary, on the grounds that it was not considered good for her to be alone. She needed a strong consort, and Bothwell was clearly that man. This document is known as the Ainslie Bond. It was signed by ten earls, eleven lords and eight bishops. George, Maitland of Lethington, Seton, Morton and Sutherland were amongst those who signed.

The following day George and the whole of the nobility, except Lennox and Moray, accompanied the Queen to the Tolbooth for the official opening of Parliament. Argyll bore the crown, Bothwell the sceptre, and Crawford the sword of honour.[48] Next day, the Estates ratified gifts of land to all those who had helped clear Bothwell of Darnley's murder, including George, Maitland of Lethington, Morton and Bothwell himself.[49] The forfeitures imposed after the battle of Corrichie were, at last, officially ratified as being reversed for George, his cousin the Earl of Sutherland, his brother Adam Gordon, George Gordon of Beldorney and his eldest son, Alexander Gordon, James Gordon of Lesmoir, James Gordon of Tillyangus, and many others.[50] Lord James had the earldom of Moray ratified, as did James Ogilvie the lands of Findlater and Deskford.[51] Queen Mary formally took the Reformed Church under her protection. Afterwards, on passing from the Tolbooth to the Abbey, George had the honour of bearing the crown, Argyll the sceptre and Bothwell the sword of honour.[52] Meanwhile, the Earl of Lennox departed to England in disgust.

When George was accompanying Queen Mary on a ride over the Almond Brig on 24 April, they were held up by Bothwell and an armed force. George was among those taken with her to Dunbar Castle, but he was soon released. Rumours were rife in Edinburgh that Mary had been abducted and 'ravished' by Bothwell. When word reached the provost in Edinburgh, the common bell was rung and the castle artillery fired. People ran to arm themselves.[53] Word even went round that Mary had been taken willingly.

Meanwhile, in Dunbar Castle, Bothwell managed to get Mary's agreement to the marriage by showing her the Ainslie Bond, which purported to prove that the nobles supported the idea. He then galloped off to Crichton Castle to obtain Jean's agreement for a divorce. They both made separate pleas, Bothwell stating that the marriage should be dissolved because they had not got dispensation from the Pope for being closely related. This was a lie, as Jean had the dispensation hidden amongst her papers, but she did not bother to produce it. Bothwell had the gall to ask John Hamilton, the Catholic Archbishop of St Andrews who had pronounced the original dispensation and had been conveniently reinstated, to say that there had been no such dispensation.

A commission of six clerics was set up to look into the case. Five were reluctant to act and judge; only one, the Canon of Dunbar Collegiate (no doubt bearing in mind that Bothwell had charge of nearby Dunbar Castle), agreed to judge and gave sentence in Bothwell's favour, on the grounds that the couple were related within the forbidden degree of consanguinity. Jean, meanwhile, filed her petition on the grounds of Bothwell's adultery with her serving maid, for which she had a witness, Thomas Craigwallis, who had guarded the door. Bothwell denied it, but when further witnesses were examined the judge decided in Jean's favour and divorce was pronounced on 3 May, in record time. Bothwell was declared an adulterer, and Jean was free to marry again whom she pleased.[54] No doubt it was a relief for both George and Jean to know that her canny marriage contract allowed her to retain the rents of Crichton, as well as her recently acquired Nether Hailes estates, for the rest of her life, meaning that she would be well supported financially.

Despite what was happening to his sister, George was still in the company of the Queen and Bothwell, part of the entourage accompanying them back to Edinburgh. As they entered the city through the West Gate, the artillery guns were fired in salute. It was noticed that Bothwell was leading Mary by her horse's bridle, as if she were his captive. George seems to have supported the idea of Mary's marriage to Bothwell: Drury, the English ambassador, reported to Cecil an incident in which George Gordon nearly 'thrust Maitland through with a sword' for insulting Bothwell's aspirations to marry the Queen. Interestingly, Mary leapt to Maitland's defence, saying that 'if a hair of his head did perish, she would make George forfeit his estates and lose his life'. This seems to suggest that she respected Maitland's reservations and his right to express them.[55]

On 11 May the banns were proclaimed. The fearless minister of St Giles', John Craig, refused to read them. He wanted assurance that Mary had not been raped or held prisoner by Bothwell in Dunbar Castle. She sent him the requested writ the next day. However, he was summoned to explain himself, and bravely admonished Bothwell. On 12 May George bore the crown to the Court of Session, for Bothwell's elevation to the titles of Duke of Orkney and Lord of Shetland.

On the eve of their wedding, Bothwell's coarse language caused the diarist Sir James Melville to walk out of the supper.[56] George was one of the very few lords present at the marriage conducted by Adam Hepburn, Bishop of Orkney, in the very early hours of 15 May in the old Chapel Royal of Holyroodhouse. It was not a happy occasion, with none of the customary celebrations.[57] Mary wrote a letter to the Pope explaining the circumstances of her marriage, signing herself 'your most devoted daughter'. However, not long after this, the Pope declared his intention to have no further communications with Mary. Her decision to marry Bothwell was another grave tactical error, especially so soon after the murder of her husband, and Bothwell still a major suspect in it, despite his trial.

Something must have occurred during the honeymoon, because it marked the end of Mary's happiness with Bothwell. Was it something he revealed? She asked for a knife to kill herself, and also threatened to drown herself. It might have been something to do with the scandalous relationship between her mother, Mary of Guise, and Bothwell's father.[58]

After the marriage, George and Crawford were the only earls to appear at council meetings.[59] On 6 June 1567, a new bond, which had been prepared before the marriage, was circulated amongst the many nobles who had signed the Ainslie Bond supporting her marriage to Bothwell. They now vowed to rescue Mary from 'her captivity' by Bothwell. The signatures included twelve earls and fourteen lords, who called themselves 'The Confederates'.

Mary and Bothwell assembled arms and set off from Holyrood for Bothwell's Borthwick Castle, which neighboured Crichton. Morton and others began to converge threateningly on Borthwick. Bothwell managed to escape to the security of Dunbar, as Mary did later, disguised as a man. The Confederates withdrew to Edinburgh, where they called the people to arms, to rescue the Queen from 'that barbarous tyrant, cruel murderer'.[60]

George was one of the few nobles to support the Queen and Bothwell when they raised a small army. She issued a series of proclamations, one of which called on all those aged between sixteen and sixty to come to her aid, on pain of death; then another, saying they should come to Edinburgh; and another stating that the rebels would be forgiven for their past misdemeanours if they departed for home. However, the latter proclamation was intercepted.[61]

Athol came to Edinburgh to join the Confederates, with a great number of followers intent on punishing Bothwell. Even Mary's secretary, Maitland of Lethington, had joined them. George attempted to hold Edinburgh for the Queen but was all too aware of the many 'unfriends' in the city. He made his way to the security of the castle, where he found others of 'the Queen's friends' taking refuge, such as the Archbishop of St Andrews, who had supported Bothwell's divorce plea, as well as George's uncle, Alexander Gordon, the reformed Bishop of Galloway, the provost of Crichton, and Claud Hamilton, youngest son of the Duke of Chatelherault.

With ill-concealed reluctance, George and the Archbishop of St Andrews attempted to raise men. However, Mary and Bothwell were overconfident about the amount of support they had and, fatally, sallied forth towards Edinburgh without waiting for reinforcements.[62] The Confederate lords, including Morton, Athol, Ruthven, Lindsay and Kirkcaldy of Grange, marched out of Edinburgh to meet them.

The van bore a banner showing the corpse of Darnley lying under a tree, with his infant son kneeling before him and bearing the legend: 'Judge and avenge my cause, O Lord.'

The result was a disastrous confrontation between the two sides at Carberry Hill, about eight miles east of the city, on 15 June 1567. The French ambassador, du Croc, was deputed by the Confederates to beg Mary to abandon Bothwell, which she furiously refused to do, saying that many of those same lords had signed the bond recommending the marriage.[63] Bothwell offered to fight in single combat against a champion chosen by the Confederates, but Mary's army was melting away.

Only after seeing Bothwell safely gallop away did she surrender herself to Kirkcaldy and the Confederates. We can only imagine how George and Mary's other friends must have felt when they saw or heard how roughly she was treated thereafter, her chapel and possessions in the palace smashed up or stolen and, worse still, her removal as a prisoner to the island of Lochleven, where no one was allowed to visit her.

George then heard that the Confederates had again demanded she divorce Bothwell, and that she had refused. Then came the startling news that she had decided to abdicate in favour of her son, James, as she did not have the heart to continue. What is more, George was told, she had begged that her brother, the Earl of Moray, now on the Continent, should take over the reigns of government; and, failing him, the Earl of Morton. Not even the English and French ambassadors were allowed to see her, no matter how urgently they demanded it, so this version of events was spread around and could not be verified. As far as they knew, it was true that Mary had decided to abdicate. George now agreed to sign the Confederacy Bond, which recapitulated the events surrounding the Darnley murder, stating that Mary was innocent but that Bothwell was guilty and had treated her badly. George would certainly have witnessed his ill-treatment at close hand.

However, by the end of June, George had deserted the Confederates and joined the lords gathering at Dumbarton on the west coast to plan Mary's rescue. He signed the Dumbarton Bond shortly after and returned north to Strathbogie, declaring himself Mary's Lieutenant of the North, as his father had been, and ordering everyone to place themselves under arms in readiness to meet her, once she was free.

On 29 July, the Confederates arranged baby James' coronation at Stirling Castle. Only five earls and eight lords were present.[64] He was anointed by the pliable Adam Hepburn, Bishop of Orkney, so soon after he had married Mary and Bothwell. John Knox preached. He, who had written of the 'monstrous rule of women', must have been most satisfied at the turn of events. The people were told by the Confederates to ignore George's call to arms, saying that his lieutenancy of the north had been rescinded.

Meanwhile, Bothwell had also come north to Strathbogie, seeking aid from his erstwhile brother-in-law, but George refused to help him. He said that he hoped Bothwell would fail in his attempt to escape, as he had been such a bad husband to his sister and to the Queen. Bothwell took refuge in the fortified Palace of Spynie with his uncle, Patrick Hepburn, the notorious Bishop of Moray. A plot was hatched to capture or kill him, which the bishop's illegitimate sons were forced to join. The plot went wrong, and during a fight Bothwell killed one of the bishop's sons. He then set off by sea, with three 'well furnished' ships for his dukedom of Orkney. Five ships were sent from Dundee to chase him, commanded by the redoubtable Kirkcaldy of Grange. They almost caught up with him in a Shetland harbour, but he just managed to slip out of it as they came in. He fled to Norway, where he was soon captured and sent to Denmark. There he was brought to justice by the family whose daughter, Anna Throndsen, he had jilted some years before. He spent the rest of his life in a wretched prison, where he went mad and died in 1578.

PART II: KING'S PARTY AND QUEEN'S PARTY

Moray's Regency

On 11 August 1567, Moray returned from the Continent and visited Mary at Lochleven. He informed her that she was in danger of being executed. In fear of her life, she gave what he called 'a voluntary confirmation' of her nomination of him as Regent. She was led to believe by England's ambassador, Sir Nicholas Throgmorton, who was now allowed to see her, that she would not be held to her abdication decision, because it had been procured under duress. However, on 22 August 1567 Moray was officially proclaimed Regent for the infant King James VI.

This was very bad news for George, who was now in the north and had been joined by his mother and his sister Jean from Edinburgh. On her way north, Jean had visited her cousin Agnes Keith, Moray's wife, and told her that she never wanted anything more to do with her ex-husband, Bothwell. With Moray now in power in Edinburgh, and in the neighbouring earldom of Moray, their position as supporters of Mary was tenuous. George obviously felt alarmed, because he took the precaution of requesting his uncle, the Bishop of Galloway, to ask Athol and Maitland of Lethington to intercede for him, to assure Regent Moray that he would not make any trouble.

At the end of September George signed an agreement to that effect and was reinstated on the Council, with Moray as the new Chancellor. On 12 December George even carried the sceptre for the opening of the first Parliament of James VI. Argyll bore the sword of honour, and the twelve-year-old Lord Angus was given the honour of bearing the crown. George was even chosen as one of the Lords of the Articles, as were Argyll, Morton, Athol and Mar, together with the bishops of Moray, Orkney, Galloway and the lords Home, Ruthven and Lindsay.[65] As time passed, more peers took their places on Moray's council. It looked as if he had successfully consolidated his power and had brought about unity at the top.

However, the Hamiltons were still hostile, but they were scattered and their chief, the Duke of Chatelheraut, remained an exile in France; the Queen's cause was not dead, however. The Duke believed that if there had to be a Regent, it should be himself, as heir apparent. The crowning of James weakened his claim to the throne, because it made Darnley's younger brother next in line. The Hamiltons took the initiative and sent an emissary to France to persuade the Duke to lead a rebellion on behalf of the beleaguered Mary.[66]

The new government formally established the Reformed Church, with the laws against the mass that had been passed by Parliament in 1560 but had not been ratified by Mary. Moray now sent drastic orders that the lead was to be stripped off the cathedrals of Aberdeen and Elgin. This was to go towards the war effort against the Spanish in Holland and to raise money for the government. George was even ordered to make sure that no one interfered with the work. This must have been particularly galling for him and all the family, with their father so recently buried in the family vault at Elgin Cathedral. Many in the north-east, Catholic or not, who saw it happening or heard about it must have been horrified. Maybe the fact that the ship carrying the lead foundered and sank was considered divine judgement. There were even rumours that the captain had scuttled it intentionally.

Early the next year, 1568, four of Bothwell's servants were publicly charged with Darnley's murder. They were hanged, drawn and quartered, and 'their bodies thrown on a great fire'.[67] On the scaffold, one of them, John Hay the younger of Tallow, revealed that a bond had been signed for the murder. He named not only his master, Bothwell, for his involvement, but also George, Argyll, Balfour and Maitland of Lethington, among others who had signed.

Meanwhile, Queen Elizabeth, who was not enthusiastic about the idea of regents, seriously considered the restoration of Mary, but only on the condition that she accepted Anglo-Scottish religious conformity.[68]

When George heard of Mary's escape from Lochleven on 2 May 1568, that she was making for Hamilton and, crucially, that the abdication had been forced on her out of fear for her life, he joined other nobles who were calling for her restoration. Nine earls, nine bishops, twelve commendators and eighteen lords, some from Moray's council, pledged their support, and up to 6,000 men joined her. George again hastened north to muster a force on her behalf. However, when he came near Perth with his 2,600 men, he was frustrated to find all the passes along the River Tay strongly guarded and that he could proceed no further. He must have been dismayed to hear that, on 13 May, Mary's force, making for the security of the Dumbarton stronghold, was defeated at the battle of Langside as they attempted to skirt Glasgow. Moray, with a much smaller force, defeated them, mostly thanks to Kirkcaldy's skilful leadership. This is ironic, as Kirkcaldy of Grange had second thoughts about the regency when he heard of the duress that Mary was under to agree to her abdication. No doubt George was horrified to discover that, against the advice of most of her followers, she had escaped by boat across the Solway Firth to England. Mary expected her cousin Elizabeth to give her support, relying on her disapproval of rebellions. However, she was to be bitterly disappointed.

Mary's Incarceration in England

Mary's presence in England was an embarrassment to Elizabeth, because she had not repudiated her claim to the English throne. Elizabeth refused to deal with Moray's administration and sent Throgmorton to negotiate for Mary's release on the condition that she divorced Bothwell, which she had strenuously refused to do at Lochleven. In June, Elizabeth wrote to Mary stating her conditions: that she face trial for her part in the murder of Darnley, and that she agree to Moray's answering for his rebellion. Mary agreed, and in July she appointed George's father-in-law, the Duke of Chatelherault, as her representative.

On 9 July, a band was circulated round the country by Moray that forced people to acknowledge James VI. George signed unwillingly in Aberdeen. However, the nobles were clearly dividing along the lines of those who did not accept the status quo and those who did. A parliament was called by Moray, at which those who had refused to sign were to be forfeited. Later in the month George met Argyll and other northern supporters of Mary at Largs. Others held a convention in Ayrshire, which decided to march against Moray in Edinburgh, to pre-empt the forfeitures.[69]

On 14 August, a Patrick Hepburn, parson of Kinnoir, great-nephew of Bothwell and illegitimate son of the Bishop of Moray (also Patrick Hepburn), was captured by Ruthven and Lindsay at Scone. He was taken to Stirling to be examined by Moray on the grounds of a conspiracy to kill him. He was then sent to Edinburgh for further questioning, where his father, who had given succour to the fleeing Bothwell, was warded in the castle.[70] There must have been no proof of the conspiracy, because the younger Patrick Hepburn was freed. He appears three years later in connection with the story of George's sister, Margaret.

In mid-August Moray held a parliament, in the traditional Edinburgh Tolbooth, and elected new Lords of the Articles. The only bishops present were of Orkney and Moray – who, having been held in the castle, were afraid not to attend. A new group now carried the royal insignia: Morton the crown, Glencairn the sceptre and Mar the sword of honour. They forfeited many Hamiltons, including the Archbishop of St Andrew's and Claud Hamilton.[71]

On 12 September 1568 George and others, calling themselves 'Assisters of the Queen's Grace', signed the Dumbarton Bond. On 4 October, Mary's first trial was held in York. However, she was not allowed to defend herself in person. She, Moray, and Elizabeth were each to have their own representatives to speak for them.

At last, on 21 October, Mary expressed a willingness to use the law to obtain an official separation from Bothwell. The trial was a convoluted affair, because Mary's representatives were not entirely sure of her innocence and Moray's were divided: Maitland of Lethington, for instance, favoured Mary's restoration and her marriage to the Duke of Norfolk. In November, the conference reassembled in Westminster and then again in December at Hampton Court.

There, Moray's side produced the Casket Letters, which had been found in June, but he now said that they proved Mary's compliance in the murder of her husband. Elizabeth's judgement was delivered by Cecil on 10 January 1569. It said that nothing detrimental to Mary's honour had been shown, and no truth could be drawn one way or the other, so the trial was adjourned indefinitely. The matter was now in abeyance. Mary had not been found innocent, but neither had she been convicted.[72] However, Moray had gained a cautious recognition for his government and a loan of £5,000.[73] Elizabeth was pleased that she had avoided provoking France to action in support of Mary.

On returning to Aberdeen, where he was Sheriff, George insisted that the Provost declare for Mary.[74] He persuaded the burgh of Aberdeen to support a bond asserting their loyalty to Mary and promising support in resisting those who opposed her.[75] He now became active as Mary's Lieutenant in the North. He captured Dingwall Castle and gained widespread support from others, including the Barclays, Leslies and Abercrombies. The Duke of Chatelherault responded to the call for his return from France on the pretext that he needed to see his physicians.[76] By March 1569, the whole of the north was held for the Queen by George. With Argyll, Cassilis, Crawford and Eglinton holding the west and south-west, and the Hamiltons the south-east, they were between them strong enough to crush Moray.

However, fatal to Mary's cause, her supporters received a message from her to disperse their followers. Queen Elizabeth claimed that she had said the same to Moray, but he did not receive her communication.[77] George took an army to Brechin, but the men of Angus and Fife complained that he was persecuting those who adhered to the King, by 'taking their places and spoiling their goods'.[78]

By April, Moray had tried to bring peace by asking the Marian lords to sign the Pacification of Edinburgh. The newly returned Duke of Chatelherault refused to sign, and was immediately arrested and imprisoned. George, who had been absent, also refused to sign. The others were so discouraged that first Argyll, then Crawford, Cassilis and several other Marian lords and lairds entered a kind of armistice and signed a Bond of Loyalty to the King. This recognised the authority of Moray as Regent, and annulled any previous bonds to any other authority.[79] Crucially, this enabled Moray to further resist Queen Elizabeth's attempt to allow Mary back, despite her having divorced Bothwell and given religious guarantees.[80] Moray toured the north-east, receiving the submission of George's vassals. Eventually, on 18 May, he too yielded to the pressure when heavy fines were imposed on him and his supporters. This time the Burgh of Aberdeen was excused from paying a fine, on the grounds that it had been coerced by George.

George was now diverted from national events by his involvement in the dramatic rescue of his young cousin, eighteen-year-old Alexander Gordon, 12th Earl of Sutherland, from the clutches of the Earl of Caithness. Alexander must have regaled George, Jean and their mother with the horrific story of how, aged only fifteen, he had returned from a hunting trip at Helmsdale Castle to find both of his parents dying, poisoned by the hand of Isabel Sinclair. Isabel's son also died, because he inadvertently took the poison intended for Alexander, who managed to escape to Skibo Castle.

However, he was later caught by the Earl of Caithness, who made him his ward and forced him to marry his daughter, who was aged thirty-two. She, meanwhile, had been carrying on a notorious relationship with someone else. The Earl of Caithness concocted another plot to have young Alexander murdered, so that his own son might become Earl of Sutherland. Alexander's friends, hearing about the plan, sent one of their number into the castle disguised as a pedlar. He told Alexander about their rescue idea, which involved a mock ambush during Alexander's morning walk. As a result, he got away with his friends, crossing the Dornoch Firth in a storm. George gave him a home at Huntly Castle, where he remained for the next few years until he came of age in 1573. George also provided for Alexander's friends, known as the Men of Murray,[81] who then supported the Gordons in Mary's cause. They were mentioned specifically as acting with Adam when the civil war reached the north-east in 1571. Alexander was able to witness George's work restoring Huntly Castle.

In view of Mary's agreement to divorce Bothwell, a convention was held at the end of July in Perth to consider a proposal for her restoration. George supported the motion, but it was overwhelmingly rejected. This demonstrates Moray's strength and the weakness of the Marians.[82]

In September Maitland of Lethington was arrested, on the grounds that he was privy to the plan to murder Darnley. He was put in the castle in the charge of his friend Kirkcaldy of Grange. Moray attempted to get Kirkcaldy removed from his post as Provost of Edinburgh, but the town council rejected the request.

In January 1570, the Northern Rising of Catholics in England was a threat to Moray as well as to Elizabeth. He was prompt to offer support for action against them. However, when they were defeated, he craftily offered to deal with any of them who crossed the border. The Earl of Northumberland did so, but was immediately arrested. Moray then used him to bargain with Elizabeth that, in exchange for his release, she would give him financial assistance and back his regime.[83]

New Hope for the Marians

In January 1570 all was to change for the Marians. While he was riding through Linlithgow, Moray was shot by James Hamilton of Bothwellhaugh from the window of the Archbishop of St Andrews' house. Moray was badly wounded and died the next day. This changed the situation dramatically and gave the Marians new hope. Mary, too, was delighted at the news and awarded a pension to the perpetrators. However, Elizabeth said that Moray's death was a disaster, and that she had lost 'the best friend she had in the world'.[84] Those who regretted his passing referred to him as 'the Good Regent', but it is hard to disentangle his services to Church and state from self-interest and ambition.[85] He was buried in St Giles'. The government was now without focus, and many of the King's party deserted. To them, what followed was six months of stalemate.

George and the other Marians were jubilant at Moray's demise, and the Hamiltons planned to rescue the duke, who was still imprisoned in the castle. They gathered supporters in Glasgow. With Moray gone, Kirkcaldy, Maitland and others, including nine earls and thirteen lords, joined the Queen's party, which renewed efforts on her behalf. At Maitland's suggestion, 'the lords of both factions' wrote a letter to Queen Elizabeth appealing for Mary's restoration. This was signed by, George, Athol, Crawford, the Lords Ogilvie, Home, Seton and George's brother-in-law, the Master of Forbes, Maitland and others.

However, things changed again in February, because the Pope issued a bull depriving Elizabeth of her 'pretended right' to the English Crown. This implied that Mary was the rightful sovereign of both kingdoms. It placed Elizabeth in danger from Catholic plots to rescue Mary and make her Queen of England, so she now supported the King's men as being more reliable allies in Scotland.

On 14 March the Council declared the Hamiltons responsible for the death of Moray. George, Maitland, Athol, the Master of Forbes and the lords Ogilvie, Home, Seton and others, 'being of one faction who will to have the Queen's grace regained', came to a convention in Edinburgh to confer with Morton and Mar on the dangerous state of affairs. However, they received no encouragement for their proposals for the Queen's recall, and they left next morning. The Council affirmed that the regency should continue.

At the end of March, George and others of the Queen's friends sent another letter to Queen Elizabeth describing in graphic terms how the country was dividing between the two factions: supporters of the mother, or of the son. The letter said: 'All are divided, not only the nobles, but also the gentlemen and commons universally, and not unequally divided.' They appealed to her as 'the princess in Christendom who had the best means . . . and the best reason' to 'quench this heat going among us before it burst into a flame, which is able before long to set both countries on fire . . . We require water at your hand to repress the rage of the flame.' In particular, they begged her not to 'bring oil, timber and other materials to increase and increase [the fire]' by supporting one faction, but 'by the reducing of the two claims to one', remove the need for the various factions to exist.[86]

The Duke was released in April. An English army entered Scotland on a punitive expedition against those who had assisted the fugitives from the English Northern Rising. Their forces did much damage in the Borders, which won them few friends in Scotland. However, Morton returned from England with the intention of making use of English help to defeat the Duke, George and others of the Queen's faction.[87]

In April, George, Argyll, Athol and the lords of the western parts of the country were made welcome in Edinburgh. However, out of fear of the English, the magistrates persuaded them all, including the Duke and the other lords, barons and gentlemen of the Queen's side to leave the city, for the sake of the burgh's safety. Meanwhile, Kirkcaldy was granted £200 by the Council to strengthen the castle's defences.

In May, Sir William Drury was sent to Scotland with a force from Berwick. It penetrated into the Hamilton lands in Lothian and Lanarkshire, and assisted the King's troops in a siege of Dumbarton Castle, which was held for Queen. Again, their actions did not make friends for England or the King's party.

The council met to decide who should be Regent in place of Moray, but they failed to reach agreement. Almost in despair, they appealed to Queen Elizabeth for a final decision. Her choice was Lennox,[88] father of the murdered Darnley and grandfather of the infant King.

The French King's representative landed at Dumbarton and gave hope to the Queen's party by thanking them for maintaining her cause, and promising aid. There was talk of invading England. Encouraged by this, George became busy in the north, enforcing universal obedience to the Queen's cause. His brother Adam led a force that succeeded in taking and fortifying Brechin in the Queen's name. They came down to Edinburgh with 3,000 men in the hope of enlisting support there, but the magistrates refused to allow the gates to be opened.

On 12 July, Maitland of Lethington won over his friend Kirkcaldy of Grange, who officially changed sides. Because Kirkcaldy was in charge of the castle, this resulted in the important outcome of putting it in the hands of the Marians. He further strengthened it against the approaching English army accompanying Lennox. He seized the Tolbooth, and was able to attend services at St Giles' when Knox withdrew to St Andrews.[89] George's uncle, Alexander Gordon, Bishop of Galloway, now occupied the pulpit. He had been the first of the Scottish bishops to embrace the Reformed faith.

At the approach of the English army, who were again harassing the Borders, the Queen's party withdrew to Linlithgow, where they proclaimed Mary's restoration. They then went to Glasgow, the Lennox heartland, to besiege the castle there. Lennox entered Scotland, supported by the English under Sir William Drury, and marched to Edinburgh, Linlithgow, Falkirk and Stirling, where Lennox's grandson, the young King, was being cared for by the Earl of Mar. Many welcomed and joined them, including Morton, Glencairn, and the lords Ruthven, Lindsay and Sempill. They then set off to relieve the siege of Glasgow Castle. Friends and kindred of Lennox came to offer their services to him. When the Duke heard of their approach, the siege broke up. About 4,000 men marched to Hamilton, where the Duke's castle, town and other houses were blown up. The English then returned to England, accompanied by Morton. Lennox and his followers returned to his base in Glasgow.[90] In July, Lennox was appointed Lord Lieutenant of Scotland at Stirling.

Meanwhile, George and Argyll continued to act successfully as Queen's lieutenants in their own spheres of the north and west respectively. Kirkcaldy and Maitland held the trump card of Edinburgh Castle. Contemporary records say that, at this time, 'the son's party daily decays, and the mother's party daily increases'.[91] Queen Elizabeth now insisted that the only way out of the impasse was for Lennox to become Regent.[92]

The Regency of Lennox

Lennox was duly elected Regent. In some ways he was the obvious choice, as he was the King's grandfather and closest relative but, if anyone was to be Regent, the Duke of Chatelherault still considered it should be himself as next in line to the throne. Lennox was not a popular choice from other points of view. He had lived in England for twenty years, following his forfeiture in 1544, and was regarded as an English subject. Maitland of Lethington asked whether 'as an Englishman sworn . . . could he be lawfully Regent of this realm?' George referred to Lennox as 'an alien, a lackey of England, a traitor, bought by English gold'. However, Lennox countered that he was 'a Scotsman of the royal blood and surname'.[93] He was formally made Regent at a convention of the Three Estates in Edinburgh. Maitland refused to work for his administration, and called for the restoration of Mary. However, he also favoured a continuation of the entente with England, which he had long worked for.[94]

Military moves were made in the Queen's name against the new Regent by the Duke, Argyll and George, who was invested as Lieutenant General. Civil war could not be avoided. George made a contract with Hugh Fraser, 6th Lord Lovat in Inverness (or possibly, in Aberdeen) that he and his followers would assist in the Queen's cause.

George called for a parliament, to which the lords of both parties were summoned, to be held in Linlithgow on 21 September. Lennox called for a rival parliament at the same place and at the same time, but in the King's name. Lennox's purpose was for his parliament to forfeit all of the Queen's lords and ruin his ancient enemies, the Hamiltons. The bait for the lords who came over to his side was a promise that they would share in the consequent spoils.

Lennox complained to the Earl of Sussex that George not only resisted the King's authority but, under the pretext of administering justice, oppressed the King's supporters within his sphere of influence. 'He sends out letters and holds courts in the Queen's name and, what is more,' he said, 'his men force reluctant officials at sword point to make a proclamation calling out all men in his area of influence to meet him in warlike manner.'[95]

Morton was sent north with 1,000 horsemen, with Lennox following, aiming to ambush George on his way south to the parliament he had called at Linlithgow. At Brechin, George was warned of their approach and managed to escape just in time. Lennox besieged the castle. George had promised to relieve those inside within eight days, but failed to do so and the besieged surrendered. Three hundred men inside the castle and hiding in the kirk steeple were captured, and thirty of the leaders were executed.[96] The Regent then went on to besiege the castle of Doune, held for the Queen, which yielded after three days. Five were executed there.

In October 1570, England, through the Earl of Sussex, mediated a six-month truce, during which George, the Duke and Argyll were instructed to cease hearing civil actions, and were told that criminal justice should be administered in the King's name only. At some point during this year Alexander Gordon, the Bishop of Galloway, John Leslie, Bishop of Ross, and Lord Livingstone went to England on Mary's behalf, hoping to bring about her release and establish peace in the country. They made various undertakings:

- Mary would renounce her claim to the throne of England while Elizabeth or any offspring of hers lived.
- Mary would agree not to admit or be in league with any foreign prince against England, nor admit foreign soldiers into Scotland .
- She would have no intelligence with the English or Irish without Queen Elizabeth's knowledge.
- Rebels and fugitives from justice who had taken refuge in Scotland would be sent back.
- The murders of Moray and Darnley would be investigated.
- The Queen's son would be delivered to England.
- Mary should undertake not to marry anyone from England without the advice and knowledge of the Queen of England, nor any other person without the consent of the nobility of Scotland.
- The Treaty of Edinburgh would be confirmed.
- They would be prepared to lose lands held in France.

It all came to nothing in the end, because agreement could not be reached over the articles. Alexander Gordon returned to Scotland, and Queen Mary appointed John Leslie, Bishop of Ross, to stay in London as her ambassador. Mary now ordered her followers and assisters in Scotland to take up arms against her enemies there, and to put no further trust in a deceitful truce.[97] After the six-month truce expired, civil war resumed.

In November, twenty-three peers, including Lord Forbes, again wrote to Elizabeth saying they were even prepared to send their sons, brothers or other next of kin to England, four at a time, as hostages, in exchange for Mary's return. The document was signed at Doune and, under George, at Strathbogie.

In 1571, Philip II of Spain plotted his 'enterprise of England'. His aim was for a fleet to sail to England with the Duke of Alba's troops from the Netherlands. They would capture Elizabeth on one of her summer progresses. A rising of the English Catholics would liberate Mary, who would then marry the Duke of Norfolk and re-establish Catholicism in both countries.

At the start of that year things looked encouraging for the Queen's party. George held power in the north-east and Angus; the Hamiltons were in control of Clydesdale; and Kirkcaldy held the castle with the country's munitions, regalia and the records of the kingdom. Meanwhile, members of the King's party based themselves in Leith.

However, the balance of power changed again in the spring, when Lennox's men dramatically took the important stronghold of Dumbarton Castle. They achieved what had previously seemed impossible because of the height of the rock and the surrounding water. They had the benefit of information supplied by an informer, and succeeded in scaling its walls. Among those captured was the ablest of the Hamiltons, the Archbishop of St Andrews, and also the French ambassador.[98] The Castle Keeper, Lord Fleming, and five others escaped by boat. 'Great munitions from the King of France' were found. The loss of Dumbarton meant that the Queen's party was less likely to receive further help from France, as that was the main port they used.[99] The Archbishop of St Andrews was taken to Stirling and hanged in his vestments for his part in the murder of Darnley, and for knowledge of the plot to assassinate Moray.

With new confidence, Lennox summoned a parliament to be held in Edinburgh. On 14 May he passed from Stirling to Linlithgow, where he met Morton and commissioners from England. From there they headed towards Edinburgh, where they were surprised to find themselves unwelcome. Kirkcaldy still held the castle for the Queen and was Provost of the town. He had been joined by George and others. Lennox now made a proclamation for all to meet him at Linlithgow, and returned to Stirling.

George heard that Lennox was expecting supplies to arrive from England by sea at Leith and had sent the Laird of Carmichael with his armed household servants to fetch it. George left Edinburgh with

Hume to ambush the party. A very hot skirmish ensued, resulting in George and Hume having to flee to the gates of Edinburgh, pursued by Carmichael. Some of their men were killed, and some taken prisoner. For revenge, George and Claud Hamilton again marched their force out of Edinburgh, meaning to attack Morton's home at Dalkeith, but Morton heard of their intention and came out to meet them. A sharp fray ensued, with many hurt on both sides. However, this time George and Claud Hamilton had more men, and took forty prisoners.[100]

England's Sir William Drury now tried to arrange another truce, but the meeting degenerated into a fight, with many killed and taken prisoner. Lennox fortified Leith to prevent help arriving for the Queen's party from France.

Kirkcaldy realised that, as he had changed sides, there were many in the castle who were not supporters of the Queen's cause, so he made a proclamation to allow those who were not with him to leave. Many took the opportunity, but then offered their services to Lennox at Leith. Kirkcaldy heard that people were calling him a traitor to king and country, so he issued a challenge to anyone to fight him, with place and time to be decided. Those in the castle said he was too important to their cause to allow him to risk his life in this way.[101]

On 17 June Alexander Gordon, Bishop of Galloway, preached a sermon on charity for the Queen.[102] He argued that Mary's moral shortcomings did not disqualify her from rule. 'No inferior subject has the power to deprive or depose their lawful magistrate,' he said. He illustrated the case of King David in the Bible, who, despite being an adulterer and a murderer, was not barred from rule.

The Queen's party now held their own parliament in the traditional place, the Tolbooth. George, the Duke, Home, Maxwell and Lord Claud Hamilton were among the nobles who attended, as well as commissioners for the bishops of Moray and Aberdeen and for the boroughs of Aberdeen, Elgin, Forres, Inverness, Jedburgh and Dumfries. Sir William Drury attended, as Queen Elizabeth's representative. There it was reiterated that the Queen had abdicated in fear of her life, having been told by England's Throgmorton that she would not be held to the abdication. The Three Estates agreed to pass an act stating that Lennox's regency was illegal.

In their formal procession from the Tolbooth to the castle, the Duke bore the crown and George the sceptre. The Queen's party made proclamations from the market cross about an act been passed by parliament that all future proclamations and letters were to be issued in the

Queen's name, and that ministers were instructed to say daily prayers for the Queen, her son and the nobility. The castle 'shot great ordinance'.[103] However, this was the last time that the Queen's party showed any sign of strength.[104] It was ominous that the rival parliaments of the King's party held in May and June were better attended than that of the Queen's.[105]

There was an incident at sea, involving Morton's soldiers arriving from Dundee, who were intercepted by ships of the Queen's party. They chased and boarded one of Morton's vessels, capturing twenty-five soldiers. The other ships escaped. After a period of hesitation and of moving further out to sea for fear of Morton's men, who were watching the coast, the Queen's party men landed at Corstorphine Crags and took their prisoners safely to the castle. They were locked in the Tolbooth, and the castle cannons were fired in triumph.[106] Drury, meanwhile, was talking to both sides and giving each the impression that England supported them.

On 22 August 1571, the King's party held their parliament in Stirling. It was more fully attended than any had been for years. The regalia were still in the castle, held by Kirkcaldy, but a substitute crown, sword and sceptre were carried before the young King. George was again forfeited, as were the bishops of Aberdeen, Moray, Ross and Galloway, the Duke, Kirkcaldy, Seton, Crichton, Walter Kerr of Ferniehurst, George's brother Adam and thirty-four of his followers.

The two armies continued skirmishing between Leith and Edinburgh. Lennox sent messages to Queen Elizabeth, mostly in code, some of which were intercepted between Edinburgh and Musselburgh.

Kirkcaldy summoned a Queen's party parliament to be held in the castle. George attended, along with the Duke, various prelates, barons and the Three Estates. They now forfeited Morton, Lennox, Mar and many others, and announced that various burghs not loyal to the Queen would lose their freedoms for ever. The forfeitures were proclaimed at the market cross. Both sides had now denounced the other as traitors and passed laws of attainder against the nobility attending the parliament of their rivals.[107]

Kirkcaldy expressed exasperation with 'Scotsmen furiously bent against each other, set on course by the practices of the English, and the extreme greed of some for their selfish designs, hoping to augment their estates and raise their own fortunes by the ruin of their neighbours'. On 3 September he hatched a plot to set off for Stirling that night, where he would arrive in the early hours. He and his men would stand guard outside the houses where the King's lords lodged, and the next morning they would take them prisoner as they emerged, take them to Edinburgh Castle, and persuade them to come to terms. George and John Hamilton begged Kirkcaldy not to accompany them, as he was too important to the cause. Kirkcaldy argued that he was used to difficult enterprises and was afraid that they would not follow his directions properly. Eventually, he gave way, and it was decided that George, as Queen's Lieutenant General, should lead the expedition. However, as Kirkcaldy had feared, it all went very wrong.

They arrived in Stirling under cover of darkness and divided the party, one half to wait outside the lodgings, and the other half to wait at the town cross under Captain Calder. He was to ensure that everyone was kept in order and none of the town houses spoiled. Buccleugh and Kerr of Ferniehurst were to take the horses from their stables and out of town. It worked as far as the capture went, but Captain Calder was late at the town cross, causing the servants to rush hither and thither in disorder and leaving their masters to take the prisoners on foot down a steep pathway to where the horses were to take them all to Edinburgh.

Kirkcaldy had only left his men on condition that they killed no one. However, the inmates of the castle heard the disorder and rushed down to rescue the captives. Lennox gave himself up to the laird of Hamilton on condition that his life would be saved, but when Captain Calder saw would-be rescuers coming down from the castle, he shot Lennox with a pistol. In the confusion, Morton and many others broke free and turned the tables on their captors, taking them prisoner. They would all have been taken if Lennox's men had their horses, but when Claud Hamilton heard of the events, he took the horses from the outskirts of town and fled, leaving everyone behind to fend for themselves.

Despite his wound, Lennox managed to ride back into the castle and call his nobles to him. He said he had only accepted their request to return to Scotland in order to defend his grandson, the King, and to see justice done to the murderers of his son, and the King's uncle, 'the good Earl of Moray'. He had given his own blood in the action, and he asked them to remember their duty to God, the King, and to maintaining the state of the commonwealth. He committed his servants to their friendship and protection, and also his dear wife Margaret, still in England. He prayed for God's mercy and died.

Lennox was buried in the King's chapel in Stirling.[108] Robert Gordon of Gordonstoun described him as 'a good and plain man, honourably minded; a good soldier who had fought in Scotland, England, France and Italy'.[109]

The Regency of Mar

On 5 September 1571, the King's lords assembled and chose John Erskine, Earl of Mar and governor to the young King, as Regent. This was against the advice of Randolph, the English ambassador, who favoured Morton. George also took part in the election. Mar was more of a conciliator than a party man, resulting in many of the Queen's men changing sides, including previously strong Marians such as Argyll, Crawford, Cassilis, Eglinton, Montrose, Caithness and Sutherland. Over eighty crossed sides at Mar's inauguration and received remissions of their forfeitures. Lord Lovat and other Highland chiefs were won over with offers of pensions from the bishoprics of Aberdeen and Moray. Argyll, Crawford, Eglinton, Cassilis and Boyd were elected to the new Privy Council.

However, George still remained a strong supporter of Mary. His brother Adam acted as his deputy in the north-east while he continued to act on Mary's behalf in and around Edinburgh, where the opposing forces were fairly even.[110] Great cruelties occurred when one side got the upper hand in the skirmishes.

Mar appealed to those in the castle under Kirkcaldy and Maitland to surrender before further bloodshed and inevitable defeat occurred. This had little effect. Mar could only foresee the wreck of the country, with the two factions pretending to support one side or the other but only concerned with their own interests, ambitions, greed and vengeance for past wrongs, rather than the King or the Queen.

Randolph asked Kirkcaldy to appoint an English captain of the castle. Because he was dealing with both sides and was seen as stirring up trouble, both sides lost trust in him. He ceased therefore to be of use to England. He was recalled, and replaced by Sir Henry Killigrew, who arrived at Leith from Berwick. He sent a message to Sir James Melville (the diarist) at the castle, who was an old friend, saying he had letters to deliver from the Earl of Leicester and Cecil for Kirkcaldy and Maitland. He wanted a meeting to discuss how to bring the two sides of the factions together. Melville suspected that that was not his real commission.[111] When Killigrew arrived at the castle, Melville asked him to deal plainly with them, unlike Randolph. Killigrew then revealed that

England put its faith in Morton. Those in the castle appreciated his plain talking, but they did not want to ally with Morton. Killigrew stated that his commission was to ask those in the castle to submit their differences to the English council for a decision, as the King's party had done. He promised that Kirkcaldy would be maintained in office and given an honourable pension. Kirkcaldy refused, saying it would prejudice his prince and country. This patriotic stance later cost him his life.[112]

On 7 September the Ridolphi plot was discovered in England by Cecil's spies. This involved plans for a Spanish landing and a rising of English Catholics, who would free Mary. She could then marry the Duke of Norfolk, which she had agreed to. As a result, Norfolk was arrested and executed.

On 10 September, Mar proclaimed Morton his Lieutenant General of the King's Forces. Their attempt to take the castle in October failed, but in the north-east, where the Gordons continued to hold sway, Morton succeeded in winning over Lord Forbes to the King's party. This led directly to the spread of the civil war there. The Forbeses had long been at feud with the Gordons, with their many grievances mostly to do with land. This presented them with an opportunity.

George, in Edinburgh, would have heard how on 17 October 1571 the Forbeses had ambushed the Gordons on their way south. His brother Adam, however, had succeeded in winning a victory over the superior Forbes forces at the battle of Tillyangus. No doubt he heard the rumours in Edinburgh when the Master of Forbes arrived at Leith, having fled the battlefield. He said that the Forbeses had merely gathered there to sort out their differences when the Gordons attacked them.

People were horrified when they heard about the burning of Corgarff Castle by Adam's men, with twenty-seven dying inside, including the Forbes laird's wife and children. When George heard that Morton was mustering a force of Lothian pikemen under the Master of Forbes, to take revenge and with a commission to enlist others en route, he sent his own reinforcements to Adam in Aberdeen by sea. How triumphant George must have felt when he heard of the resounding victory they had won in the battle of Craibstone, on the outskirts of Aberdeen, on 20 November. Not only that, but John, their brother-in-law, the Master of Forbes, had been captured and taken to Spynie Palace. This victory greatly strengthened the obedience of the north-east to the Queen's authority under Adam, George's deputy Lieutenant of the

North. George must have been gratified to hear that his brother's word was law 'fra the water of the Dee north'.[113]

Meanwhile, Cecil was at work in England. He arranged for the dossier recounting the King's party version of events in Mary's recent life written by the humanist George Buchanan, tutor to young James, to be translated from Latin into imitation Scots. The translation was in order to give the false impression that it was authorised by the lords in Scotland, not by anyone in England. It had a damning anonymous oration against Mary, referring to her as 'this Jezebel', 'Athalia',[114] 'Idolatress' and 'this most wicked and filthy woman'.[115] These sounded very like John Knox's words.

In February 1572, Maxwell and Herries submitted to Morton. Athol, Rothes, Elphinstone and others now declared themselves neutral, and two of Mary's most loyal friends were out of the country: Fleming in France and Seton in Flanders. Elizabeth had been careful not to offend France in relation to Mary. By the Treaty of Blois in April, France agreed to support action for the pacification of Scotland. There would thus be no further help for Mary's supporters from that quarter.

The Queen's party was becoming greatly reduced, but there was still a lot of activity.[116] In June, they took Castle Douglas, and on 5 July George's brother Adam retook Brechin. He captured several of the leaders and 200 men. He harangued them for the wrongs done to his family, which had resulted in the deaths of his father and his brother John. He then dismissed them. He marched on Montrose and imposed an enormous ransom of £2,000 and 2 tons of wine.

However, on 1 August a one-year truce was arranged between the two sides. On the 12th of the month, Argyll made his final capitulation. Cassilus signed a bond with Mar and Morton. Episcopacy was reintroduced, with bishops to be nominated by the Crown. On 24 August, St Bartholemew's Day, thousands of Protestants in Paris were massacred. This increased Elizabeth's need to bring about a final settlement in Scotland, but it gave hope to the Marians that a more militant anti-Protestantism in France would result in help for their cause. Between August and October, George, the duke, Claud Hamilton and Seton left Edinburgh. On 4 October, Aberdeen city gave George 600 marks, on condition that he remove his soldiers from the city.

That autumn, Elizabeth was still seriously considering handing Mary over to the Scottish government.[117] In Stirling, Mar asked Ambassador Killigrew to acts as go-between and to ask those in the castle to deal with him, for the good of the country. Mar 'made a heavy moan . . . for the craft and malice of some in England and some in Scotland, taking the colour of this or that authority, merely for their own advantage to the hurt of both King, Queen and country'. Through his friend James Melville, Killigrew got those in the castle to come to terms with Mar, and to accept the King's authority, but only while the Queen was captive. If she was freed, they said, they would decide what to do. Mar agreed for his party to pay for repairs to the castle and artillery. They shook hands in front of witnesses, and informed the Lords of the Council. However, on 28 October 1572, Mar became sick after a feast with Morton at Dalkeith. He left suddenly to ride to Stirling, and died. He had become a disappointed man, 'because he loved peace and could not have it'.[118]

The Regency of Morton

On 24 November 1572, Morton was elected Regent unopposed. Unlike Mar, he was not a conciliator. He was strongly on the side of the Reformation and the alliance with England. He was exceedingly tough, and was favoured by Queen Elizabeth. He was helped by the weakening of the Catholic cause and the paranoia in England about a Catholic resurgence in the north as a result of the St Bartholomew's Day massacre. Morton, therefore, had unusually active support from Scotland's neighbour.[119] Many other lords, lairds and commendators abandoned the Marians. This was a promising start for Morton. He was able to reoccupy Edinburgh, and John Knox returned to his home in the city, where he died shortly after. Morton made Argyll his Chancellor and Errol joined the Council. Order and stability were being achieved.[120] As Elizabeth did not have to worry about France coming to the help of Mary or the Catholics in Scotland, she was now in favour of securing Morton's regime without reference to Mary at all.

However, the castle was still held by the Marians under Kirkcaldy of Grange and Maitland of Lethington. Morton offered them the same conditions as Mar had, but they were suspicious of him, considering him too close to England. Kirkcaldy was offered the bishopric of St Andrews or Blackness Castle as inducements. He said that he did not want either, just his own lands and time to bring round others of the Queen's faction, who had asked for his protection. Morton refused this, saying that he did not want to bring George or the Hamiltons round, but to punish them for the wrongs they had committed and to take their lands. His aim was to divide them, as otherwise they were too strong and might later combine against him. Kirkcaldy must only come to terms without them, said Morton, or he would come to terms with them instead. Kirkcaldy was very angry, saying it was ungodly to lay blame on those with riches just to gain their lands and goods. Oddly, he then said that they had always been ready to come to agreement but had not been allowed to do so. Does this mean that George and the Duke had been shunned by members of the King's party? Morton agreed that if Kirkcaldy would give up the castle within six months, he would allow him to keep it for a cooling-down period. Morton left triumphant with this concession, approaching the rest of the faction to get them to come to terms.

In January 1573 a new Act of Conformity was passed, with a more vigorous line against Roman Catholics. All holders of church benefices had to subscribe to the Reformed faith on pain of being deprived of them. This resulted in the first heavy submission of Marians.

Morton used Argyll to enter into communication with George, and managed to persuade him and Chatelherault that Mary's cause was hopeless. Morton's terms were that there would be no further enquiry into the murder of Darnley, and pardon for all those involved in the murder of Lennox. George now decided to seek the best terms he could for himself and his friends. On 18 December 1572, George, Seton, the Duke and his sons all agreed to leave the castle and renew the truce. They wrote to Kirkcaldy to explain why they had done this, and thanked him for his protection and assistance. However, George secretly sent a message to France to seek help.

On 18 February, with the help of the English ambassador Killigrew, George met Morton at Aberdour and agreed terms. George and Arbroath acted as representatives of the two factions and reached agreement in the Pacification of Perth on 23 February 1573.[121] Under this agreement, they and other members of the Queen's party surrendered to the authority of the Regent and the King, and recognised the Presbyterian settlement. They had to 'acknowledge, affirm and profess the trew religioun' professed in Scotland, established by Acts of Parliament. In exchange, they were given a blanket indemnity for anything that had happened in the civil wars since 1567. The Master of Forbes and other prisoners were to be freed. The House of Spynie was to be handed over by the Gordons, in the name of the King and his Regent. Huntly and Hamilton were to discharge their 'men of war' so they could 'return to their awin dwellingis'.[122]

They also had to acknowledge that everything done by them under any authority other than the King's was unlawful and invalid. Those who had been dispossessed of their houses were allowed to repossess them. Forfeitures imposed on George, Adam, the Hamiltons, William Bishop of Aberdeen, Alexander Bishop of Galloway and George Barclay of Gartly, stretching back to 15 June 1567 when Mary was taken to Lochleven, were all reversed. They could now 'enjoy them as freely as before'. What is more, anyone who acted openly or secretly against or supported 'ony tressonabill fact, uprore or hostilities' against the true religion or the person of the King or his Regent, would lose the benefits of the remission.[123] The civil war was virtually at an end. However, Adam was still not reconciled.

On 12 April the agreement was ratified by parliament at the Palace of Holyroodhouse. George, the Duke, his sons, the Hamilton lairds, the Bishop of Galloway, Barclay of Gartly, and even Adam, undertook to accept the King's authority and support the Reformed Church, also on behalf of their kin, friends and servants. As a result, they were now able to regain their forfeited property.

Morton had succeeded in dividing and dissolving the Queen's party. Now, he would have nothing to do with Kirkcaldy, saying that those in the castle were too proud and wilful to accept the King, or himself as Regent. This was published and preached, though the opposite was true:[124] they would have been willing to accept any reasonable appointment, and he could have gained the castle peacefully. Kirkcaldy had offered the keys to the Earl of Rothes, to be delivered to Morton, but he appealed to England for help. Drury, the English Marshall of Berwick, again crossed the border into Scotland. Siege guns were sent to Leith. England and Scotland agreed not to grant terms to those in the castle without consulting each other, and also agreed that Kirkcaldy, his brother John, James Melville's brother John, and five others in the castle would have to stand trial in Scotland. Those inside realised that they had no hope but to hold out as long as possible, but water ran out due to the summer drought. They let people over the walls to a well on the outside, but it had been poisoned and so many fell sick and died.

On 28 May 1573, after eleven days of bombardment, Drury agreed with those in the castle that they would have safe passage if they came out with their arms and armoury. Kirkcaldy and Maitland gave themselves up to the protection of Drury, but they refused to give him the keys of the castle, which the English wanted. They were given to

Captain Hume and Crawford. However, after three days, Kirkcaldy
and Maitland were arrested, as Morton had secured Queen Elizabeth's
agreement that they should be executed. Drury was dismayed, as he
respected Kirkcaldy and had made promises to him.[125] Kirkcaldy of
Grange was hanged on 3 August. Maitland died in prison, possibly by
his own hand. The French King Henry II had said of Kirkcaldy: 'Yonder
is one of the most valiant men of our time.' It was also said by a fellow
Scot that he was 'as gentle and meek as a lamb in the house but like a
lion in the field'.[126]

Peace at Last

George now returned to Strathbogie and took hardly any further part
in national affairs.[127] His brother-in-law, the Master of Forbes, was
released from Spynie Palace, and immediately set about obtaining a
divorce from Margaret Gordon, George's sister, citing her adultery
with his captor's illegitimate son, Patrick Hepburn, the parson of
Kinnoir.

The Forbeses complained that they could not get fair judgment from
George as Sheriff of Aberdeen, because of the divorce proceedings and
longstanding land issues. They appealed to the Lords of the Council,
and on 27 June they and forty-nine lairds and their allies gained exemp-
tion from George's traditional jurisdiction over them.

In March 1574, John, Master of Forbes appealed to the Privy
Council against Adam Gordon's insistence that he should pay £705
for his expenses during his forced custody in Spynie! He complained
that this was against the agreements in the Pacification at Perth. His
appeal was successful.[128] The same month he gained his divorce,
Margaret having declined to defend herself against the charge of adultery. She attempted, though, to retain the lands she had gained in her
tocher. The judgement seems unclear on this matter, giving rise to
future action. As was usual when a wife was divorced, Margaret had
to abandon her two sons and two daughters, the youngest of whom
was only four years old. William, Lord Forbes, gained a charter for
new lands, ostensibly as a reward for his loyalty and support of the
Regent.

George's young cousin Alexander, Earl of Sutherland, to whom he
had given a home in Huntly Castle, was now able to return to Sutherland, where he reclaimed his earldom without bloodshed. He gained
the love of George's sister Jean, the divorced wife of Bothwell. At the

end of the year they married and she became Countess of Sutherland. He was not strong, so she soon took over as factor of his extensive estates.[129]

Early in 1574 Adam, Lord Ogilvie, Thomas Kerr of Ferniehurst and other irreconcilables had set off for France, disgusted that they were expected to come to terms with the Regent even though they had not been defeated in the north-east. Adam sold Auchindoun to his younger brother Patrick.

On 11 July George was warded in Galloway, accused of abetting Adam in 'raising an uproar' in France. He wrote to Queen Elizabeth explaining that he was no threat and could not be held responsible for his brother's actions in France, although he was sure that Adam was innocent of the accusations. He was released in December, after giving sureties for his good behaviour.

In July, Adam returned to Scotland with twenty companions, but he, Ogilvie, and Maxwell were immediately imprisoned in Blackness Castle, a grim fortress overlooking the Forth.[130] In January the following year, Adam was released but had to remain in Kirkudbright, with George giving surety for him. However, by early October Adam was in Aberdeen acting as deputy sheriff, presiding over the Michaelmas court.

Morton came north to ensure conformity to the Reformed Kirk. He ordered that only the sabbath was to be celebrated, with other festivals prohibited. The parish church of St Nicholas in Aberdeen, where George's brother John was buried, was ordered to have the pews, images and crucifixes removed. However, it was said that once Morton left, the orders were 'tardily executed'.[131]

On 20 October 1576, George collapsed when he was taking part in a friendly football game at Huntly Castle. He had gone out hunting that morning, killing a fox and three hares, and had seemed in the best of health. He was helped inside but coughed up quantities of black blood. He died later that evening. He was outlived by three sons and a daughter. Before he died, he asked Adam to take charge of his eldest son and heir, aged sixteen and also named George, and to send him to complete his education in Paris under their Jesuit brother James. George's body was embalmed and taken to Elgin to await a fitting burial for an Earl of Huntly.

George had been one of Queen Mary's most constant supporters, despite the fact that she was responsible for the death of his father and his brother John, albeit influenced by Moray; and also despite having been held in custody for nearly three years even though he had not been present at the battle of Corrichie. He wavered once or twice, perhaps understandably when it was falsely made out that Mary had abdicated of her own free will, and also when Moray's power seemed overwhelming. He was thinking pragmatically. It was really the actions of the Hamiltons that brought him back to her cause. While Mary was imprisoned in England, he had continued to be her loyal and dutiful subject. He defended her cause to the last extremity in her trials.

In the end, he was a man whose loyalty to Mary lasted longer than that of most of his fellow peers. However, ultimately, Mary became a lost cause once it became clear that Scotland would not take her back, that Elizabeth could not contemplate releasing her without endangering her own position, and that Mary's supporters could no longer expect help from France. Then his priorities altered. The pragmatist within forced him to think of his own survival and that of his family, his heirs and his lands, and so he had to come to terms. He had sacrificed most of his remaining adult life and had little time to spend on his responsibilities in the north, nor with his wife and family at home in Strathbogie. It is a sad fact that, after such a turbulent life, he was left with only three years to make up for lost time.

3

Adam Gordon – Triumphs

CIVIL WAR IN THE NORTH

Youth

Adam Gordon was the sixth son of the 4th Earl of Huntly and Elizabeth Keith. He is known more popularly as Edom o'Gordon, from the ballad of that name, referring to the notorious burning of Corgarff Castle. Like his brother George, the 5th Earl of Huntly, he was very active on the political and military scene on Mary's behalf. For Adam, his work was in the north-east, especially after Mary was exiled and imprisoned in England. This led to conflict with the family of his brother-in-law, the Forbeses, when they became active on behalf of the Regent and the infant King James VI.

As he grew up in Huntly Castle, Adam must have been aware of the scandal surrounding his much older brother John (see Chapter 1) and his dispute with James Ogilvie, whose own father had disinherited him in John's favour. This happened at about the time of Adam's birth, and the consequences almost led to his death. John had taken on the name and arms of Ogilvie of Deskford and, on the death of old Alexander, had married his widow, who was a Gordon relative of theirs. No doubt Adam visited his brother in the lands he controlled, including Auchindoun and Keithmore. Little did he know how important those lands were to become to him.

At the age of seventeen, Adam would have been well aware that James Ogilvie of Cardell was fighting to retrieve his inheritance. He would certainly have known about his brother's fight in the streets of Edinburgh, and Lord Ogilvie's injuries that resulted in the loss of an arm. Perhaps he was even present at the brawl. Then there was John's consequent imprisonment, and the excitement of his escape and return to the north-east and the protection of their father.

It would have been disappointing for of all the family that the Queen refused their mother's invitation to visit them on her journey north. Adam would have hoped to gain her notice, perhaps so that he could enter her service. There was no hope of that with the family out of favour, and his important father publicly declared an outlaw. This would have been a disaster for a young man on the cusp of adulthood. Each subsequent event made matters worse. Having submitted to Mary when she arrived in Aberdeen, John escaped prison a second time and was then said to be following her on her tour of the north; George was the cause of her being refused entrance to Inverness Castle; and John refused to give up the keys of Findlater and Auchindoun, attacked the Queen's men and stole their armaments. Adam might have helped his father flee Huntly Castle to escape capture by Kirkcaldy of Grange; and possibly he witnessed his mother unwisely encouraging his father and his brother John to fight the Queen's force, because it was commanded by their enemy James Stewart, now Earl of Moray. If he were to be defeated and killed, their family could return to position and influence.

Young Adam fought at the battle of Corrichie on 28 October 1562. Perhaps he helped his father squeeze his corpulent body into his armour that morning, and saw him, having overslept, in a state of confusion. Adam witnessed the Gordons' complete defeat and his father's collapse, probably from a heart attack brought on by the stress of events. Adam and John surrendered and were taken to the Tolbooth in Aberdeen, their father's body slung ignominiously over the back of an ass carrying fish baskets. Adam was condemned to death along with other captured Gordons, and although the sentence was commuted, he might well have had to suffer the sight of his brother's gruesome execution. It was Maitland of Lethington's wife (or, rather, his prospective wife, Mary Fleming) who appealed for Adam's life, on the grounds of his 'extreme youth'.[1] There may have been some who came to regret that clemency in future years.

Whether Adam continued to languish in prison like his eldest brother George, who was not even present at the battle, we do not know. His cousin Robert Gordon of Gordonstoun states in his book *The Genealogical History of the Earldom of Sutherland* (1603) that Adam was imprisoned, along with other nobles. He records also that the Duke of Chatelherault was banished from court; his son, the Earl of Arran, was imprisoned; and the Earl of Sutherland was banished to Flanders and forfeited. Bothwell, who had also not been at the battle, was again banished to France, suspected of intending to raise a rebellion with

George. The Archbishop of St Andrews and other nobles were imprisoned.[2]

The rest of the family might have been warded by a person trusted by Parliament, such as Adam's maternal uncle, the Earl Marischal. The following spring, Adam had to witness his family's humiliation in front of the Three Estates of the Parliament, at the farcical trial which saw his father's embalmed corpse propped up in its coffin and declared a traitor to the Queen. The family arms were torn to pieces, and their name struck from the herald's roll. The lands of all the Gordons who had followed his father had their lands forfeited.

However, Adam's fortunes changed dramatically three years later, in August 1565, when his brother George was released from prison and restored to favour. This followed the defection of the Earl of Moray and others, which meant that Mary needed new friends and supporters. She brought George onto the Privy Council, and his mother and sister Jean to Court. At the age of twenty-one Adam, who might have been Jean's twin, would almost certainly have attended her very grand wedding to James Hepburn, Earl of Bothwell, and no doubt took enthusiastic part in the five days of jousting and tournaments that followed.

After his brother George was made Chancellor, following in his father's footsteps, on 20 March 1566, he had influence enough to help sort out the long-running Ogilvie dispute. This was done through compromise, which greatly benefited the family. A new decree was passed, confirming that the baronies of Deskford and Findlater belonged to James Ogilvie, but excluding Auchindoun and Keithmore.[3] They were to go to Adam, who had been mentioned in the original will, in case of his brother John's death. No doubt Ogilvie complained about this, as he had wanted to regain all the Findlater estates, but he was ordered to sell Auchindoun and Keithmore to Adam. He may have had no choice, given Huntly's new position of power and the pro-Gordon witnesses to the decree.[4] The baronies of Auchindoun and Keithmore were greatly to the Gordons' advantage, as well as Adam's.

Although restored to royal favour, the Gordons did not have their own lands formally restored until the following month. Their mother, Elizabeth Keith, had made an appeal for this,[5] but the restoration might also have been a reward for George's co-operation in the exceptionally quick divorce between their sister Jean and Bothwell, so soon after their marriage, so that Mary could marry him.

On 21 July 1566, the lands and barony of Auchindoun and Keithmore were formally chartered to Adam. The barony of Auchindoun included the tower, manor and crofts of Auchindoun; a small part of the Cabrach, north of the rivers Deveron and the Blackwater; and the lands and mills of Beldorney, Lymebane and the Gouls, with woods, forests, parks, fishings and tenants. Adam could now call himself Adam of Auchindoun, which was how he was known from then on. What triumphs for the Gordons!

Civil War in the North-East

Although the Gordon lands were now restored, George Gordon, 5th Earl of Huntly, was unable to spend much time in his earldom, because he was closely tied up with the unfolding events of Mary's life in Edinburgh. However, he returned to the north, along with his mother and sister Jean after Moray was declared Regent. Until Mary's escape, the family did not realise that her abdication had been forced. George had even returned to Edinburgh to join Moray's administration for a while, but once Mary had escaped the truth was known and he returned north to collect a force to help restore her to the throne. Adam was probably part of the troops that he collected. However, frustratingly for them, they and their 2,600 men found the passes blocked along the Tay and were unable to proceed in time to prevent Mary's disastrous defeat at the battle of Langside and her fatal flight to England.[6]

There were two periods of virtual civil war in Scotland between 1567 and 1573, but action was mainly confined to Edinburgh and environs, and to the areas of her lieutenants: the Earl of Argyll in the north-west, the Duke of Chatelherault in the south-west, and the Earl of Huntly, ostensibly in the north. In reality, George was mostly active in and around Edinburgh, and in some of Angus. Throughout these areas, there was remarkably little fighting or material damage until 1571. Adam, aged twenty-five, held the north-east, in a relatively peaceful regime, on his brother's behalf,[7] despite ongoing tensions between Gordons and Forbeses. What was it, then, that lit the fuse and brought the civil war to these parts in 1571? We will first look at events surrounding it, and then attempt to answer that question.

Following the assassination of Moray, the Regent, in 1570, the unpopular Earl of Lennox became Regent on behalf of his young grandson, James VI. Certain incidents showed that conflict was moving nearer to the north. Adam was a witness in Inverness (or possibly Aberdeen) to the contract between his brother George and Hugh Fraser, 6th Lord Lovat, under which Lovat bound himself to 'concur, assist and take part, with his friends and servants, in the earl's actions and causes'. In exchange, Huntly would 'assist, fortify and maintain Lovat: in particular he will procure the Abbot of Kinloss to feu to Lovat some land and mains in Beauly'.[8] Obviously, the Gordons were collecting supporters.

What is more, Adam and his followers took action in the Mearns, where they fortified the castle and steeple of Brechin. Lennox declared this a treasonable act and summoned reinforcements. His main purpose was to prevent George and his followers from reaching Linlithgow, where they proposed to hold their rival parliament. However, George received a warning and managed to escape in time. Lennox successfully stormed the castle at Brechin, hanging thirty-four of the garrison. He then went on to take Doune Castle, which had also been held for the Queen.

In August 1571, the temperature rose when many members of the Queen's party were forfeited for treason by Lennox's Parliament, which was held in the Great Hall of Stirling Castle. Those forfeited included Adam, Huntly, thirty-four other Gordons and followers, such as their great uncle, William Gordon, Bishop of Aberdeen; Patrick Bothwell, who was Bishop of Moray; George Barclay of Gartly; Kirkcaldy of Grange (who now changed sides and held Edinburgh Castle on behalf of the Queen); the Duke of Chatelherault; and Sir Thomas Kerr of Ferniehurst.[9] This sets the scene for the three bloody events that took place in the autumn of that year.

The first incident was the battle of Tillyangus on 10 October, in the vicinity of the White Hill, above the village of Clatt and the present-day farm of Tillyangus, on the north edge of the Correen hills. Versions of the story vary, according to which side the sources support. The Forbeses said that they were merely gathering there, not far from the Forbes seat of Druminnor Castle, to sort out their differences, when they were attacked by the Gordons. The Gordons insisted they had informed the Forbeses that they would be passing peacefully through their lands on their way south.

Acting as George's deputy Lieutenant of the North, Adam collected a force of about 1,000 Gordons and supporters at Strathbogie and proceeded to join the Mar road, which ran from Auchindoir (near the present village of Lumsden) across the side of the Correen hills to join the north–south road at the Suie hill. En route, they met a smaller force of about 300 Forbeses, who the Gordons later claimed were waiting to ambush them on their way south. It does seem likely that the Gordon intention might well have been to 'to cum upoun the Mernes, as thai have done befoir, and so to Dundie, to truble all the kingis trew lieges that would not assist in their factione',[10] and then to take reinforcements to George in Edinburgh, in an attempt to lift the Regent's siege of Edinburgh Castle. Or perhaps they planned to retake Brechin.

Adam had divided his men into two groups. One group was under the command of his younger brother Robert, and initially it was to keep out of sight. His own section was to take on the Forbeses, who were led by Black Arthur, brother of William, 7th Lord Forbes. This man must have been of unusual stature and strength to have wielded the immense sword traditionally held to be his and still hanging on the wall of Castle Forbes. The Gordons 'fell upon the Forbes spears and entrenchments'. The Forbeses, thinking 'the enemies sa few' emerged, upon which Robert Gordon's group descended on the Forbeses putting them to flight towards the safety of Druminnor Castle.[11] Black Arthur bravely defended their retreat. He bent to take a drink from a burn (probably the spring now called Black Arthur's well), but was surprised by William Gordon of Terpersie.[12] William, a relatively near neighbour of Arthur's, with whom he might well have had a land dispute, stabbed Black Arthur to death through a joint in his armour. About thirty Forbeses were killed or captured, as was William, the second son of Lord Forbes. Although Adam had been stopped on his supposed route south and had lost about twenty of his men, he must have considered the encounter a triumph. Arthur, a virulent hater of his family and 'by far the most important military leader among the Forbeses',[13] was dead; and Lord Forbes' second son was captured, as well as all the horse and munitions – these, presumably, were taken back to Huntly, Auchindoun or other Gordon strongholds.

Meanwhile, John, Master of Forbes, who had only just managed to escape with his life, hastened south to complain to the Regent, Mar, about the suffering brought on the country as a result of Gordon oppression. There was little response from Mar to the Master's pleas until news was received of the horrific burning of Corgarff Castle, probably in early November. This lonely tower house guarded the confluence of the passes of the Don, the Dee and the Avon. It therefore controlled almost all the high routes from Moray, Banff and Strathavon south and was accordingly a valuable asset. It was held by John Forbes of Towie, who was the Regent's tenant.

The Gordon version of the story says that Adam Gordon was not present but sent his captain, Thomas Kerr, with troops from Elgin to demand it be given up in the name of the Queen. Forbes of Towie was away, but his pregnant wife Margaret Campbell refused in no uncertain terms to comply. Apparently the lady fired a shot which hit a soldier's knee, infuriating Captain Kerr, who ordered bundles of wood and heather to be placed all around the castle. A twelve-hour truce was agreed with the lady, so that a messenger could go to the laird to ask him on what conditions she should surrender the castle or hold it. A daughter attempted to escape down on a rope made of sheets, but she was speared when she arrived at the bottom. It is not clear whether Margaret Campbell received an answer to her message or whether the captain ordered the fire to be lit when the truce expired. The whole affair took place over two or three days. Twenty-seven people died from the conflagration, including Margaret Campbell, her daughters, her stepson John Towie the younger (her husband's natural son), and her servants.[14] This outrageous deed sent a chill throughout the country. It is commemorated in the Ballad 'Edom o Gordon', which places Adam firmly in command, as do Forbes sources and subsequent legal appeals for redress.

Possibly because of the Corgarff scandal, and because Forbes of Towie was his tenant and theoretically in the earldom of Mar,[15] the Regent was now provoked into action. He made the Master of Forbes a rival Lieutenant of the North, in the name of the King. He gave him command of five companies of foot from Leith, including 200 harquebusiers, and a troop of horse under Alexander Campbell (probably a relative of the deceased Margaret Campbell), who had permission to raise 700 gentlemen volunteers from the Mearns. Mar gave Campbell instructions to use two thirds of the income of the recently forfeited bishopric of Aberdeen for his expenses. The Leith force was under a Captain Chisholm.

Forbes's forces included Adam's uncle William Keith, Master of Marischal. His movements are unclear. He and the Laird of Drum were mysteriously called back to Leith by the Regent; there is a hint that Forbes would 'nocht follow the Master of Marischal's 'counsall'.[16] It seems they might have been leadership rivals. The force gathered at Brechin, which had been retaken by Lennox that summer, and were now in a much stronger position to challenge the Gordons and revenge the Tillyangus humiliation and the Corgarff outrage on behalf of the Regent and the King. They were particularly keen to take on 'Adam Gordone, who playis king Herrot in the north, upoun the kingis freindis and guid subjectis, bot in speciall upoun the Forbesses, whois rowmes he is going about to destroye with fyre and sword, as he hes done pairt alreadie'.[17]

They marched at night over the Cairn o'Mount and crossed the Dee, but Adam had advance warning of their approach and was well prepared. He had taken the precaution of laying waste the lands round the lower Dee, burning the orchards and grain stores. As a result the exhausted troops went hungry, as 'for two days they were very scairce of victuals'.[18] The movements of John Keith – possibly the Master of Marischal's brother or son, if not the Master himself but with a different name – are a bit of a mystery, as sources vary. Robert Lindsay of Pitscottie says that the Forbes force divided in two, with John Keith taking his half of the 500 horse north into Gordon lands, whereas Bannatyne reports that he 'departed to his house', which would probably refer to the Keith stronghold of Dunnotar Castle. 'Whidder he was not willing to enter in battell against the said Adam, I know not,' says Bannatyne.[19] If this was so, it might have been because of his close relationship to Adam, whose mother Elizabeth Keith was the Earl Marischal's sister, possibly making them cousins. Alternatively, he might have just needed to take his men to his own area to find a source of sustenance, realising it was unwise to risk a battle with the Gordons when the men were exhausted and hungry.

Despite the reduced size of his troop and feeling somewhat let down by his allies, Forbes being 'ane manlie man' continued to march his remaining men overnight along the Dee, hoping to reach Old Aberdeen the following afternoon before dark. They approached the city by the Hardback, the main approach road from the south or the west, planning to cross the Denburn at the Bow Brig. They would have reached Aberdeen by a wide street known as the Green, passing an ancient stone boundary marker to the Crab family that had been there since the time of Bruce. They arrived at the Green in the afternoon of 20 November 1571.

Adam, in Aberdeen, had been reinforced with a detachment of seaborne troops sent by George from Edinburgh 'with a commandment to offend the Forbeses all that they can'.[20] He now had about 1,500 armed men, including 'citizens from Elgin' (also mentioned as being at Corgarff) and the Earl of Sutherland, accompanied by ninety-eight 'Murrays' displaying banners 'in warlike manner'.[21] Adam had also conscripted citizens of Aberdeen to 'make the number of his army look greater'.[22] With all of these forces, he headed out of Aberdeen to block the way of the approaching Forbeses. The Gordon force crossed the Denburn at the Bow Brig and lined up on the Green. They must have been quite a sight, with their banners blowing in the November wind. However, they hesitated to attack first because they saw that the Forbeses had three times as many harquebusiers as they had.

Despite having ridden all that night without food, and being now a much smaller force, Forbes and his royal footmen from Leith went into the attack, 'desirous more hastily than wisely to fight', and 'foulishlie wold gae upon thane and skirmish'.[23] The battle only lasted an hour before the Forbes powder was all spent. The exhausted and hungry forces were overcome, for 'the maister and his small companied beand rydand all that nicht bypast and nathir had gottin meit nor drink all that day'.[24] They turned and fled, pursued by Gordon horsemen and bowmen. Some of them were separated from their own side: 'The King's footmen . . . adventuring further in following of the Gordons than their shot of powder would continue, they went so far that in the end, being out of reach of defence or help of their company, they were put to fearful flight by the bowmen of the Gordons, who pursued them eagerly and continued the battell until night.'[25] It seems clear that Forbes was not such a good tactician or commander of men as his opponent Adam Gordon. Nevertheless, the chronicler Pitscottie commented: 'Nochtwithstanding, the maister of forbus faught that day verie manfullie.'

Captain Chisholm and a great many of his best soldiers died, as did a popular burgess of Aberdeen known as 'meikle' Duncan Forbes. After being chased for four miles, the Master of Forbes was amongst many taken prisoner. That night, he was locked up in the Tolbooth, where Adam's brother John, as well as probably Adam himself, and his father's body had lain nearly ten years before in 1562, after the battle of Corrichie. It seems that about sixty were killed on each side at what became known as the battle of Craibstone. The next day, the provost of Aberdeen gave £10 Scots to bury 'the deat with great pitie'.[26]

It was a triumph for Adam to capture the King's Lieutenant of the North. He was taken to Spynie Palace near Elgin. This was the seat of the Bishop of Moray, Patrick Hepburn, which had recently been fortified by the Gordons. Forbes seems to have been treated with courtesy and respect during the fifteen months of his incarceration, but he had the indignity of knowing that his Gordon wife, Adam's sister Margaret, was having an affair with the bishop's natural son, Patrick Hepburn, parson of Kinnoir. Alexander Forbes of Strathgirnock and many other Forbeses were imprisoned in Auchindoun Castle.[27] Because of fears that reprisals would be taken on the Forbes' hostages, there was no further challenge to Adam's power. It was said that, by means of this victory, 'Adam Gordon thinks to play the king'.[28] He was now unopposed in the north. 'Adam 'passit to all placeis of the Forbes and tuik thame perforce and causit thame to be keipit in his name.'[29] This was probably when Druminnor Castle was sacked. Forbes properties were despoiled of their valuables, and livestock was driven off. Aberdeen was occupied and Adam's word was law 'fra the water of Dee north'.[30] He had succeeded in saving the north-east for the Queen.

Adam, with 1,200 men, successfully retook Brechin in 1572. Several notables were killed and wounded, and 200 prisoners taken. He harangued them for the wrongs done to his family, showing how much the deaths of his father and brother John had affected him, even though they had occurred many years before. He also took control of Arbroath, and imposed a large ransom of £2,000, and 2 tons of wine from the town of Montrose.

However, the situation was changing in Scotland. The horrific massacre of Huguenots on St Bartholomew's Day in France in August 1572 greatly strengthened the hands of those determined not to risk a return of the country to Catholicism along with the restoration of Mary, despite her assurances. After the Pope declared Mary the rightful Queen of both Scotland and England, it became extremely unlikely that she would be released by Elizabeth. And, of course, many who had gained from the redistribution of Church lands in both England and Scotland did not want to risk losing them.

Chief among those who had gained from the acquisition of Church lands in Scotland was the Earl of Morton, who became Regent after the sudden death of Mar on 28 October 1572. Morton was much more determined than Mar to bring the threat of Mary's return to an end. The production of Mary's Casket Letters, which supposedly showed her involvement in the Darnley plot, meant that many of Mary's erstwhile supporters turned away, thinking that she had been party to the murder of her husband. Then, crucially, the Act of Conformity in January 1573 ordered all holders of Church benefices to subscribe to the Reformed Confession of Faith. Both sides now came to terms in the Pacification of Perth on 23 February 1573. Its generous terms were meant to ensure that the events of the civil wars would not give rise to further conflicts and feuds.[31] The only crimes not remitted (forgiven) were fire raising, incest, witchcraft and the murders of Moray, Lennox, Darnley and others.[32]

However, Adam was still victorious in the north and did not submit to the Pacification of Perth, even after his brother had given up the struggle. He refused to sign. Even as the Pacification agreement was in progress, he was fighting and defeating Lord Forbes in Aberdeen, in order to ensure that he did not attempt to exploit the triumph of the King's party.[33]

On April 10 Adam sold the lands and barony of Auchindoun and the forest of Glenfiddich to his younger brother Patrick. The nucleus of the Cabrach was leased to George Gordon of Lesmoir. It was said that Adam, 'in disgust, went into voluntary exile with Sir Thomas Kerr of Ferniehurst and six other gentlemen, "for their pleasure"'.[34] In France, they were welcomed and entertained by the King, Charles IX, Queen Mary's brother-in-law.

However, Adam was followed to Paris by Arthur Forbes, 4th son of Lord Forbes, who was determined to revenge the death of his uncle and namesake, Black Arthur. In Paris, Arthur hired some unemployed cut-throats and lay in wait for Adam and his party to leave the home of the exiled Archbishop of Glasgow, Archbishop Beaton. They 'discharged their pistols' upon Adam and 'wounded him in the thigh'. His servants gave chase but failed to catch anyone, although they were lucky enough to find a dropped hat, belonging to Forbes, with a note in it indicating where the plotters were to meet up after the deed. John Gordon, Lord of Glenluce, happened to be Lord of the King of France's Bedchamber. He was informed of the ambush and immediately reported it to the French King, who sent an officer with guards to accompany them to the place of meeting. 'Being impatient', Adam's servant rushed 'violently into the house' and killed Arthur. His accomplices were arrested and punished by the cruel death of being 'broke on the wheel'.[35]

Adam soon recovered and appealed to Queen Elizabeth to intercede for him. He returned to Scotland in late 1575,[36] but was immediately arrested and incarcerated in Blackness Castle, a stronghold overlooking the Firth of Forth. It was a bleak garrison fortress and state prison, used for people of high status. He was charged with plotting in France for Mary's restoration. He remained there for some months. He was released in January 1576, but was commanded to remain in ward at Kirkudbright,[37] probably with Gordon of Lochinvar, who was a trusted Protestant and King's man. He was still there six months later.

After the Civil War

Meanwhile, thanks to the Pacification of Perth, George had at last been able to return to Strathbogie to enjoy a more peaceful life and take up his many responsibilities, including his sheriffdom of Aberdeen. However, the Forbeses were bringing cases to his jurisdiction against the Gordons, as a result of grievances from the civil war period, and wanted redress for the injuries they had incurred at the hands of the Gordons under Adam.

There were also the sensitive divorce proceedings brought by the Master of Forbes against Adam's sister Margaret, as well as his challenge to Adam's insistence that he pay the expenses of his time as a prisoner in Spynie. It was clear to the Forbeses that they would not get an objective hearing from George as Sherriff. In June 1573, as a result of their appeal, they gained the right to have their cases heard by the Lords of the Council in Edinburgh. The Master of Forbes achieved a favourable result in both the Spynie payment and his divorce settlement.

Adam's own return to Aberdeen and ensuing public respectability, in the wake of his imprisonment and warding, is demonstrated by the fact that he presided as a deputy sheriff over the Michaelmas sheriff court in Aberdeen on 2 October 1576.[38] George, however, was not able to enjoying his family, lands and responsibilities in Strathbogie for long. Adam was present on 24 October 1576 when his eldest brother, who seemed in good health, was taking part in a friendly football game outside Huntly Castle. Having kicked the ball two or three times, he suddenly fell flat on his face. He was conveyed to a room in the castle, where he died three hours later. This must have been a shock for the family and everyone around him. His embalmed body lay in the castle chapel for a few days and was then taken to the traditional family burial place of Elgin Cathedral. Adam immediately took charge as head of the house and managed the affairs of the family, which included charge of his nephew, the sixteen-year-old heir George, now 6th Earl of Huntly. Following his brother's dying wish, Adam sent George to Paris and into the care of his Jesuit brother James, in order to complete his education.

Despite acting as deputy sheriff in Aberdeen, there must still have been a need for Adam and his followers to be publicly and officially pardoned for the civil war events of the autumn of 1571. In May 1577, nearly six years after the events, there was a 'precept for a remission' for Adam, and for ninety-eight Murrays and others of the Earl of Sutherland's tenants for treasonably acting with Adam Gordon of Auchindoun in his rebellion against the King, as well as attacking John, Master of Forbes at the field of Craibstone, and other offences. In July there was another 'precept for a remission' for the citizens of Elgin, including the provost, for their treasonable acts in accompanying Adam Gordon to Corgarff, besieging it for three days, starting a fire and murdering Margaret Campbell.[39] That Adam was now being officially pardoned for the event seems to confirm that he was present at Corgarff.

In July 1578, the Forbeses were still not satisfied, writing a long letter to the Parliament at Perth detailing their complaints against the Gordons from the time of the civil war onwards. Much of the letter concerns the possession of the old Church lands associated with Keig and Monymusk. The Forbeses had occupied these lands as tenants under the Archbishop of St Andrews, but he had come to some agreement with the Gordons that allowed them to take possession instead. The Forbeses had also not received any compensation for all the damage done to their properties, farms, mills and other possessions from the civil war period. All they wanted now was to be able to return to their native lands and homes.[40]

A judicial commission of six judges was set up to look into all the complaints and reach a final decision on all issues before 1 May 1580.[41] On 25 March of that year, it was decreed that the stipulations of the Pacification of Perth should remain in place, and therefore that the Forbeses must remove themselves from Keig and Monymusk.[42]

In January 1580, George Gordon of Gight and Alexander Forbes, younger of Tollie (Towie) had quarrelled in front of the King at council at Holyroodhouse, and ended up killing each other shortly after. There were complaints that more trouble was likely to follow from their relatives: 'Gretar inconvenientis is abill to follow, to the trubling of the gude and quiet estait of the haill cuntrie.'[43] This sounded like a repeat of fears expressed before the civil war period, and there was obviously a need to avoid another outbreak of hostilities in the north-east. Accordingly, William Lord Forbes, John Master of Forbes and Adam Gordon were charged to appear at Edinburgh before the Privy Council on 10 April, accompanied by the 'most honest, wise and discreet persons, their principal friends, not exceeding forty persons, to settle the feud'.[44]

On 22 April there was a special meeting of the King (now aged fourteen) and council at Edinburgh, at which Adam Gordon and the Master of Forbes undertook to return by 31 May the submission subscribed by their friends. Adam promised to ask his nephew, the 6th Earl, who was still in Paris, to sign. Then the noblemen chosen by each party could begin negotiating a settlement of the issues.[45]

The next day, at the council meeting at Stirling Castle, the steps taken by the King and Council to put an end to the deadly feud between the Gordons and Forbes were recited, outlining the 'divers slaughters, bloodshed and other displeasures happened amongst them'. Both parties had submitted their quarrels to the Lords of the Privy Council, and both agreed to be bound by the arbitrators' decision. By 1 July, each party had to submit its formal case to the clerk of the Privy Council, who would send a copy to the other side. By 1 August they would deliver their answers to each other's cases. Between 10 August and 1 November 1580. the arbitrators were to meet in the King's presence and debate the cases, delivering their judgement by 1 November. Both sides were to refrain from any violence or legal proceedings against the other until 1 December, on pain of perjury, infamy and loss of honour in perpetuity.[46]

However, on 27 October 1580, just days before the final judgement was to be delivered by the arbitraters in front of King and council, Adam died of 'ane bledin'.[47] He was only thirty-five. Thus ended the turbulent career of the most successful and resolute captain in the cause of Mary Queen of Scots.

Analysis

So what turned an ancient feud between the Gordons and the Forbeses into the violent events of 1571?

Some sources suggest that it was set in train by the Protestant Master of Forbes' repudiation of his Catholic wife Margaret, Adam Gordon's sister. Certainly, their marital problems might have caused tempers to rise, but it seems unlikely that it would lead to open war.

Was it, then, a religious conflict, as in France between Catholics and Protestants in the Thirty Years' War and, therefore, part of wider European troubles?[48] To some, no doubt, it was. Morton had tried to create a faction in the council, portraying the Queen's friends as wanting to restore 'Popery', knowing that this claim would antagonise his listeners and arouse greed for the spoils of war.[49] In reality, though, religion played only a small part in determining loyalties. There were Catholics in the King's party and many Protestants in the Queen's.[50] George had himself joined the Reformed faith. Kirkcaldy of Grange and Maitland of Lethington, who changed sides to hold the castle for Mary, were champions of the Reformed Church, and the Queen's party were not hostile to it: St Giles' Cathedral was held for the Queen for its military use, but Reformed services continued to be held there, some of which they attended. The supporters of the Queen's party were those who recognised Mary's authority and wanted her restoration, believing that no subject had the right to depose a reigning monarch however much she might deserve to be overthrown.[51] Indeed, Alexander Gordon, the Reforming Bishop of Galloway, preached a sermon on charity in St Giles' on 17 June 1571 in which he pointed out: 'Look at King David; he was a sinner, an adulterer and a murderer.'[52] The King's party, on the other hand, believed that they did have the right to depose an unworthy monarch[53] and had forced Mary to abdicate, crowning her infant son as James VI. The last thing they wanted was Mary's return.[54]

Many dithered about which side to support. George had not been totally consistent in his loyalty to Mary. When her cause seemed hopeless in the spring of 1569, he signed a bond recognising Moray as Regent and acknowledging the King's authority. This bond resulted in Moray being able to resist Elizabeth's move to return Mary, despite her religious guarantees and a promise to divorce Bothwell.[55] However, in July George was one of only nine who voted for her restoration against forty who opposed it. Mostly, he was loyal to her, which was probably the result of strong personal attachment, having been part of her inner circle during the most dramatic moments of her life.

The Master of Forbes was not always in the King's party. He had signed himself with Huntly, as one of the Queen's Lords, in letters written to Queen Elizabeth after Moray's assassination in July 1568, and again in the spring of 1570, begging her intervention. This was the letter that described in such graphic terms 'the tinder box that could become a conflagration' because of the divisions caused by conflicting loyalties between supporters of mother and son.[56] Elizabeth had it in her power to ensure that there was only one claim to the throne, they said. In November that year, Forbes was one of twenty-three peers who offered to send their son, brother or next of kin as hostage for Mary if Elizabeth sent her back to Scotland. As late as September 1571, it was said that Lord Forbes was (for a short time) an ardent supporter of Mary. But his uncle, Black Arthur, had always followed the King 'to his utmost, from the first time of the discord'.[57] Mary's return was the last thing that the Earl of Morton, encouraged by Cecil in England, wanted.

Was it significant that the Earl of Mar was elected Regent in 1571, the year that conflict broke out in the north-east? Did he offer inducements of land in the earldom of Mar to bring the Forbeses into action against the Gordons? During the previous century, it was an Earl of Mar who had given his friend and vassal Sir Alexander Forbes land on the Don in the old earldom of Mar, which then covered the Don and the Dee. However, the Crown had given away almost all of the earldom's lands between 1457 and 1563. Most of Strathdon went into Lord Elphinstone's Lordship of Kildrummy in 1509, including Kildrummy Castle. Mary's mother, Mary of Guise, had granted Braemar and Strathdee in feu to Adam's father, the 4th Earl of Huntly. The lands of Strathavon, Strathdon, Auchindoir and the Cabrach had all been acquired by him. Thus, the Earl of Mar had little land in Mar to offer anyone. Mary had restored the title of Earl of Mar to him in 1565, but he had been unable to dispossess the Elphinstones and their vassals.

Was it possible that Mar wanted the Forbeses to challenge Huntly in the field, in the hope of regaining that land? If so, his strategy didn't work, but later his son embarked on a long and ultimately successful campaign to reconstitute the earldom of Mar to the state it had enjoyed in 1404, with the result that vast swathes of Aberdeenshire were restored to Mar's ownership or superiority.[58] This might have been a case of a son fulfilling his father's failed ambitions to harness the help of the Forbeses, in the name of the King, for their family cause, especially the chance of taking back Mar land held by the Gordons.

Perhaps the Forbes–Gordon feud ignited because Morton was appointed Lieutenant General of the Forces and was determined to bring the remaining rebels under control, having 'laboured violently to draw Forbes to him'.[59] It would be very much in accord with Morton's methods if he used as bait the possibility of aggrandising the Forbes estates at the Gordons' expense, their lands having been forfeited that summer, along with those belonging to the bishops of Aberdeen, Moray, and Ross and Galloway. The Bishop of Aberdeen had made

his nephew, the 4th Earl of Huntly, bailey of the Aberdeen bishopric's
lands at the time of the Reformation. He benefited his Gordon kin with
Church lands and revenues within the earldom of Mar, very close to
the Forbes stronghold of Druminnor, including Tillyangus, Clatt,
Knockespock, Terpersie, Cluny and Towie.[60] Many Forbes tenants
were ousted or had to pay rent to the Gordons. It might have been
suggested that this state of affairs could be redressed – certainly, the
struggle for land in the old earldom of Mar was at the root of the feud
between the Forbes and the Gordons. Ironically, it was said that Mar
was disgusted that many pretended to support the King or Queen
merely to enlarge their estates at their neighbours' expense. Did this
apply to Mar himself, or to the Master of Forbes and his father, urged
on by Black Arthur?

Mar and Morton were preoccupied with the Queen's party's hold
on Edinburgh Castle under Kirkcaldy of Grange and Maitland of Lethington, supported by George. It might be that Mar and Morton
concocted a plot to create a diversion in the north-east, causing Huntly
to withdraw his troops from Edinburgh in order to defend his heartland, thereby making it easier for them to retake the castle.

Did Forbes gain confidence as a result of the important defections to
the King's party that were taking place at the time? Some, including
Lord Lovat and a number of Highland chiefs, were offered the bait of
benefits, such as pensions from the forfeited bishoprics of Aberdeen
and Moray. Forbes was probably urged to act quickly so that he could
regain what he had lost of these lands before someone else procured
them. Following the Reformation, there was a continuous scramble by
the opportunists for their share of any spoils, and they would not want
to risk losing such opportunities if Catholicism was restored.

The Forbeses might have been moved to bold action as a result of
Black Arthur's leadership. Arthur was not only a strong supporter of
the King's party from the beginning but was also a man of great
courage and ambition, ready to undertake anything to advance his
family's interests. It was at his instigation that the Forbeses gathered at
Druminnor, prepared to take on the Gordons at Tillyangus in October
1571.[61] He was the son of John, 6th Lord Forbes and his third wife
Elizabeth Barlow, widow of the 1st Lord Elphinstone and Lady of
Kildrummy in her own right. For much of the 1540s and 1550s Black
Arthur held the office of Baillie of Kildrummy on behalf of his nephew,
the infant and absentee 3rd Lord Elphinstone, which enabled him to
establish himself as the natural leader in Strathdon. By 1571, he was

by far the most prominent military captain among the Forbeses, commanding the loyalty of much of the Highland country of Strathdoun and adjacent districts.[62] He naturally took the lead at Tillyangus, and may well have initiated the attempt to block the Gordon march south as the Forbes' contribution to the King's war effort.

I believe that all of these factors played a part in the turmoil in the north-east during the late sixteenth century. They were influenced by the feud and by competition for land, and exacerbated by Morton and Mar encouraging the Forbeses to play their part in defeating the remaining vestiges of the Queen's party in the north-east; the Forbeses took up the challenge using a good military leader, probably envisaging the prospect of redistributed lands. These events were essentially a reflection of national politics and part of the struggle between Mary's supporters and those of the Regent of the time who served her infant son, King James VI. Nevertheless, because the Forbeses did not succeed in changing the status quo, even with added reinforcements and authority from the south, the three incidents – the battle of Tillyangus, the burning of Corgarff Castle, and the battle of Craibstone – made no difference to the national political scene, and are not even mentioned in most books on the history of that time.

The Gordons continued to hold the north for the Queen until they were eventually persuaded by Argyll that the Queen's cause was hopeless, and the two sides came to terms at the Pacification of Perth on 18 February 1573. The Gordons, along with other members of the Queen's party, were pardoned and their forfeitures lifted. Even Adam was eventually pardoned. Forbes received a charter of new lands as 'rewards for loyalties'.[63]

4

Margaret Gordon – Sinner or Saint?

Childhood, Youth and Marriage

Margaret is an enigma. One theory holds that she was a wild young woman, acting tomboyishly with her younger brothers and the illegitimate sons of the Hepburn Bishop of Moray, and that she was the mistress of the eldest of these. However, Catholic sources write about her as a wronged saint. This chapter explores her life in the hope of coming nearer to the truth.

It is thought that she was born in 1544, the second daughter of George Gordon, 4th Earl of Huntly, which would make her about a year older than her sister Jean. When she was three years old, an official contract was drawn up for a marriage between the eldest son (aged seven) of Lord Forbes to 'ane of my Lord Huntly's daughters'. The Earl of Huntly was in England at the time of the signing, having been captured after the disastrous battle of Pinkie. In his absence, the contract was signed by Margaret's mother, Lady Elizabeth Keith, Countess of Huntly, and also by Margaret's eldest brother, Alexander. Papal dispensation for consanguinity was required, as the two children were third cousins once removed.[1]

Margaret grew up in Huntly Castle in a family of two sisters and nine brothers. Tragically, Alexander died soon after his marriage to the eldest daughter of the Duke of Chatelherault.[2] However, when Margaret was fourteen she saw her next eldest brother, George, marry the third daughter of the Duke.

At fourteen, Margaret was considered of marriageable age herself, and in November 1558 she was married to the seventeen-year-old John, Master of Forbes. Typical of women of her position at the time, Margaret would have been obliged to submit to an arranged marriage whatever her own private feelings about it. Because family feuding was so widespread in Scottish society, such marriages were often intended to end a dispute, in a similar fashion to peace agreements between two countries. This was the case for Margaret, where her marriage was aimed at healing the age-old feud between her family and the Forbeses, who both 'had long striven for mastery in the county of Aberdeen'.[3] The rivalry was exacerbated by the redistribution of Church lands amongst the nobility. The Forbeses had long tenanted Church lands of the bishopric of Aberdeen and St Andrews, which now came under the 4th Earl of Huntly's jurisdiction and had been portioned out to members of the Gordons of Huntly clan. The marriage was meant to defuse the inevitable sense of grievance and antagonism. However, it was a particularly unfortunate match for Margaret, because her spouse's family, who lived in Druminnor Castle near Rhynie, were enthusiastic supporters of John Knox, while she must have already been an ardent young Catholic: she had once been hit in the face for telling her mother that she wanted to be a nun in a foreign country.[4] The seeds of her future were already sown.

The wedding service and the law of the time stated that Margaret must 'be in subjection and under governance of her husband, so long as they continue to live'.[5] Further, her mother-in-law, Elizabeth Keith of Inverugie, Lady Forbes, was a famous Presbyterian, politically active and a woman of strong personality,[6] who would not have viewed the Catholic practices of her daughter-in-law favourably.

The Battle of Corrichie and its Aftermath

Although the marriage was intended to bring the two families together, it was unfortunate for Margaret that they continued to take opposite sides in the ensuing conflicts. The first of these was the battle of Corrichie in 1562, when Margaret was pregnant with her first child. She must have been well aware of tensions between her family and the government when Mary Queen of Scots refused her mother's invitation to stay at Huntly Castle on her royal progress to the north. There must have been plenty of talk in Druminnor Castle about her brother John and also her father, the 4th Earl, being put to the horn and declared rebels for intransigence. She must have heard that the Forbeses were mustering, ready to join the Queen's force under the Earl of Moray, with her father-in-law as second-in-command, ready to confront her father's force. Moray may have been cleverly exploiting the Forbeses' existing resentments against the Gordons in order to bring them on to the royal side, as the government released them from their feudal obligation to follow the Earl of Huntly. They would now be at liberty to use force against the Gordons.[7]

It must have been a painful time for Margaret, being caught in the middle between her own family and that of her husband, followed by the Gordon defeat, her father's tragic death on the battlefield and her brother John's execution in Aberdeen. No doubt it was widely reported that her mother-in-law Lady Forbes had viewed her father's body lying in the Tolbooth in Aberdeen, exclaiming: 'There lieth he, that yester-day, at morn, was esteemed the wisest, richest and most powerful man in Scotland!'[8]

How relieved Margaret must have been that Adam, the brother closest to her in age, had narrowly escaped execution thanks to the appeal of Mary's companion, because of his young age. Also that her eldest brother George had escaped Moray's cruel ruling that he should be hanged, drawn and quartered, despite his absence from the battle. The Queen commuted this to ward in Dunbar Castle. John Knox said that it was Moray who appealed to the Queen on George's behalf, but this seems unlikely.

But Margaret had to hear about and even witness her old home of Huntly Castle being bombarded and stripped of its valuables: it would have been devastating for her to see her childhood home so desecrated. There was further humiliation for her family in 1563 when her father's embalmed body was put on trial, along with her brothers and those who had supported them. All of their lands were forfeited, and a charter was issued under which the Gordon lands were to be held in the hands of her father-in-law Lord Forbes, with his obligations to Huntly swept away.[9] This must have given the Forbes family much satisfaction. How could a marriage survive such a situation? Unfortu-nately it did not, as we shall see in the conflicts that lay ahead.

The main purpose of marriage was procreation. Because so many children died, the aim then was to have as many as possible so that there would be someone to provide care for parents in their old age, to carry on the family name and, in the case of the nobility, to create new alliances. Wives were often pregnant soon after marriage, but in Margaret's case there had been a curious five-year delay before she gave birth to their first child. It was a son and heir, whom they named William after his grandfather, Lord Forbes. Little did they realise what lay in store for him.

The Gordon Family Restored

In 1565, two years after the terrible humiliation and downfall of her family, it would have been gratifying for Margaret to hear that their enemy, the Earl of Moray, who had done much to bring about the disaster, was now out of favour with the Queen, having rebelled along with other influential people who opposed her marriage to Catholic Lord Darnley.

Better still was the cheering news that her brother George had been released from Dunbar Castle and had been restored to the Queen's favour as the 5th Earl of Huntly, despite the Corrichie trial ruling. Her mother the Countess was brought to court, where she became a close confidante of the Queen; and her sister Jean was to be married in style to the Earl of Bothwell. Did Margaret sympathise with her sister's regret for her first love, Alexander Ogilvie of Boyne? Perhaps, as an older sister, she may have encouraged Jean to regard the marriage to Bothwell as beneficial to their family's full rehabilitation, as it had been arranged by the Queen. The Forbes family might well have been amongst the many opposed to Lord Darnley but perhaps overcame their objections in order to attend Jean's grand wedding, which was to be graced by both of their majesties.

While George and Jean became closely involved in the dramas of Mary's life, Margaret was busy during the next five years giving birth to four more children: three girls and, in 1570, a second son, completing the family. The boy was named John, after his father. Margaret was now twenty-six. She must have been delighted to see her Gordon family home and land being restored, along with those of other Gordons in the district, including their neighbour, James Gordon of Tillyangus. Additionally, on 20 March 1566, her brother George was elevated to the position of Chancellor, the same post that their father had held during her childhood. Probably as a result of this, her younger brother Adam had the pleasure of gaining official title to Auchindoun and Keithmore in a compromise deal with James Ogilvie. Surely, also, she must have attended when her father's embalmed body was at last brought north for burial in Elgin Cathedral, with the full honours due to an earl of Huntly? Her family's place in society was truly restored and the future looked good. However, this pleasant situation was not to last long.

The Tinderbox

Although no doubt somewhat preoccupied with childbirth and her growing family, Margaret must have been aware of the shocking goings-on at court, especially the horrific murders of Riccio and then, most startling of all, Lord Darnley. News must soon have spread north of the scandalous relationship between her brother-in-law, the Earl of Bothwell, and the Queen, leading to his unusually rapid divorce from her sister so that he could marry Mary. The break-up of her sister's marriage, difficult as it had been, might have given Margaret ambivalent feelings towards Mary. Her husband's uncle, Black Arthur, and her husband must have had plenty to say about it in the Forbes household, as they were followers of John Knox, who railed against Mary from many a pulpit. At least Jean was financially well provided for, as she had managed to hold on to her dowry lands and property. Margaret was not to be so lucky.

Once he realised that Mary's abdication had been forced on her, George returned home, firmly committed to the Queen's cause. He was followed north by Jean and their mother, as things were becoming uncomfortable in Edinburgh for Mary's supporters. How fascinating it would have been to be a fly on the wall, listening as her returned relatives told Margaret their versions of what actually went on at Court, especially given all the conjecture and controversy there has since been about Mary's life. Did George think she was a willing accomplice when Bothwell abducted her? Did he seduce or rape her in Dumbarton Castle? At which point did they think she became committed to him? Was Darnley as bad as everyone said? Who of all those around her knew about the plot to murder him, and who actually carried it out? Above all, did Mary know about and connive in it? No doubt members of the Forbes family had strong ideas about these questions, particularly if Black Arthur had anything to do with it. To followers of John Knox, Mary was a 'Jezebel' and had forfeited her right to be Queen. They believed that her people had the right to depose her. To them, it was much better that the country be ruled by a Regent and his council on behalf of a powerless infant monarch. It was, after all, Scotland's way.

News must have soon spread north of Mary's capture at Carberry Hill, and her erstwhile brother-in-law's arrival at Huntly Castle in his vain attempt to win support from her brother. No doubt she was told that George hoped Bothwell would come to grief, so ridding their sister and the Queen of such a wicked husband.

Margaret would have met a new member of the household when she visited her family at Huntly Castle: their cousin Alexander Gordon, Earl of Sutherland, who came as a refugee, having been rescued by George from ugly plots for his murder. He had previously avoided being poisoned along with his parents at the hands of the Sinclairs of Caithness. George also gave succour to other escapees from the north: Alexander's followers, known as 'the men of Moray', who helpfully provided reinforcements in the conflicts ahead. He and Alexander now joined others committed to Mary's cause, although they arrived too late to fight for her at the crucial battle of Langside on 13 May 1568. Some sources say that the Forbeses blocked their way, but the delay may well have been due to the death of their mother, the Countess of Huntly, which occurred just then.[10]

Margaret's father-in-law, Lord Forbes, appeared to be unsure of which side he was on. On 28 July 1568 his name appeared on a letter sent to Queen Elizabeth, who was holding Mary captive. It was signed by twenty lords and three bishops, and asked her to free Mary and allow her to return to Scotland. The signatories also asked Elizabeth to help 'with certain men, money and munitions instantly, whereby she may recover her strengths falsely taken from her, and stablish her again in her own realm'.[11] A couple of days later, on 30 July, another letter was composed by Argyll and the western lords in Largs, this time to the Duke of Alva. It complains of the inhuman and barbarous treatment of their sovereign by the Queen of the English, and begs him to to ask Philip II of Spain to write a sharp letter to Elizabeth demanding that Mary be allowed to return to Scotland or France. The letter also requested military aid for the Marians to retake some castles. Because time was short, Argyll explained later, the names of the eastern lords were included without their knowledge, and they were expected to ratify it afterwards. These speculative inclusions included both Huntly and Lord Forbes, so it is not clear if Forbes really did support the request.

Tensions must have risen in the Forbes household when contradictory proclamations were made at the market crosses in all the main burghs. One was from George, as Earl of Huntly, urging all the people in the north to join him in Perth prepared to fight those opposed to Mary. The Confederate lords, on the other hand, urged people, even at the market cross in Aberdeen, to disobey Huntly's call to arms, and proclaimed they were discharging him of his Lieutenancy of the North.[12] Which of these exhortations would Margaret's husband, the Master of Forbes, obey?

By April 1569, he had decided. Along with other nobles in Aberdeen, Inverness, St Andrews and Edinburgh, John signed a bond acknowledging the infant King James as 'oure onelie Soveraine Lord; and his dearest uncle, James Erll of Murray – Regent to his Hienes, his realme and lieges thairof during his Majesteis minoritie', promising 'never to harm them, and to forgo all former bandis for obedience of ony uther authoritie'.[13] By the following month, even her brother George and his followers had signed, having previously been made to pay huge fines for disobeying. For the moment they felt obliged to sign.

However, on 23 January 1570 the atmosphere in the Forbes household would have been inflamed by the news that the Regent, the Earl of Moray, had been assassinated in St Andrews. The Forbes family must have been devastated and, as Protestant Reformers, had held high hopes for him. The temperature would then have risen further, as in the rest of the country and in England, with news of the Papal bull that referred to Queen Elizabeth's 'pretended right' to the English throne. This, of course, implied that the imprisoned Mary was the rightful queen of England as well as Scotland.

Margaret would have seen little of her eldest brother George from now on, as he was mostly in and around Edinburgh. He was now fully committed to military means as a method of bringing about Mary's restoration, especially after the French King's representative landed at Dumbarton to promise aid and thank them for maintaining her cause. Adam assumed leadership in the north in place of his brother, taking Brechin Castle in the Mary's name. In fact, it was declared that the Queen had 'universal obedience' in the north.

It appears that Margaret's father-in-law Lord Forbes and her brother George were so concerned about the country dividing in two that on 3 March both of their signatures appeared on the letter from the Scottish nobles, appealing in graphic terms to Queen Elizabeth for her help in calming matters. It is possible that some of the names were forged, including those of Lord Forbes and Huntly,[14] but her brother would have been sure to support the appeal at this point, if not her father-in-law.

Margaret would have heard, probably from her husband's family, that George had narrowly missed capture at Brechin Castle by the large force sent north by the new Regent, Darnley's father, the Earl of

Lennox, intending to block George's route south to attend the rival parliament he had called at Linlithgow. No doubt there were conflicting reactions to the news that 300 of George's men were caught inside, and that thirty of those sheltering in the church and steeple were brutally executed by Lennox and his men.

Perhaps it was because of this shocking event that Lord Forbes became for a short while an ardent Marian. So much so that on 20 November 1570 he put his name to another appeal to Queen Elizabeth, along with other lords, stating that he would be prepared to send four members of his family, including next of kin, to England as surety if she would send Mary back to Scotland. Elizabeth did seriously consider returning Mary to act as joint sovereign with her son. However, the tinderbox was not yet made safe.

Civil War in the North

On 1 July 1571, Margaret's brothers, George and Adam, were both accused of treason by Lennox's parliament, along with her great-uncle, the Bishop of Aberdeen, and Patrick Hepburn, Bishop of Moray, who sheltered his nephew Bothwell on his flight north. In August, the Gordons and others were again forfeited. The Queen's party retaliated by forfeiting members of the King's party. To add to the turmoil, Margaret then heard that her brother George had led an attempt to capture the King's party at Stirling Castle, during which Lennox had been accidentally shot in a skirmish. By the middle of the year the Queen's party was powerful, especially as it held Edinburgh Castle, but things changed after Elizabeth released incriminating versions of Mary's Casket Letters, purportedly showing connivance in the plot to murder Darnley.

The Forbes household was soon to be affected when the Earl of Mar was elected Regent on 5 September 1571 and appointed the hard-line Earl of Morton as his Lieutenant General of the Forces. Margaret must have been aware of a tug of war between Morton and George for Forbes support.[15] In fact, it was said that Morton 'laboured violently' to draw Forbes to him, obviously believing the theory that 'the Forbeses were the key to the north'.[16] He succeeded, because in May the following year Forbes appeared with 'KP' (King's party) written by his name on a list of 'Earls that are Protestant' sent to William Cecil, now Lord Burghley. They were asking for England's intervention. Lord Randolph, the English ambassador, promised help. Attitudes must have been hardening in the Forbes household.

The autumn of 1571 was a turning point in Margaret's life. She again had to face seeing her husband and brothers gathering their forces on opposite sides. This time Adam was leading the Gordons, as George was involved in military action in and around Edinburgh. Adam was accompanied by her other younger brothers, Robert and Patrick. In October her father-in-law, Lord Forbes, received a message from Adam saying that the Gordons would be passing peacefully through Forbes lands. This was a chance for the Forbeses to obey Morton's appeals and prevent the Gordons proceeding south and causing more trouble in the Mearns. Black Arthur would no doubt have been urging action, probably delighted to have the opportunity to use his military skills to fight the hated Gordons once more.

Animated discussions must have taken place in the Forbes household on how to set about the ambush. Finally, it was decided to halt the advancing Gordons at a point on the Mar Road called the White Hill of Tillyangus on the edge of the Correen hills, where there was an ancient stone circle atop an area of rock and gullies, which would provide excellent cover. It was on 10 October 1571 that the Forbeses, led by Black Arthur, left the castle to set up their ambush. Imagine the conflicting loyalties this would have aroused in Margaret. All she could do was await the outcome – which turned out to be witnessing her husband's fleeing forces returning to the castle, badly defeated and reporting news of many dead. Amongst the deceased was Black Arthur, stabbed through a gap in his armour, the best military leader they had.

Her husband had only just escaped with his life and was fleeing south to appeal to Morton for more military support against Margaret's family, and to relieve the hardships suffered by the country from 'the oppression of the Gordons'. It was even considered important enough to report to Queen Elizabeth that: 'The Maister of Forbes is with the Regent, soliciting to have horsemen and footmen sent into the North against the Gordons.'[17] How could any marriage survive such eventualities? It must have made life extremely difficult for Margaret at home.

Added to this was the news of the horrific burning of Corgarff Castle by Adam's men, purportedly led by Adam himself, and the twenty-seven people, including women and children, trapped inside. This would have inflamed the Forbes household even more, because the castle in question belonged to a leading Forbes, John Forbes of Towie, who was a tenant of none other than Mar, the Regent. His wife

Margaret Campbell, who was pregnant, and her daughters and stepson were burnt to death. The enormity of this event must have contributed to the success of her husband's appeal for help against her brother Adam, who was being referred to as 'the Herot of the North'. Her husband was made Lieutenant of the King's Forces in the north, with a large number of the Regent's forces, and was given freedom to raise more in the Mearns, to be paid for by proceeds taken from two thirds of the bishopric of her great-uncle, the forfeited Bishop of Aberdeen.

Margaret would have heard that her husband was marching north with a huge force in an attempt to destroy Gordon hegemony in the north-east and break its loyalty to the Queen. But did she know that George had sent reinforcements to Adam by sea from Edinburgh? He also had young Alexander Sutherland's 'men of Moray', as well as most of the Gordons collecting in Aberdeen.

What was her reaction when she heard that her husband's force had been decisively defeated by her brother and his Gordons at the battle of Craibstone? He had been captured, and many of his 'kyne and frendis slayne'.[18] No doubt she would have known many of those who had been killed. Her husband was taken to Spynie Palace, seat of Patrick Hepburn, Bishop of Moray, great-uncle of Jean's former husband, and equally notorious. Spynie had been taken over and forti-fied by the Gordons, aided by the bishop's bastard sons.[19]

The Forbeses were now at the mercy of the Gordons, whose control was again unchallenged in the north. Druminnor was bombarded and sacked. For some unknown reason, Adam went looking for Margaret's mother-in-law Lady Forbes, 'who now beiris the blame of all the wrake of the Forbessis', and if he had found her 'nothing suld have savet her lyfe'.[20] From this report, it looks as though Margaret's mother-in-law must have been behind the challenge to Gordon hegemony, presuma-bly by urging her husband to take up arms against the Gordons at Tillyangus. The project had failed, though, and now their eldest son and heir was captured.

The Affair

Margaret was without her husband John for fifteen months while he was incarcerated in Spynie Palace. It appears that, from December 1571 to May the following year, Margaret was involved in an affair with none other than one of the bastard sons of her husband's captor, also named Patrick Hepburn, parson of Kinnoir. The term 'parson of

Kinnoir' was merely titular and gave the holder access to land rent. Parsonages were often granted to lay holders, leaving the pastoral duties in each parish to be performed by vicars (which means 'deputies'). These vicars were invariably badly paid and usually badly educated. The 'parsons' were generally connected to the person who had the right of nomination to the benefice, in this case the Bishop of Moray, who provided his bastard sons with healthy incomes in this way. The many parsonages in the gift of William Gordon, Bishop of Aberdeen, were similarly parcelled out to his allies by the Earl of Huntly, as the bishop's hereditary baillie.[21] The Hepburn bastards behaved as if they were beyond the reach of the law, leaving dozens of murders, rapes and acts of arson in their wake. At times they were joined in their wild behaviour by Margaret's younger brothers.[22]

January 1573 brought the Act of Conformity, which placed more restrictions on Catholics, including Margaret and other members of her family, such as Jean and their Jesuit brother James. Those who failed to conform to the Reformed faith were to lose their entitlement to the Church lands they held. This brought the first heavy remission of Marians.

With English help, Morton managed to bring the two sides together, even Margaret's brother George, to acknowledge James as King by signing the Pacification of Perth.

A letter written by Morton, then the Regent, in the following month shows that he intended to take a military force north to deal with this continued non-compliance. The letter made particular reference to the incarceration of Margaret's husband.

> Having deliberated with the nobilities at the Parliament about the troubled state of the north country, where so many honest men have experience sa gret outrage and appression as they are not able to endure it, and amongis all otheris, *the Maister of Forbes, a young Gentilman is sa straitlie detenit captice and upon na band can be gotten relievit* – it is concludit that . . . we sall pass north and convene at Brechin the first of March next with a substantious force of the Kingis Majestis Guid Subjectis for redeeming of that discordant countire to his hieniess dutifull obedience.[23]

Morton asks that his followers meet with their kin, tenants and followers 'in warlike manner'.

However, in May, before the force had gathered, Margaret's husband managed to extract a promise from members of his family and friends to pay the £750 ransom, thereby freeing himself. He was now able to hear the whole story of his wife's infidelity.

He wasted no time in getting divorce proceedings drawn up the following month, at the end of June 1573, in the Commissary Court of Edinburgh. This courrt had replaced the now defunct Ecclesiastical Courts, although canon law remained the basis of matrimonial law.[24] Adultery had been the only possible reason for divorce before the Reformation. The Reformers were even more anxious than the previous ecclesiastical regime to condemn adultery. The 1563 parliament had passed an act declaring it to be punishable by death, but matters were never taken to that extreme.[25] The prosecution detailed how Margaret had committed adultery many times with Patrick Hepburn during the period of her husband's captivity up until May 1872, both in Druminnor and Rinnalloch.[26] Rinnalloch was on the edge of the Correen hills and was probably a house built on lands settled on her at the time of her marriage as part of her jointure (marriage settlement).[27] Margaret's partner in adultery is described as the 'umquhil' Patrick Hepburn in the divorce paper dated 29 June 1573, which means former, late or dead.[28] This may be why their affair stopped well before John was released.

Margaret must have known that her husband's family had also initiated proceedings against her brothers for settlement of their grievances. Many of the complaints related to the period of conflict, particularly damage to Druminnor, but also to longstanding land issues. The Forbeses must have celebrated when they heard that the Lords of the Council and Session had agreed that forty-nine Forbes lairds and thirty-three of their allies should be exempted from the jurisdiction of the Earl of Huntly, because tensions were running so high between the two families that the Forbeses were unlikely to receive a fair hearing.

The divorce document drawn up by Mr Robert Maitland, Dean of Aberdeen, still exists and goes into striking and colourful detail about Margaret's alleged misdemeanours, clearly stating incidents of adultery. It says that from at least the month of December 1571 until May 1572 she

did diverse and many times keep companie with umquhill Patrick Hepburn persoun off Kynnor suspect and sladerit off audultyeries with dyvers personis of before – And that not onelie in suspect places in secreyt maner and upon day lycht bot be contenuall resorting and hanting with him during the tyme forsaid be the space of auchteen, fifteen and XX days togethair boithe nyt and day. In the placis of Druminnor and Rannalloch within the Sheriffdom off Aberdein and sum tymes being sa convoyit that no persoun knew of him but the said Margat and her serving woman familiar unto her in thair unlauchfull doings as they supposit. Within the quhilkis placis the said Margrat during the space forsaid and in the absence of her said spouse resavit and harborit the said Patrick mony and dyvers nytis with quhom she committed adulterie – Lykas for the better accomplishment thairof the said Margrat having lytill or na regard to her schame and at all tymis and nytis quhar the said umquhill Patrick repairit lyid and harberit in Drumminour, he lay in the uter chalmer within the hall nixt to the said Margratis chalmer quherin he myt have enterit at his plesir he beand soetar within the said uter chalmer and the hall dour steikit upon him within and the said Margrat havand na persoun with her bot her servand womane pertesepant and beand upon the cusall off the said filthie crym for accomplischment quherof sche left her awin chalmer quherin sche was accostomit to remain befoir.

Lyk as the said Patrick quhen he was in Ranalachie quhilk was upon the fford, fyft and saxt dayis of mai the said yeir of God, being resavit and harborit in the said place of Ranalachie lay nytlie in ane chalmer with the said Margrat to whom he have had access at his pleasor, for perpetrating of the said crym quherof he was most vehementlie suspect be public fame and common voice during the tyme foresaid and was maist quietlie keepit in the said place of Ranalchie that very few knew of him the tyme of his remaining.[29]

John, Master of Forbes, asked to divorce Margaret and be considered a free man, and that Margaret should lose the right to her tocher, as well as all the goods and lands given to her when they married for her life rent.

Unlike Bothwell's hasty divorce from Margaret's sister Jean, most divorces took a long time to accomplish. The process needed persistence and financial resources, and the number of divorces granted at that time were very few.[30] The sittings for John's divorce from Margaret took eight months from when the proceedings were first called on 28 July 1573, being considered at intervals until 22 March 1574. Unfortunately, we do not know what Margaret pleaded in her defence, or even whether she did defend herself.

However, there is an interesting anomaly in the record, because it states that the adultery plea was not accepted. Instead, 'differences of religion' was given as the reason for the divorce. It goes on to say that after hearing further witnesses, the adultery plea was accepted. On 24 June 1574 their marriage was officially dissolved by decree.[31] This was good news for John, because it meant that he could retain her tocher property but, of course, it was very bad news for Margaret. As was usual at the time, a wife who was divorced by her husband lost her right to any of the land settled on her at her marriage, and also the right to her children, who would have stayed with their father whatever the background of the case. He would only lose them if he was found unfit, or if his religious beliefs were 'unsatisfactory'. There would also have been much disapproval of Margaret, both public and private, as marriage vows had been broken.[32] She would therefore be in a sorry situation, both financially and emotionally, especially having to leave behind all five of her children, aged between four and eleven. She was now aged twenty-nine.

In the same month, her husband was explaining to the Privy Council that he had been released from Spynie after his friends promised to pay £750, and it was reported that 'the said erle is claiming this sum from the sureties'. John claimed that, under the terms of the Pacification of Perth, the 'obligation should be null and void'. This plea was accepted by the Council and confirmed by the Regent at Holyrood.[33]

Meanwhile, Margaret's cousin, the young Alexander Gordon, Earl of Sutherland, had been pursuing a legal claim against the Sinclairs of Caithness, saying that his forced marriage to the much older Barbara Sinclair should be annulled, as he had been under age at the time. He was also successful in claiming his legal right to the earldom of Sutherland. Once achieved, he and Margaret's sister Jean were married. Was Margaret able to face her family and enjoy the wedding when it was solemnised at Huntly Castle on 13 December of that fateful year 1573? Adam must have been present, as he did not set off for France until early the following year. Shortly afterwards, George was warded for five months in Galloway, suspected of 'abetting' Adam in Paris.

Margaret's youngest child was only four years old, but she would have been compelled to leave him and the other four children. Where she lived afterwards is not known.[34] Did she take refuge in Huntly Castle? Her mother, Elizabeth Keith, had died five years before, in May 1568. Her Keith maternal grandparents would have been unlikely to help because her uncle, William Keith, Earl Marischal, was a recluse who lived in a tower in Dunnottar Castle. The family were ultra-Protestants, and the Master of Marischal had originally joined the force sent against her brothers before the battle of Craibstone. Her mother-in-law was also a Keith, and would have sided with her son. Margaret's sister Jean, now the Countess of Sutherland, was closest to her in age and might have provided a possible refuge. She had gone through the humiliation of a divorce herself, from the unfaithful Earl of Bothwell, but in that case he was the guilty party. Jean was now pregnant with their first child, and may not have wanted a scandal-tainted sister tarnishing her new family's reputation.

Two years later Margaret lost her brother George when he died suddenly and unexpectedly at Huntly Castle of what was then called apoplexy, just as their father had on the battlefield of Corrichie. Returned and rehabilitated, Adam took charge of the family and their affairs, including George's eldest son, aged only sixteen, who was to complete his education in Paris in the charge of their renowned Jesuit brother James. Perhaps Adam gave her a home.

However, the long-running grievances between the Forbeses and the Gordons continued, aggravated by the divorce. How frustrated the Forbeses must have been when Adam died five years later of 'ane bleeding', just days before the King and Council were to give their final arbitration on their case. It was deferred to the following year, when the more favourable regime of the young James and his favourite, Esmé Stewart, arbitrated in the Gordon's favour. But did Margaret benefit? In the Catholic accounts, we are told that she lived a life of penury.

Margaret's Sons

Meanwhile Margaret's sons were growing up and having trouble at home. The eldest boy, William, fell out with his father and his grandfather John, 7th Lord Forbes, as a result of disputes over his mother's treatment.[35] While he was still quite young, he left home and went to fight on the Protestant side in the Wars of Religion in the Low Countries. At first his father sent considerable sums for his living expenses, but William then deserted to the Catholic side and cut off communications with his father.[36] He became a favourite of the Duke of Parma, who led the Spanish troops.[37] The Netherlands were nearly all under Spanish control. William then decided to abandon the military life and entered instead, on 13 February 1589, a Capuchin convent newly established by the Duke of Parma. The word 'convent' comes from the

Latin 'conventus' and was used interchangeably for male or female religious houses; in fact 'monastery' was often used for women.[38] The Capuchin Order of Friars was an offshoot of the Franciscan Order. Their main aim was to work amongst the poor. William was known from then on as Brother Archangelus and led a most holy life, 'remarkable for severe abstinence and fervour in prayer'. He renounced all rights as heir to his father's title and estates in favour of his younger brother John Forbes, then aged eighteen.[39]

William had managed to keep in touch with John, and was 'like a father' to him in spiritual matters. He advised John to get in touch with their uncle, Father James Gordon. Fr James' presence in the country, secretly ministering to Catholics, 'was winked at because of his noble birth and the connivance of his family members'.[40] He was surprised at being approached by John and asked how it had come about. John replied that it must have been due to the prayers of his mother and his brother William.

John explained to his uncle that he had seen how his father's life did not measure up to what he read at the daily mealtime Bible readings. His uncle instructed him secretly in the Catholic faith, 'delivering him from the corruption of heresy and, finally, by the benefit of absolution, reconciled him to his mother, the Holy Church'. Later he gave him some 'little devout images and an Agnes Dei, to wear round his neck'.[41] His father was horrified when he happened to see it as his son got out of bed one morning. He said nothing, but tried to distract him with rich clothes, money, sports, lively company and a beautiful young bride-to-be. Once, when John was out hunting with friends his own age, he grew tired, fell back and had a vision of men 'in a poor habit'. Later, in Antwerp, he saw some Capuchins similar to those he had seen in his vision.

John decided that all those round him – his father, sisters and step-mother Janet Seton – were heretics. Warned by his mother of the dangers in adhering to his new-found faith in Scotland at that time, and strengthened by his uncle James, John decided to follow his brother's example and go into voluntary exile. After a feast with his parents and those of his bride-to-be, he drew the young woman aside 'with loving words and sighs', and remarked how young they were to be committed to each other, saying: 'The state of marriage requireth more prudence and maturity of judgment then is incident to our tender age.' He asked her to release him, so that he could travel in foreign parts. She seemed quite happy with the idea, replying: 'Your proposition is very reasonable. And if, happily, you shall change your mind and affection, I wish you better fortune than you should have if you had lived with me.' Encouraged by this reaction, he took the young girl further into his confidence and asked her to keep another secret. To her amazement, he revealed that he was actually a Catholic and wanted her to become one too. She was astonished and said that she would need to think about it. He suggested that his uncle James would be a good adviser for her, saying she would soon notice, 'the difference between that which is only in speech and that which is truly powerful and effectual'. She was so influenced by this that she did indeed convert to Catholicism later, and became a nun after instruction from Fr James.[42]

John went to bed, but could not sleep. In the early hours he walked about his father's castle, wondering how to make his escape and deciding on flight. He meditated on what he would be giving up, in the following vein:

Oh noble heart fear not . . .
Leaving thy father and thy dear sisters, and thy best beloved spouse, Without bidding thy dear mother farewell, abandoning thy father's home, All thy familiar friends and kinsmen, quitting all thy right and title to all those domains and possessions, which were thine by right of inheritance [left to him by his elder brother] . . .
He was relinquishing, moreover, his sweet country, the grace of the King, his spouse of equal rank, who was to him the one half of his soul.[43]

In 1587, on the eve of another feast, John left the castle as if he was embarking on some 'running and youthful exercise'. He came across one of this father's shepherds and persuaded the man to change clothes with him, so that he could disguise himself.[44] He set off for the coast, and only just avoided being recognised by people he knew at a lodging house by pulling his shepherd's cape over his eyes and sitting in the chimney nook, pretending to be sick.[45] He met some English and Scottish soldiers who wanted to employ him in their guard, but he declined. Having found a ship to cross the North Sea, he landed at Noorda but was soon arrested by Spanish soldiers. They had seen his silk stockings and found he had no passport, so they brought him before Mondragone, the governor of the citadel of Antwerp, who took him for a runaway solder and sent him to prison.[46] He was lucky to avoid torture and death. Meanwhile, the poor young shepherd boy also found himself in trouble. He was locked up for two years on suspicion of having murdered and buried his master. Graves were opened, and a search was made in many parts of Europe.[47]

In the meantime John was set free, and his ardour in prayer was noticed by a priest. John told him that he wanted to join the Capuchins. He was informed that he would have to first learn Latin, and also either Dutch or French. He replied that he only wanted to be a lay brother, but it was doubted that he had the stamina. He was still poorly dressed in the shepherd's rough clothes and clogs, and was careful not to reveal where he came from. He was advised to join other poor scholars to learn Dutch. He ate what his fellow students rejected, helped the serving maids in the kitchen and, in exchange for food, began to carve figures in lead or wood for fellow students. In time, his tutor found someone to sponsor him, and thereafter his living conditions improved while he pursued his studies in Latin and Dutch.

John then begged the Capuchins to accept him as a lay brother, which they did, in August 1591. He was now aged twenty.[48] Meanwhile, his father and his future spouse's father were half dead with grief. His father sent agents, who eventually found him and tried to induce him to return home, but his only response was to say that he would retire to some other more secluded convent. They then planned to kidnap him, but the abbot sent him to another Capuchin convent.[49]

Meanwhile, Margaret's ex-husband was giving her a hard time. It was said that Forbes 'increased his cruelty' towards Margaret, 'giving much cause for complaint amongst good men'.[50] This was probably caused by his understandable anger at losing both of his sons, thanks to both her and her Jesuit brother's influence. He believed that she and her family had hidden the boys, and he may have hoped that the pressure would result in her revealing where they were.

Margaret was now without husband, daughters or sons in a country paranoid about Catholics and Jesuits. This religious tension had taken on an international aspect because England had become involved, fearing French and Spanish plans to use Scotland as leverage to bring England back to the Catholic faith. Jesuits were being sent over from the Continent to act as agents working from within.

However, in the late 1580s Margaret was again a centre of scandal, because she was cited in court proceedings as a recent lover of Sir John Gordon of Pitlurg, husband of her erstwhile sister-in-law, Isabel

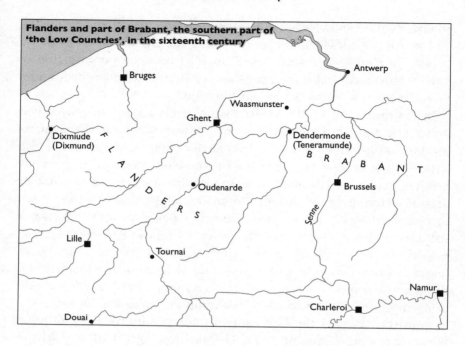

Forbes.[51] And her eldest son William did not long enjoy the strict life of abstinence he had chosen. Margaret and her former husband must have been horrified to learn that he had died on 21 March 1592 during the evening service at his convent in Ghent. This was a year before his father succeeded to the title as 8th Lord Forbes, when William would have become Master of Forbes had he not renounced the title in favour of his younger brother.[52] But John Forbes and his second wife Janet Seton started a new family, which included a male heir named Arthur, possibly after his uncle or cousin, who were both killed by the actions of Margaret's brother Adam.

Margaret's youngest son John took his solemn vows and adopted the habit of a Capuchin novice at Tournai on 2 August 1593, aged twenty-three.[53] He had been declared missing all this time, and his father had spent a great deal of money and a year of his time travelling round Europe trying to find him. He also conducted an extensive correspondence for decades, trying to find hints of where his son might be.[54] Eventually, John was tracked down by some Catholic noblemen at a convent at Douai, Flanders (now in France), where he had been for a year. Philip II of Spain had founded the university there in the 1560s, after the French-speaking area became incorporated into the Spanish Netherlands. It had become a centre for educating English Catholics, and there were also Irish and Scottish colleges, as well as Benedictine, Franciscan and Jesuit houses.

The Scottish noblemen sent by John's father pleaded with John to return to Scotland, where he could take up his responsibilities as Master of Forbes and do far more for his cause than retreating into obscurity. The professors at Douai agreed, but John refused, saying that if they pursued him further he would find a more obscure convent and pursue the contemplative life in peace. He was transferred to another monastery at Bruges to study philosophy and theology under a famous professor. He then resided in a succession of houses of his order, including at Antwerp. He was sent to a monastery at Teneramund, which had been built with the alms of Spanish soldiers. It was walled, with a pleasant garden and a tidal river that ebbed and flowed twice a day.

Margaret the Penitent

Margaret also left the country and made her way to Antwerp after letters from John urged her to come, just as his brother William had previously urged him. John was concerned about his mother's spiritual welfare, as she had been living as 'a desolate matron in her own country'. He decided to offer her spiritual comfort, as his brother had given him, persuading her to 'seek after perfectin of vertue to which she was very much disposed, having tasted the bitter cup of affliction'. As it would have been difficult for her to leave the country unobserved, she had to do so secretly, accompanied by a maidservant and carrying some jewels with her.[55]

She had a joyful reunion with John, witnessed by his seniors. They 'were unable to speak as they embraced with exceeding joy'. She found him greatly changed. He had left Scotland as an ignorant young man, but after two years of hardship as a poor student he was now proficient in Dutch and Latin. He had managed to keep his noble background secret, as the Superior had agreed not to reveal it. It was assumed that he was a poor man's son and used to menial tasks. Certainly, he seemed to take delight in a life of hardship and deprivation, and took every chance to do the most humble and menial tasks in order to serve others. It was said that he subjected himself to the severe discipline and penances of the Capuchin order with 'sweetness and patience'. Having entered the noviciate in 1592, he took his full vows on 2 August 1594, adopting the same name of Brother Archangel that his late brother William had used.[56]

John's fellow monks made Margaret welcome and were instructed to help her all they could. At first, she survived by sewing and accepting alms, but the Catholic princes helped her later and John succeeded in gaining her a pension from Philip II of Spain. Her maidservant learnt Dutch very fast, was converted to Catholicism, and wanted to be received by the Sisters of St Brigit at Teneremund in Flanders.[57] John didn't discourage her, despite the loss of her company and assistance to his mother. Instead, he encouraged her to be obedient to God's will.

At about the same time in Scotland, Margaret's former husband, now Lord Forbes, was commissioned to raise a force of 1,000 men under the young Earl of Argyll. They were to confront Margaret's nephew, the 6th Earl of Huntly, because he was suspected of plotting with Spain. King James, now aged twenty-eight, had been persuaded to put a force together to pursue his friend and other 'popish lords'. In October 1594, the King's advance guard marched north, with Lord Forbes as second in command, ever happy to take action against the Gordons, especially as Margaret had been the cause of the break-up of his sister's marriage as well as his own. However, they were soundly defeated by Huntly's much smaller, but more disciplined, force at the battle of Glenlivet. Sadly for Margaret, her brother Patrick of Auchindoun died in the battle. Despite his military victory, Huntly did not wish to confront his friend the King, who was proceeding north with heavy heart and was joined by Lord Forbes. Having first celebrated mass in Elgin, the 6th Earl and Fr James retreated to Caithness, and then left the country in voluntary exile.

On 28 December 1598, his father made a formal renunciation of John's claim to the Forbes title and lands, and executed a deed in favour of Arthur, his eldest son by his second marriage. In 1600, Arthur signed himself Master of Forbes when he replied to a letter from John. However, he did not officially succeed to the title until John's death in 1606.

Whatever had been the truth of Margaret's behaviour during her husband's absence as a captive and afterwards, she now lived the life of a devout penitent, prepared to endure anything for spiritual gain. John had received special permission to minister to her spiritually, because she could not find a priest who understood Scots and did not understand Dutch. He was sent to Antwerp as vicar of the convent there; she followed him then, and again when he went to Lisle in Flanders. Once, at an Ash Wednesday mass, thieves attempted to rob her. They could find nothing of value in her purse, so stole her precious fur mantle, lined in white skins and speckled with black. She bore the loss stoically. Her son and the Capuchins said she should pray and, miraculously, the thieves' consciences were pricked and they returned the cloak and slipped away![58]

John might have felt Margaret was becoming too dependent on him, because he later found her an English Catholic priest in Antwerp and persuaded her to move there, as she was now 'well advanced in spiritual life'. He began little by little to withdraw himself, 'for her better perfection'. The little book on the *Life of Father Archangell* (1623) describes how Margaret became increasingly sick and weak. Another exiled Scot, Alexander Caston, who befriended her, asked if he should send for her son, now Superior of the monastery at Teneramund.[59] She declined. Her disease become worse every day and her strength began to fail, but she 'grew and increased much in spirit'. As she weakened, she requested Caston to ask John to give thanks to the Catholic princes for their charity towards her, and for procuring a pension from Philip II. She died on 1 January 1606 and was buried by the Capuchins beside the body of her eldest son William in the Abbey of St Bavan in Ghent. John gave public thanks to God for the manner of her death, and that he had been able to give her spiritual strength.[60]

There were other momentous family events that year. John successfully broke up a confrontation between Scots and Spanish armies. He was sent to preach to the Scottish soldiers who were garrisoned at Dixmund with Spanish soldiers, serving the Catholic princes of the Low Countries. He brought more than 300 of them to the Catholic faith, and converted eighteen others at Mennen. Neither the soldiers, nor the governor, could persuade him to come to the table to eat, and he took only one small meal a day.[61]

His father died on 29 June 1606, and was buried at Kearn beside Druminnor.[62] This made John, Father Archangel ostensibly 9th Lord Forbes – but, as it turned out, only for six weeks. (However, this has now been reversed, so Arthur has that title.)

Father Archangel was a devoted nurse of the sick and comforter of the dying. In August 1606 he travelled from Teneramund to Waasmunster, a town two leagues away, to nurse those sick from the plague. He returned 'with a burning heat'. As he knew he must be contagious, he asked his fellow monks to take him to house at some distance from the convent. But he died on 2 August 1606 as they carried him across a little bridge. He was buried in the nave of the Capuchin church at Teneramund, Ghent, aged thirty-six.[63] He is considered a distinguished ornament of the Capuchin branch of the Franciscan order, as was his brother William.

It is sad to read of Margaret dying in a foreign country, without the presence of her remaining son or other family members. In her life, she was a victim of the feuds between the Gordons and the Forbeses, instigated and exacerbated by the political and religious conflicts of the time. In combination, this made her arranged marriage to John, Master of Forbes, particularly difficult for both of them. One hopes that she really did finally achieve happiness through inner spiritual fulfilment, her apparent aspiration as a young girl.

5

Jean Gordon – Thrice Married

BOTHWELL, SUTHERLAND AND OGILVIE OF BOYNE

Alexander Ogilvie of Boyne courted and won the heart of Jean Gordon before she was twenty. He was the love of her life, but she had to submit to the wishes of Queen Mary and her brother George, and instead marry the notorious James Hepburn, Earl of Bothwell – a man who many said should be kept away from wives and daughters. He had already abandoned one young woman to whom he was espoused in Denmark, the daughter of an admiral.

Jean led a fascinating and varied life, deeply affected by the drama of national events. At one stage her life was closely tied up with that of Queen Mary, during the most troublesome time of her brief personal reign.

Childhood

Jean (sometimes called Jane) was born in 1545, the third daughter of the 4th Earl of Huntly and Elizabeth Keith. As mentioned in the previous chapter, when she was only two years old her mother and her eldest brother, Alexander, signed a contract on her father's behalf with Lord Forbes, by which she would marry his eldest son should anything happen to her sister Margaret, who was two years older. This contract was aimed at healing the ancient feud between the two families.

When she was nine years old, her father took an active role in national events, leading the armies of King James V in defending the country against an English invasion. Later, after the battle of Pinkie, he was captured and imprisoned in England. Being a perceptive and kind girl, she would have sensed her mother's worry. Many aristocratic women of the time would have had to take over running the affairs of the family and estates when their husbands were away fighting. Jean would have to do the same, for different reasons, in the future.

The year 1558 was one of marriages, an exciting time for a girl of thirteen, especially when one wedding involved a sister so close in age. Margaret, now fourteen, married John, Master of Forbes, aged only seventeen. Then in November that year, her eldest brother George had the honour of marrying Anna Hamilton, the third daughter of the Duke of Chatelherault. The wedding was celebrated at his sumptuous mansion of Hamilton.

By 1562, when Jean was seventeen, she was being courted by Alexander Ogilvie of Boyne, who must have been about thirty-two. However, her hopes in that direction were destroyed when her brother John injured Lord James Ogilvie of Airlie during a fight in the streets of Edinburgh. This was a result of the long-running dispute between John and Lord James' cousin, James Ogilvie of Cardell, on the matter of the latter's inheritance. As described in previous chapters, James' father had overlooked him in his will in favour of Jean's brother John.

This was a sad time for the seventeen-year-old Jean. She must have been excited at the thought of helping to entertain Queen Mary and her retinue at Huntly Castle as part of Mary's northern progress, but the family was deeply out of favour because of John having escaped from prison to their father's protection and refusing to give himself up. John's further actions resulted in disaster for the family as they tried to battle it out with the Queen's forces, commanded by their enemy, the Earl of Moray.

Jean and the family had to face not only their defeat at Corrichie, but also the horror of the sudden and unexpected death of her father on the battlefield. Added to that was the grisly execution of her handsome brother, John. Being a wise young woman, she would have realised that she could not wallow in misery but must instead be a strong support for her mother. Mercifully, her younger brother Adam narrowly escaped the same fate thanks to the intervention of Mary Fleming, who pleaded for him on the grounds of his youth. Luckily, her eldest brother George was not at the battle, because he was with his father-in-law, the Duke of Chatelherault, pleading for his intervention in the whole unfortunate affair. The family pinned their hopes on the Duke's influence with Mary when he went to meet her at Dundee on her journey south, but she said that George's fate would depend on the decision of Parliament. This was not encouraging news, because Moray would be holding sway there: he who was anxious to destroy the Gordon family and fill the vacuum by expanding his own power base in the north. Instead they had to wait until May the following year, when the macabre trial took place in the Tolbooth in Edinburgh, with her father's corpse being put on trial, along with her brothers and the other prominent Gordons who had rallied to their leader's call to arms. Jean and her sister may well have been present, as their names were included in the list of Gordon family members to be forfeited and humiliated. She was to lose her family home of Huntly Castle, which was bombarded and ransacked, the family possessions taken away to be shared between the Queen and Moray, the latter for his newly acquired palace of Darnaway.

It was some small relief that George was saved from execution for treason by Mary's clemency, but he still had to go to prison in the Dunbar stronghold. The future looked gloomy for Jean, particularly in relation to her marriage prospects. Who would want to marry a girl from a destroyed and humiliated family with no land? The two cheering events of that time were the births of two nephews: one a son and heir to her sister Margaret and her husband John, Master of Forbes; and one to George and his wife Anna Hamilton. He, too, was to be called George, like his father and grandfather, and he should have been the son and heir – although it seemed unlikely that he would ever be the 6th Earl of Huntly, with the family lands forfeited and their titles expunged. Jean's support for her sister-in-law would be particularly important while her husband was in ward at Dunbar Castle.

Two years later, in 1565, everything changed for Jean and the rest of the family when the Earl of Moray and most of the other influential lords abandoned the Queen. They were disgusted at her marriage to the despicable Lord Darnley, ostensibly because of his dangerous initiatives towards the European Catholic powers. Mary's need to build a new power base was the cause of the family's reinstatement. When George was brought out of ward and restored to his title as 5th Earl of Huntly, Jean, now twenty, and their mother, the Countess of Huntly, were called to Court. That autumn, everything looked promising.

Marriage

Jean had grown into an attractive young woman: tall and brown-haired, with an oval face, large dark eyes and a long elegant nose. She displayed a calm and self-possessed air. Now that the family was rehabilitated and their forfeited estates due to be returned, with all the financial benefit that that entailed, she would make a good catch. With her brother on the Privy Council, her mother a confidante of the Queen, and she herself now at Court, she had the benefit of exposure to all the young bloods there. The world appeared to be her oyster. What is more, her first love, Alexander Ogilvie of Boyne, was one of the gallants attached to the Court. There were rumours that he had entered into a contract to marry Elizabeth, sister of Margaret's husband, but also that he had second thoughts about the commitment. Despite the tensions at Court, with so many of Mary's erstwhile followers rebelling against her and massing their troops, the future looked rosy for young Jean Gordon – quite exciting, in fact.

However, a dark cloud appeared on the horizon. Arriving at Court was the already notorious James, Earl of Bothwell, who Mary had called back to Scotland from disgrace and exile. Although a Protestant himself, he was reputedly heartily disliked by the Lords of the Congregation because, during the regency of Mary's mother, he had waylaid a messenger from England, robbing him of funds sent by Cecil to support the Protestant revolution against her. Mary had been exposed to his wild attractions in France. Like Huntly, Bothwell was now brought onto the Privy Council. However, having been in exile so long, he was seriously in debt.

The Queen concocted a plan that would help resolve Bothwell's financial problems and strengthen her power base. She suggested a marriage between him and young Jean Gordon. Part of Jean's dowry would pay off Bothwell's debts and take Crichton Castle in Midlothian out of the hands of his Edinburgh merchant creditors. It would unite her two most powerful supporters: Bothwell with his influence in the Borders, and George Gordon, when he was restored to his position in the north. Crichton was a fine castle set on moorland fifteen miles from the centre of Edinburgh. It was to be in Jean's name for her lifetime. Bothwell was not unattractive. He could be considered one of the greatest nobles of sixteenth-century Scotland, but he could also be rough and aggressive. Jean heard that he had abandoned a girl whom he had previously promised to marry in Denmark, the daughter of a retired Norwegian admiral.[1] He was a restless, violent man, not comfortable to be married to, especially for someone with Jean's thoughtful character. Nor would she be the type of woman that would really appeal to him. Also, Jean was still deeply attached to Alexander Ogilvie of Boyne, but her brother and her mother must have insisted that it would be very good for the family if she fell in with the Queen's plans. Being an intelligent young woman, Jean realised that for the sake of the whole family, so recently restored to favour, she could hardly refuse. A contract was drawn up. The Queen was the first to sign, then her brother George, then Bothwell, her mother and Jean herself.

Mary took a great interest in the plans for the winter wedding, to be held on 24 February 1566. She gave Jean cloth of silver for her wedding dress, to be lined with white taffeta. The celebrations were to last five days. She proposed that, as Jean was Catholic, they have a Catholic wedding ceremony in the royal chapel. Bothwell flatly refused to agree. As a result, Jean had to accept that the ceremony would take place a short distance from the royal chapel in part of the abbey of Holyrood used by the Protestant congregation of the Canongate. The wedding was performed by Jean's uncle, the Reforming Bishop of Galloway.[2] The Queen paid for and came to the sumptuous banquet on the first day accompanied by her husband Lord Darnley, now referred to as 'the King'. Then there were joustings and tournaments, at which Jean's brothers Adam, Robert and Patrick must have played prominent parts as young squires.

Wedding miniatures show Jean to be pale-skinned with a fresh complexion, and wearing a fashionable, though not elaborate, dress. She has a kind face and a wise, insightful look. Bothwell was of stocky build, with a moustache and a ruddy complexion. He looks hyperactive, as if unable to sit still. He is wearing a gold doublet. Papers believed to refer to Jean's marriage suggest that it was not a happy occasion for her.

The couple spent their honeymoon at Seton House on the Firth of Forth, the home of George, 5th Lord Seton, a close friend and firm supporter of the Queen. Mary often chose to relax there, playing golf and archery.

Jean and Bothwell set up home in Crichton Castle, her first experience of running an independent household. Bothwell was only too aware of his new wife's preoccupation with thoughts of her lost suitor, Alexander Ogilvie. Two months later, she had to witness his marriage to the beautiful Mary Beaton, one of the Queen's 'Four Maries'.[3]

Although Crichton was only fifteen miles from the centre of Edinburgh, it is likely that Jean was often at Court and had lodgings in town, possibly in the palace of Holyrood itself, because her husband, brother and mother were so closely involved with the Queen and certainly had rooms there. Only two weeks after Jean's wedding, her world turned upside down with the murder of Mary's Italian secretary, Riccio. She would have heard all about the terrifying event from her mother, as well as the probability that her husband and brother were also intended victims, due to jealousy over their new influence with the Queen. They had only just managed to escape out of a back window. Jean's mother stayed with the distraught but calm Queen through the night, until ordered to leave her.

No doubt the Countess told Jean how she had suggested ways for Mary to escape,[4] and also how she had hidden a note to Bothwell and George from Mary in her underwear, asking them to meet her at Seton House the following night. They sent a note back suggesting she be let down over the wall by a rope secured to a chair, a common practice for people escaping fires at the time. However, Mary cleverly managed to win Darnley to her side, by convincing him that his life would also be in danger and promising him her favours. Together they managed to creep out by a back way. Bothwell and George then accompanied them on the five-hour ride to the safety of Dunbar Castle on the coast, a gruelling ride for Mary, who was pregnant with the future King of Scotland and England. She had to stop several times due to nausea. It was from this point onwards that Mary saw the contrast between her weak and ineffectual husband and, as she considered him, the resourceful and trustworthy Earl of Bothwell. It was said that, from then on: 'He of all men had the greatest access and familiarity with the Queen, so nothing of importance was done without him.'[5]

In March, Jean had the good news that her brother George had been made Chancellor in place of the Earl of Morton, following the latter's flight with others closely involved in the murder of Riccio. George was now in a position of real power. He was at last able to sort out the long-running dispute with James Ogilvie, with a compromise that was to the advantage of their brother, Adam. He achieved the lands and castle of Auchindoun and Keithmore at least, and from then on he would be known as Adam of Auchindoun. They were all pleased to hear that George had arranged for a fitting burial for their father, the 4th Earl. When the weather improved in April, his body was taken from Edinburgh to be reburied in the family tomb in Elgin Cathedral. This would have been a special occasion for all the family, bringing some conclusion to the sad memories following the battle of Corrichie. No doubt there was a big gathering of all the Gordons and their supporters from a wide area around Strathbogie and the north to bury the 4th Earl of Huntly, with the honour due to one who had been so important in the past. Perhaps the rebel Moray was blamed for events leading to the unfortunate battle of Corrichie. Jean's family must have been aware that all was not well with her in her marriage.

Trouble in the Marriage

It was during that month, perhaps while she was back in the north and preoccupied with the burial of her father, that her husband started his liaison with her serving maid Bessie Crawford, daughter of a Hadding-ton smith. Jean was incensed when she heard about it. However, wives of political marriages could not easily abandon their husbands. They had to make the best of things, despite the strain of living with an unfaithful husband. In June Bothwell attempted to placate her by giving her the life rent for the castle, houses and lands of Nether Hailes. Hailes Castle near East Linton had been the traditional base of the Hepburns since the time of Robert the Bruce. This gesture seemed to mollify her, because in the winter of 1566 they were described as 'living friendly and quietly together'.[6]

However, it must have been clear to Jean at the lavish and showy three-day celebration of baby James's christening in the royal chapel at Stirling Castle that the Queen was depending more and more on Bothwell. The significant role he was taking was obvious to all, includ-ing the visiting ambassadors and dignitaries, whom he greeted at the entrance to the chapel while Darnley sulked and opted out of any involvement in his son's baptism. They reported it back to their own countries, and people began to mutter.

Did Jean see the Queen try to lead Bothwell and George by the hand in an attempt to persuade them to come into the chapel for the Catho-lic ceremony? They were both Protestants and stood firmly outside the door, along with the newly forgiven Moray. But the three stood behind her chair at the banquet.[7] Did Jean feel proud of the important role her husband was taking at Court, or did she feel jealous and worried about its implications?

The following year, 1567, must have been the worst of Jean's life. First, in February, there was the terrible shock of Darnley's murder. Worse still was the fact that all suspicion pointed to her husband's involvement. He and George were playing cards in the Kirk o'Fields house where Darnley lay on that fateful night. It was Bothwell's men who carried the gunpowder to the basement. As rumours circulated and accusatory placards began to appear around Edinburgh, Jean became seriously ill. It was rumoured that she was dying of poisoning. Meanwhile, her husband and brother George were at Seton House with the Queen, who had gone there to recover from the shock. They played golf, and Bothwell partnered the Queen against George and Lord Seton in archery matches.

Jean may have felt some relief at Bothwell's official acquittal at the trial, set up to prove he was innocent of Darnley's murder, but she was astute enough to realise that it was rigged. The main accuser, Darnley's father, the Earl of Lennox, refused to attend when he heard the town was heavily packed with Bothwell's armed supporters, while he was allowed to bring only a few.

Did George explain to his sister the shocking story about what happened at the Ainslie Tavern after the trial – how Bothwell had invited him to the tavern, along with many of the other nobles, and how he had feasted and plied them with drink? He had then unexpectedly urged the men to sign a long, detailed bond, giving reasons why he would be a fitting husband for the Queen and urging him to facilitate this.

Jean must have seen little of her husband in these days. However, she would have heard the scandalous news that he had abducted the Queen and taken her off to Dunbar Castle, the very place where George had been incarcerated for so long. There, Bothwell had reportedly seduced or even raped Mary, and got her eventual agreement to marry him, by showing her the Ainslie Bond with all the signatures of her nobles, urging that marriage to him was necessary for her protection and the good of the realm. Much later, before his death, a document appeared that purportedly came from him, saying that he had drugged Mary to get her agreement – and all this happened while he was still married to Jean.[8]

Divorce

Once Bothwell had obtained Mary's reluctant agreement, he purportedly galloped to Edinburgh to ask Jean to initiate proceedings for a divorce. Jean filed her petition that very day, on the grounds of Bothwell's infidelity with her maid not long after their marriage the previous year. She spared no detail in describing how Bothwell had enjoyed 'the bonny black-eyed Bessie Crawford', in the precincts of Haddington Abbey in broad daylight.[9] Bothwell denied it, but the judge decided in her favour. Divorces were unusual in the sixteenth century and usually took a very long time to achieve. This one was achieved in record time.

Bothwell brought his own case for annulment of the marriage on the grounds of consanguinity, they being distantly related within the forbidden degree in canon law. He persuaded the newly reinstated John Hamilton, Archbishop of St Andrew's, who had originally obtained dispensation, to deny that he had ever achieved it. Jean did not reveal that she had the dispensation in her own possession.[10] A commission of six clerics was set up to look into the matter. Five of them were reluctant to act, but John Manderston, Canon of Dunbar Collegiate Church, confirmed that they had indeed married without dispensation. Bothwell had the means to persuade anyone to do what he wanted, especially when they were so close to hand as Dunbar. Jean kept the dispensation hidden amongst her papers for the rest of her life.[11] This suggests her collusion, as she was probably glad to be free of her husband, but possibly she had no choice.

Bothwell returned to Dunbar, where he found that the Queen and Huntly had had a violent quarrel. Jean's brother might not have fully realised what he had agreed to in signing the Ainslie Bond, with all its implications for his sister. His support for Bothwell was clearly wavering. His reluctance to take up arms on Mary's behalf was unconcealed. Naturally, he would have been concerned about where his sister would live and her financial security. Maybe he insisted during the quarrel that the divorce settlement allow her to retain ownership of Crichton Castle and its lands for her lifetime. It had, after all, been part of her marriage settlement tocher and that is where she continued to live – for a while, anyway. The Queen now settled Dunbar Castle on Bothwell.

Huntly's co-operation in facilitating the easy divorce from his sister was soon rewarded with the formal official reversal of the forfeiture on the Gordon lands. This was not only for him, but also for the other Gordons who had been involved in the battle of Corrichie, including the Earl of Sutherland, Alexander Gordon of Strathdon, George Gordon of Beldorny and his eldest son Alexander Gordon, James Gordon of Lesmoir and James Gordon of Tillyangus. All of their lands were restored at last, five years after the event. So even if Jean had not wanted to divorce Bothwell, it is unlikely that she would have been able to resist his will in the matter for the sake of her wider family, as well as that of the Queen.

The divorce on the grounds of adultery and annulment were all received in the first week in May. Nevertheless, although the official annulment had not yet come from Rome, the marriage banns between Mary and Bothwell were proclaimed the following week, and the marriage took place privately seven days later. It was only fifteen months since Bothwell's marriage to Jean. The night before the wedding, Bothwell's filthy language caused Sir James Melville to walk out of their company.[12] The unseemly haste showed how little the couple cared about public opinion. This was to prove fatal for Mary's future.

Last Days in Edinburgh

Shortly after Mary and Bothwell's marriage in the early hours of the morning, George, who was one of the few to attend, asked permission to leave Court. He found Bothwell too arrogant. Mary's reaction was a furious refusal.[13]

The following month, rumours reached Jean in peaceful Crichton of the dramatic and disastrous events unfolding nearby. Many of the lords had formed a confederacy and signed a new bond, in which they agreed to call the masses to arms, ostensibly to rescue Mary from Bothwell. They declared that she had been kidnapped by Bothwell, who they described as a 'barbarous tyrant' and 'cruel murderer'. Jean heard how he and Mary had fled in disguise back to the safety of Dunbar Castle, how her brother was trying vainly to raise support for them in Edinburgh, and how Mary and Bothwell had ridden out of Dunbar only to be confronted at Carberry Hill. She learned how Bothwell had been allowed to escape, and Mary transported ignominiously to Holyroodhouse with scant attention to her comfort or dignity, and then roughly taken to be incarcerated on Lochleven island. These were tragic, disturbing, sad and frightening events.

Jean would have heard how her brother George had turned against Bothwell and signed a new bond with those who came to be known as the Confederate Lords. The lords not only agreed Bothwell's guilt in Darnley's murder, but also his ill treatment of the innocent Mary, which George had witnessed at first hand. Then she heard the surprising and shocking news, publicly announced at the market cross in Edinburgh, that Mary had abdicated in favour of her baby son and how, a few days later, an official coronation of James had taken place, with the Earl of Moray made Regent. Surprised as he may have been, George was still on the Privy Council and, on 12 December, he even carried the sceptre for the infant James VI at the opening of the first parliament in his name.

Nevertheless, by the end of June, George had deserted the Confederate Lords and signed the Hamilton Bond along with those who wanted to rescue Mary from Lochleven. It was also signed by Jean's Alexander Ogilvie of Boyne. George now returned to Strathbogie in order to raise arms on Mary's behalf.

Back to Strathbogie

Life was becoming uncomfortable in Edinburgh for supporters of the imprisoned Queen. George had returned to the north and put together a force to come to her aid. However, the Privy Council rescinded his Lieutenancy of the North, and the people were told to ignore his call to arms. Jean's mother, the Dowager Countess, had also left court and returned home to Huntly Castle. Some of it was still ruinous, and the contents looted after the bombarding that followed Corrichie. However, Jean decided to return there also. We hear of her passing through Edinburgh on the way and visiting her cousin Agnes Keith, Moray's wife, and telling her that she would never want to live with Bothwell again. Rumours had it that he was with George in the north. Perhaps Jean witnessed her brother rebuffing Bothwell and expressing his hope that he would 'miscarye, to ryd the queen and hys sister of so wicked a husbande'.[14] No doubt they heard how Kirkcaldy of Grange, in command of five ships sent to pursue Bothwell up to the Orkney Isles, had very nearly managed to trap him in a Shetland harbour, but he had just managed to slip out of the bay in time.

They must all have been shocked to hear that Moray and other lords were now busy implicating Mary in the murder of Darnley, referring to certain letters between her and Bothwell, the originals of which were not produced.

George had to report to Jean that the new council had re-enacted the legislation of 1560, by which the Reformed Church was officially established, and the mass was again forbidden.

In early May of the following year, 1568, there was the good news of Mary's successful escape from Lochleven. Jean would have been well aware that George had gathered his followers and rushed to give her support, but their euphoria would have been shattered when they heard that the passes on their route had been blocked; they were unable to get south in time to help her in the crucial battle of Langside, resulting in her final defeat. But at least she had managed to escape to the hoped-for protection of her cousin Queen Elizabeth in England. However, the Gordons were probably cynical about the wisdom of choosing that route. Where they were concerned, France would have been a much better choice.

In July, Moray circulated a bond, which he ordered all to sign, to acknowledge James VI as King. Jean's brother George signed unwillingly in Aberdeen but, only the following month, he forced the Provost to declare for Mary. In the autumn, he resumed his role as the Queen's Lieutenant of the North and captured Dingwell Castle in her name, with widespread support.

Bad news arrived in December that Mary's Casket Letters were said to thoroughly incriminate her in the plot for Darnley's murder. It was suspicious that eighteen months had passed since they were found. However, some small relief would have been felt in the family that, by Christmas 1568, Mary's trial in England, held in absentia, had adjourned indefinitely. She had not been found guilty – but neither had she been declared innocent.

In April 1569, tensions rose in the household of Huntly Castle when the demands arrived for a new bond of loyalty to the King to be signed. This time George refused, as did his father-in-law, Chatelherault, who was then arrested. However, by the following month, George gave way when heavy fines were imposed on him and his supporters for their earlier refusal.

Alexander Gordon, Earl of Sutherland

The year 1569 was an exciting one for Jean, now aged twenty-four, with the arrival at Huntly Castle of another refugee from other people's schemes. This was her young cousin Alexander Gordon, Earl of Sutherland, who was eighteen. He brought with him dramatic tales of twice narrowly escaping death and finally being rescued by George and friends.

Jean would have heard how, two years before, at the age of fifteen, Alexander had witnessed the poisoning of both his parents at Helmsdale Castle by Isabel Sinclair, who was attempting to gain the earldom for her son.[15] By mistake, this boy was also given the poisoned chalice by a servant, unaware of the plot, and died two days later.[16] The poison had been meant for Alexander, but his dying parents managed to cover the food and drink on the table with a cloth so that he would not take any when he returned late from the hunt. They sent him home to Dunrobin

Castle without food. The earl and his pregnant wife were conveyed there too, but died the next morning.[17] Alexander's father was later described by his grandson Robert Gordon of Gordonstoun as 'the good Earl John of Sutherland, so kind and courteous towards all men, so full of mildness and affability, and well beloved of all good men'.[18]

Alexander took refuge in Skibo Castle. However, he was found there by George Sinclair, the 4th Earl of Caithness, who removed him to Caithness, took over the castles of Dunrobin and Skibo, harassed the Sutherland tenants and made Alexander his ward. Caithness forcibly married Alexander to his 32-year-old daughter, Lady Barbara Sinclair. The Sinclairs wanted to get rid of the Sutherland Gordons, because they resented the good use they had made of Church charters, particularly from the bishopric of Caithness, to expand their territory from Skibo in the south to Dounreay in the north.

The latest threat to Alexander was the Earl of Caithness' plan to marry his second son, William Sinclair, to Lady Margaret Gordon, Alexander's elder sister, who he now held. William Sinclair had a chance of becoming Earl of Sutherland if Alexander was out of the way. Fortunately, Alexander's friends had heard of the plot to bring about his death and resolved to rescue him. One of them had entered Dunrobin disguised as a pedlar and secretly told young Alexander of their plan: they would pretend to ambush him as he took his morning walk with his servants.

He was duly seized and taken safely across the Dornoch Firth in a storm. He was then taken to Huntly Castle to his cousin George, who made a home for him there over the next four years. George also welcomed the friends who had helped him escape, referred to as 'the Men of Murray'.[19] Later, these men supported George and Adam in Mary's cause. Alexander based himself at Huntly Castle for four years, until his minority expired in 1573. This gave him opportunity to form a relationship with Jean who, like him, was a refugee from a forced marriage to a notorious and unfaithful spouse.

Civil War in the North-East

Although 1570 brought the pleasure of a new nephew for Jean, born to her sister Margaret Forbes, the year brought fear to them both, because they saw their families and the country dividing between those who wanted Mary's restoration and those who opposed it. George and young Alexander Gordon were deeply committed to Mary's cause.

They were rarely at home, as they spent most of their time with their forces, involved in skirmishes in and around Edinburgh or Glasgow.

The household would then have heard the startling news that on 23 January 1570, Moray was shot dead from a window in Linlithgow as he rode past, and that George and young Alexander were both present. After a period of indecision, the Earl of Lennox, grandfather of the infant King James, was chosen to replace Moray as Regent.

The following month, there came the momentous news that the Pope had issued a bull in which he referred to Elizabeth's 'pretended right' to the English throne, which in effect meant that Catholics would regard the captive Mary the rightful sovereign of both kingdoms. Jean must have realised that this made Mary's position doubly dangerous. Despite this, the 'lords of both factions', including George and Alexander, sent a letter to Queen Elizabeth requesting that Mary be sent back in order to save Scotland from 'conflagration'. Elizabeth seriously considered the idea of allowing her to go, so that she and James could be joint rulers. However Cecil, as always, considered Mary too dangerous a threat to Elizabeth to let free, especially after this new papal bull.

Jean now saw her brother Adam begin to take positive action in the north on Mary's behalf. Triumphant and exciting news filtered north that Edinburgh Castle had become a Marian stronghold thanks to its holder, Kirkcaldy of Grange, being persuaded by his captive friend, Maitland of Lethington, to change sides. Things were looking up for the Marians.

In September, Jean saw George summon a parliament at Linlithgow in the name of the Queen and then heading south. She heard how Lennox, as new Regent, did the same but in the name of the King, and how he had marched north to intercept George. She heard how George was warned at Brechin and just managed to escape in time, how 300 of his men were besieged within the fortress, and how they and the thirty-one who had taken refuge in the kirk steeple were all cruelly executed.

Added to this horror was the shocking news that John Hamilton, the last Roman Catholic Archbishop of St Andrews, had been hanged in his vestments for having foreknowledge of the plot to shoot Moray from his house in Linlithgow. On top of that, Jean and her mother heard that George, accompanied by young Alexander Gordon, was the leader of the debacle at Stirling when Lennox, so recently appointed Regent, was also shot dead.

Both George and Alexander took part in the election for a new Regent. They chose the Earl of Mar, who was the official guardian of the infant James in Stirling Castle. Mar appointed the Earl of Morton as his Lieutenant General of the King's forces.

As a result of this particularly appointment, 1571 was the year when things took a serious turn for the worse in the north-east, which had been relatively peaceful up until then. Morton succeeded in winning Margaret's father-in-law, Lord Forbes, to the King's party. Jean saw her brother Adam taking on a much more prominent role, acting as George's deputy Lieutenant of the North for the Queen. It was good that Jean was able to be at home and support her mother in Huntly Castle during that year of Gordon conflict with her Forbes brother-in-law's family. It was also good to see Gordon victories in the battles of Tillyangus and Craibstone, but at the cost of many deaths on both sides, with many Gordons being buried at Dunbennan burial ground. It was shameful to hear accusations that Adam's orders had led to the appalling twenty-seven deaths in the burning of Corgarff Castle, including the Forbes laird's pregnant wife and children – even if her brother denied his involvement, saying that his captain, Thomas Kerr, had exceeded his orders. Then there was the capture of Margaret's husband, the Master of Forbes, and his imprisonment in the newly fortified Spynie Palace. Now, at least, a ransom could be demanded, and Adam was triumphant in the north-east.

Countess of Sutherland

No doubt there were arguments in Huntly Castle the following year, 1572, when Morton became Regent following the sudden death of Mar. He was managing to bring members of the Queen's party round to accepting James as King. George tried to persuade Adam to accept that Mary's cause was hopeless, and that they should all come to terms and sign the Pacification of Perth. However, Adam and his friends went off to France in disgust.

Having come to terms, Alexander Gordon was officially recognised as the Earl of Sutherland. He began a legal action against Barbara Sinclair for forcing him into marriage when he was under age, but she died before judgement was pronounced. Alexander sent a messenger to warn the Sinclairs off the land of Sutherland, but they killed him. However, Alexander himself now succeeded in 'pacifying Sutherland without bloodshed', and 'procured the love of Jean'. He had been part of the family at Huntly Castle on and off for four years, so she had got to know him well. They had much in common. Both were Roman Catholics, had been through unhappy marriages as pawns in other people's games, and had the interests of the Gordons at heart.[20] It was a pleasing match for all parties. The marriage was solemnised at Huntly Castle on 13 December,[21] Jean's second winter wedding. They went up north soon after, to make their home at Dunrobin Castle.

It soon became clear to Jean that Alexander, although seven years her junior, was not physically strong enough to manage the affairs of such a large estate. Within two years she took over as his factor.[22] It was not unusual for wives to run their husband's estates, because the men tended to be often away fighting, or at Court in Edinburgh. There was a great variety of business, including handling the payment of feu duties, payment of creditors, buying oxen and payment of merchants' bills, as well as overseeing house and garden improvements. Evidently she made a very competent job of it, as described later by her second son, Robert Gordon of Gordonstoun:

> Schoe wes in a manner constrained and forced to tak upoun her the manageing of all the effaris of that hous, a good whyle, which schoe did performe with greate care, to her owne credit and the weill of that familie; all being committed to her charge by reassoun of the sincular affectioun which schoe did carie to the preservatioun of that hous, as lykwise for her dexteritie in the managing of business.[23]

Their rental income amounted to £1,702 0s 4d, nearly half of which were accrued from the properties from her marriage to Bothwell, such as Crichton and Nether Hailes.[24]

Jean was now a long way from the rest of the family, but letters from home kept her in touch with news of major events, such as the divorce of her sister Margaret from the Master of Forbes on the grounds of her adultery with Patrick Hepburn. She also heard that George had been warded in Galloway for five months, accused of abetting Adam in Paris, where he was suspected of attempting to procure French help to rescue Mary. George denied being responsible for his brother and was released. She heard of Adam's return to Scotland with twenty friends, only to be imprisoned in the grim Blackness Castle on the Forth for six months through the winter. Then she had the good news of his regained freedom. He was able to return to his castle of Auchindoun and even take up duties as Deputy Sheriff of Aberdeen. Then there was the great shock in October 1576 of George's sudden death from a heart attack following a friendly football game at Huntly Castle. It was so quick, just like the death of their father. She heard that her nephew, George's sixteen-year-old heir, now the 6th Earl, had been sent off to Paris to complete his education in the care of their Jesuit brother James, while Adam took charge of Gordon affairs at home.

Not until 1577, six years after the event, did Alexander's ninety-eight Murrays and other tenants receive official remission for their involvement in the burning of Corgarff Castle, and for accompanying him to fight the battle of Craibstone in 1571.

In 1580, Jean's husband Alexander Gordon, 12th Earl of Sutherland,[25] had to go to Edinburgh as one of Adam's forty supporters in order to hear the many disputes between him and the Master of Forbes being publicly aired in front of the young King, the Council and Morton. The Master of Forbes also brought forty supporters. The case was to be publicly arbitrated, with the intention of bringing the long-running feud between them to a final resolution. However, Alexander soon returned north with the shocking news that Adam had died suddenly, three days before the hearing. As a result, the arbitration was deferred until the following spring.

Young King James was now under the influence of his Catholic cousin Esmé Stewart, who came over from France. Jean's nephew, George Gordon, 6th Earl of Huntly, also returned from France, having completed his education in Paris. He formed a strong friendship with young King James, who was taking more power into his own hands. Morton's situation was becoming increasingly threatened, and at the end of the year he was arrested on the charge of complicity in the murder of Darnley. He was executed the following June. Things were looking more favourable for Catholics.

Jean had borne Alexander seven children, five of them sons (two of whom died in infancy) and two daughters. In 1580, Alexander had taken the precaution, no doubt because of his poor health, of transferring the right to the earldom and its lands to his oldest son John, reserving his own life rent. This was a common safety device that was meant to ensure the safe transfer of the property to the next generation when the time came.[26] In John's name, the sheriffdom of Sutherland and Strathnaver was purchased from the earldom of Huntly, in exchange for the Lordship of Aboyne. This swap was a sensible consolidation for both families.

In 1587, Jean heard the tragic news of Mary's execution at Fothering-
hay. It would have revised memories of how, twenty years before, she
had been closely involved in Mary's life for a short, traumatic period.
Mary had acknowledged their friendship in her will. Maybe Jean's
feelings about Mary were ambivalent. It would be interesting to know
what she really thought about the Queen's relationship with Bothwell
while he was still married to her.

That same year Jean, who was a determined Catholic all her life,
found herself in trouble with the authorities. She, her husband and
friends were mentioned in an investigation initiated by the General
Assembly into the extent of Catholic practice in the country. Following
the failure of the Spanish Armada in 1588, she would have heard about
the suspected activities of her Catholic nephew George, 6th Earl of
Huntly in aiding Jesuits, and of letters discovered on a boat, purportedly
from him to Philip II, encouraging another attempt at invading England,
this time through Scotland. King James had resisted taking this seriously, until finally agreeing to send a force against George in 1594.

That would have been a terrible year for Jean, with the death of her
brother Patrick of Auchindoun at the consequent battle of Glenlivet,
and then the 6th Earl of Huntly's retreat north in order to avoid having
to face his friend the King in person. No doubt he spent time with her
in Sutherland before his self-imposed exile in France. She would have
heard of his forfeiture and the new bombardment of her old home,
Huntly Castle, recently restored by her brother.

Worst of all that year was the death of her husband Alexander, aged
only forty-three. He was buried in Dornoch Cathedral. Jean was now
on her own again, caring for the three boys (John, Robert and Alexander Gordon) and the two girls (Jane and Mary) She sent John, now the
13th Earl of Sutherland, who was eighteen years old, to France to
complete his education there.[27] She sent her two younger sons, Robert
and Alexander, to university 'to be instructed in learning and virtue'[28]
– first to St Andrews, where they only stayed six months, and then on
to Edinburgh.

In 1597, the three northern countesses of Sutherland, Caithness and
Huntly were all ordered to subscribe to the Confession of Faith, under
pain of excommunication. Despite their non-compliance, the threat
was not carried out. Later, Jean was in trouble for giving assistance to
Jesuits, including her brother James and other priests from abroad.
James was put on trial in Edinburgh for saying mass in Dunrobin
Castle and other private houses.

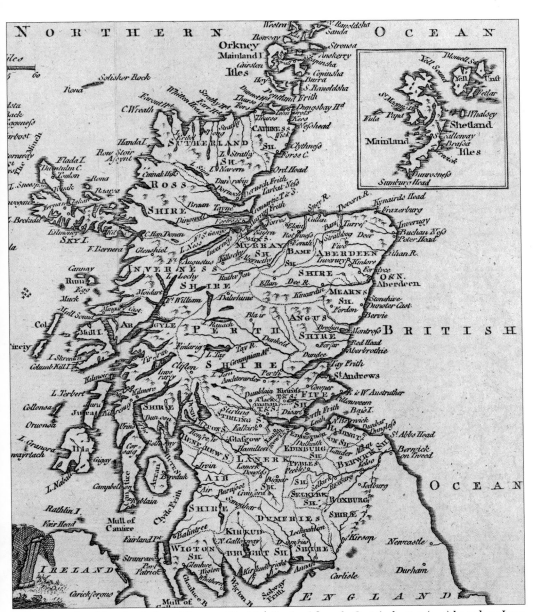

Plate 1. Mainland Scotland, from Thomas Kitchin's *Scotland from the Best Authorities* (1771) based on Joan Blaeu's work of nearly 120 years earlier (much of which was based on maps by Robert Gordon of Straloch and Timothy Pont).

Plate 2. Strathbogie, the centre of Gordon power, extracted from Robert Gordon of Straloch's map of *Aberdonia & Banfia* (1654). Auchindoun and Keithmore are due west of Strathbogie (Huntly). Bog of Gight, the Gordon 2nd base in Ainie (Ainze or Enzie), is due north-west.

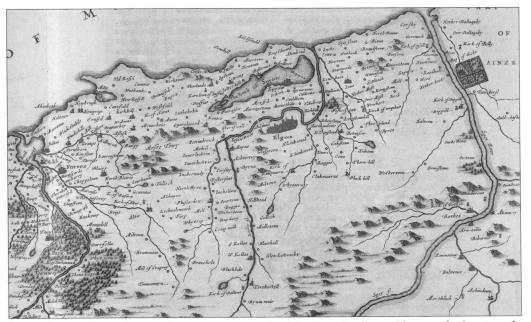

Plate 3. Part of Moray showing Darnaway (Tarnway) on the River Findhorn, Elgin on the Lossie and Bog of Gight on the Spey in Ainze (Ainie or Enzie), from Joan Blaeu's *Moravia Scotiae provincia* ex Timothy Pont, and Robert Gordon of Straloch. 1654.

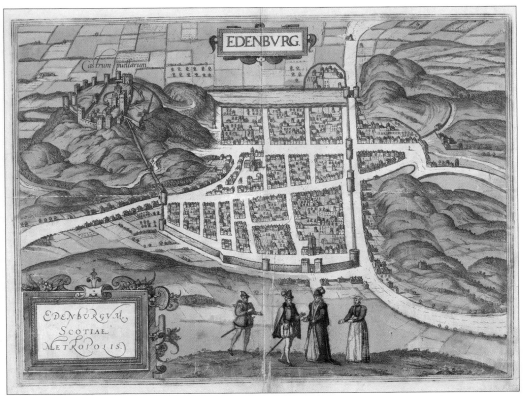

Plate 4. Edinburgh by Georg Braun and Franz Hogenberg, *Edenburgum, Scotiae Metropolis*, 1581.

Plate 5. James Stewart, 1st Earl of Moray, half-brother of Mary Queen of Scots, 1st Regent for the young James VI (1567), by Hugo Munro; after unknown artist.

Plate 6. James Hamilton, 2nd Earl of Arran, 1st Duke of Chatelherault, by William Holl Sn; after Comeles Ketel. He was George Gordon's father-in-law, leader of the Queen's Party till 1573.

Plate 7. *New Aberdene from the Block house*, in *Theatrum Scotiae*, by John Slezer, 1693. Old Aberdeen is seen in the distance on the right; both were visited by Mary Queen of Scots in 1562.

Plate 8. Inverness: *The Prospect of ye town of Innerness*, in *Theatrum Scotiae* by John Slezer, 1693. The castle withheld permission for Queen Mary to enter in 1562.

Plate 9. Sir William Kirkcaldy of Grange, by Jean Clouet. He came to Huntly Castle looking for John Gordon (1562), joined rebellion against Mary on marriage to Darnley, pursued Bothwell to Shetland, held Edinburgh Castle for Mary, and was hanged after its fall.

Plate 10. Sir William Maitland of Lethington, Secretary of State for Queen Mary, by T. Blood, 1825.

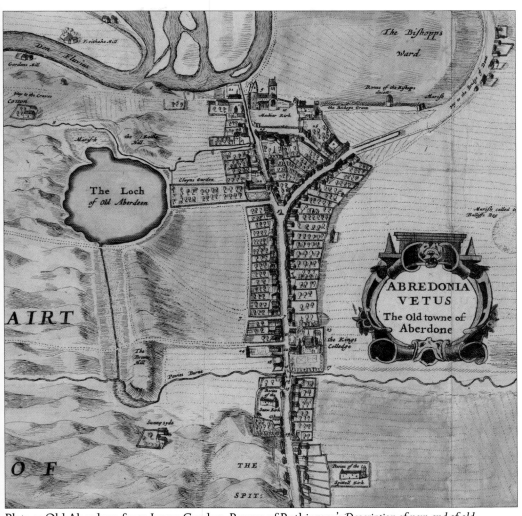

Plate 11. Old Aberdeen from James Gordon, Parson of Rothiemay's *Description of new and of old Aberdeens with the places of nearest adjacent*, 1661. Queen Mary gifted books to King's College in 1562. St Machar's Cathedral is seen in the north and King's College in the south.

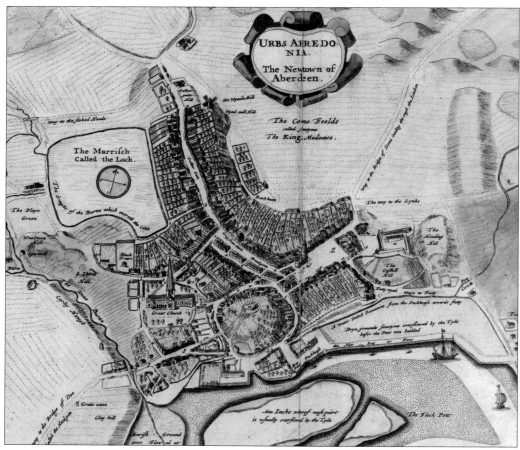

Plate 12. New Town of Aberdeen from James Gordon, Parson of Rothiemay's *Description of new and of old Aberdeens with the places of nearest adjacent*, 1661. John Gordon was beheaded here in 1562 on Heading Hill on the south-eastern edge of the city. The battle of Craibstone took place on the south-western outskirts.

Plate 13. *Execution of John Gordon* in Aberdeen, on Heading Hill, in 1562; woodcut in Raphael Holinshed's *Historie of Scotland unto the year 1571*, 1577.

Plate 14. Area round Edinburgh from *The Kingdome of Scotland, performed by John Speed*, 1610. George Gordon, 5th Earl of Huntly, was active here during the civil war between supporters and opposers of Queen Mary. Seton House can be seen north-east of Edinburgh, on the Firth of Forth, and Dunbar Castle east of that, on the coast.

Plate 15. *George, 5th Lord Seton*, aged 27, attributed to Adrian Vanson. Oil on Panel in 1570s. Holding a staff with a royal monogram MR in token of his office as Master of the Queen's Household; a friend and supporter of Queen Mary.

Plate 16. 'Seton Palace and the Forth Estuary' by Alexander Keirincx, where Queen Mary often went for leisure and sport such as archery, accompanied by Bothwell and the 5th Earl of Huntly.

Plate 17. Linlithgow, where Queen Mary was born, 'The Prospect of their Ma'ties Palace of Linlithgow', by John Slezer in *Theatrum Scotiae*, 1693.

Plate 18. Stirling, where the baby James VI was kept in the care of John Erskine, Earl of Mar. 'The Prospect of their Ma'ties Castle of Sterling from the East', by John Slezer in *Theatrum Scotiae*, 1693.

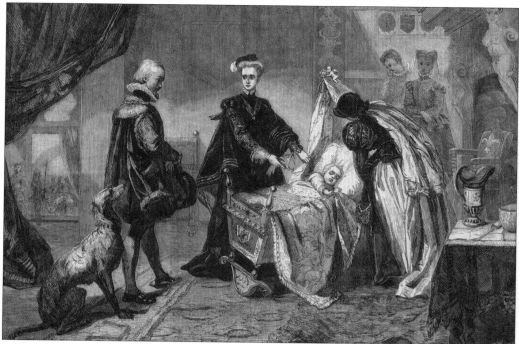

Plate 19. Artist's impression of *Queen Mary Quitting Stirling Castle*, by William Luson Thomas; after Henrietta Ada Ward. Queen Mary left the baby James there, in the care of the Earl of Mar.

Plate 20. John Leslie (1527–1596), Parson of Oyne, Bishop of Ross (1566), Queen Mary's emissary in France and England.

Plate 21. Matthew Stewart, 4th Earl of Lennox, Darnley's father and 2nd Regent for his grandson, the young James VI (1570). Artist unknown.

Plate 22. Queen Elizabeth I, with William Cecil, 1st Baron Burghley, and Sir Francis Walsingham, who all kept a close eye on events in Scotland through her ambassadors. Artist unknown.

Plate 23. John Erskine, 1st Earl of Mar, Governor of Stirling Castle, where he had care of the infant James VI ; 3rd Regent for the young king (1571–72). Copy of John Scougall.

Plate 24. James Douglas, 4th Earl of Morton, attributed to Arnold Bronckhorst (c. 1580). 4th Regent for the young James VI (1572–78), executed as an accessory to murder of Darnley.

Plate 25. James VI aged fourteen, who presided over the Council attempting to resolve the Gordon–Forbes feud in 1580. Artist unknown.

Plate 26. James Hepburn, 4th Earl of Bothwell, 1st husband of Lady Jean Gordon, 3rd husband of Mary Queen of Scots (1566); wedding miniature for his marriage to Jean. Artist unknown.

Plate 27. Lady Jean Gordon, Countess of Bothwell – wedding miniature; later Countess of Sutherland. Artist unknown.

Plate 28. Jean Gordon, Countess of Sutherland. Artist unknown.

Plate 29. Robert Gordon of Gordonstoun, second son of Jean Gordon and Alexander, 12th Earl of Sutherland; author of *A Genealogical History of the Earldom of Sutherland from its Origin to 1603; with a Continuation to the Year 1651.* Artist unknown.

IACOBVS · 6 · D · G
SCOTORVM
ÆTA · 29 ·
1595 ·

Plate 30. King James VI aged 29, later King James I of England, friend and supporter of the 6th Earl of Huntly. Attributed to Adrian Vanson (c. 1595).

Plate 31. Anne of Denmark aged 19, Queen of Scotland and later Queen of England, attributed to
Adrian Vanson (c. 1593).

Plate 32 George Gordon, 6th Earl and later 1st Marquis of Huntly. Artist unknown.

Plate 33. 'The Erle of Huntlye' coat of arms from *The Dublin Armorial of Scottish Nobility*, edited by Leslie Hodgson, published by The Heraldry Society of Scotland in 2006.

Heraldic explanation:

The Gordon heraldic shield is divided into four quarters: 1 (top left), 2 (top right), 3 (bottom left) and 4 (bottom right):

1. Three boars' heads associated with the surname of Gordon
2. Three lions' heads for the lordship of Badenoch
3. Three crescents within a double tressure flory counter flory for Seton
4. Three cinquefoils (strawberry flowers) for Fraser (from the French word for strawberry: *fraise*)

The supporters are collared deer hounds, the crest is a hart's head and the motto is 'Bydand' which means 'Remaining'.

Plate 34. Coat of Arms of the 'Marqweis of Huntlie' from *Kings and Nobility Arms*, compiled in 1638. Motto 'Bydand' meaning 'remaining' not in this view.

Plate 35. Huntly Castle showing the embossed names: GEORGE GORDOUN FIRST MARQUIS OF HU (Huntly) and beneath it HENRIETTE STEWART MARQUISSE OF HU (Huntly) by Robert William Billings from *The Baronial and Ecclesiastical Antiquities of Scotland*, published in four volumes in 1847–52.

Her son John had committed the management of his affairs to his mother during his absence in France. In 1598 she started up the enterprises of mining coal and salt panning at Brora.[29] Her father-in-law John, 11th Earl of Sutherland had found the coal, but his untimely death prevented him from doing anything about it.[30] The seam ran under a river and out to sea. It was industrial coal and very sulphurous. Mining went on there till the 1970s.[31] Jean also had a natural loch undammed and drained the land by diverting the Loth Burn so that it went directly out to sea.[32] This created the best farming land in Sutherland, which was only 3 per cent arable. Good salt was made there, which served not only Sutherland but the neighbouring provinces, and was also sold to England and elsewhere. Later, when John returned after two years in France, he added many more salt pans.[33] The salt was also used to salt herring.

In 1599, Jean's nephew George, 6th Earl of Huntly, agreed to be formally received into the Reformed Church. As a result, he was restored to the King's favour, had his forfeitures revoked and, what is more, was created a marquess.[34] He then began his restoration of Huntly Castle, inspired by the French chateau of Blois. No doubt Jean heard and even saw how he had his own and his wife's names emblazoned across the front of 'the palace' in embossed stone. The magnificent front piece over the main doorway blatantly trumpeted Catholic symbols.[35]

Alexander Ogilvie of Boyne

In December 1599 Jean, aged fifty-four, had the happiness of finally marrying her first love and childhood suitor, Alexander Ogilvie of Boyne. She said that it was for the sake of her family (Gordon family?). Like her brother John's marriage to Elizabeth of Findlater, it would have extended Gordon influence to the coast. Alexander was fifteen years older than Jean. His first wife, Mary Beaton, had died, so he was now a widower. It was Jean's third winter wedding.

Because Jean's son John, 13th Earl of Sutherland, had returned from Paris, she would have been able to leave her Sutherland duties to make a home with Alexander in Banffshire. The barony or thanedom of Boyne was vast, stretching many miles along the coast, and included the Forest of Boyne. It is probably when Alexander was married to Mary Beaton that the ambitiously grand Castle of Boyne was begun, to replace the old castle of Craig of Boyne on the coast, but it was never finished because the expenditure caused financial difficulties for many years. As a result, Jean's new husband had become financially beholden to his kinsman George Ogilvie of Dunlugas, who had helped him out.

In 1600 Jean's son John married Agnes Elphinstone, daughter of Lord Elphinstone of Kildrummy, Lord High Treasurer of Scotland. The wedding was attended by King James and his Queen, Anne of Denmark. The couple had many children, but five died in infancy.[36]

Tragically, Jean and Alexander Ogilvie of Boyne's time together lasted only two or three years before he, too, died and Jean was again left a widow.

Back in Sutherland

Jean decided to return to Sutherland. She had a house, Crackaig, built on a promontory north of Brora, perhaps so that she could keep an eye on the coal mining, salt panning and fish curing.[37] The foundations of her house are still there.

In 1603 her capable second son, Robert Gordon, was bidden to London in the entourage of King James VI when he became James I of England. Robert then went to France to continue his studies in civil law, and to travel there.[38] Three years later, in October 1605, he returned through England and became so valued by King James that the King appointed him gentleman of the honourable Privy Chamber. He was knighted Sir Robert Gordon of Gordonstoun in 1609, and awarded him a yearly pension of £200 sterling.[39] Jean found Robert very useful for sending things they wanted from London, such as the finest double virginal for her daughters Elizabeth and Anne, the finest tobacco – which was the most appreciated gift – and a spyglass. In return, Sir Robert would send requests for strong Scottish linen to be sent from the north. Money would be paid to 'posts' to carry mail – and even money, for example to her daughter-in-law's father, Lord Elphinstone, and also to Aberdeen or Edinburgh to pay creditors. Mail took about a month from Dunrobin to London.

In 1605, Jean had the sadness of seeing the death of her second daughter, Mary, known as the Lady of Balnagowan. Mary had married David Ross, Laird of Balnagowan, a few years earlier. They had no children.[40]

The years from 1615 to 1617 involved difficulty and more tragedy for the family. Jean's Catholic eldest son John, 13th Earl of Sutherland was in trouble with the church authorities. He wrote to his brother Robert complaining that he had gone to St Andrews, then to Edinburgh to make peace. 'I have done beyond all those of my profession in Scotland to please the authorities,' he commented, adding 'outwardly, at least.'[41]

Further tragedies in those years were the deaths of John's youngest son and, the following year, John himself. In a portrait at Dunrobin, he looks a bit like his brother, Sir Robert. He had pale brown hair, a straight moustache and a pointed beard, and brown eyes in a round gentle face. Sir Robert was made tutor or guardian of his fatherless nephew, now the 14th Earl of Sutherland. Jean and her daughter-in-law Agnes Elphinstone had a big disagreement about the young earl's future education. Agnes wanted him to go to the care of her father, Lord Elphinstone of Kildrummy, but Jean preferred the less expensive option, which was to be schooled locally in Dornoch. The nobility usually made sure that their sons were educated at grammar schools, where they studied the classics, Latin, Greek and French. They would then go on to university, after which they would take a modified version of the Grand Tour, going at least to France. Daughters were not even sent to local schools, but were kept at home, free from temptation. The first skill for them to learn was reading, so that they could read their Bibles. Girls often did not learn writing till much later in life. A writing and arithmetic master might be employed for a short while. Accounts were often kept in a mixture of Arabic and Roman numerals. Writing was Italic. Few women wrote journals or letters.[42] Much more usual activities for girls were playing music with guitar, virginal and harpsichord, and singing and dancing. Other leisure activities were embroidery, and playing cards. In September 1617, Agnes Elphinstone also died, aged only forty, in Jean's home of Crackaig. She too was buried at Dornoch Cathedral.[43] It was just as well that Jean was available to care for her orphaned grandchildren.

In 1617, Sir Robert planned to come up to Scotland in the entourage of King James, on the King's only return visit to Scotland. Jean and her third son, Alexander of Navidale, wrote to Robert urging him to write to them soon so that they could book lodgings in Edinburgh, because everything was filling up for the royal visit. Robert stayed in Scotland for the next two years, seeing to his nephew's affairs as his tutor, or guardian. It was then that he began writing his magnum opus, *A Genealogical History of the Earldom of Sutherland.*

Jean, aged seventy-one, was again in trouble because of her Catholic faith. This time it was for giving hospitality and assistance to members of the Jesuit mission, including her brother James and other priests from abroad in their work in the north of Scotland, and for general non-conformity. She was summoned before the High Commission in Edinburgh. Robert was a member of the Reformed Church, and therefore 'of a contrarie opinion with her in religion'.[44] It never impaired affection between them, but occasionally put him in a good deal of trouble. Husbands were responsible for their wives' ecclesiastical misdemeanours, and had to pay fines for them.[45] As she was a widow, this responsibility was placed on her eldest surviving son, Sir Robert. He stood surety for her, and purchased 'from his Majesty an oversight and toleration of her religion for the rest of her days, providing she would not harbour Jesuits'.[46] While in Edinburgh, Robert attended a meeting of the Commissioners for the Plantation of Kirks. It was concerned with the building of Reformed churches and the appointment of ministers.

After Robert's departure, Jean took the new young earl back into her care and managed the affairs of the earldom with the help of her third son, Alexander of Navidale. As she had wanted to do earlier, she sent the young earl to board at school in Dornoch, at a cost of £67 13s 4d a year and £12 for bows, arrows, golf clubs, balls, books, paper and other necessities. Recreation was taken on the links of Dornoch, which were described by Sir Robert as 'the fairest and largest links or green feildis of any part of Scotland, fit for archery, jogging, ryding and all iethir exercise, they do surpasse the feildis of Montrose or St Andrews'. Later John was sent to St Salvator's Collage at St Andrews. There is a portrait of him in Dunrobin Castle, painted in 1631 when he was twenty-two, and another when he was sixty. He was responsible for building the magnificent seventeenth-century part of that castle.

Alexander of Navidale kept his brother Robert informed about the affairs of the estate by letter. There were periodic bad harvests to report, and sometimes famine. In one letter he lamented the difficulty of making money in that part of the country, and suggested asking poor tenants for less grain, or else the land would lie fallow. He also let him know that there was an amount owing of nearly £2,000 from their father's debts. He had incurred considerable expense in confirming his legal right to the earldom.

In 1619, there was the wedding of Jean's granddaughter Elizabeth to Crichton of Frendraught. Sir Robert came back up to Scotland to arrange and sign the contract at Huntly and Frendraught castles. Her aunt, the Marchioness of Huntly, Henrietta Stewart, took Elizabeth to Elgin to buy her wedding clothes. The gown material cost £82 and, with 'two other gowns and necessaries', amounted to £266 13s 4d.[47]

In 1621 Jean, now aged seventy-six, travelled again to Elgin to buy her second granddaughter Anne a riding gown, and to hand her over to her grandfather Lord Elphinstone, who was to take her to Huntly Castle. She was to live there in the care of her uncle George and his wife Henrietta, now the Marquis and Marchioness of Huntly. Two years later, Jean asked Robert to bring Anne back with him when he came up north for his homecoming.

In 1627, aged eighty-one, Jean was excommunicated from the pulpit by the Golspie minister, Alexander Duff. However, on 19 October 1627, she was again absolved after Robert gave surety that she would not receive Jesuits or hear mass in the future. In the autumn of the following year, Sir Alexander of Navidale wrote to his brother Sir Robert, saying that their mother had a serious illness. He wrote of his desire to give her an honourable burial when the time came, but that he and the local lairds were worried about the probable expense.

Jean lived on until the following spring, and died on 14 May 1629 in Dunrobin Castle. Sir Robert arrived just in time, and was happy to be able to receive her last blessing before her death. She was buried in Dornoch Cathedral in the sepulchre of the earls of Dornoch, and given the full honours usually accorded to an earl of Sutherland.

There is a portrait of her in old age at Dunrobin. Wearing black and holding a rosary, she still looks much as she did as a younger woman: wise, knowing, practical and intelligent – an example of a self-possessed woman of character.

She led a fascinating life, and was for a period closely involved with national events. She emerged triumphant from her unhappy first marriage to Bothwell, the traumatic events of the last years of Mary's reign, the political conflicts during the minority of James VI, and the religious pressures of his adult reign, as well as having to endure two long periods of widowhood. Much of her time was spent efficiently managing the affairs of her husband, her son and finally her grandson in Sutherland.

What better than to finish with the words of her son, Sir Robert, in his book entitled the *Genealogical History of the Earldom of*

Sutherland. There he described her warmly as 'a virtuous and comelie lady, judicious, of excellent memorie and of great understanding above the capacitie of her sex'. High praise indeed for the time! He continued, saying that she was

> in this much to be commended, that during the continual changes and particular factions of the Court in the reign of Queen Mary and in the minorities of King James Sixt (which wer many), schoe alwise managed her affaris with so great prudence and foresign, that the enemies of her family culd nevir prevaile against her . . . Further, shoe hath, by her great care and diligence, brought to a prosperous end many hard and difficult business, of great consequence appertenying to the house of Sutherland . . . Shoe was, during her dayes, a great ornament to the familie . . . and shoe lived with great credit and reputation, so shoe dyed happily.[48]

What more could one want?

6

James Gordon – Jesuit Traitor?

ATTEMPTS TO BRING COUNTER-REFORMATION TO SCOTLAND

PART I

The question about Father James Gordon, the Jesuit, is whether to regard him as a dangerous traitor, secretly trying to influence people in positions of power, including the young King himself; or, instead, as a dedicated and courageous pastor, willing to come over from the Continent at great risk to himself in order to bring comfort and ministry to the persecuted Catholics in Scotland, and the truth to those in authority.

James Gordon was the fifth of the nine sons of the 4th Earl of Huntly, after Alexander, George, John and William. We know that James died in 1620 aged seventy-seven, which would mean that he was born in about 1543, making him a year older than his sister Margaret. He grew up in Huntly Castle in a firmly Catholic household that had its own chapel, and he was a teenager during the religious upheavals of the Reformation. His father was even asked by Archbishop Beaton to oversee attempts to stamp out Reformist heresy. His uncle William, Bishop of Aberdeen, remained unreformed to the end of his days.

Calvinism was formally established in 1560, without consulting Queen Mary in France, despite the act of Parliament which stipulated that any changes to Scotland's religious status quo should be decided by mutual agreement between the sovereign and a commission appointed by Parliament.[1] The new act instituted draconian rules against the Catholic Church. Priests had to either accept Presbyterian doctrine or leave the country. Those who accepted it were then able to marry. If they, or the people, were discovered hearing mass, they could be severely punished. For the first offence, their possessions could be confiscated, for the second offence they could be banished from the country, and for the third offence they risked a death sentence.[2] This act was not ratified by Mary.

The Arrival of Father Nicholas de Gouda

In the summer of 1562, a year after Mary arrived back in Scotland, the Dutch Papal Legate, Father Nicholas de Gouda, came with a mission to invite the Queen to send representatives to the reconvened Council of Trent. The council was an attempt by the Catholic Church to reform itself from inside. It was certainly necessary. Its shortcomings were an immediate cause of the revolution. De Gouda noticed with dismay that the monastic buildings were nearly all in ruins. He wrote a description of what he considered to be 'Scotland's miserable condition', saying that 'the churches, altars and sanctuaries were overthrown and profaned, images broken and in dust', and that mass was only allowed in the Queen's personal chapel. He attributed the Reformers' success to the scandal of benefices to laymen, the ignorance of the clergy, and the low standard of their morality.[3] The people of Scotland, he thought, were like sheep without a shepherd, and the only hope now was for a new generation of priests.[4]

To de Gouda, the Jesuit order to which he belonged was the answer, with its emphasis on spiritual self-discipline, and respect for education and learning. The order had been formed by the Spaniards Ignatius Loyola and St Francis Xavier in 1534 and had gained papal approval in 1540. The order concentrated on education and discipline, setting up seminaries for the training of priests. Its members then infiltrated the newly Protestant nations in Europe, and engaged in underground warfare against Protestantism. Mary was advised by her brother that, in order not to antagonise Queen Elizabeth, she should not agree to send any representatives to the Council of Trent. And the bishops either refused to meet him, or declined to go the council.[5]

Although the Council of Trent was sparsely attended by mostly Italian bishops and was marked by adjournments, often lasting years on end, it emerged with a more clearly defined Catholic Church doctrine, strengthened discipline, and services enriched by the exquisite music of Palestrina. The differences between it – with its emphasis on the importance of the Eucharist – and the Protestant Church, with its emphasis on justification by faith and the authority of the Bible, became more clearly defined. It has never been revised since and remains the doctrine of the Catholic Church today.[6] The Council of Trent launched the greatest force operating in Europe during the second half of the sixteenth century – the Counter-Reformation. The Catholic Church set itself to recover its lost dominions. Philip II, the hero of the movement, also sought political domination. Both England and France feared Spanish imperialism and were therefore bound to oppose him. Rather than open warfare, Queen Elizabeth counteracted with surreptitious support of the Protestant parties in France, the Low Countries (dominated by Spain), Portugal and Scotland.[7]

James Gordon Joins the Jesuits

All of these events must have generated fervent debate while James Gordon was a student at St Mary's School of Divinity at St Andrews University.

De Gouda had been accompanied on his mission by two other Jesuits, both from Scotland: Edmund Hay, a member of the Errol family; and his cousin, William Crichton. Hay's parents sheltered De Gouda for two months. Whilst there, he recruited four other young St Andrews graduates to take back to the Continent. One of these was James Gordon, aged about nineteen. The others were James Tyrie, Robert Abercrombie and William Murdoch. The names of all six are important in the story that follows.

They left for the Continent on 3 August 1562, and so James missed the final dramas leading to the battle of Corrichie and the resultant death of his father, the execution of his brother John, and the imprisonment of his eldest surviving brother, George. He also missed the trial in May the following year that brought about the downfall of his family.

When they arrived on the Continent, James Gordon, Tyrie, Abercrombie and Murdoch were sent to the Scots College of Louvain for further studies. Edmund Hay and William Crichton were exempted and went on to Rome to complete their novitiate. These two later became particularly important in the effort to return Scotland to the Catholic Church. James Gordon entered the Society of Jesus on 20 September 1562. He and the other five spent the next twenty years on the Continent making important contributions to the Jesuit order. James Gordon (whom we refer to as Fr James from here on, to distinguish him from King James) gained a great reputation for learning in the various colleges of his order, including the Sorbonne and Vienna.

He was Professor of Hebrew and Divinity in Paris, Bordeaux and Rome.

He must have heard that his eldest brother George had been freed in the summer of 1565 and formally recognised as the 5th Earl of Huntly. Fr Edmund Hay returned to Scotland in 1566 along with the unreformed Bishop of Dunblane, William Chisholm, the pair acting as papal envoys to see what could be done to induce Mary to break with Moray, Maitland of Lethington and the other Protestant ministers. Their conduct in the murder of Riccio had shown they were capable of the most appalling crimes. The Bishop of Dunblane called for their execution, but that was too much for Mary to contemplate.

No doubt Fr James would have been anxious to hear if the envoys had brought news of his family and especially his mother, who was a confidante of the Queen. They could have taken back details of how she had helped the Queen escape Court with Lord Darnley on the fateful night of Riccio's murder. At the time of the infant Prince James's christening, the Bishop and Fr Edmund Hay had an interview with the Queen. Darnley's murder happened as they prepared to leave the country.[8] They must have informed Fr James that his brother-in-law Bothwell was a prime suspect in this latest murder.

Not long after that, Fr James would have been appalled to hear of more shocking events, with Bothwell's sudden divorce from his sister Jean, followed by his rapid marriage to the Queen, their capitulation at Carberry, her capture and imprisonment on Lochleven, her forced abdication, escape, flight to England, and incarceration there. Then there was the civil war breaking out in his country, with his brother George deeply involved on Mary's side. Finally there was the news that, in 1571, the civil war had spread briefly to his home area, with his younger brother Adam leading Gordons and others for the Queen against their old enemies, the Forbeses, who supported the Regency. This must have caused Fr James great concern, and frustration at being so far away. However, it seemed that Adam was succeeding in holding the north for the Queen – that is, until 1573, when her supporters came to terms with Morton, the Regent. As a result, Adam and his friends had left Scotland with a group of like-minded people and joined Fr James in France, disgusted at the turn of events. Fr James was the first of their family to know about the failed attempt on Adam's life in Paris.

Meanwhile, opinion in Counter-Reformation Europe was hardening against Protestants. James must have been aware of the cruelties carried out by the Duke of Alva, on behalf of Spain, against Protestants in the Netherlands. The ascetic Pope Pius V had approved, and said that no quarter should be given to the Huguenots in France; the following year came the appalling massacre of three to four thousand in Paris. Philip II called for a special Te Deum to be sung, and the Pope directed that a commemorative medal be cut.

As a result, the Counter-Reformation was viewed with fear by Protestants in Scotland and England, especially after the Pope excommunicated Queen Elizabeth and declared her reign illegal. In the eyes of many Catholics, this made Mary the rightful Queen of England, as well as Scotland. They had to ask themselves to whom their ultimate allegiance was owed.[9]

However, to suffering Catholics in both Scotland and England, a more active, aggressive Catholicism gave hope that their situation might change. They thought that Catholic powers – in particular France, the Spanish Netherlands and Spain under Philip II – were possible sources of help in their predicament. Mary, imprisoned in England, had the same hopes. Despite its riches from the gold and silver obtained in Peru and Mexico, Spain was in financial straits because much had been frittered away by embezzlement and wars in the Netherlands and Turkey.[10] As a result, the mission to restore Catholicism to England and Scotland could only be carried out by means of influence and intrigue.[11] In Scotland, hope sprang from the Jesuit mission in England, from where a Fr William Holt arrived at Seton House in 1574, to investigate the possibilities of mission there.[12] Fr James was to become deeply involved in the resulting endeavours.

The New 6th Earl of Huntly

In 1576, there was the shock for Fr James when he heard that his eldest brother George had died suddenly of a heart attack, as their father had done. The cheering news for him was that his younger brother Adam, now back in Scotland, was able to take control of their father's estate on behalf of their sixteen-year-old nephew, now the 6th Earl of Huntly. What is more, it was his brother's dying wish that the young lad be sent to his care in Paris to continue his education there.

A couple of years later John Leslie, Catholic Bishop of Ross, wrote of his high hopes of the lad, saying: 'The chief of the Gordons is the Earl of Huntly, a young man of eighteen years of age, of excellent disposition, and well brought up in the Christian faith . . . We shall keep him for better times, like another Joas rescued from the cruelty of Athaliah,[13] in hopes that he may restore the worship of God in Scotland one of these days.'[14] It was probably his attempt to fulfil these aspirations that led the future marquis into so much trouble in subsequent years.

In 1578, Protestant hardliner Andrew Melville was made Moderator of the General Assembly in Scotland. He, too, had been educated at St Andrews and then Paris. He went on to be a professor at the universities of Geneva and Glasgow. He did much to reorganise university education. In 1580, he was made Principal of Fr James' old St Andrews college, St Mary's, where he taught Theology, Hebrew, Chaldee and Syrian.[15] Although he was strongly pro-English, and worked to bring about legislative union, he advocated a Presbyterian form of Church government and was responsible for the particularly Scottish form of Calvinism. He and others compiled the Second Book of Discipline, which would make life even more difficult for Catholics, including James's mother, the Countess of Huntly, and his sister Jean, now married to the Earl of Sutherland. Nevertheless, both of them continued as practising Catholics, despite the restrictions.

In 1580, Fr James' brother Adam also died suddenly, just before the final judgement was to be given in the Gordons' legal disputes with the Forbeses in the presence of the young King James, who was hoping to bring the Gordon–Forbes feud to a close after a protracted series of legal wrangles. As a result of Adam's death, Auchindoun and Keithmore passed officially to his next brother, Patrick, to whom he had sold the estate when he went to France. Patrick now became known as Patrick Gordon of Auchindoun. He married an illegitimate daughter of the exiled Catholic Archbishop Beaton.

The Catholic Resurgence

Fr James must have been very encouraged to hear news from Scotland that the thirteen-year-old King James was reacting against the severe Presbyterianism taught to him by his tutor, the ageing George Buchanan, and was confiding in his French relative the Duke of Guise, a champion of French Catholicism. Even more significant was the news that young King James had formed a strong personal attachment to his father's Catholic first cousin Esmé Stewart, Seigneur d'Aubigny, who had come to Scotland from France the previous year, 1579. He was in his late thirties and may have acted as a father figure, giving James the affection he had been unable to receive from his parents. Esmé Stewart's continental sophistication would naturally have appealed to a youth in his teens, especially as a contrast to the prevailing Calvinist atmosphere.

Esmé Stewart had good reason to return to Scotland, because he was an heir to the earldom of Lennox and probably hoped to gain from the forfeiture of his family's traditional rivals, the Hamiltons. Indeed, King James made him Commendator of Arbroath Abbey, forfeited from John Hamilton, and made sure that he was soon able to inherit the earldom of Lennox in place of an ageing relative. He also made him Keeper of the important Dumbarton Castle and other fortresses. Stewart was admitted to the Privy Council in 1580, where he led the party moving against the former Regent, Morton, who had held power for so long. Morton was arrested on 31 December 1580, charged with complicity in the murder of the King's father and Lennox's first cousin, Lord Darnley. He, who had accused so many others of that murder, was himself caught at last.

The same year, young George Gordon completed his education in Paris and returned to Scotland to take up his role as 6th Earl of Huntly. He took an active part in the plot to bring down Morton, who had activated the north, and particularly the Forbeses, against his uncle Adam. Morton was executed in June the following year by the very contraption he had introduced, known as the Halifax Maiden.[16] Although a hardliner with respect to Mary and the moves for her restoration, Morton was a moderate compared with Andrew Melville and the Kirk leaders, who also contributed to his downfall.

Without Morton's moderating influence, the Church Assembly now abolished the Episcopalian system, complete with its bishops, and published the Second Book of Discipline, but it still needed to be sanctioned by Parliament. In the Book, claims were made for the Presbyterian Kirk at the expense of the prevailing civil powers. This led to a prolonged struggle between those who supported the Presbyterian principle of a combination of democratic and theocratic authority, and those who supported Episcopacy, which preached about the need for bishops and believed in the divine right of kings. King James, of course, felt much more in tune with those who favoured Episcopacy, such as his cousin Esmé Stewart.[17]

King James was beginning to enjoy his hold on the monarchy and rejected the idea of 'an Association', or joint rule, between him and his mother, as suggested by Mary. This strategy was disastrous for her, because it was now less likely that Elizabeth would release her. As a result, Mary determined to commit herself, her son and her realm to the protection of Philip II. However, Philip urged the necessity of James's conversion to Catholicism in the first instance. Mary assured him that this would probably come about.

In 1581, Pope Gregory XIII was 'solicitous for poor Scotland'[18] and gave approval for a Scottish mission. He communicated with Archbishop Beaton in Paris. The English Jesuit Fr Parsons, who had sent Fr Holt to Scotland, wrote to the General of the Society of Jesus saying that the country should be the key target, because 'on the conversion of Scotland depends every hope, humanly speaking, for the conversion of England'.[19] They decided to send two Jesuits to investigate the possibilities further. Those chosen were two of the original six who had gone to France with de Gouda in 1561: Fr Edmund Hay and Fr William Crichton who now, twenty years later in February 1581, arrived back in their home country. William Crichton became a pivotal figure in the story that follows.

James Stewart, another of the King's cousins, was created Earl of Arran and brought onto the Privy Council. He and Esmé Stewart represented a conservative aristocratic core gathering round young King James, along with former supporters of Mary such as Lord Seton, Maitland of Thirlestane (younger brother of Mary's one-time secretary, Maitland of Lethington), Lord Maxwell and Kerr of Ferniehurst. They were not necessarily practising Catholics, except for Seton and Maxwell, but they, like the King, tended to dislike the extreme Protestantism, which was supported by the anglophile lords and lairds from the south-east and Ayrshire.[20] In October that year, the returned young Huntly had the honour of carrying the sceptre for King James's first Parliament.[21]

Esmé Stewart, now Earl of Lennox, became a focal point of Catholic intrigue, and with the two Jesuit emissaries, Hay and Crichton, he concocted a plot known as the 'Enterprise of England'. This aimed to make Scotland the springboard for a Catholic re-conquest of England, backed, they hoped, by Spain, the Pope and the Guise faction in France. The Jesuits were to be the main channel of communication. Their principal task was to bring those with influence over others to join them in the plan.[22]

When the English Jesuit Fr Holt arrived back in England ready to report to Fr Parsons on the state of the Catholic Church in Scotland, he found that Parsons had retired and so he saw the Spanish ambassador, Mendoza, instead. Holt told Mendoza that only six Catholic priests were at work in the whole of Scotland. Mendoza sent him back north with words of caution. There, Holt met Fr William Crichton, who informed him that he had come to Scotland on a mission from the Pope.

Although Lennox had, for appearances sake, declared himself to be of the Reformed faith, he soon became angry with the Kirk and the pro-English party. He become over-enthusiastic when he heard from Fr Crichton of the Pope's goodwill and the zeal of the Duke of Guise and other Catholics on the Continent. Fr Holt contributed to Lennox's ardour by showing him how his plans coincided with what Mendoza had indicated were the intentions of Spain.[23] Esmé Stewart, now Earl of Lennox, pledged himself to bring about the conversion of young King James and the re-establishment of Catholicism in Scotland. He drew up a plan for raising an army against the dominant Protestant faction, if sufficient aid was received. Understandably, Queen Elizabeth became uneasy about young King James's friendship with Lennox and tried to dislodge him from favour.[24] The Duke of Guise took an interest in Lennox, and he became a focus for foreign intrigue.[25]

Fr Holt returned to England, and reported to Mendoza that magnates such as Lennox, Seton, Argyll, Caithness, Eglinton and young Huntly would accept Spanish and papal help to bring about the King's conversion. Holt again returned to Scotland and secretly met the King to find out where he stood. James professed to favour Spain, but he gave no hope of his own conversion. Ambassador Mendoza wrote to Philip II telling him of the secret pact with six Scottish nobles, saying that the only hope for England was through Scotland. Philip II responded that they should send a trusted priest to young King James to tell him that, if he joined the Catholic Church, he would be supported by many in England, who would put him on the throne. However, Philip said James should be warned that if he remained Protestant, the Catholics would vehemently oppose him and would attempt to promote the claims of some other person.[26] He was, no doubt, thinking of his own claim to the English throne.

Lennox now asked Philip II to pay for an army of 20,000 mercenaries – Spanish, Italian, German and Swiss – for eighteen months, as well as funding for the raising of Scottish troops and equipment to restore Catholicism and liberate Mary. Lennox was convinced that King James would co-operate with vigour.[27] However, Philip II was frightened off by such a grandiose, over-ambitious scheme involving such great sums of money. He did not have much faith in Lennox, who he had been warned was untrustworthy. He also distrusted the Guises, so he withdrew his support from the scheme.[28]

However, in May 1582 Fr William Crichton returned to the Continent, where he discussed the plans further with Archbishop Beaton, the retired Fr Parsons, the head of English Catholics (Cardinal Allen), and the Duke of Guise. Crichton went on to Rome, and was encouraged to find Pope Gregory XIII enthusiastic and in crusading mood. He seemed to entirely approve of the plans. However, two weeks later, the fired-up Fr Crichton was disappointed to be told that the scheme was beyond papal resources.

Meanwhile, England began to feel surrounded and vulnerable when Portugal and all its possessions came to the Spanish crown, which already controlled part of the Netherlands and was in touch with the disaffected in Ireland. Elizabeth began making new overtures to France, and even considered marriage to the King's brother, the Duke of Anjou.

Fr Holt remained in Scotland waiting for more Jesuits to arrive. He was befriended by the young Earl of Huntly and Lord Seton. He seemed safe while the King was under the influence of Catholics. However, Holt was kidnapped and was to be sent to London, but the King intervened and let him escape. Much hope was placed on the King's sympathy to the cause. Holt reported that 'the King, having quarrelled with the ministers, the greater part of the country have abandoned them and asked for Catholic preachers'.[29] As a result of this, the Jesuits made a great effort to help the Scottish Catholics.

Fr Crichton managed to persuade Lennox that the young King should have a Catholic education. Lennox signed an agreement to send him abroad or else provide the education in Scotland. Crichton believed that Pope Gregory would put forward the money. He took the document to France and forwarded it to Rome. The Pope agreed in principle but, much to Crichton's bitter dismay, he crucially delayed action for two years. This was another major disappointment to the Catholic cause.

Queen Elizabeth got to hear about this scheme which, along with the conflict between the King's government and the priorities of the Kirk, resulted in the Ruthven Raid. On 23 August 1582, young King James was invited to Gowrie Castle. There he was seized by a group of pro-English Protestant nobles, led by William Ruthven, 1st Earl of Gowrie, who kept him for ten months. This became known as the Ruthven Raid.

Fr Crichton did all he could to interest the Pope and Catholic sovereigns in a scheme to rescue the King from the Ruthven Raiders and have him educated as a Catholic.[30] Philip II was sympathetic but did not give his consent, and Mendoza opposed it. The scheme was aborted due, in many respects, to the vigilance of Queen Elizabeth and her ministers, especially William Cecil, Lord Burghley, who hated and feared the agents of the Counter-Reformation. Meanwhile, Lennox, seeing the change in the status quo and fearing for his life, fled the country. He died not long after, in France.[31] It looked as if efforts for a Counter-Reformation in Scotland had come to an end.

The King Rescued from the Ruthven Raiders (June 1583)

However, in June 1583 the young 6th Earl of Huntly was one of the leaders of a group that liberated the King from the Raiders.[32] Crawford, Argyll, Montrose, Rothes and Marischal rallied to him. Once James was reinstated to power, he announced that he wanted to unify his nobility and 'be a universal king above faction'.[33] Ruthven was put on trial and executed. At last the King had been able to take the revenge promised by his pregnant mother when Ruthven had acted so violently against her at the time of Riccio's murder. In March 1584 Andrew Melville, the outspoken Presbyterian religious and political reformer, was summoned for trial, accused of preaching a seditious sermon. However, he fled to England to avoid the jurisdiction of a hostile council and probable imprisonment.[34]

Despite the indoctrination during the time of his incarceration, the King still appeared sympathetic to the Catholic cause. Many exiles returned to Scotland, including John and Claud Hamilton. The 'Enterprise' idea was renewed. Fr Crichton, now in Rouen, suggested that friars should go about in disguise, without their habits, and that the Pope should allow small pensions to relieve the poverty-stricken Catholic priests still in the country.[35] Crichton continued to believe that, because all power was in the hands of the nobles, their support must first be gained. Many of them had submitted to the Reformers simply to protect their property from confiscation.

The King made his cousin James Stewart, Earl of Arran, his Chancellor on 15 May 1584, and young Huntly became a member of his

Privy Council. Maitland of Thirlestane was made Secretary. He resembled his older brother Maitland of Lethington in his ability and in his pro-English policy.[36] There were rumours that the King was prepared to grant toleration to Catholics. Fr Crichton assured the Pope and the Duke of Guise that the King's conversion was likely. He mooted the 'new idea' of using Scotland for an invasion of England. As a result of the King's favourable attitude, Archbishop Beaton wrote from Paris to Pope Gregory XIII, asking him to use his influence to obtain, not domestic chaplains, but missionaries, and specifically asked that Fr Crichton be sent, accompanied by Frs James Gordon, Edmund Hay and James Tyrie.[37] Meanwhile, twenty exiled priests also wrote to the Pope, asking for the means to go to Scotland 'even at the risk of our lives'.[38]

In May, King James asserted his power over all persons and estates by means of 'the Black Acts', so called by the people who opposed them. Under these acts, he denounced the 'new pretended presbyteries' and reaffirmed the authority of bishops and, through them, his own authority. Nearly a score of ministers followed Andrew Melville into exile.[39]

Father James Returns to Scotland

In 1585, the Pope agreed to Archbishop Beaton's plea to send missionary priests to Scotland, including Crichton and Fr James. However, on their way there they were captured at sea by Dutch sailors. Fr James was allowed to escape as a result of his important family connections, in that the Earl of Huntly was his nephew and close to the King. Fr Crichton just escaped execution for his supposed part in the murder of the Prince of Orange. He was handed over to Queen Elizabeth as part of a treaty agreement with the Dutch, and was imprisoned in the Tower of London for two years.

When Fr James landed he was taken to the home of David Graham, Master of Fintray, who was a nephew of Archbishop Beaton. He had hosted Fr Holt from England, and was described by Catholic sources as 'one of the staunchest laymen of the day'.[40]

There were exaggerated rumours about how many Jesuits had been in their boat, the amount of chalices they had brought, and that they were subverting the King, who now heard mass daily, and so on. As a result, the King felt pressured to react and issued a proclamation forbidding Jesuits to enter Scotland in future. He ordered Fr James not to come within ten miles of court, and to leave the country within a month.[41] However, Fintray assured Fr James that he had no need to worry about the order, because he would have the protection of his nephew, the 6th Earl of Huntly: he knew he had the King's affection. Huntly was made High Chamberlain and Lieutenant of the North, as his father and grandfather had been. Fr James' arrival and influence kept him faithful to the Catholic cause.

As had been agreed, the half-dozen or more Jesuits now in the country aimed to convert influential nobility. Fr Edmund Hay was put in overall charge of the project. They went about in disguise, and led lives of extreme danger and often heroism. They generally lived amongst and were hidden by the aristocrats who remained loyal to the faith.[42] It was Fr James' aim to convert the King. He even followed him for six months, hoping for an opportunity. His aim was to procure royal protection for Catholics and freedom of discussion. He believed that the nobles were still Catholic at heart, and that the destiny of Scotland lay in their hands. One third of the barons still adhered to the Catholic faith. As a result of his work, a large number returned to the faith and were encouraged to continue in it, and there were also many converts. Queen Elizabeth's spies informed her of everything, saying: 'The King is the mark they shoot at.'[43] She and the Presbyterian ministers became alarmed.

Father James Debates Publicly with a Top Presbyterian Minister

Despite the order that Fr James not come within ten miles of court and that he leave the country, Huntly used his influence with the King to allow his uncle, Fr James, to demonstrate his brilliant debating skills in front of him and an audience. The debate was to be with George Hay, the intellectual champion of the Presbyterian cause. Hay sent a cartload of books from his home to back up his arguments. These were mainly that the Church had been right for its first few hundred years but then went astray with false doctrine not backed up by scripture. Francis Hay, 9th Earl of Errol was so impressed by the way that Fr James was able to fully complete lines of scripture quoted by Hay that he became ardent in the Catholic cause.[44]

However, in 1584 a significant new player appeared on the scene. This was the Master of Gray, a diplomat and political schemer. He had spent many years in France, nominally in the service of Mary, who was again proposing joint rule with her son. Gray indoctrinated the King against the Jesuits and Archbishop Beaton.[45] In May 1585, King James categorically repudiated the idea of 'the Association' with his mother. Gray did not believe Philip II would invade in order to hand the throne of England to James, because he had begun to consider his own claim to the throne of England. Philip's attitude to Mary became cold, and he discouraged her escape.

Gray soothed Queen Elizabeth's doubts about the reliability of the Scottish administration by advocating that Scotland negotiate a formal alliance with England. She sent an offer of £4,000 down and £4,000 yearly, with agreement to the terms of a treaty that was formulated in July 1585.[46] With promises of English military support, Gray and Maitland of Thirlestane began to plot against the King's cousin, Chancellor Arran, on the grounds that he was not sincere about the treaty with England. The King surrendered to pressure and Arran fled. The exiled lords then returned to power and took over the government in the interests of England.[47]

Fr James had advised Frs Edmund Hay and James Tyrie to delay their return to Scotland, and pointed out that it would be less embarrassing to the King if arriving Jesuits were not home-grown Scots, but instead came up from England. Despite this advice, Hay came with Drury. They landed in Aberdeen, disguised as servants of one of Archbishop Beaton' adherents. Hay took a letter to the King from the Duke of Guise.

Queen Elizabeth heard about the two Jesuits' arrival and demanded their banishment. Gray had been appointed a Gentleman of the Privy Chamber and was made Master of the King's Wardrobe and Menagerie, setting him in charge of the King's jewels, clothing and tapestries, as well as the employment of tailors and shoemakers. He was told to arrest the Jesuits. New proclamations were made, but the men could not be found. Fr Hay had taken refuge with Fr James in their home areas in the north-east, where it was reported that 'they say mass openly and lead great numbers of people to visit chapels and relics here and there, to the great scandal of all honest men in the realm, and nothing is done for their apprehension'.[48] Fr Drury had succeeded in converting Lord Maxwell, Governor of Dumfries, to the cause, and was then able to work in the south-west under his protection.

The 'Catholic League' proclaimed by Philip II and the Duke of Guise 'for the extirpation of heresy', caused horror, alarm and fear in England and Scotland. This was because of the inquisition in Spain and the Netherlands, especially as the Duke of Parma was winning back most of the Netherlands for Spain. People feared that this represented a threat, especially to Scotland, being nearer to the Netherlands.

Queen Elizabeth began to give the King the promised subsidy of £4,000 from her personal income. She was careful not to put anything in writing, nor to mention the accession. It was referred to as 'a gratuity', but the King preferred to call it 'an annuity'. It was paid in gold coins and was therefore ready cash, which he badly needed. This was not a universally popular move in Scotland, because it made the country even more prone to English interference. Historically, England usually aimed to control Scottish policy by subsidising either the crown or nobles and courtiers (usually those who were discontented), or by military intervention. Queen Elizabeth pursued all three methods. Nevertheless, the Jesuit mission continued to prosper.[49]

Parson of Clatt

Fr James lived quietly as 'Parson of Clatt', ministering to Catholics in the north-east along with Fr Hay and under the protection of Huntly. Two more of the original six who had gone to the Continent with de Gouda – Fr Robert Abercrombie and Fr James Tyrie – worked under the protection of Lord Maxwell in the south-west, with astounding success. The Bishop of Derry came over from Ireland and confirmed 10,000 in the area. Fr Drury blatantly celebrated three solemn masses over Christmas 1585 in New Abbey, Dumfries and midnight mass in the ruined church of Lincluden, three miles from Dumfries. Many came from the north of England, crossing a waist-high swollen river to avoid guards posted on the bridge. Despite the cold, they slept overnight in the ruined church.[50] Queen Elizabeth realised the danger to England should the King become Catholic, so she contrived a return of the Ruthven raiders.[51] James realised his tolerance towards the Catholics could endanger his present and future crown, so he now allied himself with the Protestants, and Lord Maxwell was warded for permitting forbidden Catholic activities in his domains.

By the end of 1585 a composite administration was formed which aimed at fulfilling the King's ideal of unity amongst his nobles. It even included leaders of the Ruthven faction who had kidnapped and kept him in captivity. The Lords John and Claud Hamilton and former members of Arran's administration were also included, such as Huntly, Gray, Maitland of Thirlestane, Montrose, Crawford and Marischal.[52]

In 1586, the Spanish ambassador, Olivares, reported to the new Pope, Sixtus V, that King James was of little value to the Catholic cause, thereby refuting France's continued confidence in the King's conversion. The English Jesuit Fr Parsons did not trust King James, and was now determined to exclude Scotland from any Spanish invasion plans. A memo from Olivares shows that Philip II had decided to push his daughter's case for the English throne, because he and the Pope dismissed the King as heretical. They urged that he be removed from the throne rather than making any further attempt to convert him.[53] The Guises were also excluded from this new 'Enterprise of England' which, ostensibly, aimed for the liberation of Queen Mary. However, they were somewhat indifferent to the possibility of her death and, after it occurred, Olivares considered it 'rather fortunate' in his letters.[54] Frs Parsons and Allen then prepared a defence of Philip's 'just claim'. Fr Allen stressed that Mary herself had disinherited James in her will as a hopeless heretic. Philip did not want the King to be publicly disinherited. He intended, in time, to attack him. However, the Francophiles continued to press King James's case, and to believe in his future conversion.[55]

In March 1586 Thomas Randolph, who had been England's ambassador in the 1560s, was sent back to Scotland to conclude the new league between the two countries. It took four months but did not include various clauses Scotland wanted, such as the recognition that King James would succeed Elizabeth, provision for mutual naturalisation of Scots and English in each others' countries, or raising the King's subsidy to £5,000, as only half had been given of what was promised. However, each country was to help the other in the event of an invasion.[56]

In May, Huntly, Claud Hamilton and Lord Maxwell followed the advice of the Duke of Guise and made contact with Spain. In August, England's ambassador to Scotland, Asheby, advised Elizabeth's Secretary of State and chief spymaster, Francis Walsingham, that, in view of the dangers from Spain and the faction that it had 'in these parts', it would be wise to make generous offers to James to keep him on side. Asheby advised Walsingham that Spain had made great offers, such as 20,000 footmen and 5,000 horses. Asheby suggested that Queen Elizabeth offer the King an English dukedom, a yearly pension of £5,000, a guard of fifty Scots and their commanders, and 100 horsemen and footmen on his borders during her lifetime. Additionally, Asheby assured Walsingham that the King intended to put his life and crown on the line for the advancement of the Protestant religion and the safety of Queen Elizabeth.[57]

However, at the end of November, a letter to the King of France said that many lords in Scotland openly declared themselves to be Catholics. The ministers complained that the King's house, council and parliament were full of papists, and that Huntly had two or three Jesuits in his house. The King took little account of the matter, simply telling the ministers to attempt to convert those concerned, and also saying that he could not stop Huntly having his uncle in his own house.[58]

A letter to Queen Elizabeth from an anonymous Scotsman refers to the King's displeasure with his Presbyterian ministers, because they were 'tending to their own preferment' and to his 'wrack and overthrow'. The letter reported that the nobility, and most barons, were either Catholics or favourers of Catholicism, but that the people of the boroughs and sea coasts were all 'heretykes'. It refers to Fr James landing, along with some 'Inglish priests at the New Town of Aberdeyne', with a message and money from the Pope. It describes their arrest by magistrates, who were then compelled by Catholic noblemen to release them, and that they then made offer of their services to Huntly.[59]

The Execution of Mary (8 February 1587)

Mary's execution reignited Scotland's old hatred of England. Banners appeared showing pictures of the execution, and at first the Chancellor and many of the lords vowed revenge. The King promised action. Huntly attempted to persuade him to open Scottish ports to Spanish ships. Philip II promised money, but continued to declare that the King's conversion was necessary.

The Duke of Parma, at the head of the Spanish forces in the Netherlands, became convinced that an invasion was practical. He and a Fr Bruce drew up a plan by which thirty wheat ships from the Baltic would unload at Dunkirk and take soldiers on board. Fr Bruce was given 10,000 crowns to take to Scotland, with a friendly message to the King from Archbishop Beaton in Paris. Bruce saw the King three times in 1588 but did not mention the wheat ships, because he became convinced that, although he was prepared to negotiate with Philip, James was a Protestant at heart. Parma abandoned the scheme because of this, and also because it had become too late in the season for wheat to be loaded.[60]

The Master of Gray brought a suggestion to England that the King's right of succession should now be publicly recognised, especially as there was a rumour that Mary had changed her will just before her execution, passing her right of succession to Philip if King James insisted on remaining a Protestant. However, when the Scottish government was accused of not taking action to avenge her death, Gray was used as a scapegoat, for taking wrong messages to England, and was imprisoned. The King's subsidy from Queen Elizabeth began at this time. The chance to avenge Mary's death was lost. It was a critical moment for Protestantism.[61]

Nevertheless, the King was more lenient towards Catholics once again after the execution, resulting in an influx of missionaries, including Frs William Ogilvie, William Murdoch and John Myrton.[62] Myrton was immediately seized and banished to Belgium. The other two found secure hiding places.[63] Fr Crichton returned to Scotland along with Fr Alexander McQuarrie. Practically the whole of the north was solidly Catholic. Pilgrimages were being revived and the mass celebrated openly, especially in the houses of the lairds.[64] With her death, Mary's pensions to the priests had ceased, so their need for money was much emphasised in Jesuit correspondence. 'The fathers can hardly live, let alone organise', was one complaint. The hard life was beginning to tell. Father Drury died from his exertions, as did William Ogilvie, not long after.[65]

Father James and his Forbes Nephews

Fr James was a strong influence on the only two sons of his sister Margaret, the estranged wife of the Master of Forbes. The eldest son, William Forbes, went to the Low Countries to join the forces of the Duke of Parma, but decided to abandon his military career and join the Capuchins. He wrote to his father renouncing all his rights and expectations as heir in favour of his brother John, then only eighteen.

Fr James was surprised to be approached by John, who told him that his older brother had suggested that he ask him for instruction in the faith, as he was disillusioned with the difference between what his father read from the Bible at table and his life. As a result of this, and despite his father's efforts to distract the boy with more worldly pursuits and an attractive young wife-to-be, John decided to follow his brother's example and left secretly for the Continent in disguise. This must have been seen as a tragedy for the Forbes family, especially as John was now the only son and heir. Despite strenuous efforts to find him and make him change his mind, the boy persisted, enduring a hard life while he learnt the language and became accepted as a novice Capuchin. Soon their mother, Fr James's sister Margaret, decided to follow him, so that she too could pursue a devout life.

Maitland of Thirlestane's Administration

In June 1587, the King attained the age of twenty-one. He made Maitland of Thirlestane his Chancellor. His middle-of-the-road administration was not so different to that of Arran. Though more conciliatory towards Presbyterians, there was no question of his returning to the ultra-Protestantism of the Ruthven Raiders: the King was careful to maintain a balance between the Catholics, the Kirk and friendship with England.[66] In August 1587, The English ambassador Asheby reported that he was told by the Chancellor that the King had accepted Elizabeth's excuses for having agreed to Mary's execution. However, James asked for all the judges' signatures to show agreement that his own right to the accession was not weakened by the judgement on his mother.

Asheby reported that there were 'many discordant persons in these parts', and went on to warn that 'great offers were made him [James] by other princes'. However, he assured Walsingham that the King had 'utterly refused' these and was 'void of all revenge'.[67] Asheby went on to suggest, though, that 'some honourable pension would quench all the rest'. In other words, opposition could be bought off.

Lord Maxwell and Colonel Semple arrived in Scotland with 5,000 crowns from Philip II and a commission from Parma to avenge Mary's death. However, the terms were deliberately vague, as King James was still not fully trusted by the Spanish. The money was only to be given to him if the Catholic earls advised it. Fr James had exploratory interviews with the King; he was friendly, but there was no sign of him changing his religion. With his eyes on the English throne, he would certainly not want to alarm Queen Elizabeth. He proved his credentials in that regard after Lord Maxwell made a premature rising in Galloway and James led an expedition against him, having Maxwell captured and imprisoned. By this action the King had shown that he was definitely committed to the Protestant cause and was now firmly in the English camp, but he continued to be lenient towards his friend

Huntly. In June, now that she was surer of him, Elizabeth reduced his subsidy to £2,000 in order to finance defences against the threatened Spanish invasion of England. Meanwhile, her ambassador was given freedom to make 'unauthorised promises'.[68]

Huntly's Marriage and Post as Captain of the King's Guard

In 1588, the King arranged for Fr James's nephew Huntly to marry Henrietta Stewart, eldest daughter of his erstwhile favourite Esmé Stewart. The Privy Council voted 5,000 merks to bring her over from France.[69] On 21 July, the wedding took place at Holyrood. The King gave her away and offered the couple the Abbey of Dumfermline as a wedding gift. The Bishop of St Andrews officiated at the ceremony but was later reprimanded by the Presbytery of Edinburgh for performing it before Huntly had fulfilled his promise to subscribe to the Presbyterian Confession.[70]

Huntly did so afterwards, but he also informed Parma that it was entirely against his wish. He was still considered 'the most persistent adherent of the old faith'.[71] The clergy did not like Huntly's continued close relationship with the King, especially as his marriage to Henrietta made him 'almost one of the royal family' and the young couple frequently stayed in the Palace of Holyroodhouse.

Huntly now urged the King to get rid of Maitland of Thirlestane and form a new administration, with himself at its head. The King resisted, standing by his Chancellor and saying that Maitland's brain was worth twice as much as Huntly's.

Frs Hay and Crichton were withdrawn for reasons of health and opposition to their work. The Jesuits were having no success in the towns, except perhaps Dumfries. However, many border chiefs were Catholic, such as Angus, Cassilis, Maxwell and Semple. The north was stronger under Huntly and Errol. Between one third and two thirds of all the nobility remained Catholic. The Privy Council complained to the King about Fr James's 'publick and privie reasoning in alluring, and perswadine, of his highness good subjects to decline from the truew religion'.[72]

On 15 October 1588, the Spanish Armada was defeated by the English fleet under Sir Francis Drake, helped by strong winds blowing the ships up the east coast of England and round the Scottish coast. Nineteen of them were wrecked off Scotland, and 500 off Fair Isle. The King was humane to the shipwrecked Spanish. He received the nephew of the Spanish admiral, Medina Sidonia, and other nobles. Two hundred Spaniards hired a ship in Fife, and forty-six were taken on Scottish ships going to France. Four hundred in all were given help to get home. Captain Semple took the opportunity to leave the Firth of Forth to speak to a Spanish captain on his ship; he was arrested on his return, but the King secured his release. He was then recaptured, but dramatically escaped. The King waited until the Armada had safely passed before rearresting him.[73]

In November, despite all the Kirk complaints about the King's close relationship with Huntly, he was made Captain of the Guard and placed in command of thirty-three foot soldiers and 300 horsemen. This demonstrates the trust in which Huntly was held. He and Henrietta resided at the Palace of Holyroodhouse all winter.[74] News arrived that the Duke of Guise and his brother, the Cardinal of Lorraine, had both been assassinated.[75] This meant that Scottish Catholics lost their most important supporters in France.

Despite this, however, they refused to accept the significance of the Armada's defeat, and clamoured for Spain to make another attempt. Even Mendoza was in favour of sending troops to Scotland and plots continued, fermented by papal emissaries and Spanish gold. Robert Bruce brought a letter to Huntly from Parma, in which he encouraged Scottish Catholics with the hope of a new invasion in the spring. Huntly was to communicate this to the others. Shortly after, 10,000 crowns were delivered by William Chisholm, Bishop of Dunblane, to Robert Bruce in Huntly's Dumfermline House, to disperse as he thought fit for the cause. Huntly said that one third should be for himself, one third for Claud Hamilton and one third for Lord Maxwell, although he was still in prison. Bruce said it was up to David Graham of Fintray to decide, although he was warded in Dundee at the time. In the end, Huntly did not get any of the funds, because he had subscribed to the Reformed faith 'at the King's desire'. Philip II does not seem to have been serious about the invasion, merely saying: 'I will have the Scottish matter you mention well considered.' Realistically, Spain had neither the mind, the means, nor the men, to help.[76] King James continued to play a double game, but was determined not to rely on Spain.[77]

The First Packet of Letters (24 January 1589)

The atmosphere became much more heated after a packet of letters bound for Spain was brought to the Privy Council when it was about to rise from a meeting. The packet had been intercepted and was accompanied by a letter from Queen Elizabeth. The letters inside it were to Philip II and were signed by Huntly, Claud Hamilton, Crawford and the Lords Maxwell and Errol. They expressed regret at the defeat of the Armada, and offered help if the Spanish made another attempt. A letter from Huntly to Parma excused himself from having submitted to the Kirk, and promised to try to make amends. There was one from Errol saying that, since his conversion to the Catholic faith, he did 'ever think of himself obliged to procure the advancement of the Catholic King's enterprises'.[78] Letters from Huntly and Crawford suggested sending two armies, one of them via Ireland to divide English forces. There were also letters from Robert Bruce to Parma and Spanish agents.

The accompanying letter from Queen Elizabeth passionately expressed astonishment that the King should 'countenance someone who was sending to a foreign king for forces to land in your land ... without your special direction – the same never punished, but rather hold fast, dear and near. Good Lord, methink I do but dream! No king a week would bear this.'[79] There was considerable consternation at the opening of the letters. Huntly and Errol were present, but the latter slipped away. Huntly offered himself for trial and committed himself to the castle. As he went up the High Street, accompanied by a friend, he seemed to linger, as if he thought better of it, or maybe to attempt an escape, but then continued forward.

The King consulted Maitland, the Chancellor, on what they should do. He visited Huntly daily for six days, he and Maitland dining with him on the last evening. The King protested that he knew Huntly was innocent and kissed him often.[80] Huntly was then transferred to Borthwick Castle for a short period of easy confinement.

As a result of these events, there was great excitement among the citizens. The General Assembly met in Edinburgh to discuss reports from every province and presbytery, especially in the north and south, that 'Poperies, superstition, bloodshed and all kinds of villanie' were abounding. The main subject was the enormous increase in Jesuit and Catholic activity in Scotland, correspondence with Spain, and preparation for a new Spanish invasion. A convention was planned to consider 'the threat to the true religion, and to devise methods of prevention'. Petitions were presented to the King for more rigorous laws against all Jesuits, and other private or public 'seducers of his Hieness' lieges'. The names of those in league with the Jesuits in places of trust within his own household were listed. Nearer to home, the petitions also asked for the removal of 'sinister suspicions' about the King's own 'sincerity in the truth'.[81]

Under pressure from Thirlestane, the King dismissed Huntly from his new post as Captain of the King's Guard. Frs Crichton and Hay advised the Catholic lords that they should attempt something on their own, to show Philip II that they were serious. They concocted a plot to get the King away from Thirlestane but also to make out that it was nothing to do with religion, but rather neglect of the nobility and bad management of public affairs, in order to attract more support. The unprincipled Francis Stewart, 5th Earl of Bothwell, nephew of Fr James's former brother-in-law, promised to join them, more from personal malice towards Queen Elizabeth than anything else. [82]

The Brig o' Dee Incident

On 14 March 1589, when the King and Huntly were out hunting near Edinburgh, they were joined by Lord Errol. Both men tried to persuade the King to go north with them, leaving Thirlestane and the Edinburgh people. He refused and returned to Edinburgh,[83] where he attended a banquet.

Huntly, Errol and Crawford went north to raise a standard of rebellion. Huntly gave out that he had a commission from the King to levy forces to march on Edinburgh. The plan was that Bothwell would surround Edinburgh and capture the King and, if necessary, kill Thirlestane, after which Huntly would march south to complete the revolution.[84]

However, the King mustered a large force 'for the suppression of a treasonable enterprise',[85] and marched north against Huntly. On the King's approach to Aberdeen, many of Huntly's followers abandoned the enterprise when they saw its true nature. He and his force melted away, fearing conflict with the King in person. This became known as the Brig o' Dee incident. The King entered Aberdeen in triumph. Huntly, Errol and Crawford then became fugitives. The King held a Privy Council meeting in Aberdeen and gave orders to crush the last relics of the insurrection. He continued pursuing Huntly to Strathbogie, which he threatened to demolish unless Huntly gave himself up, which he did unconditionally. He was taken to Edinburgh, and again held captive in Borthwick Castle. Bothwell and Crawford also surrendered. Huntly defended himself in front of three members of the council, explaining his conduct and motives. Meanwhile, the King continued on to Inverness and Cromarty, which he saw for the first time. Like his mother, he was in excellent humour and much enjoyed himself in northern parts. Gordons, Hays and Errol came to tender their submissions. Thus the conspiracy was defused and the Thirlestane government confirmed in power. The King's leniency was regretted by the Privy Council, but they were generally satisfied with the situation and cordial relations were resumed with England, as it was considered that the King had acted firmly.

Huntly was put on trial and on 24 May and was found guilty of a very large number of charges. These included 'practising with Jesuits, seminary priests and other strangers against religion; receiving of Spanish gold, and hiring soldiers therewith to disturb the quiet of the realm'; entering 'in bond and confederacy with the earls of Erroll, Montrose, and others, contrary to the laws . . . and treasonably [surprising] the town of Perth, of purpose to have fortified the same against his majesty'; conspiring 'to take the King prisoner at Halyrudhouse, and kill his servants and counsellors', especially Thirlestane; besieging 'the house of Kirkhill [and setting] fire to the same'; capturing the Treasurer, the Master of Glamis; proclaiming that the King was 'detained a prisoner against his will'; coming with banners 'to the Bridge of Dee, of mind to invade the King, whom they knew to be upon an expedition to the north parts'; and taking 'the King's herald at arms in Aberdeen, spoiling him of his coat and letters, when he was about to proclaim them'.[86] Surely all of this was treason enough?

Bothwell was charged with hiring Scots soldiers, as well as 'strangers', entertaining them at Dalkeith, and threatening to invade the town of Leith, while the King was in the north. Bothwell admitted hiring soldiers and making bonds with noblemen, but denied the rest. Huntly admitted it all and was found guilty of everything. He was committed to Edinburgh Castle, and his co-consiprators elsewhere. The King wrote Huntly a letter full of reproach, more in sorrow than anger, but reminding him of his submission to the Reformed faith and asked for a prodigal son-like confession, in acknowledgment of his fault. However, the clergy and others were disappointed that the rebels were not executed. An English informant wrote: 'The King hath a strange extraordinary affection to Huntly, as yet unremovable.' The King said that he also loved his Chancellor, Thirlestane, and tried to keep the two men as friends, 'but it never lasted more than forty days without some suspicion or jar'.[87] 'This reflected,' the informant said, 'the enmity between Thirlestane and the pro-Catholic contingent, especially Huntly.'[88]

In June, the King attended the General Assembly of the Church in Edinburgh, and assured it of his 'good affection' towards it. The assembly was grateful for the beginnings he had made in suppressing 'the enemies of religion', and entreated him to prosecute the business. However, they later complained again about the Bishop of St Andrews officiating at the marriage between Huntly and Henrietta Stewart. This angered the King so much that he released most of the rebels, including Crawford, and pardoned Errol. However, he deferred freeing Huntly and Bothwell, 'to keep them in awe', he said. Maxwell and others, who had offended the Kirk and government, had to sign a bond in their defence, pledging themselves to defend King and Kirk against all enemies and to pursue Jesuits. They had to pledge a bond of £100,000, guaranteeing their good behaviour in these respects.[89] The King supervised the signing of the pledges.

Huntly wrote about it to William Douglas, the 9th Earl of Angus, who had not been there. He dismissed it all as, 'a gawk's storm', meaning that the trouble they were in would be of short duration. He apologised to Parma immediately after the reconciliation and compromise with the King, and promised to work as before. He continued to correspond with Spain and Parma.[90]

In August 1589 the King, now aged twenty-three, married Anne of Denmark, who was aged almost fifteen, by proxy. She set off for Scotland, but her ship was driven back to Sweden by bad weather. The King went to Oslo to fetch her, taking Thirlestane with him. They did not return until the following spring. He left the country in the charge of Henrietta's brother, Ludovic Stewart, Duke of Lennox, with the erstwhile rebel, the released Bothwell, made second in charge. John Hamilton was in charge of the Borders. Robert Bruce, the eminent minister in Edinburgh, was also given charge 'for good order', with the help of his brethren. They took the opportunity of the King's absence to confirm and reissue all of the former acts against Jesuits and seminary priests, and reconstituted a large commission of lords and gentlemen to enforce the acts.

On 17 December Huntly was given a remission for all his crimes of May and the Brig o' Dee affair. He retired north to build himself a castle in Badenoch at Ruthven, close to his hunting forests. He, Argyll and Athol were commissioned to pursue the clan Gregor.[91] However, trouble arose because the Macintoshes resented this as as danger to themselves, and then a dispute arose between Huntly and the Grants of Ballindaloch Castle, which he captured, because he alleged outrages against himself. Athol and Moray, son-in-law of Regent Moray, now united against him and went to the aid of the Grants.[92]

While in Scandinavia, the King and Thirlestane had conferred on how to bring good governance to Scotland. Thirlestane had impressed on the King the need for stricter government to bring all ranks into orderly obedience to the law. As a result, they arrived back in Scotland with a new zeal for order and discipline. It would be a hard task, because so many nobles were used to independent power, jealous of the crown and at feud with one another. They decided that the 950 landed proprietors were to be listed and made responsible for the good behaviour of their tenants and adherents, in accordance with the pledged agreement of a General Band adopted in 1587. There were twenty-one sheriffdoms and other judiciary districts.[93] Thirlestane brought the King into friendly relations with the Kirk, ready to use courts and presbyteries for discipline and purposes of social order. There were also to be new acts against Jesuits and seminary priests.

The King had brought his young bride, Anne of Denmark, home to Scotland in May, where they had a Scots marriage by Lutheran rites. At her coronation, Anne was anointed by Robert Bruce despite the objections of the Kirk to such a popish ceremony. The King passed the crown to Thirlestane to place on her head. Lord John Hamilton gave her the sceptre and Angus the sword of state. Chancellor Maitland was now elevated to the peerage as Lord Thirlestane. Huntly's wife Henrietta, who had come from the Continent herself as a new bride, took the lonely young queen under her wing. She became one of Anne's ladies-in-waiting, and they spent a lot of time together.

On 28 May 1590 Fr James, his brother-in-law, the Earl of Sutherland, and his brothers Patrick of Auchindoun and Huntly, were summoned by the Privy Council to present themselves before the King and Council to answer charges. These were that, despite the act of July 1587 forbidding the mass, receiving Jesuits and seminary priests, and so forth, Fr James had continually remained in Scotland since then, 'occupied in public and privae reasoning, alluring and perswading of his highenes good subjects to decline from the true religion, mostly the said people and their friends and dependers'. They were to answer charges on 22 June.[94] This was all reported to Cecil, now Lord Burghley.

The King expressed confidence that Fr James would come on the appointed day so that he might receive the King's promise to depart without harm. He also believed that Huntly and his uncle, Patrick of Auchindoun, would obey him in all things. However, Huntly wanted recompense from the King because he had taken the Abbey of Dumfermline. This had been the King's wedding present to him and Henrietta. James now wanted to give it instead as a wedding gift to his new Queen.[95] On 21 June, the day before they were due to arrive before the Privy Council, Lady Auchindoun came, on the advice of Huntly's friends, to plead for her husband, as he was sick and unable to attend the following day. It was said that 'she returned home contented'.[96]

Fr James was brought secretly to see the King, and promised to depart quietly if that would bring the King's favour towards Huntly. Otherwise he would put himself in the King's hands, because he knew that he was the chief reason for disfavour shown towards Huntly.[97] Fr James told the King that Huntly had offered Dumfermline back to him and had promised to be loyal and obedient, and to make peace with Thirlestane. Huntly also sought permission for himself and his wife to leave the country if he could not obtain the King's favour. Thirlestane warned the King against trusting Huntly's promises, as he had broken them so often before.

Father James to Depart for Flanders

Fr James was now ready to depart, with the charge not to return. He made preparations to go to Flanders. Thirlestane remonstrated with the King about the necessity to be firm with the earls, saying that 'the best sort begin to fear over his great clemency'. The Privy Council passed a motion that Huntly, Bothwell, Crawford and Montrose be warded, and also required to give their assurance of obedience in the future. The new English ambassador, Bowes, wrote to Burghley reporting his doubts that this would be carried out, because of the influence they could command.

However, the King asked the Council whether he should receive those involved in the Brig o' Dee incident, who had answered for their actions at the time and had since agreed to be of good behaviour. Bowes reported to Burghley that Huntly was expected back at Court soon and that Fr James was at Leith, pretending to embark at the King's command, 'but hopes to find some favour to either remain secretly in the realm or depart shortly'. Meanwhile, Patrick of Auchindoun was at Lord Seton's house, hoping for a good outcome, his friends pleading for him in the chamber.

Bowes then reported that Huntly had permission to come to the King 'at his pleasure' but had not rushed to do so; and that Fr James had gone north on 4 July but that on 11 July the King 'still pretendeth that he shall be openlie embarked at Leith to pass out of this country to content the Church'. He also said that Auchindoun had delivered the band promising good behaviour to the King and had gained the King's remission for the Brig o' Dee incident.

The King revealed that Fr James had come to him at Dumfermline and that he had sent him to Burntisland, from where he was ready to be immediately shipped. However, Fr James was still in the country on 1 August. Apparently Huntly had wanted to speak to the King privately in a wood, but was not able to do so; it was surmised that he probably still wanted the King to return Dumfermline Abbey to him. One of the King's pro-English councillors urged the King to 'hold a good course with Huntly and his faction'.[98]

Bowes informed Thirlestane that Fr James and other Catholics had been seen in the Canongate but escaped capture. The King issued a warrant for James' apprehension. On 14 August Bowes reported that Fr James was to be presented to the Council and told to depart the realm. However, a month later, on 17 September, he was still at Burntisland, and even held a mass there.[99] Although Huntly was not now in office, he attempted to make peace with the Chancellor, as promised, and was expected to be received at Court. In contrast, David Graham, Earl of Fintray, was going to leave the country, also as promised.[100]

The King, the State and the Chancellor Fear They are in Danger

In October, Bowes reported that many of the nobility planned to winter in town and that the papists plotted to draw many secret friends, who favoured their plots, into the assembly. He stated that they wanted to overthrow the Chancellor and put someone in his place who was more favourable towards their plans. They were amassing money. They aimed to bring Huntly back to Court, and to let Fr James stay in Scotland. It was feared that there would be a sudden attempt on the Chancellor and the state. The King had been warned. Fr James was to leave Scotland immediately, Bowes reported. The King made excuses for past delays in relation to the papists which, he said, were due to particular councillors, who had prevented the execution of his commands. Thirlestane was resolved to find a solution because the King, the state and he himself were in danger. He hoped to trap the plotters.[101]

On 7 November, Bowes reported that Fr Edmund Hay was in Rome, getting money from a cardinal to bring over to Scotland in May the following year. He also said that papists were contributing money, which they hoped would eventually be repaid. They had even offered Thirlestane 10,000 crowns and a yearly pension if he agreed that Catholics could have freedom of conscience and an end to harassment. They assured him that they would not attempt anything against the Protestant religion, the King's person, the state, or the peace of the realm. They appealed for Catholics who were censured by the Church to have the issue overlooked and not be coerced into subscribing to the articles of the Presbyterian Church. They also requested that Fr James be permitted to remain in the country, at least for the winter. To the last request, Thirlestane replied that Fr James must either leave the country or put himself in custody in Edinburgh.

On 28 November, Bowes reported hearing intelligence that a barque had arrived in the north with 12,000 crowns on board for the papists. The money had been brought by two men, a Fleming and an Englishman, possibly Holt, who had recently been with Parma. They had met Fr James and three noblemen. Thirlestane was seeking their arrests, but could not find any truth in the reports. He promised that Fr James would be committed to ward at Seton and, later, a more secure place.[102] In December, Bowes reported that Fr James had come secretly to Aberdour in Fife, where the King was, but was advised to depart quickly. Lord Maxwell recommended to Huntly that he should 'quench his correspondence with the King of Spain, Parma and the Pope, which was ever bringing him trouble and endangering his life and possessions'.[103]

On 17 December Huntly gained a remission for all his crimes over the Brig o' Dee incident in May. Shortly afterwards there was a riot in Edinburgh, because the King was again raising Catholics to power. There was even a report that he had sent Frs James and Crichton to Pope Clement VIII with a request for funds and advice on restoring Catholicism to Scotland. Queen Elizabeth heard about this, but the King insisted that he knew nothing about it. He blamed his secretary, Balmerino, for having surreptitiously put the communication among his papers for signing. Balmerino admitted it and was disgraced, ruined and condemned to death, although the sentence was never carried out.

Meanwhile, Fr Abercrombie, who is noteworthy for the later conversion of Queen Anne, wrote graphically to the General of the Jesuit order about the difficulties they all faced in their endeavours. He said: 'We live in caves in secret and unfrequented places, perpetually moving from place to place, like gypsies, and we never lodge two nights in the same locality for fear of falling into the hands of the enemy.' Spies were posted everywhere, he said. They had to travel by night, by unfrequented paths, over wild and desolate hills. 'This is rather hard for me, since I completed my sixtieth year,' he complained. Abercrombie laboured for eighteen years in constant threat of arrest and banishment. Despite all these hardships, he survived until he was eighty-one, dying in East Prussia.[104]

The Irish were appealing for help from the islands and other parts of Scotland against the forces of Queen Elizabeth I in Ireland.[105] It was noticed that Fr James had been conferring with the Bishop of Derry, who was trying to raise 'the Spanish faction' amongst Scottish Catholics. On 13 January 1591, Bowes reported that there was an order in council to denounce Fr James. The King had agreed to be harder on the papists and seditioners, to remove the Masters of Angus and Fintray to stricter ward, and to imprison 'all other excommunicated and seditious persons', promising to 'hunt out Fr James and other Jesuits in this realm, so that they shall have little comfort to remain here'.[106]

The following month Bowes reported that, despite all his promises, the King continued to favour Huntly, allowing him him to return to Court. It was given out that Fr James was in Flanders, but he was actually still in Scotland under Huntly's protection, saying mass daily. 'The punishment threatened to the papists is likely to be easily passed over,' commented Bowes. However, Fr James and those with him were now publicly declared as rebels.

No doubt, though, Fr James eventually got to hear the sad news that his nephew, the Capuchin William Forbes, eldest son of his sister Margaret and the Master of Forbes, had died during evening compline at his convent in Ghent on 20 March 1591.

Despite being declared a rebel, Fr James must have remained in Scotland in August, because Huntly assured Bowes of his devotion to Queen Elizabeth and said that he would banish Fr James and would instead receive Protestant preachers. Nevertheless, in November Francis Stewart, Earl of Bothwell and High Admiral of Scotland, came over to the Catholic lobby, more interested in acting against his cousin the King, and Queen Elizabeth (because of Mary's execution), than from personal conviction.

Fr James encouraged Bothwell to make overtures to Spain. Fr Abercrombie wrote to Fr Crichton, who was in Spain, explaining their hopes that Bothwell would become a good Catholic, and would one day even be entertained by Philip II. On 27 December 1591 Bothwell, who had been denounced a rebel and declared an outlaw, mounted a night raid on Holyroodhouse, the result of which was the death of the Master Stabler, who was killed defending the King.

Meanwhile, a Leith dyer used by Fr James was described as 'a busy instrument for the papists and knew about their plots'. He had been caught, Bowes reported, and was likely to be executed, although the papists were trying to safeguard his life. Intelligence was increasing daily between England and Scotland, the dispatches expressing resentment that Huntly, Montrose and Maxwell were still holding sway.[107]

The Murder of the Earl of Moray (8 February 1592)

The 6th Earl of Huntly has gone down in history as the murderer of the 'bonny Earl of Moray', immortalised in the ballad of that name. This Moray, James Stewart, was the son of Sir James Stewart of Doune. He received the title at his marriage to the eldest daughter of Regent Moray and Agnes Keith. He continued his father-in-law's policies, aiming to extend his influence in the north-east at Huntly's expense. The King resolved to settle the resultant feud between them. They were both called to Edinburgh to submit to arbitration. The ballad says that the King sent Huntly to bring Moray to him, but 'forbade him to slay'. However, during the fray, Huntly set fire to Moray's house of Donibristle, on the north coast of the Firth of Forth, and when the inmates were forced to come out, Moray escaped and hid behind rocks on the foreshore, but he was seen because the tassel on his helmet was on fire. In the skirmish, he was killed by Huntly, after John Gordon of Buckie had slashed his handsome face.

The King seemed remarkably unconcerned, and went hunting. Rumour circulated that he had instigated the incident because he wanted Moray arrested for sheltering Bothwell, who was his bête noir. There was great indignation and anger amongst the people, which moved the King to action. He interviewed Huntly, and withdrew his Lieutenancy and Judiciary of the North. Huntly agreed to go into ward, or nominal imprisonment, in the gloomy Blackness Castle to await trial, after which he would be given his freedom – or so he understood.

Meanwhile, there was an outcry in Kirk sermons against Huntly for the murder of the bonny Earl. In the north, Argyll, Athol, the Grants and the Macintoshes made use of the opportunity to take revenge by ravaging Huntly's lands. Angus was appointed Lieutenant of the North to sort it out. According to *The Historie and Life of James the Sext* (1825), Thirlestane had stirred up trouble between Huntly and Moray in the hope they would destroy each other.[108] The King tried to bring the feud with the Gordons to an end by arranging for the new Earl of Moray's son, also James Stewart, to marry Huntly's eldest daughter, Anne Gordon.

A Flemish barque arrived in Montrose with Spanish gold in the hands of two Scotsmen and one Spaniard. From there, they rode post-haste to Aberdeen in order to make contact with Huntly and Fr James.[109] An association of nobility was formed against 'the traitors', who were named as not only Huntly, Errol, Father James and Patrick of Auchindoun, but also William Chisholm, Bishop of Dunblane, and Frs William Ogilvie and Abercrombie, as well as others, even including the new Lieutenant of the North, the Earl of Angus. Bowes reported that Fr James was not found, and that Spanish money could tempt some, but that most named had refused to accept it. Crawford confessed that he was tempted by the 3,000 crowns offered, but had refused them for himself and given them to his servants. Bowes went on to say that the Catholics had been pressed to take arms to change the government and break with England. However, in July he reported that Philip II was not keen on any involvement with such schemes that year, as he had too many commitments elsewhere, such as in France and the Low Countries. Nevertheless, Bowes warned: 'Parma sought to stir in all places and was much keener than previously.'

In June, after being forfeited by Parliament, the King's chief enemy, Bothwell, attacked Falkland Palace and nearly captured the King but was beaten off.[110] As a result of the need to quash a threatened alliance between Bothwell and the Presbyterians, who were angered by Moray's murder, the King agreed to what became known as the 'Golden Acts'. It was essentially Thirlestane's achievement, and was the first thorough legal establishment of the Presbyterian system in Scotland. By these acts, the Presbyterians regained some of the privileges they had lost.[111] However, the King feared the seditious influence of the ministers and would not give an inch more than he had to. He does seem to have believed that the Presbyterian system would be best for the good of Scotland, but under his overall control. Nevertheless, he did make a private list of the pros and cons of Spanish intervention at this time.

Bowes went on to say that the King sought more funds from Queen Elizabeth in order to 'avoid present dangers threatened to religion and estate'. He assured her that the King had remained on her side of late, and although some had tried to persuade him that she cared little for him or his standing, he refused to listen. However, Bowes said: 'I found the scar of some offence sticking and appearing in him.'[112]

The King used Bowes, with his very efficient spy network, to obtain information about whether Fr Crichton had come from Spain with gold and comfort for the Catholics. Bowes had told him that Fr McQuhirrie had landed in Montrose to 'negotiate' with Fr James, who Bowes had often said should be chased up.[113] Huntly now sought leave for himself and his three brothers to exile themselves. The King agreed, but others pleaded for him to remain in order to protect them. Fr Crichton now wrote from Spain to say that Bothwell would be welcome there.[114]

On 23 October, Bowes reported that the King had excused Huntly for the murder of Moray – because it was the result of a particular feud – but that he would not excuse him partaking in the mass, so he ordered the Presbyterian minister Mr Robert Bruce and others to go to him. Huntly, Bowes said, had broken his promises to the Kirk (for which the King was a cautioner) and also the oath made on his knees to the King. Bowes commented on his failure to persuade the King of the dangers involved, because he continued to believe Spain would not dare do anything if he had not agreed to it. However, he again ordered Fr James to depart within ten days, but few believed it would happen until they witnessed it themselves.[115]

Indeed, Fr James must still have been in the country on 11 November because Bowes reported that he and other Jesuits were working to bring Spanish forces and gold to Scotland, and that 'they depend much on a party in England'. Bowes said that the principal parties involved were not as far advanced in the enterprise as the Fathers wished, because the plots had been found out, but they did not want the Huntly and Gordon troubles to hinder their cause.[116]

Between 15 and 20 November 1592, there was a meeting of ministers to discuss the Kirk's difficulties, and also plans to set up a network for information to pass from the periphery to the centre and visa versa.

Ministers were instructed to inform their congregations of the cruelties resulting from the Council of Trent in other countries, which would be likely to happen to them also if the Catholics got the upper hand.[117]

Even while that meeting was in progress, Bowes was writing to Burleigh to say that Fr James and the other Jesuits had met and resolved to stay in Scotland. Fr James was planning to take a petition from them to the King and Council asking for liberty of conscience for Catholics if they swore loyalty and obedience. The many nobles supporting that petition resolved to be in Edinburgh at the end of the month. They were confident of success. Bowes added there were fears that the Catholics would attempt to establish their policy by slaughtering the Protestants, and that Thirlestane might be accused and taken away before the petition was presented.[118]

On 17 December Bowes reported that Huntly, Angus and Errol met together 'in such secret manner that some suspicion is concerned therein'.[119] A convention of brethren from all parts of the country was held in Edinburgh to prevent danger to the country and to plan their next move. They resolved to set up a fast, with prayers for the discovery of plots, and to concentrate people's minds on the consequences of the Council of Trent. These would include the 'fearful defection of a great many people of all estates to papistry and atheism through the actions of the Jesuits and others, and the general disorder in the country'.[120]

Every Presbytery was to inform 'the best affected gentlemen' among them of the practices of the enemies, and to be on their guard 'in readiness for the defence of religion'. They set up a network of informers about all papists and 'practicers against the religion'. They agreed that all decisions of the Council were to be carried out by the Presbyteries and reported back to the council; all proceedings between the King and the Kirk were to be noted; all packets of letters taken on ships were to be reported; that a sufficient number of the wisest of the noblemen, baronies and best affected to religion were to be appointed to the secret council and to reside in Edinburgh that winter; and that all papists and practisers against the religion were to be removed from his Majesty's company and be debarred from all public charge, commission, lieutenancies and public office.[121] Finally, a petition was sent to the King urging him to proclaim support for the Presbyterian religion, and to promise to defend it.

PART II: TRAFFICKING WITH SPAIN

The Spanish Blanks (December 1592)

The climax of the anti-Catholic ferment was the discovery of what became known as the 'Spanish Blanks'. At the end of December 1592, Andrew Knox, minister of Paisley, learned that a young Catholic gentleman named George Kerr was about to embark on a ship to Spain. Kerr was the brother of the Abbot of Newbattle, who was an emissary of the Catholic lords. It appeared that Kerr stood in for Sir James Chisholm, one of the Masters of the King's household, who was unable to go himself.[122] George Kerr had been excommunicated by the minister of Haddington – excommunication meant that a person would:

> in the presence of the whole people assembled in the Kirk, be given over by the ministers into the hands of Satan, as not worthy of Christian society and, therefore, made odious to all men, that they should avoid his company, refuse him all kinds of hospitality and the person, thus continuing in refusal by the space of a whole year, his goods would appertain to the King, so long as his disobedience lasts.[123]

As a result, Kerr considered that he could not live quietly within his native country, and so he decided instead to 'pass beyond the sea'.

However, Kerr's loose talk put him under suspicion, and he was afterwards known to be commissioned by 'sum Scotes noblemen by word and wryt to the King of Spain'.[124] He was traced to Glasgow and then to the island of Cumrie off the west coast. Andrew Knox came with twenty-four armed men and arrested George Kerr on a ship, finding him in possession of two great packets of letters bound for Spain. Among the letters were eight blank sheets of paper with eight wax seals of Scottish earls, including those of Huntly, Angus and Errol, and also Patrick of Auchindoun. The seals were interpreted as showing Philip II the earls' commitment. In other words, this was what Fr Crichton, who was still in Spain, had asked for. Also with Kerr were David Graham of Fintray and Barclay of Ladyland. All three were taken to the Tolbooth of Edinburgh.[125] Kerr said that the letters were so that he could introduce himself abroad, because he was destitute as a result of his excommunication, which had denied him rental income.

The news reached Edinburgh on a Sunday, so the excitement caused the ministers to cut short their sermons, 'as they were not accustomed to do'. Most of the letters looked quite innocuous. For example, there was a testimonial from Fr James about George Kerr, another from Fr Abercrombie, and letters from Fr James to two Spanish Jesuits, dated 20 November. There were two letters from Sir James Chisholm: one to his brother John, and one to George Kerr, dated 24 October. There were others from 'Christeson' (which was the alias of Fr James) and George Crawford (the alias of Fr William Crichton, who was in good standing in Spain). There was one in code from Fr James to Fr Crichton, which when deciphered revealed suspicious phrases such as references to bringing over 'your friends as soon as possible'; 'they would find much support'; 'we have delayed too long'; and:

> Next best is that you use all expedition against next summer. If you come, you will find more friends than ever you had; but next summer many are bound for other countries and will wait no longer for you. Send word to your friends that we may put them in good hope of you and they will tarry the longer . . . You have got all that you desired [presumed to relate to the signed blanks] therefore make haste.[126]

There was also: 'I would ye brought the rest of your friendis with you that are beyond the sea' (interpreted as the Spanish army or its allies), and 'your wife & children look to see you shortly' (interpreted as Catholics and their confederates).

Kerr was tortured and admitted to a conspiracy, though he later recanted. Bowes had asked to be present, but this was refused and he was later told the official version. Kerr had confessed to all he knew, which was:

> That upon a letter sent from Mr William Crichton the Jesuit, then residing in Spain, and assurance given of the king of Spain's aid for the alteration of religion in Scotland, Mr James Gordon and Mr Robert Abercrombie, Jesuits, had devised to send one to Spain, to certify the king of the concurrence of the Scottish catholics in his service, and that for the greater secrecy, the three forenamed earls should undertake for the rest, and by their letters testify the same.[127]

The three earls agreed that the blanks signified six letters from them to Philip II, and the others were for 'procurations, one for the messenger's credit, the other for the articles that should be drawn up in Spain'. The filling in of the blanks was trusted to Fr Crichton in Spain and to Fr Tyrie. Sir James Chisholm should have gone to Spain as well, but had been detained. Angus and Errol had also revealed to Kerr that the plan was for Philip II to send 30,000 men, with 15,000 to remain in Scotland and, with the help of Catholics, make sure that Catholicism became the official religion, or would at the very least be tolerated. The rest of the army was to invade England, being taken there by the Catholic lords, who would meet them at Kirkudbright or at the mouth of the Clyde.

Kerr signed the confession implicating the earls, but he later said that he had only confessed to implicating Fr James and that some letters were merely letters of credit to Philip II, the Pope and others. Another of the letters, he said, asked for a Spanish ambassador to come with money to relieve the Jesuits, to tempt the King to grant toleration, and to grant them a place where they could meet.

During this time, Huntly was in the north fighting the Macintoshes.[128] Meanwhile, there was high excitement amongst the ministers and the people. The King was out of town on a visit to the Earl of Mar and his young wife, the sister of Huntly's wife Henrietta. Before he came back, the ministers took precipitate action without his permission. They wrote to all of their main brethren, asking them to ensure that the noblemen, gentlemen, barons and burgesses were assembled in Edinburgh on 8 January, and if they were unable to come they should send a commissioner. They asked the lords of the Privy Council to inform the King of their actions. When he arrived in Edinburgh, he was told all, partly by Bowes and partly by Robert Bruce, principal minister of Edinburgh, that the 'cuntrie was in apperant daynger of spanyartis to be brought in by the earls, being papists, and both his crown to be in danger, and the established religion in hazard'.[129]

The King read the letters but appeared remarkably unconcerned. He refused to be dragooned into what he called 'major error'. During the first fortnight in January, he thought about how to exploit the situation. He seemed more concerned about the cessation of the full payment of Queen Elizabeth's gratuity, and how to capture Bothwell (who was in England), than the perceived dangers. Calderwood reported suspiciously that 'it appeareth the cheafe conspirators have the King's express or tacit consent, or at least have perceived him inclined that way, where upon they have presumed'.[130] It has also even been suggested that the whole scheme was the work of the Kirk, aimed at trapping the papists, and that the King was privy to the plot.

Queen Elizabeth sent Bowes to beg the King to renounce his clemency, for his own security and for the preservation of the Kirk. He was to declare the popish lords enemies of the public peace, and to confiscate their goods and make examples of them. David Graham of Fintray and Barclay of Ladyland were imprisoned in the Edinburgh Tolbooth with George Kerr, but the latter managed to escape.[131] The King wrote to Queen Elizabeth, seeming unconcerned and saying that he only required assurances of the lords' good behaviour in future. Elizabeth continued to call him a 'seduced king'.

Angus held that the blank letters were forged, but David Graham of Fintray admitted that Fr Abercrombie had revealed their purpose to him. This finally animated the King. He published his resolution to spare 'none that should be guilty of treason'. He asked his ministers' advice on the course to take. They said Parliament should call the subscribers of the blanks to attend. As they were not expected to agree, the King would then be compelled to pursue them by force of arms. However, the earls accepted and a proclamation was made for them to meet him on 20 February 1593 in Aberdeen.[132]

Angus and Errol had maintained that they were merely asking the Catholic princes for payment of the debts advanced to Jesuits such as Fr Crichton, and to urge them to fulfil their promises. Although Angus was warned by the King not to risk going to Edinburgh unless he wanted to be imprisoned, he arrived there on New Year's Eve, thinking that no one would dare to imprison him if the King wasn't there. He was duly arrested, however, and the council wanted to ward him, but he refused to co-operate, saying that he had been with the King and had been sent away 'with his favour and good countenance'. However, the angry populace managed to persuade him to go to the castle.[133]

Huntly utterly denied any dealings with foreign princes since the Brig o' Dee incident and offered himself for trial. He wrote to warn Fr James's Jesuit superiors that his uncle would be compelled to leave the country sooner than expected, for fear of the 'strictness of the laws', and because the ministers had blackened his name so much that he didn't dare to remain any longer.

The Privy Council, meeting at Holyroodhouse on 5 January 1593, complained to the King that the Jesuits had taken the opportunity to persuade sundry of his Highness's subjects to apostasy from that religion which they were well instructed and grounded in, and had seduced them to cast off their due obedience, which they owe to his Majesty, and to enter treasonable conspiracy for bringing in stranger Spaniards into this realm next spring, or sooner, to overthrow of his Highness and all professing the said true religion with him. This would result in the ruin of the ancient kingdom and slavery of the people, as had been shown in other places who had called on Spain for help.[134]

They agreed that proclamations should be made at the market cross at the main burghs and other appropriate places, to keep watch for the Jesuits and not to listen to 'their perswasionis, nor to entertain or help them, under pain of treason'. The Council informed the King that in his absence they had apprehended Angus on suspicion of treasonable conspiracy. The King thanked them for their good and acceptable service.

On 8 January the King was annoyed to see the great gathering called by the ministers without his knowledge, to which they responded 'that it was tyme to attend to warnings when thair religion, prince, countrey, thair lyves, lands and all was brought in jeopardy by sic treasonable delling'. At first, he concealed his irritation, and assured them that his intention was to remain with the true religion to the end of his life, and to resist all those who adopted a different course. 'Nevertheless,' it was reported, 'the Erle of Angus escaped out of the Castle of Edinburgh . . . which wrought a grait suspicion and miscontentment in the harts of all the guid subjects of the land towards the King.'[135] Goaded by the Kirk, he had those named denounced as rebels and put to the horn, but they were released the following month.[136]

On 13 January, Bowes reported that the King was expressing his usual complaints about Queen Elizabeth's failure to pay his gratuity, and the insufficiency of his funds. 'All exhortations are likely to be fruitless,' he reportedly said, 'until some satisfaction had been given him on a number of outstanding matters touching the receipt of his enemy Bothwell (who had taken refuge in England) and the payment of his pension'. The King was informed that unless he took strong action, English money would not be forthcoming. As a result he again removed Huntly from the Lieutenancy of the North and sent Argyll to see who had supported the Catholic earls in the north-east.[137]

Firmer action was promised on 17 January, when a proclamation was issued from Holyroodhouse announcing the King's intention 'to pass northwards for suppression of rebellion and conspiracy, with orders for musters to attend him in progress, and to bring thirty days worth of food'.[138] On 25 January, Huntly, his brother Patrick Gordon of Auchindoun, and Errol were ordered to appear at St Andrews on 5 February to answer 'upon their practising and trafficquing against the estate of the trew religioun'. Nevertheless, the King and council were careful to protect them by stipulating that they were not to be charged with any other action or crime while they were there, and they wouldn't be searched, warded or 'troubled in body or goods' for any other reason during the time specified.[139] Despite this assurance, Huntly and Errol failed to appear at St Andrews 'touching their treasonable practising with Jesuits and other excommunicated and trafficquing papists, and are to be denounced rebels.[140]

The King Proceeds North against the Earls

On 10 February 1593, the King set off north against Huntly, Errol and Angus and 'made his residence in Aberdene', though it was reported that this was only 'for appearance's sake'.[141] He was actually still much more interested in the capture of Bothwell than the Catholic earls. Huntly, with a few of his followers, went further north to Caithness, perhaps staying with his aunt Jean at Dunrobin on the way. Despite their husbands being denounced as rebels, the King granted the countesses of Huntly and Angus the keeping of their own 'special houses and rents, which pleased them'.[142]

Meanwhile, David Graham, Earl of Fintray, had written a long letter to the King. In this he took the bold step of admitting that he and the other earls had assumed the burden, along with other Catholics, of supplying a number of soldiers, as well as money for raising men in Scotland to invade England or stay in Scotland to reform religion and obtain liberty of conscience. The matter had been communicated to him, he said, by Fr James, Abercrombie and George Kerr. As a result of this admission, the King ordered his execution. Fintray appealed for the King's mercy, but the jury was told to proceed. The members of the jury found that they could not acquit him because of his written confession, so they referred the matter back to the King. The result was that on 16 February 1593 David

Graham of Fintray was executed, 'the unlucky single minor culprit'. The King, thus able to show Queen Elizabeth that he was taking action, asked for money to meet the threat of 'a dangerous conspiracy' but delayed doing anything further.[143]

The same day, there was a declaration by the King and council, once again protecting the rights of the earls, that no promises were to be made of lands, goods or rents of any person who had been denounced, or at any other time denounced to the horn, or otherwise taken and declared fugitive. Such measures were only to be dealt with by the King's officers. An exception was to be made in the case of John Cockburn of Ormiston, Justice Clerk, 'for his pains in the discovery of the said treasonable practices'.

The King's lords of northern Scotland were ordered to meet him in Aberdeen and to appear at the Aberdeen court on 28 February.[144] The Gordons said they dare not appear 'for daingar to thair lyves' and sought leave to stay at home, or else to be assured of their safety. The King conceded that the Gordons, not 'already at the horn', could remain at home, 'uncommanded to meet him'. On 26 February, Angus was denounced for failing to appear at the Aberdeen court. Jean's husband, the Earl of Sutherland, was again excused from appearing due to 'disease and inability'.

On 3 March cautions were issued to various Gordons and others, including Alexander Gordon of Beldorney (1,000 merks) and Walter Barclay of Drumdelgie (500 merks), ensuring their promise to 'do nothing to the hurt of his Majesty's government and the true religion', and not to take the part of Huntly, Angus, Errol, Patrick of Auchindoun, Sir James Chisholm, Frs James, William Ogilvie and Abercrombie, 'or other Jesuits, seminary priests or trafficking papists and, when required, shall assist in persuite of thame with all rigour and extremites, to thair utter powers, and shall appear before the King and Council, when charged with seven days warning'.

By mid-March the King was giving the distinct impression that he intended to take action but also leaving Queen Elizabeth's special ambassador, Lord Burgh, with the sense that action would not be forthcoming, except at the price of substantial subsidy from England. Bowes got the same idea from members of the Council. However, the Queen would not 'be drawn' over the money, because her representatives were cynical about James's 'pretended severity'.[145] The case was deferred until 15 May.[146]

Relaxed from the Horn

This cynicism was obviously well merited, because on 16 March the King ordered letters to be issued relaxing the following from the horn: Huntly, Angus and Errol; Patrick Gordon of Auchindoun; Frs James, Abercrombie, Crichton, Tyrie and McQuhirrie; and a long list of others 'for any cause bygone and to receive them to the King's peace'. However, they were summoned to appear before Parliament on 2 June.[147] The Countess of Huntly then came to Court with a great train of ladies. Queen Elizabeth was annoyed to hear that she was honourably entertained and, what was more, 'shown tender affection' by the King. The King sent Sir Robert Melville to England to pacify the Queen, and told the Countess to stay away from Court until further notice. Elizabeth was still not satisfied. She sent her new ambassador, Baron Zouch, to insist that the popish lords be brought to judgement or an army be sent against them.

On 3 April the King's nemesis, Bothwell, raided Leith then fled north to seek refuge from Huntly, claiming kinship through his uncle's marriage to Huntly's aunt, Jean Gordon. Motivated at least on this score, the King decided to muster a force to pursue him. In May, the King expressed anger when someone compared Huntly to Bothwell in terms of their wickedness.[148] In June, the King's financial demands of England became more explicit: he asked for funds to support 600 armed men for six months.[149]

On 24 July Bothwell, who was now to be tried for witchcraft, again attacked Holyroodhouse. He insinuated himself into the palace and successfully seized the King, taking him into what he called 'protective custody' until after his trial. He had now become the self-constituted champion of the Presbyterian clergy, who called him a 'sanctified plague', chastising the King for his leniency towards the Catholic earls.[150]

In August Alexander Ogilvie of Boyne, Jean's first love (whom she later married), was called to assist in pursuing the rebels.[151] That same month Bothwell was acquitted of witchcraft, because the only evidence against him was the testimony of a proven liar. Bothwell then told the King that he would remain under the 'protection' of himself and his associates until they were relaxed from the horn and restored to their lands and offices, and also until Moray's murderers were punished. He said that not only those who had wielded the weapons in that murder but also those who subscribed to the warrant should hang, and that all of their identities were known. They included Thirlestane and Sir Robert Melville. Much to the King's fury, Bothwell made unsubtle insinuations that he, the King, was behind the murder. James consented to pardon them, but resisted the pressure to appoint him and Athol as Lieutenants of the South and North, respectively. This would have enabled them to pursue Huntly.

Huntly was still supreme in the north, having successfully seen off the Mackenzies and Grants. The King agreed to meet him secretly at Falkland Palace, much to England's despair that he was still so 'addict and inclined' to Huntly and his papist faction. The King needed reliable supporters against Bothwell, and the Catholic earls were the most trustworthy and eager. However, he was soon strong enough to free himself from Bothwell and his associates without their help.

Meanwhile, in August 1593, Fr James was doubtless pleased to hear that his nephew John Forbes, only surviving son of his sister Margaret and the Master of Forbes, had been accepted as a novice in the Capuchin monastery at Tournai.

When the King was heading south to quell troubles at the border, the Catholic lords saw their chance and intercepted him at Fala Moor in Midlothian, where they 'threw themselves at his feet, entreating pardon, protesting their innocence of the Spanish Blanks, or of any conspiracy to bring in foreign forces, and asserting their fidelity to their creed'. They claimed to be both good Catholics and loyal subjects. They petitioned the King for a speedy trial, because they were confident of clearing their names and regaining their positions.[152] The King was fearful of anyone thinking that the meeting had been pre-arranged. With the advice of his attendant councillors, he made arrangements that the lords should stand trial at the Convention of Estates in Perth in order to clear themselves, and to agree to remain there until tried. They considered this a triumph and 'left rejoicing'.[153]

This decision caused great excitement at a meeting in Edinburgh of the 'zealous lairds, clergy and commissioners of burghs', who then sent a deputation to the King at Jedburgh asking for the trial to be a real one, not a pretence, and to delay it for a while. They also asked that he prevent the earls mustering a large gathering of friends, that they be held in a proper prison, and that the jury should not be packed with their supporters. The King was 'greatly incensed' at the unauthorised meeting in Edinburgh, and showed his feelings by issuing 'sharp words to the deputation'. He told them that he would reply in writing. He decided on a trial organised legally and properly by a Convention of Estates at Linlithgow. The clergy, lairds and commissioners of burghs agreed, but again insisted on armed enforcement of justice, and that the King shouldn't allow the earls to summon their friends and supporters. Orders were issued to stop an armed gathering there, as the Catholic lords were assembling their forces at Perth, alarming the clergy and lieges by intimating that they would be content with nothing short of 'toleration of religion'.[154] The ministers refused to agree to the lords' request to have a trial in Perth, but agreed on Linlithgow as a compromise.

However, despite everything, the King still did not take the accusations of treason seriously and temporarily shelved the project.[155] In an undated letter to Huntly, he conceded 'seeing what you did, ye did it not without my allowance', and gave him advice via a messenger about 'your proceedings'.[156] Is it possible that the Spanish Blanks were merely a ploy to force Elizabeth to increase her annuity?

The Act of Abolition

Thirlestane suggested that the best way out of the impasse was to introduce an act, drafted by himself, Henrietta's brother, the Earl of Lennox and Mar, by which terms would be offered the earls that they must either accept or, if they wouldn't, go into exile. This caused fury, especially in the Kirk, as 'everyone knew that it was collusive'.[157] On 26 November the terms were published and referred to as an 'Act of Abolition'. Everyone was either to agree to embrace the 'trew religion' by 1 February 1594 or go into exile. Thus by professing belief – or, at least, recanting – they would be making their peace with the King and Kirk. Forgiveness would be on condition that they did not repeat their offences. They could then retain their property. A concession, believed to have been added by the King, much to the fury of the Kirk, was that in the meantime, the earls and their heirs could keep hold of their lands and livings. Once agreements had been made to the terms, there would then be no prosecutions in the affair of the Spanish Blanks, as long as no pledges had been sent out of the kingdom.

There were stipulations in the Act. Huntly and Errol must expel their Jesuit friends and relatives, and keep them out of the realm. They must also be answerable for all their men, tenants and servants who were accused of popery. What is more, if they accepted the terms and stayed in the country, they must take a minister as a house guest, 'to resolve them of their doubts', and the earls were to pay £40,000, and the knights £10,000 each, as surety for their continued good behaviour. They were given until 1 January 1594 to inform the government of their choice. This was all to be ratified by the next parliament, but 'his Majesty and the Commissioners think it the best way forward'.[158] Bothwell, on the other hand, was to be exiled without hope of redemption, and his friends hunted down and imprisoned. Queen Elizabeth and the Kirk loudly condemned the arrangements for the Catholic earls, saying that the 'seduced king corrected miscreants with benefits'.

However, despite this, no answer had been received from the earls by January 1594. On 18 January the Act of Abolition was officially withdrawn, and it was declared that the earls had wilfully deprived themselves of the act's benefits. They countered that they had rejected it because they could not find the vast sums required to guarantee their good behaviour.

Aftermath of the Earls' Rejection of the Act of Abolition

Events began to move quickly. There was a Privy Council meeting at Holyroodhouse, where the earls were declared to have acted contemptuously when they disdained to accept the act. Therefore, the King, on the advice of the Council and Estates, declared that they had forfeited all benefit and favour granted to them by the edict, and that they would be pursued for the crimes contained in the summons raised against them, just as if the edict had never been passed.[159] This put a stop to the clergy's passionate denunciation of the Act of Abolition.

On 26 January 1594, the Privy Council told Huntly, Angus, Errol and Patrick Gordon of Auchindoun to ward themselves in different castles. For Huntly, it was to be the stronghold of Dumbarton. On 19 February the country was distracted by the joyful news that a son and heir, to be named Prince Henry, had been born to Queen Anne; but on 8 March, the earls had still not warded themselves, and therefore had 'not only shown contempt to his Majesty and his authority but also, plainly, accepted the crimes of treason'. They were thus to be pursued as traitors, and the process of forfeiture to be laid against them.

On 3 April 1594, Bothwell made another attempt to seize the King. He rode with 600 men to Leith in the hope of meeting up with Athol and Argyll, and crossing the Firth of Forth with the northern troops. The King raised his own force to march again Bothwell, and forced his rapid retreat to Kelso. Bothwell disbanded his troops and again took refuge in England. In St Giles' Kirk, the King announced that if he had victory over Bothwell, he would never rest until he 'passed upon Huntly and the other excommunicated lords'. He was now resolved to move against those who were so ungrateful as to spurn his compromise in the Act of Abolition.[160]

On 30 May 1594, the Catholic lords were officially declared traitors, forfeited and stripped of their estates. Henrietta, Countess of Huntly, was dismissed from Court. Even then, rumours circulated that the King had dispatched Home to borrow £2,000–£3,000 sterling from Huntly. Huntly, Errol and Angus communicated with the King, offering to leave the realm under royal warrant, provided their wives and children were left in possession of their properties, with no reprisal against friends and followers. The King wrote back more in sorrow than anger, saying that he 'had many times and with great care sought to preserve you from ruin', and 'greatly hazarded himself, his life, estate and honour: whereof Huntly had no regard, but always abused him with fair words and pretences'. He told Huntly flatly that he 'could not condition or capitulate with him in any sort, but would prosecute him and Bothwell by all means in his power'; with this, he dismissed his messenger, 'much discontented'.[161] Clearly, he is saddened, exasperated and ready for action.

Landing in Aberdeen with Gold from the Pope

On 9 April the King resolved, on the advice of the Council, to go north in person to ensure the repression of 'the chief authors of treasonable conspiracies'. There would be proclamations made for men to meet the King at Dundee on 29 April, coming well armed and with thirty days' food. However, a month later, pressure from the ministers forced the King to bring the matter of the popish lords to Parliament, where a debate was held. The ministers wanted the earls to be declared enemies of the public, their houses demolished and their estates forfeited. Very few noblemen were present. Various individuals were brought to the Tolbooth 'for the crime of hearing mass' and had to pay fines: John Gordon of Newton, for example, had to pay £1,000 for having his children baptised by Jesuits.[162]

Frs James and Crichton, meanwhile, had been busy seeking help for the earls on the Continent. On 16 July 1594 they landed at Aberdeen along with the papal legate, George Sampiretti, carrying large sums of money in gold (10,000 crowns) intended for the earls, who could use it to raise solders to defend them selves.[163] Fr James also brought a letter from the Pope offering a monthly allowance to the King if he would guarantee freedom and protection to Catholics, and would permit them to 'remain unmolested in the exercise of their faith'.[164] The papal legate, money and letters were seized, but Fr James, as usual, was able to slip away.

Errol and Angus, joined three days later by Huntly, went with a force to Aberdeen and threatened to set fire to the town unless those who had come with Fr James were released, and the gold turned over to themselves.[165]

The Kirk urged precipitate action, suspecting the King of prevarication. On 25 July, Archibald Campbell, the eighteen-year-old 7th Earl of Argyll, was proclaimed the King's new Lieutenant in the North, and the Earl of Athol his Justicia of the North. Both of them were Huntly's most determined enemies, and they were given powers to act against the rebels. Athol and Lord Forbes were given powers to repress Jesuits and 'traitors'. All of these moves would, of course, seriously jeopardise Huntly's position in the area. Those appointed disliked their new positions, and Bowes reported that they were likely to refuse, which Argyll did, but the clergy persuaded him to accept.[166] The King appealed to the clergy for the utmost activity against Jesuits and other enemies of 'the true religion', on the grounds that they had brought money and strangers in pursuit of war against the Kirk. The Kerrs were all told to enter ward at Dumbarton.

In August 1594 Lord Forbes died and was succeeded by John, Master of Forbes as the 8th Lord Forbes. That same month his heir, also John (Fr James' nephew), took his solemn vows as a Capuchin in the Low Countries. Perhaps Fr James was among the Scottish Catholics who tracked him down, and tried to persuade him that his duty lay in returning to Scotland, as the new Master of Forbes, to further the Catholic cause. The professors at his college of Douai agreed, but John refused, saying he would retire to a secret spot to pursue the contemplative life. He was sent to another monastery in Bruges to study philosophy and theology. He was then transferred to Lille, as there was a risk that he might be kidnapped. His mother Margaret joined him there, and later they both went to Antwerp.

King and Kirk now made common cause against the three Catholic earls and Queen Elizabeth, at last, sent the King a large sum of money 'not of her liberality, but his proper revenues from his own inheritance in England due'.[167] This was, of course, a promising development for him.

However, on 25 September 1594 the Provincial Assembly in St Andrews was again informed of 'the bissines and dangerus delling of the papist Erles and Lords, throw impunitie and oversight of the Prince'. They were annoyed that the lords had been to the King and spoken to him before the Assembly. They all agreed to the excommunication, of 'certean of the cheiff of them', including Huntly, Angus, Errol, Patrick of Auchindoun, Sir James Chisholm and Lord Home.[168]

The Provincial Assembly asked that a meeting of commissioners appointed from among themselves be held in Edinburgh in October to prosecute the matter. Most refused to act as messengers to the King to inform him of their decisions and requests, but eventually James Melville, who was acting as Moderator for a time, agreed to go, accompanied by two barons, two burgesses and one other. However, when they did so, the King railed against the Assembly. James Melville, answering for them all, appeased him. However, the King then turned on the two barons and burgesses and complained about the convention in Edinburgh. They countered that all their efforts were for the 'preventing of imminent evill and danger to his Stat, Relligion and Countrey'.[169]

They waited in fear for his answer next morning. His eventual response was that when he returned from the Borders, he would personally hold a convention in Linlithgow, where he would deal with the matters they brought up. However, the ministers complained that the lords were 'making grait preparation of armes and amassing thair friends to repair to the King and . . . be about his persone'.[170] They were all told to return home and inform the barons and boroughs of the King's answer, and that the commissioners should be ready to go to Edinburgh a few days before the meeting to receive instructions. As the Catholic earls had disobeyed the summons to place themselves in ward, they were condemned by Parliament, attainted and outlawed.

The Battle of Glenlivet (13 October 1594)

The King called a Council meeting which voted that Huntly's enemies – Argyll, who had been made Lieutenant of the North; Athol, Justiciar of the North; and the Forbeses – should raise an army and pursue him. Various Gordons (such as Alexander Gordon of Beldorney) and others, including the Barclays, Leslies and Alexander Ogilvie of Boyne, were charged to appear before the King and council. A few days later, it was agreed that the lands of the Catholic earls were to be awarded in feu to 'kindly tenants'.[171] The Aberdeen provost, baillies and council now proclaimed 'non-complicity with Huntly, Angus and Errol, and other traitors'. They promised to actively pursue them at the horn and make them fugitives from the law for the murder of Moray and the burning of his Donibristle house two years earlier, in 1592.[172] It was even declared that those who wilfully heard mass would be put to death, and that papists who refused to satisfy presbyteries would be summoned before the Council.

The King said that after the christening of his baby son, Prince Henry, he would join his force in the north. Argyll, head of the most powerful clan in Scotland and a personal rival of Huntly, was commissioned to lead the expedition. The King was not really in favour of this, fearing the Highlander's usual insolvency, but he had to yield to the ministers, and especially to the influential Mr Robert Bruce, who gave Argyll money and promised him that he would have some of Huntly's estates for himself and his heirs.

Argyll summoned musketeers, spearmen and archers under Lachlan MacLean of Duart, an eminent chief and experienced fighter. Angus MacDonald promised 500 bowmen. The King called various clans, those most envious of Huntly, to take part, such as the Macintoshes, Grants and Mackenzies. Argyll headed for Inverness to await the King. The English ambassador reckoned that Argyll had about 8,000 foot, but no artillery and very few horse.[173] He hoped to recruit some when Lord Forbes, who would be eager to avenge past Gordon 'outrages', joined them. The only reason given for the muster was Huntly's 'obstinacy in the Popish religion'. Proclamations were made all over the country but were ignored by all except the Forbeses, and the Baron of Drum along with his Irvines. However, a quarrel arose when one of the Irvines was shot in the dark, so they departed. Some thought that bloodshed was no way to enforce conversion.[174]

Huntly made commendable efforts to avoid the unnecessary spilling of innocent blood, sending Cameron of Lochiel to plead for peace in order to 'to spare the spoil and slaughter of poor tenants'. He argued that the King could adjudicate between them. Argyll would not be placated, and interpreted this disinclination to fight as a sign of weakness.[175]

As winter approached, Robert Bruce urged haste. Four thousand men set off on 21 September 1594 and were joined by the clans Grant, Chattan and Tillibarton, the Macleans of Mull, and the young Earl of Moray. The first encounter was at Huntly's castle of Ruthven, in Badenoch, which was strongly fortified and well garrisoned. When Huntly returned to Strathbogie, the Forbeses and Lesleys were forced to remain at home in order to disguise their intentions from their feudal overlord.

Errol, Huntly's brother-in-law, rushed to help with six score of horsemen, first going to his own house at Turriff for provisions. Huntly had no word of Argyll's whereabouts, so he sent Patrick of Auchindoun on a reconnaissance. Within two days, he heard that Argyll had besieged Ruthven Castle, but that the siege had been unsuccessful.

On 1 October, Fr James led his fellow Jesuits to accompany Errol and Huntly,[176] marching their men from Strathbogie to Cairnborrow, where they set up camp. In the glow of the cooking fires, 'each earl drew his sword, and swore a solemn oath to the other, that it should not be sheathed till the enemy was vanquished, or he died in the attempt'.[177] It seems likely that Fr James conducted the mass celebrated there. They then marched to Auchindoun but had to leave two cannons behind because of the difficulty of the terrain. An eyewitness reported that, next morning, 'the Catholics in the army went into the castle of Auchindoun to celebrate mass, after which each person's arms were blessed and consecrated, as were the standards of the noblemen'.[178] They were joined by old Gordon of Cairnborrow who, even though he had been told to stay at home, was determined to accompany his eight sons. The Gordon force now consisted of 1,000 men, all on horseback, 'with no men of the meaner sort'.

Argyll marched towards Strathbogie at the head of 6,000 men, with instructions to 'ravage the Gordon country with fire and sword'.[179] However, the King had surreptitiously sent word to Huntly, forewarning him. Huntly was an experienced commander, as was Patrick of Auchindoun, who was described as a man of 'singular courage'.[180] They were determined to engage the enemy before they were reinforced.

Although in Argyll's troop, Cameron of Lochiel was in secret communication with Huntly. John Grant of Gartinbeg was called to join Argyll, but he was a faithful vassal of Huntly and came in the night to ask him what he could do to help. He was instructed to take up a place with his 500 archers on Argyll's left wing. Bothwell, who had been expelled by Queen Elizabeth, undertook to create a diversion in the south on Huntly's behalf and, if possible, seize the King and young prince.[181] Thomas Kerr, a veteran of Flanders, was sent to spy out the enemy. He returned to say that they were four miles further on, marching in battle order near the Glenrinnes border. Huntly's force divided in two. The vanguard was led by Errol, described as 'a nobleman of great prudence and courage', with his friends and followers, and about 400 of the best horsemen. Huntly was in the main battle formation. Patrick of Auchindoun was in command of the rear. Huntly and Errol swore on their drawn swords not to leave one another, or the battle, until victory was won.

They marched six miles, 'but with much ado, by reason of the ruggedness of the way and the steepness of the hills',[182] which impeded the carriage of the cannon. Errol got about a mile ahead, so Huntly sent a message to say that if Errol did not wait for him he would leave the cannon and look for the first occasion to fight without his troops. However, they were still uncertain of the enemy's location. Patrick of Auchindoun and Captain Thomas Kerr returned and reported that Argyll and his army were at the Castle of Drumin in Strathavon, attempting to meet up with the Forbes and Lesley horsemen but, due to thick fog, they were unsure which way to go. They were attempting to advance, with great difficulty, up the side of a mossy, rocky hill.

Huntly had decided that they should move to lower country to cut off the Forbeses, when they saw the van of Argyll's men coming over the top of the same hill. Argyll descended to the crown of the lower hills. He had divided his force into three, with the vanguard of about 3,000 islanders, led by MacLean of Duart. Two thousand were hagbutters,[183] a third of them made up of bowmen and swordsmen, with darts and targets. The last were mostly protected with coats of mail reaching to their knees. The Bishop of Argyll and two ministers, including Andrew Melville, were with them. Argyll was in the rear.

The Catholic earls decided to fight before Argyll discovered how small their army was, being between a quarter and a third of the royal army. They saw Argyll's main force approaching, having at first mistaken it for a wood. Huntly spoke to his men, urging them to remember 'their quality, as being all well born gentlemen' and that they should consider 'the weakness of their enemy, howsoever more in number, yet naturally such as knew no order, nor could hearken to any discipline, and mostly ill armed, so open to wounds, all on foot, so easily broken and over run by horses; [and that] they should fight for their estates and posterity. Finally, they should keep in mind 'that it was God's cause, for religion was their quarrel, wherein God would not fail to protect them'. The call to charge was 'Virgin Mary'.[184] The field of battle was a little hill, not steep but full of stones and covered over with heather. On the south side was a rocky precipice and below it, at the bottom of the hill, a little winding burn.

Fr James' brother-in-law John, Lord Forbes, now arrived and was second-in-command of Argyll's force. Argyll steyed on the gentler slope, the south side of which was secured by the precipice. Huntly was on the exposed lower ground to the north-west. Errol made the first advance. Some of Argyll's forces were protected by a wall of rock. Errol covered considerable ground and got to the end of the rocky wall, followed by his men. The enemy fired small shot, but Errol and his men kept their ground. Huntly ordered his two cannon to fire, aiming at Argyll's yellow standard and hitting the standard bearer and the front ranks of his Highlanders.[185] Errol and his men charged on foot, beating the enemy down with spears and 'made a great slaughter'. However, Errol was badly wounded by an arrow in his arm and left foot, and lost his pennon[186] to Maclean of Duart.

Patrick Gordon of Auchindoun and his men galloped boldly straight up the hill towards MacLean of Duart, who held him off from the superior position he occupied. An eyewitness attributed Auchindoun's suicidal gallop to an unmanageable horse, which ran off with its rider into the midst of the enemy. He and his men got bogged down in the mossy ground, and were subjected to a blistering fire. He was unhorsed by a shot and dirked to death by the Highlanders. They severed his head and displayed it in taunting triumph.

With this tragic loss, the remnants of Errol's horse wheeled back, to join the main body of Huntly's army. There was then a pause, while both sides regrouped. Fighting resumed in the afternoon, the Highlanders still having the tactical advantages of terrain, sun, and a following wind.

MacLean of Duart asked Argyll for 500 men, to attempt to capture Huntly. He tried to encircle Huntly's vanguard, using a pincer movement to trap the troops between his own men and Argyll's. During this manoeuvre, Gordon of Gight was badly wounded by three bullets. The situation was becoming desperate for Huntly's force.

However, the elements came to their rescue. The wind changed direction, blowing a smog of gunsmoke into the eyes of Argyll's men, and cloud obscured the low October sun. Seizing the opportunity, Huntly galloped ahead of his men into the close columns of the enemy and, singling out the most prominent opponent, struck him with the last thrust of his spear before coming under direct attack from a powerful blow at his side. However, he managed to parry this with his broadsword, leaving a deep cut in the blade, before it struck the protective plates in his boot. His horse was shot from under him and he was only saved from the same fate as his uncle Patrick by Gordon of Innermarky, who managed to extract and reseat him on his horse.

Unable to see because of the gunsmoke blown into their eyes, the ranks of Argyll's infantry aimed their arrows into the air and fired volley after volley, which mostly landed harmlessly behind Huntly's force. John Grant of Gartinbeg now fulfilled his promise to Huntly, attacking his erstwhile ally by sending flights of arrows into Argyll's ranks, thus adding confusion to the carnage. Argyll's main force broke and fled, casting aside their weapons, shields and plaids, being driven by the Gordons down the far side of the hill. They died in droves as they were cut down in their flight. MacLean of Duart made a last dash through to Huntly's standard, embedded the spike end of his axe in the mount, sliced the bearer of the standard in two, and made off with the trophy.

However, Moray of Tullibardine seized the bridle of Argyll's horse and forced him off the field, leading Argyll away in tears as he still implored his men to stand and fight. Sir Robert Fraser, bearing the royal standard as the Lyon Herald of Scotland, was not so fortunate. He stood out conspicuously, dressed in his tabard with its emblazoned red lion, the emblem of his office and his safeguard. With a shout of 'Have at the Lion', a contingent of Gordon horse surrounded him and speared him to death on the spot. The royal ensign he bore was later taken with other spoils to Huntly Castle and placed triumphantly on the top of the great tower.

Thus, the King's force was defeated, but it was a pyrrhic victory for the Gordons, because they had suffered the loss of Patrick Gordon of Auchindoun and 'uther diverse gentlemen of his ken, their horses all spoiled, and a great number of the best heavily wounded'.[187] Nevertheless, the Gordons knelt down on the hillside and sang a triumphant *Te Deum* in gratitude for their victory, their voices echoing through the glen and their solemn chant soaring over a field strewn with the dying and the dead, whom they then buried on the spot.[188] It was said that the King was not displeased at Argyll's defeat.[189] A few days after the battle, Lennox, Huntly's brother-in-law, brought the earls a secret remission from the King.

The King Comes North

However, the King still felt that he was under pressure from Queen Elizabeth – especially through her continued manipulation of subsidies – to align himself with the Protestant rather than the Catholic interest. He was persuaded to go in person to pursue the rebels, and so headed north with a fresh force – a paid army gathered by proclamation. However, a letter Huntly wrote to the Earl of Angus showed that he did not take the King's advance seriously.

The letter came into the King's hands, so he resolved to teach Huntly a lesson.[190] His army included the hardliner Andrew Melville and his nephew James Melville the diarist, whom the King brought with him to witness his firm reaction, 'because the people were jealous of his perceived favouritism towards Huntly'.[191] The King held a council meeting in Aberdeen, where bad weather kept him for almost a month. It was commonly believed that the King only pretended to go after the earls and that he would not really demolish their houses but would have them taken over by the crown instead and put in the charge of his own officers.[192] However, at the end of October, an act was passed for the demolition of Huntly Castle.

Because the King had to pay his soldiers for a second month, he sent James Melville to Edinburgh to ask 'the well affected of all ranks' to send funds. He also gave him instructions to inform Ambassador Bowes, and to assure all the brethren of the ministry in Edinburgh, that 'the rebels were fugitives; their principal houses said to be demolished; . . . [and] there was utter indignation against them'. However, James Melville commented that: 'I was not more than two days on my journey when I was told that no more was done but a viewing of the places and returning again.'

At Strathbogie, the King had 'swithered between razing or garrisoning the castle'.[193] However, he yielded to Argyll, Lord Lindsay and, in particular, the irascible Andrew Melville, who all 'pressed hard for the destruction of this soaring symbol of Huntly's pride'.[194] Master William Shaw, the King's Master of Works, was in charge. Reports said that on 29 October 1594, 'it was cast down and made equal with the ground . . . and all men were made free to the spoyle thereof'. However, we are told that the King, 'struck by the beauty of the place, was unwilling to visit it with the drastic fate of the ruder Errol fortalice'.[195] This, the castle of Slains, was burnt and completely demolished, and Newton and Abergeldy were razed to the ground.[196] But, in fact, damage to Huntly's main house was limited.[197] It was only the original great tower that was dismantled, defaced and blown up with gunpowder. It was said that it took two days to destroy what had taken fourteen years to build. Taken and fortified were the strongholds of Bog of Gight, Ruthven in Badenoch, Glenbucket, the Craig of Auchindoun, Haddo, Cluny, Cairnborrow, Inverness, Spynie, Craneston, Muiresk,

Gartully and Turriff.[198] The Gordons who had taken part in the battle of Glenlivet were ordered to appear and promise good behaviour.[199]

On 14 November, the King disbanded the army and returned to Stirling. Henrietta, Countess of Huntly, continued to have access to the King as much as she pleased, and she made the utmost effort to obtain her husband's pardon. He agreed to offer Huntly full pardon if he would hand over Bothwell, but Huntly cited the obligations of kinship and demurred long enough for Bothwell to escape. He escaped abroad and ended his life in Naples.[200]

Thanksgiving at Elgin Cathedral

Meanwhile, Huntly and Fr James attended a solemn mass of thanksgiving for their victory in the ruined Elgin Cathedral. Fr James pleaded with Huntly not to flee but to stay and continue the struggle – to venture everything for their faith. However, the Catholic army was dispersed and Huntly, feeling that there was no hope of toleration, fled to Caithness. He and Errol sent news of their victory to Flanders, Rome and Spain, and requested aid.[201] The King did not attempt to pursue them.[202] In fact, he protected Huntly's followers and put the earl's estates and properties in Henrietta's charge, a clear signal of eventual and full restoration.[203] He made Henrietta's brother, Ludovic Lennox, Lieutenant of the North, with the commission to seek out the Catholics and exact fines.[204] The Act of Forfeiture was never acted upon, and Huntly was provided with a private remission and a general pardon if he paid fines dating back almost to the time of the battle. He and Errol lingered, hoping for help from Spain.

On 6 December 1594 Fr James's brother-in-law, Alexander, Earl of Sutherland died at Dunrobin. This made his sister Jean a widow with five sons and two daughters.

Leaving the Country

Leaders of the Kirk put the blame on Fr James as the author of the rebellion, and again demanded he be banished.[205] On 19 March 1595 Fr James, Huntly and sixteen others departed the country from Aberdeen for Denmark, despairing of the King ever granting them liberty of conscience. Errol left from Peterhead. Angus went into hiding rather than exile. It was rumoured that there was a private agreement between the King and themselves that the exile would not exceed six months.

The rebels toured France and Germany, and continued to intrigue.[206] Meanwhile, Henrietta continued to do her best to obtain their pardon, as she still had access to court, being a great favourite with the King and Queen. Meanwhile, she also managed Huntly's affairs at home. He and the others sent appeals to be absolved from excommunication. Fr Murdoch took Fr James' place as head of the mission in Scotland, where there was a campaign to demolish every building where the mass had been offered.[207]

Huntly's Return to Scotland

Only three months later, in June 1595, Huntly returned secretly. He was seen at Bog of Gight, his wife's residence. The King had said that they could return home but must keep themselves private until they received new orders. In October of that year, Maitland of Thirlestane died. On 19 October 1596, two years after the Battle of Glenlivet, Henrietta formally presented offers to the General Assembly on her husband's behalf.

Meanwhile, the General Assembly condemned the state of Scotland where, they complained, 'thirty-six years after the Reformation, there was a universal coldness, lack of zeal, ignorance, and contempt of the Word, prayers and the singing of psalms. The word of God was profaned and abused; the people perish in atheism and profanity.' A minister named Black even denounced Queen Elizabeth as an atheist, and said that religion in England was 'an empty show, Satan ruled both Court and Council'. He declared that 'all kings were devil's bairns, Lords of Session were miscreants, nobles cormorants' and that 'there was vain hope for any good thing from Queen Elizabeth'.[208] Despite the Privy Council condemning his sermon, Black persisted in his opinions.

In December, the Assembly was incensed about what they called 'the King's connivance' in Huntly's return. It caused a tumult in Edinburgh. They organised a public humiliation of the King on the first Sunday in December, crying 'no popery, not in Edinburgh'. The King left the city, announcing that it would be his capital no more. The burgesses had to pay a huge sum to recover its status. Meanwhile the King made generous grants from church lands to the nobles.

On 31 December 1596 Huntly wrote to the King saying that he had returned to Scotland with the intention of submitting himself to the King's will and, also, to the will of the Kirk, country and party.[209] The

King replied that Huntly must not expect better conditions by the 'lingering of time', nor that 'your wife and your allies shall get better conditions. I must love myself and my own state better than all the world, and think not,' he continued, 'that I will suffer any professing a contrary religion to dwell in this land.'[210] At last, it was quite clear that Huntly could not expect to return to his wife, family, home and lands unless he complied totally. He must either embrace Protestantism or leave for ever, and he must also publicly ask for God's mercy for the murder of the Earl of Moray.[211] To save their estates from confiscation, the exiles decided to return, subscribe to the Confession of Faith, and publicly recant their errors.

On 10 May 1596 the General Assembly met in Dundee to discuss conditions for the admission of Huntly, Errol, Angus and also the Gordon laird of Gight. A commission was appointed to receive them into the Church. In June, there was a great ceremony of reconciliation in the Old Church of Aberdeen, where Huntly was formally received into the Reformed Church, after which he took communion.[212] Many noblemen and gentry of the county were present. Immediately before the sermon, the earls publicly and loudly confessed their defection and apostasy, and professed their present conviction of the truth of the Protestant faith and their resolution to adhere to it. Then Huntly declared 'before God, the King and Church, his penitence for the slaughter of the Earl of Moray'. Consequently, his forfeiture was rescinded. From then on, he played no further part in Catholic intrigues.

Father James' Return to Scotland

Fr James returned to Scotland in July, landing close to the English border. He was dismayed when he heard that his nephew had come to terms with the Reformed Kirk and publicly confessed his Protestant faith. He regretted not having arrived earlier and prevented it, which shows the influence he thought he had. 'This is what I had feared,' he said 'and it is a great misfortune for the Catholic cause.' He also complained that 'Huntly listened to the blandishments of the King and his heretical friends and was persuaded to confer with the ministers; then went to their temples to hear their sermons and ended by openly, at least in words, if not sincerely, renouncing the Catholic religion, for which he had so gloriously combated.'[213] The 'apostasy' of Huntly and his fellow earls was also a great shock to their fellow Catholics.[214] Most subsequently followed their example and three Catholic fathers had to flee, as they knew they would no longer have the protection of the earls.[215]

However, Fr James was not going to give up.[216] He issued a public challenge to the ministers in an open letter to the King aimed at rallying the Catholics. There were public proclamations warning people not to take him in or feed him, so he had to leave Edinburgh but promised to return for an answer to his challenge.[217]

Huntly told him not to come to the north-east. Instead he sailed up to Cromarty, where he was welcomed by the people, and many did look after him. His sister Jean, Countess of Sutherland, got into trouble for giving hospitality to him and Fr William Murdoch (who was later put on trial in Edinburgh for saying mass in private houses in the north of Scotland, including Dunrobin). Henrietta, Countess of Huntly, Jean, Countess of Sutherland, and the Countess of Caithness were ordered to subscribe to the Confession of Faith, under pain of excommunication. Jean did not obey, but she was not excommunicated at this point.

Huntly managed to obtain a withdrawal of the proclamation prohibiting people from offering Fr James hospitality, on condition that he left the country. He took lodgings in Aberdeen and many came to see him, including the bishop. The bishop even agreed that he should be allowed to preach. However, the ministers were so angry about this that he had to announce that only they would be able to hear him, with the condition that they be allowed to refute what he said. The ministers first searched his lodging house and then rejected the text he had chosen to preach on, on the incorrect grounds that it was not from the Bible. Fr James said that they could give him any text they chose and he would preach on it! They replied that his text must be from the Word, and not from tradition. In the end, when he did preach, the bishop failed to attend. It was not until Fr James was on his ship and about to sail that he received the ministers' written refutation. He promised to return in about eight days to respond. However, icy seas and bad weather prevented this.[218]

Huntly Restored to his Former Estate

The King called a parliament on 16 December 1597 at which Huntly, Angus and Errol were officially restored to their former dignity and estates. They solemnly swore to keep order in all respects and to ensure that justice was carried out in their areas. In the parliamentary procession, Angus carried the crown and Huntly the sceptre, thus demonstrating publicly their restoration to royal favour. Huntly regained his place on the Privy Council. Their final relaxation from the horn and withdrawal of their forfeitures were announced to the public at the market cross in Edinburgh, accompanied by the sound of the trumpet. At the Castle Gate 'a great assemblage of the people shouted, drank the health of the earls and tossed their glasses'.[219] Huntly was now able to return north and start the refurbishment of Huntly Castle, whose old tower had been blown up after the battle of Glenlivet three years previously. His lordship was still intact, and he expanded his power base into Moray and Argyll's domains. He was a virtual prince in his own region, as his grandfather the 4th Earl had been. What a triumph!

Catholicism was now extinguished as a political danger, and the King could turn his attention to limiting the political threats of ultra-Protestantism. He needed Huntly to help balance the power of the Kirk.[220] The General Assembly requested the representation of ministers in Parliament. The King replied that this would be fulfilled by those he chose to be bishops.

Father James back in Scotland in Disguise

Fr James returned to Scotland again, on 10 December 1598. He came in disguise to the door of the King's chamber in the Palace of Holyroodhouse, where a Privy Council meeting was taking place. He sent a message to a kinsman saying who he was and asking to be allowed to dispute in front of King and Council with any minister who would accept the challenge. He was seized and taken to Edinburgh Castle for defying the laws forbidding his return. From there, he issued a challenge saying that if he was allowed to have the debate and won the argument, Catholics should be allowed liberty of conscience. However, if he lost the argument he was prepared to forfeit his life. The King was amused by his boldness and agreed, much to the indignation of the ministers of the Kirk.[221]

Meanwhile, whilst in prison, he carried on engaging in argument with the Presbyterian brethren. Various ministers agreed to debate with him, but failed to appear. Instead, they called for his death. When Huntly heard about the affair, he organised his uncle's release. He took him to lodging in town and insisted on paying his expenses. People had free access to him there, and a top minister offered a book he had written for Fr James to comment on, which he did. This man offered to debate, but in private. Various other preachers approached and said that they were willing to debate with him, but then made excuses. Fr James decided that since no one was going to take up the challenge of the public debate, he might as well leave. He went to the home of Lord Seton.

The Privy Council passed an act of perpetual banishment on Fr James. He decided to obey, because he feared a public rupture between the King, the ministers and his host, Lord Seton. When he was told the ships were ready he left for Leith, but they were actually not ready to depart, so he had a whole month waiting in Leith. Many people came to visit him there. Some friends persuaded a minister who was under the influence of drink to agree to engage in a discussion. Fr James went prepared to do so, but once again the man failed to appear.

Final Departure

Huntly paid the expenses of Fr James's ship. He left on 10 May 1599, having been in Scotland five months. He had with him letters of protection from the King addressed to the state of Zeeland and Holland. Queen Anne sent a letter to her brother, the King of Denmark. He was away from home, so it was given to the Danish Chancellor, who asked what assistance Fr James needed. He said he required nothing but permission to travel by land to Germany. Four carriages were supplied for himself and six companions, to take them through Denmark and Holstein at no expense, not even for boat hire to cross the straits.[222] From exile, Fr James acted as an agent for the Scottish mission.[223]

Queen Anne's Conversion

Queen Anne had been brought up as a rigid Lutheran but was not satisfied with the Presbyterian Church. She had fond memories of going with her grandmother to a Catholic chapel. Before Father James left the country, she sought his advice.[224] He recommended Fr Abercrombie, who then obtained the position of official Keeper of the King's Falcons at Holyroodhouse. From 1598 she received instruction from him in the early mornings. A few Catholic ladies at court were privy to the secret. These no doubt included Huntly's wife, Henrietta, who was the Queen's greatest friend and would have encouraged her in her new faith. In fact, her conversion was often attributed to Henrietta.[225]

Henrietta had charge of the Princess Elizabeth, whose godmother she was. The King was severely criticised for allowing his Queen to be surrounded by Catholic ladies. However, Fr Abercrombie, in a letter explaining her conversion, reported Henrietta's revelation that when she informed the King about it, he 'behaved to me with greater gentleness and kindness'. He had said to her: 'Well, wife, if you cannot live without this sort of thing, do your best to keep things quiet as possible for, if you don't, our crown is in danger.'[226] This would have given the Catholics high hopes for the King's conversion, especially as Huntly was known to have such influence over him.[227] The King's Principal Secretary of State, Lord Elphinstone, was Catholic, as was Lord Seton, the President of the Session.

The King was always suspected of Catholic leanings, and in 1598 he made overtures to the Pope seeking his friendship, which stirred up the hopes of Catholics. Fr Alexander McQuhirrie reported that the King was 'inclined to wink at our proceedings and was well acquainted with the affairs of our mission. He urges our friends to act with great caution lest his ministers should compel him, by solicitation or by threats, which they did not shrink from using, to take some violent measures against us, and of this he would greatly regret.'[228] 'He was then suddenly seized with fear of incurring the hatred of the reformers,' continued McQhirrie, 'which might have led to a fearful persecution of his Catholic friends.'[229] Queen Anne tried to persuade her husband to allow toleration for Catholics, but without much effect. Fr McQhirrie became cynical about the King, but thought papal gold might encourage his conversion.[230] He was a shrewd judge of the King's character, and commented that 'the sole object of his ambition is the crown of England, which he would gladly take from the hand of the devil himself'.[231]

The King considered Presbyterianism a threat to monarchy. He had come to the conclusion that the best solution was to bring Scotland's system of Church government into line with that of the Church of England, with bishops chosen by himself.[232] This approach was to prove a disaster for Scotland during the reign of his son, Charles I.

In December 1599 Fr James's sister Jean, aged fifty-four, married the suitor of her youth, Alexander Ogilvie of Boyne, in Elgin Cathedral. Sadly, the marriage did not last long, because he died within a few years, leaving her a widow once again. However, she was soon needed back in Sutherland.

Huntly Created a Marquis

Huntly was invited to be godfather to the King's new daughter, Princess Margaret, which shows the favour in which he was still held, despite everything. Then, to crown it all, during celebrations following the princess's baptism on 17 April 1599, the King made Huntly a marquis, to show appreciation of his 'obedient friendship'. The Earl of Angus was created a marquis at the same time. Huntly's titles were now Marquis of Huntly, Earl of Enzie and Viscount of Inverness (the first introduction of this title in Scotland). He was also appointed joint Lieutenant and Judiciar for the North with Lennox. The marquisate caused a stir, but the King justified it on the grounds that it had been long promised and would 'comfort him in that good course of loyalty and conformity in religion, which he doubts not he will continue'.[233] Despite all that had happened, the King still had faith in him.

However, despite this and all the celebrations welcoming him into the Reformed Kirk, Huntly continued to disregard its sensitivities. Not long after his elevation he held a celebration that included a very public mass in his house in Edinburgh, which many attended. The anger of the Kirk was sufficiently strong to induce him to leave Court. Spats with the Kirk continued until the end of his life.

It took the King a great deal of effort to bring about a reconciliation between Huntly and the young Moray, and more particularly Moray's uncle, the murdered earl's brother. The King also aimed to make peace between Huntly and Argyll. He resorted to the age-old practice of arranging marriages: the twenty-year-old Moray would marry Huntly's eldest daughter, Lady Ann Gordon; and Huntly's eldest son (the future 2nd Marquis) would marry Lady Ann Campbell, Argyll's eldest daughter. The double weddings were to take place in Strathbogie the following April. In fact, the combined wedding did not occur until a few years later.[234]

With the start of the new century, Huntly undertook a major building programme, restoring and embellishing Huntly Castle in a manner befitting his newly elevated status. He did the same for his castles of Aboyne, Ruthven, Bog of Gight and his town houses in Aberdeen and Elgin. He was one of the great builders of his age. Having rebuilt and embellished Huntly Castle, he built Gordon Castle at Bog of Gight (Fochabers) and worked on Gordonstoun at Plewlands, Morayshire. He later sold it to his cousin Robert Gordon, Jean's third son (who was made 1st Baronet of Gordonstoun in 1638). Huntly planted large areas of forest and built bridges and roads. All this ambitious development caused him and his heir serious financial problems in the future. Huntly also spent considerable time with the King, who came north to enjoy his hospitality.[235] The King must have been impressed by the work of Huntly's painter at his properties, because he wanted to borrow him to work on his Palace of Falkland, but the man had failed to appear and so the plan was frustrated. Feelings must have been strong on the matter, because the painter was ordered to report to the Master of Works at the palace within six days. If he did not, he would be branded a rebel.

The King gave Huntly special charge of the colonisation of Lewis, which Parliament had taken possession of in 1600, sending colonists to develop it.[236] The King was prepared to overlook Huntly's continued non-compliance in matters of religion if he was of use to him, such as in the administration of the Western Isles.[237]

In 1601, in order to guarantee Scotland's neutrality in England's war in Ireland, Queen Elizabeth raised the King's subsidy to £5,000 and promised regular payments. This war with Ireland cost her more than five times the money that had been necessary to defeat the Spanish Armada. The King received £58,500 in all from Elizabeth, averaging £3,000 per year. He spent much of it on the royal guard. Queen Elizabeth thought that Scottish politics rested on a knife edge, so it would have been a huge risk to treat Scotland with indifference. The King would have preferred the income to have come through an English estate or dukedom, especially Cornwall, as that was the traditional way for an heir. However, she cannily went out of her way to deny him this. The anti-English faction in his court would have preferred him to do without the subsidy altogether, so that Scotland would be less prone to English interference.[238]

The General Assembly of the Church of Scotland decreed that papists should be excluded from the King's council, session, and household. It decreed that ministers were to live with his Catholic nobles to catechise, purge their homes and plant kirks in their areas.

News reached Scotland that a letter, purportedly from the King, had been taken to the Pope asking for advice on returning Scotland to Catholicism. The King denied knowledge of it, saying that his secretary must have hidden it amongst a pile of letters for his signature. However, on 31 July 1601 Queen Anne wrote to Cardinal Borghese, saying that the letter was indeed written by her husband's authority in reply to letters from the Pope. His instructions to the bearer of the letter, printed in Rome, said that he could not reply himself as he was afraid of Queen Elizabeth. The letter stated that Scotland was ripe for a return to the Catholic faith, but urged caution in publicising this because of Queen Elizabeth's spies.[239] The King's intention seems to have been to encourage the belief in the papal court of his actual or impending conversion, while at the same time knowing this could be avoided. It seems that he was also quite prepared to make use of his wife's religious inclinations for his own ends.

King James I of England

When Elizabeth died on 2 April 1603, James achieved his overriding ambition to become King of England. Two days later he set off south, and when he reached Berwick he sent word that Huntly should be ready to wait upon the Queen in London. In June, the King arrived in his new capital with a retinue of nobles and vassals, as well as two of his children, Prince Henry and Henrietta's god-daughter, Princess Elizabeth.

The King often found the means to extricate Huntly from the difficulties that his religion brought him. He tried to get Huntly's excommunication revoked by the Archbishop of Canterbury, but was told it was a matter for the Church that had excommunicated him. Eventually, the Bishop of Caithness consented to do so in the name of the whole Church of Scotland. On 7 July 1603, Huntly was publicly absolved in the chapel of Lambeth by the Archbishop of Canterbury, in the presence of the primates of Ireland and the Bishop of London. He stayed for a while in London but, as a Catholic, he was still precluded from public office and returned home to Scotland. However, he was frequently called back by the King for consultation about Scottish affairs.

A letter dated 1605 from Fr Crichton to a Fr Claud Aquaviva said that Fr James believed 'the King himself had actually been a Catholic at one point'.[240] The King had told him he could not yield to a Catholic conversion unless Fr James could find 'a means whereby I may be safe from myne enemies, and then I will willingly hear your reasoning'. In a letter to Cecil, the King said that he did not approve of dealing with religious diversity with the sword; it was far better to send people abroad than remove heads from bodies. 'No, I'm so far from any intentional persecution as I protest to God,' he said. 'I do reverence their church as our mother church, although clogged with many infirmities and corruptions. Besides that, I ever did hold persecution as one of the infallible notes of a false church.'[241]

However, despite this, once he became King of England, James was bent on introducing Episcopacy into Scotland, and persecution against Catholics intensified. This might also have been an overreaction on the part of the leading Episcopalians in the country who, being accused of encouraging popery, attempted to prove the opposite in order to reconcile the Presbyterians.

The discovery of the gunpowder plot in 1605 ended any chance of the Jesuits achieving lasting good for Catholicism in Scotland. Many Catholics fled the country, never to return. Fr Abercrombie returned to the College of Braunsberg, in Eastern Prussia, where many young Scottish Jesuits received training for missionary work in their native land. The Catholic exiles did all in their power to promote the cause of religion in Scotland, by means of benefactions, political negotiations and writing. The most famous of these was John Leslie, Bishop of Ross, who had died in 1596. He acted for Queen Mary during her imprisonment in England. He was gaoled in England but fled back to France, where he was made Vicar General of the Archdiocese of Rouen and raised to the See of Coutances in Normandy. John Leslie's *History of Scotland* was a standard authority for many years. The English College of Douai, twenty miles south of Lille, became the chief centre for those who had been exiled from England and Scotland for their faith. The Archbishop of Glasgow, James Beaton, had lived in Paris since 1560 and was a great benefactor of the Scots College there, as was Bishop William Chisholm of Dunblane, who resigned to become a Carthusian monk. A colony of Scots collected around him, and he continued to take an interest in Scottish affairs.

Back in Scotland, in 1606 the Marquis of Huntly was ordered to reside in Aberdeen for instruction by ministers from the Kirk. The following year he and his wife had to reside within ten miles of Elgin for ten days each month, which had to include two Sundays for church attendance. Their residence at Bog of Gight, Fochabers, would have been useful for observing this requirement.

Meanwhile, 1606 would have been a tragic year for Fr James on the Continent. His sister Margaret Forbes died, and it was also a year of plague in the Low Countries. Perhaps he was present when his sister was buried by the Capuchins in the abbey of St Bavan in Ghent, near the grave of his nephew and her eldest son William. Then, on 2 August that same year, came the death of his younger nephew John, also known as Brother Archangel, who succumbed to plague after nursing other sufferers. This was only two months after the death of their father, Lord Forbes, and John should have been the 9th Lord Forbes. However, Fr James's former brother-in-law had remarried and produced a new heir to inherit his title and lands.

It was reported that the Marquis and Marchioness of Huntly were still much attached to the Catholic faith. This is amply shown in the defiant and triumphant Catholic symbolism with which the marquis embellished Huntly Castle during the early years of the seventeenth century. What remains of this since the Covenanter's chiselling destruction in the next century is particularly evident in the magnificent 'frontispiece' over the main doorway, dated 1602 and still there for us to admire along with the fine decorated great fireplaces in the hall of the Marchioness's apartment.[242] A verse from Romans 8:28 remains: 'Sen God doth us defend / ve sal prevail until the end / To thaes that love God / Al thingis virkis to the best.'

Indeed, the marquis had his and his wife's names emblazoned ostentatiously across the south front of the castle for all to see, much of it still there now, 400 years on: 'George Gordoun, Marquis of Huntlie and Henrietta Stewart, Marquisse of Huntlie.' A hand points towards each name as if to say: 'Look at this – despite all our struggles and troubles, and the trials we have been through, see what heights we have reached!' A triumph indeed.

Death of Father James (1626)

As Fr James had been a frequent visitor to his sister Jean, Countess of Sutherland, perhaps she kept him informed of her family's struggles over religion. In 1615 her eldest son John, 13th Earl of Sutherland had to go to St Andrews and then Edinburgh to make his peace with the Kirk, outwardly at least. She had sad news to report over the next few years, with the deaths of three of her family: her son, the 13th earl; youngest grand-daughter; and her daughter-in-law Agnes Elphinstone. She now had to look after her orphaned grandchildren.

No doubt she complained to Fr James about the religious trials she continued to endure because of her non-compliance, and of being summoned before a commission in Edinburgh. Her third son, Sir Robert, who was a Protestant, stood surety for her and purchased 'from his Majesty an oversight and toleration of her religion for the rest of her days . . . providing that she would not harbour nore receive any Jesuits'.[243] She was now seventy-one.

Fr James died in Paris in 1626, aged seventy-seven. He was described on the Continent as 'greatly esteemed'. If he had lived ten years longer, he would have been gratified to hear that, despite all the pressure heaped on his nephew and against his apostasy, when he was dying, Huntly, the 1st Marquis declared himself with his last breath to be still a Catholic. During his life, Huntly had done all he could to help and protect his uncle until he was unable to do so any more. We should not underestimate the influence Fr James had on him and other members of the family, such as his sisters, Margaret and Jean, and his Forbes nephews, as well as many others. One has to admire his determination and courage in doing all he could to stay in the country and pursue his aims despite repeated orders to depart. As for whether he was a traitor, it was certainly a traitorous act if he really did appeal to other powers to mount a military invasion of his own country. However, he also showed saintly qualities in his devotion to his faith, doing everything in his power – including public debate and argument – to enlighten those in authority about the truth of what he believed in, even to the extent of putting his life in grave danger. It was to take many more years before the religious toleration that he struggled so resolutely to achieve was won.

Postscript

The 1st Marquis of Huntly continued to have trials, in both senses of the word, until the end of his life – not so much because of religion, but because of the aftermath of the heartbreaking loss of his youngest son in the cruel fire at Frendraught Castle.[1]

On his way north from his latest trials in Edinburgh, with his health failing fast, and too ill to ride, he had to travel in a 'wand bed within his chariot', accompanied by his faithful wife, Henrietta. He died at Dundee on 16 June 1636. The coffin, covered in black taffeta, was moved north by horse litter to his chapel at Huntly Castle. The following day it was moved to the Kirk of Belly, near Bog of Gight, and then to his house in Elgin, where it lay in state for funeral arrangements to be made. This took place at night on 30 August 1536, with a grand procession through the streets of Elgin.

His coffin was on a funerary carriage, draped with a 'rich mortcloth of black velvet, whereon were wrought two white crosses'. It was escorted on its long slow procession by 300 of his friends and local gentry, each carrying a lighted torch. Had his old friend King James the peacemaker lived to see the occasion, he would have been pleased to see, walking together, Huntly's son and the young Earl of Moray, son-in-law of the murdered 'Bonnie Earl', as pallbearers leading the funeral procession. Thus the 1st Marquis of Huntly was 'carried to the east Kirk stile of the College Kirk, in at the south Kirk door, and buried in his own aisle, with much mourning and lamentation'. The chronicler comments that 'the like form of burial with torch light was seldom seen here before'.[2]

Thus a man died who had risked much and suffered much for persisting in his Catholic faith. In light of the risks he took, it was surprising that he survived as long as he did. This was because he had been forgiven much by his friend the King who, despite all, trusted him and had so much affection for him to the end of his days. In the end Huntly could persist in his intransigence no longer without losing everything. However, he was well rewarded for his submission, superficial though it was.

Like his predecessors, his close friendship with the monarch resulted in his receiving considerable reward in the form of status, although nothing like the power and riches his grandfather, the 4th Earl of Huntly, had been granted in his heyday. However, he had enough to enable him to indulge in extravagant building ambitions, particularly in what remains of his fine embellishments of Huntly Castle, where his name and that of his wife Henrietta were triumphantly emblazoned in relief across the front, and can still be seen today.

GENEALOGIES

I. THE GORDONS OF HUNTLY

Key characters from the story are shown in **bold**

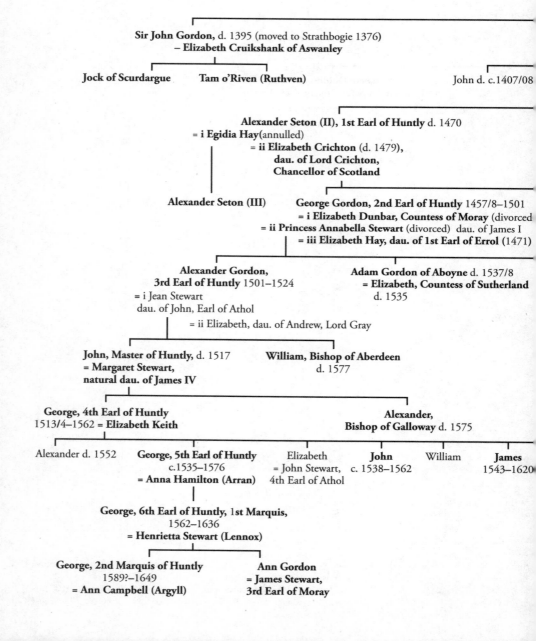

Sir John Gordon, d. 1395 (moved to Strathbogie 1376)
– Elizabeth Cruikshank of Aswanley

Jock of Scurdargue   **Tam o'Riven (Ruthven)**   John d. c.1407/08

Alexander Seton (II), 1st Earl of Huntly d. 1470
= i Egidia Hay(annulled)
= ii Elizabeth Crichton (d. 1479),
dau. of Lord Crichton,
Chancellor of Scotland

Alexander Seton (III)   **George Gordon, 2nd Earl of Huntly** 1457/8–1501
= i Elizabeth Dunbar, Countess of Moray (divorced
= ii Princess Annabella Stewart (divorced) dau. of James I
= iii Elizabeth Hay, dau. of 1st Earl of Errol (1471)

Alexander Gordon,   **Adam Gordon of Aboyne** d. 1537/8
3rd Earl of Huntly 1501–1524   **= Elizabeth, Countess of Sutherland**
= i Jean Stewart   d. 1535
dau. of John, Earl of Athol
= ii Elizabeth, dau. of Andrew, Lord Gray

John, Master of Huntly, d. 1517   **William, Bishop of Aberdeen**
= Margaret Stewart,   d. 1577
natural dau. of James IV

George, 4th Earl of Huntly   **Alexander,**
1513/4–1562 **= Elizabeth Keith**   **Bishop of Galloway** d. 1575

Alexander d. 1552   **George, 5th Earl of Huntly**   Elizabeth   **John**   William   **James**
c.1535–1576   = John Stewart,   c. 1538–1562   1543–1620
= Anna Hamilton (Arran)   4th Earl of Athol

George, 6th Earl of Huntly, 1st Marquis,
1562–1636
= Henrietta Stewart (Lennox)

George, 2nd Marquis of Huntly   **Ann Gordon**
1589?–1649   **= James Stewart,**
= Ann Campbell (Argyll)   **3rd Earl of Moray**

Sir Adam Gordon of Berwickshire d. 1333
(granted lands of Strathbogie by Robert the Bruce 1320)
= Amabilla

Sir Adam Gordon d. c.1551

Sir John Gordon (Strathbogie lands confirmed by David II) ,
d. before 1560–1 = Elizabeth

Sir Adam Gordon of Huntly d. 1402 (killed at Homildon)
= Elizabeth Keith, of Aboyne

Elizabeth Gordon d. 1436
= Sir Alexander Seton (fought at Harlow 1411)

William Seton   Elizabeth

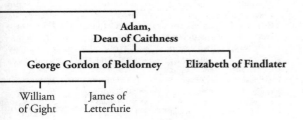

**Adam,
Dean of Caithness**

George Gordon of Beldorney   **Elizabeth of Findlater**

William   James of
of Gight   Letterfurie

Margaret 1544–1606   **Adam**   **Jean** 1545–1629   **Patrick** d. 1594   Robert   Thomas
= John, Master of Forbes   1545–1580   **= i Earl of Bothwell**   = i Agnes Betoun   d. 1572   d. 1584
                                             = ii E. of Sutherland   = ii Mariola Ogilvie
William   John   **= iii Alexander Ogilvie**
d. 1592   d. 1606   **of Boyne**

Sources: *The Scots Peerage* (founded on Wood's Edition of Sir Robert Douglas's *Peerage of Scotland)*, edited by Sir James Balfour Paul (Edinburgh, 1907) IV. pp.508–523 is the source for information on the early Gordons. *Scots Peerage* quotes earlier sources such as *Ferrerius, Records of Aboyne* and *House of Gordon,* New Spalding Club and works by J.M. Bulloch, but gives convincing evidence when challenging their facts. Harry Potter, *Bloodfeud: The Stewarts and Gordons at War* (Stroud, 2002) also used.

Chart 1 From the supposedly illegitimate line of 'Jock' and 'Tam' (but possibly the result of a handfast union recognised in the Highlands but not by the Church or the civil authorities of the time)

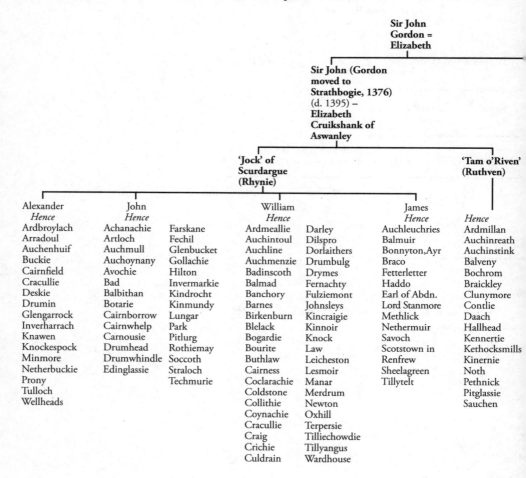

Sir John Gordon = Elizabeth

Sir John (Gordon moved to Strathbogie, 1376) (d. 1395) – Elizabeth Cruikshank of Aswanley

'Jock' of Scurdargue (Rhynie) · 'Tam o'Riven' (Ruthven)

Alexander *Hence*	John *Hence*		William *Hence*		James *Hence*	*Hence*
Ardbroylach	Achanachie	Farskane	Ardmeallie	Darley	Auchleuchries	Ardmillan
Arradoul	Artloch	Fechil	Auchintoul	Dilspro	Balmuir	Auchinreath
Auchenhuif	Auchmull	Glenbucket	Auchline	Dorlaithers	Bonnyton,Ayr	Auchinstink
Buckie	Auchoynany	Gollachie	Auchmenzie	Drumbulg	Braco	Balveny
Cairnfield	Avochie	Hilton	Badinscoth	Drymes	Fetterletter	Bochrom
Cracullie	Bad	Invermarkie	Balmad	Fernachty	Haddo	Braickley
Deskie	Balbithan	Kindrocht	Banchory	Fulziemont	Earl of Abdn.	Clunymore
Drumin	Botarie	Kinmundy	Barnes	Johnsleys	Lord Stanmore	Contlie
Glengarrock	Cairnborrow	Lungar	Birkenburn	Kincraigie	Methlick	Daach
Inverharrach	Cairnwhelp	Park	Blelack	Kinnoir	Nethermuir	Hallhead
Knawen	Carnousie	Pitlurg	Bogardie	Knock	Savoch	Kennertie
Knockespock	Drumhead	Rothiemay	Bourite	Law	Scotstown in Renfrew	Kethocksmills
Minmore	Drumwhindle	Soccoth	Buthlaw	Leicheston	Sheelagreen	Kinernie
Netherbuckie	Edinglassie	Straloch	Cairness	Lesmoir	Tillytelt	Noth
Prony		Techmurie	Coclarachie	Manar		Pethnick
Tulloch			Coldstone	Merdrum		Pitglassie
Wellheads			Collithie	Newton		Sauchen
			Coynachie	Oxhill		
			Cracullie	Terpersie		
			Craig	Tilliechowdie		
			Crichie	Tillyangus		
			Culdrain	Wardhouse		

Source: John Malcolm Bulloch, *House of Gordon,* Vol. I, pp. x–xi (Aberdeen, 1937), described as 'tentative'.

Chart 2 From Elizabeth Gordon and Alexander Seton's line

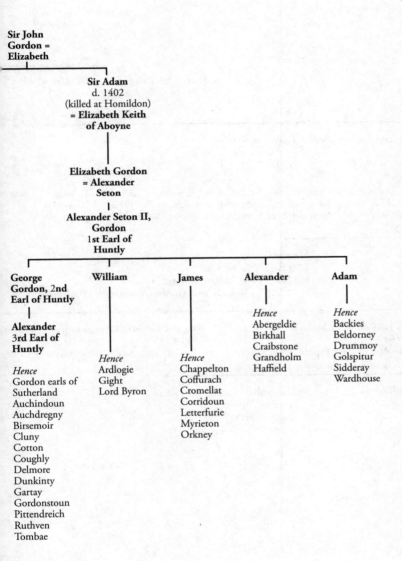

**Sir John
Gordon =
Elizabeth**

Sir Adam
d. 1402
(killed at Homildon)
**= Elizabeth Keith
of Aboyne**

**Elizabeth Gordon
= Alexander
Seton**

**Alexander Seton II,
Gordon
1st Earl of
Huntly**

**George
Gordon, 2nd
Earl of Huntly**

**Alexander
3rd Earl of
Huntly**

Hence
Gordon earls of
Sutherland
Auchindoun
Auchdregny
Birsemoir
Cluny
Cotton
Coughly
Delmore
Dunkinty
Gartay
Gordonstoun
Pittendreich
Ruthven
Tombae

William

Hence
Ardlogie
Gight
Lord Byron

James

Hence
Chappelton
Coffurach
Cromellat
Corridoun
Letterfurie
Myrieton
Orkney

Alexander

Hence
Abergeldie
Birkhall
Craibstone
Grandholm
Haffield

Adam

Hence
Backies
Beldorney
Drummoy
Golspitur
Sidderay
Wardhouse

III. EARLDOM OF SUTHERLAND

John, 9th Earl of Sutherland d. unm. 1514

Alexander, Master of Sutherland 1501–1529/30 = Lady Jane Stewart

**John, 11th Earl
of Sutherland** 1525–1567
= i. Elizabeth Campbell (1546) dau. of Colin, 3rd Earl of Argyll, widow of James Earl of Moray (d. 1544)
= ii. Lady Helen Stewart d. 1567, dau. of John, Earl of Lennox, widow of William Hay, 6th Earl of Errol
= iii Marion Seton, dau. of George, 4th Lord Seton, widow of John Graham, 4th Earl of Menteith

John (died young)

**Alexander,
12th Earl of Sutherland**
1552–1594 = i. Barbara Sinclair
= ii. Lady Jean Gordon, Countess of Bothwell (1573)

John, 13th Earl of Sutherland
1576–1615
= Agnes dau. of Lord Elphinstone

Robert Gordon of Gordonstoun
1580–1656
= Louisa Gordon dau. of Dean of Salisbury

John, 14th Earl of Sutherland
1609–1679
= Lady Jean Drummond

Elizabeth
= James Crichton
of Frendraught (1619)

Anne

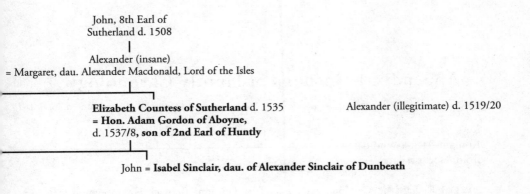

John, 8th Earl of
Sutherland d. 1508

Alexander (insane)
= Margaret, dau. Alexander Macdonald, Lord of the Isles

Elizabeth Countess of Sutherland d. 1535   Alexander (illegitimate) d. 1519/20
= Hon. Adam Gordon of Aboyne,
d. 1537/8, son of 2nd Earl of Huntly

John = **Isabel Sinclair, dau. of Alexander Sinclair of Dunbeath**

Alexander of Navidale (b. 1585)   **Jane** b. 1574   **Mary** 1582–1605
= David Ross of Balnagowan

Appendix 1 Gordons of Huntly Chronology

Key
Roman: Background dates
Bold: Gordon dates

1150 **Richard de Gordon granted land at Gordon, Berwickshire, to monks at Kelso.**

1296 **Sir Adam Gordon of Berwickshire did homage to Edward I at Elgin.**

1296 Wars of Independence broke out.

1306 Robert the Bruce inaugurated as King of Scotland.

1313 **Adam Gordon of Berwickshire changed sides to support Bruce.**

1314 Battle of Bannockburn.

1320 Declaration of Arbroath **taken to the Pope by Adam Gordon.**

1320 **Adam Gordon granted land in Strathbogie by Robert the Bruce.**

1333 Battle of Halidon Hill.

1357/8 **David II confirmed grant of Strathbogie lands to Sir Adam's grandson, Sir John Gordon.**

1376 **Robert II confirmed Strathbogie lands to Sir Adam's great-grandson, Sir John Gordon, who took possession.**

1388 Battle of Otterburn.

1395 **Death of Sir John Gordon; succeeded by his brother, Sir Adam Gordon, who married Elizabeth Keith of Aboyne.**

1402 Battle of Homildon Hill.

1408 **Sir Adam's daughter, Elizabeth Gordon, (heritrix of Strathbogie) married Alexander Seton.**

c.1437 **Alexander Seton created Lord Gordon by James I.**

1411 Battle of Harlaw. **Alexander Seton fought for Earl of Mar.**

1449 **Alexander Seton (II) created 1st Earl of Huntly.**

1458 **Alexander, 1st Earl of Huntly adopted the Gordon family name.**

1460 James II killed by bursting of his own cannon.

1470 **Death of 1st Earl of Huntly.**

1476 **2nd Earl of Huntly made Lieutenant of the North by James III.**

1488 **2nd Earl of Huntly made Judiciar of the North.**

1497 **2nd Earl of Huntly made Chancellor of Scotland.**

1502 **Death of 2nd Earl of Huntly.**

Alexander Gordon, 3rd Earl of Huntly made Chancellor by James IV.

1513 James IV died at Flodden.

1514 **Birth of George Gordon, son of John Gordon, heir to 3rd Earl of Huntly.**

1515 Adam Gordon of Aboyne, brother of 3rd Earl of Huntly, became Earl of Sutherland by right of his wife, the Countess of Sutherland.

1517 Death of John Gordon, heir to 3rd Earl of Huntly.

1524 Death of Alexander, 3rd Earl of Huntly.
He was succeeded by his grandson, George Gordon, as 4th Earl of Huntly.

1535 4th Earl made a Governor for James V, when he went to France.

1542 Birth of Mary (later Queen of France and Scotland) to James V and Mary of Guise.

1542 4th Earl fought at Battle of Haldonrig.
James V killed at Battle of Solway Moss.

1546 4th Earl of Huntly made Chancellor, after Cardinal Beaton assassinated.

1548–9 4th Earl of Huntly gained lands and administration of earldoms of Mar and Moray.

1550 4th Earl of Huntly went to France with Mary of Guise to visit her daughter, Mary.

1552 Death of 4th Earl of Huntly's heir, Alexander.

1555 4th Earl of Huntly regained lands and administration of earldoms of Mar and Moray from Mary of Guise.

1561 Return of Queen Mary to Scotland on death of her husband, Francis II of France.

1562 Battle of Corrichie, where 4th Earl of Huntly died. Son, Sir John, executed.

1565 Marriage of Queen Mary to Lord Darnley. Moray and others rebelled against her. George Gordon restored as 5th Earl of Huntly.

1566 Jean Gordon married James Hepburn, 4th Earl of Bothwell.

1566 Birth of James (VI), son of Mary Queen of Scots and Darnley.

1567 Murder of Lord Darnley. Marriage of Queen Mary to Bothwell, after his divorce from Jean Gordon.

1567 Carberry Hill confrontation between Queen Mary, Bothwell and the Confederates.

1567 Mary's enforced abdication. James crowned James VI. Moray made Regent.

1568 Mary's escape from Lochleven; defeated at Battle of Langside. Escape to England.

1568–9 Mary's trials in England. 5th Earl of Huntly her Lieutenant of the North.

1570 5th Earl of Huntly Mary's Lieutenant General. Moray shot dead.
Pope issued Bull depriving Elizabeth of her 'pretended right' to English throne.

1570 Lennox made Regent.
Civil war in Scotland. Siege of Brechin.

1571 Dumbarton Castle captured by King's Party.
Archbishop of St Andrews hanged in his vestments.
'Casket Letters' released, incriminating Mary.
Gordons fought against Forbeses in Battles of Tillyangus and Battle of Craibstone.
Burning of Corgarff Castle.
Master of Forbes, rival Lieutenant of the North, captured at Craibstone and imprisoned in Spynie Palace.

1572 Massacre of St Bartholomew's Day.
Death of Regent Mar. Morton elected Regent. Death of John Knox.

1573   Act of Conformity.
       Pacification of Perth ended civil war. Fall of Edinburgh Castle.
       Jean Gordon married Alexander, 12th Earl of Sutherland.
       John, Master of Forbes released from Spynie; divorced Margaret Gordon.
1576   **Death of 5th Earl of Huntly.**
1580   **Death of Adam Gordon, before judgement by King and council on feud**
       with Forbeses.
1580   Final fall of Morton.
1581   Morton beheaded.
1582   Ruthven Raid. Capture of James VI.
1586   Mary beheaded at Fotheringay.
       William, eldest son of Master of Forbes, joined Capuchins in Low Countries.
1589   **Brig o' Dee rebellion by Huntly, Errol and Crawford.**
1592   **6th Earl murdered 2nd Earl of Moray, 'the bonnie earl'.**
1592   **Huntly, Errol and others involved in the 'Spanish Blanks' affair.**
1593   **John, 2nd son of Master of Forbes, joined Capuchins at Tournai.**
1594   **Battle of Glenlivet – 6th Earl of Huntly's force defeated royal force under**
       Argyll. Patrick Gordon of Auchindoun killed.
1597   **6th Earl of Huntly made peace with James VI and submitted to Kirk.**
1599   **6th Earl of Huntly created 1st Marquis of Huntly.**
       Jean Gordon married Alexander Ogilvie of Boyne.
1602   **1st Marquis embellishing Huntly Castle.**
1603   James VI became James I of England.
1606   **Death of Margaret Gordon.**
1617   James VI and I's only visit to Scotland.
1620   **Death of Fr James Gordon.**
1629   **Death of Jean, Countess of Sutherland.**
1636   **Death of 6th Earl, 1st Marquis of Huntly.**

Appendix 2 Monarchs of Scotland

William I (the Lion)	1165–1214
Alexander II	1214–1249
Alexander III	1249–1286
Margaret (Maid of Norway)	1286–1290
Interregnum	1290–1292
John (Baliol)	1292–1296
Interregnum	1296–1306
Robert I	1306–1329
David II	1329–1371
Robert II	1371–1390
Robert III	1390–1406
James I	1406–1437
James II	1437–1460
James III	1460–1488
James IV	1488–1513
James V	1513–1542
Mary I	1542–1567
James VI	1567–1625
Charles I	1625–1649

Appendix 3 Supporters of George Gordon, 4th Earl of Huntly, at the Battle of Corrichie (October 1562)

From the records of forfeitures in 1563 (all Gordons, plus others whose forfeitures were sold for over 50 merks)[1]

	Value (merks)	Status
George, 4th Earl of Huntly		
John, Earl of Sutherland		
John Gordoun de Carneburro	1,250	
Sir John Gordon of Findlater	1,000	Executed
John Kempty of Carmuk	750	Constable of Abdn. (not at battle)
James Gordoun de Tulyangus	500	
Thomas Gordoun de Cragcullo	400	Killed
Mr George Gordon of Beldorney	300	Brother of Elizabeth, Lady Ogilvy-Findlater
Patrick Bissett de Lessindrom	300	Killed
George Gordoun de Cowclaroquhy	150	Executed
William Gordoun de Auchaunaquhy	150	
Patrick Gordon, son of James of Lesmoir	150	
John Gordon of Megstrath	70	(the future John Gordon of Cluny?)
George Gordoun of Prony	70	Not at the battle
James Gordoun de Blalak	70	Killed
Donald Macfersane in Cluny	60	Killed
Robert Trowp in Newy	60	Killed
John Gordon in Buky	60	
Alexander and Mr Patrick Dunbrek	60	Alex killed
James Gordoun de Blerak	40	Killed
James Gordoun in Cluny	40	
George Gordoun in Dawath	30	Not at battle
James Gordoun in Cragmylne	30	
James Duncan in New Merdrum	30	
James Gordoun in Dawath	20	Killed
James Gordoun at the mill of Monymusk	20	
William Gordoun, bro. of Alex of Abirzeldie	15	
____ Gordon of Blackhauch	—	

1 Forbes, 'Notes' I, Appendix VI.

Loyalists who submitted to Queen Mary and gave caution in October 1562

Name	Caution (merks)	Cautioner
Sir George Gordoun of Gicht	5,000	William Chene of Straloch
Alexander G. of Strathowne	5,000	None given (Pitsligo?)
(Alexander) G. of Abiryeldy	5,000	Alexander Irwin of Drum
James G. of Haddo	5,000	Thomas Menzies of Petfodellis
William G. of Craig	3,000	William Chene of Straloch
(by Alexander G, as pledge for his bro. William)		
George G. of Lesmoir	2,000	William Forbes of Tochquhone
(by Alexander G., his s. & h.a. 'as plege for his fader')		
James G. of Creichie	1,500	Alex. Knowis burg. of Edinburgh
Alexander G. of Birkenburn, his bro. for both		
(by George G. s. & h.a. of James of Creichie, as pledge for his father & Birkenburn)		
George G. of Correchieis	2,000	Maister Robert Lummisdene of Tulycarn
Patrick G. of Auchmanye	for both	
(by Patrick G., s& h.a. of George of Corrichie, for both)		

Abbreviations

APS	*Acts of the Parliament of Scotland, 1124–1770*
ASCB	Aberdeen Sheriff Court Book
CSP	*Calendar of State Papers*
CSPS	*Calendar of State Papers Relating to Scotland*
Diurnal	*Diurnal of Remarkable Occurents in Scotland since the Death of King James IV till the Year 1587, from a Manuscript of the Sixteenth Century*, edited by T. Thompson (Bannatyne Club, Edinburgh, 1833)
RMS	*Register of the Great Seal of Scotland (Registrum Magni Sigilli Regum Scotorum)*
RPCS	*Register of the Privy Council of Scotland*
RSS	*Register of the Secret Seal of Scotland (Registrum Secreti Sigilli Regum Scotorum)*
Scots Peerage	*The Scots Peerage: Founded on Wood's Edition of Sir Robert Douglas's Peerage of Scotland*, edited by Sir James Balfour Paul, 9 vols (Edinburgh, 1909–14)

Notes

Introduction

1. Grant Simpson, 'The Earliest Gordons', Lecture at the Gordon 2000 event.
2. Sir Robert Gordon, *A Genealogical History of the Earldom of Sutherland to 1603 with a Continuation to the Year 1651* (Edinburgh, 1813).
3. Sir James Balfour Paul (ed.), *The Scots Peerage, founded on Wood's Edition of Sir Robert Douglas's Peerage of Scotland* (Edinburgh, 1907), p. 507 (hereafter *Scots Peerage*); Harry Potter, *Blood Feud: The Stewarts & Gordons at War* (Stroud, 2002), p. 17.
4. Simpson, 'Earliest Gordons'.
5. Sir Bernard Burke, *Burke's Peerage and Barontage of the British Empire* (London 1860), p. 440.
6. Chilham's Castle website, 'History' page, URL <http://www.chilham-castle.co.uk/history.aspx>, accessed February 2012.
7. *Scots Peerage*, IV, p. 515.
8. Ibid., pp. 515–16.
9. Alexander Forbes, 'The Rise of the House of Huntly' (unpublished document), p. 2.
10. Ibid., p. 518.
11. Ibid., p. 1.
12. Ibid., p. 2.
13. Alexander Forbes, 'Notes', IV (unpublished document).
14. *Scots Peerage*, IV, p. 523.
15. Ibid., p. 525.
16. Ibid., p. 526.
17. Harry Potter, *Blood Feud: The Stewarts and Gordons at War in the Age of Mary Queen of Scots* (Stroud, 2002), p. 18.
18. *Scots Peerage*, IV, p. 526.
19. Potter, *Blood Feud*, p. 20.
20. Ibid., p. 20.
21. Simpson, 'Earliest Gordons'.
22. *Scots Peerage*, IV, p. 532.
23. Gordon Donaldson, *A Dictionary of Scottish History* (Edinburgh, 1977).
24. Forbes, 'Notes', IV.
25. *Scots Peerage*, IV, p. 532.
26. C.A. Gordon, *The House of Gordon* (Aberdeen, 1890).

27. Potter, *Blood Feud*, p. 27.
28. Records in the Gordon Charter Chest, in *The Records of Aboyne, 1230–1681*, edited by Charles, 11th Marquis of Huntly, Earl of Aboyne (Aberdeen, 1894), cited in Potter, *Blood Feud*, p. 27.
29. Potter, *Blood Feud*, p. 27; This may, however, have been the 'grassum' or entry fee, for the grant of the Mar lordships, or else a loan and the grant of the lands was to give Huntly security for the repayment of the 2000 merks. Forbes, 'Notes', V.
30. *Register of the Privy Council of Scotland (RPCS), XXV*, in *Records of Aboyne*, cited in Potter, *Blood Feud*, p. 28.
31. 'Goodman' means under-tenant.
32. Forbes, 'Notes', IV, p. 3.
33. Potter, *Blood Feud*, p. 45; Jenny Wormald, *Mary Queen of Scots: A Study of Failure* (London, 1988).
34. C.A. Gordon, *History of the House of Gordon* (Aberdeen, 1924).
35. Gordon, *Genealogical History of the Earldom of Sutherland*, p. 132.
36. Potter, *Blood Feud*, p. 28.
37. Jenny Wormald, *Lords and Men in Scotland, Bonds of Manrent 1442–1603* (Edinburgh, 1985), p. 117.

Chapter 1 John Gordon

1. J. Robertson, *The Inventories of Mary Queen of Scots* (Bannatyne Club, 1874), cited in Margaret H.B. Sanderson, *Mary Stewart's People* (Alabama, 1987), p. 36.
2. George Buchanan, *The History of Scotland* (1582), translated from the Latin by James Aikman, 2 vols (London, 1827–9).
3. *Scots Peerage*, IV, p. 23.
4. *Calendar of State Papers Relating to Scotland and Mary Queen of Scots 1547–1603 (CSPS)*,14 vols, I, 1562, p. 656: Randolph to Cecil, 30 Sept.
5. *Scots Peerage*, IV, p. 21.
6. Charter of John Ogilvy of Durne to John Ogilvy (previously Gordon). Papers of the Abercromby Family of Forglen and Birkenbog, National Archives of Scotland, GD185/9/7, Sasine no. 7.
7. Forbes 'Notes', I, p. 2.
8. C.A. Gordon, *History of the House of Gordon*. p. 35.
9. Gordon, *Genealogical History of the Earldom of Sutherland*, p. 130.
10. John Knox, *The Works of John Knox*, collected and edited by David Laing, 6 vols (Woodrow Society, Edinburgh 1846–64), II, p. 345.
11. *Register of the Privy Council of Scotland*, 36 vols, in three series (1545–1689) (1877–1933), 12 Feb. 1564 (retelling the story).
12. *Diurnal of Remarkable Occurents in Scotland since the Death of King James IV till the Year 1587*, edited by T. Thompson (Bannatyne Club, Edinburgh, 1833, p. 50; Knox, *Works*, II, p. 360.
13. *CSPS*, I, p. 656.
14. A tack is a lease of land for a fixed term of years, traditionally 19 years. In the Highlands, a 'tacksman' was a member of the chief's family, who was granted

a 'tack' of a portion of the clan land by the chief. Queen Mary of Guise had set the earldom 'in tack', i.e., she had granted him the lease of the earldom for however many years.

15. *Diurnal*, p. 51.
16. Potter, *Blood Feud*, p. 48.
17. *Scots Peerage*, IV, p. 23.
18. Antonia Fraser, *Mary Queen of Scots* (London, 1970), p. 236.
19. Gordon Donaldson, *Scotland, James V to James VII*, 4 Vols (Edinburgh, 1990), III, p. 86.
20. Knox, *Works*, I, pp. 314–15.
21. Donaldson, *Scotland, James V to James VII*, III, p. 101.
22. Sanderson, *Mary Stewart's People*.
23. J.H. Burton, *The History of Scotland from Agricola to the Revolution*, 7 vols (1553), IV, p. 199, n. 27.
24. *Diurnal*, p. 70.
25. E. Russell, *Maitland of Lethington* (London, 1912), p. 162.
26. Gordon, *Genealogical History of the Earldom of Sutherland*, p. 140.
27. Knox, *Works*, II, p. 345, n. 3.
28. John Hill Burton, nineteenth-century Scots historian, quoted in Charles Joseph Galliari Rampini, *A History of Moray and Nairn* (Edinburgh, 1897), p. 151
29. Fraser, *Mary Queen of Scots*, p. 235.
30. Gordon, *Genealogical History of the Earldom of Sutherland*, p. 140.
31. David Calderwood, *History of the Kirk of Scotland (1524–1625)*, 8 vols (Edinburgh, 1842–9), II, p. 194.
32. Russell, *Maitland of Lethington*, p. 162.
33. Robert Keith, *History of the Affairs of Church and State in Scotland to 1567*, 3 vols (Spottiswood Society, Edinburgh, 1845), II, pp. 158–9.
34. George Chalmers, *The Life of Mary Queen of Scots, Drawn from State Papers* (London, 1818), I, p. 81.
35. Calderwood, *History of the Kirk*, II, p. 195.
36. Treasurer's Accounts, XI, p. 194.
37. Chalmers, *Life of Mary Queen of Scots*, II, p. 82.
38. CSPS, I, p. 651
39. Fraser, *Mary Queen of Scots*, p. 238.
40. RPCS, I, p. 218.
41. RPCS, I, pp. 218–19.
42. David Breeze, *A Queen's Progress* (HMSO, 1987) p. 46.
43. CSPS, I, p. 649.
44. Potter, *Blood Feud*, p. 3.
45. RPCS, I, p. 219.
46. *Scots Peerage*, IV, p. 23.
47. Calderwood, *History of the Kirk*, II, p. 197.
48. CSPS, I, p. 649.
49. Leslie in *Scotland from Contemporary Documents*, edited by P.H. Brown (Edinburgh, 1927), cited in Potter, *Blood Feud*, p. 63.

50. *Calendar of State Papers* (CSP) (Foreign), I, 1562, p. 330, Randolph to Cecil, 30 Sept. 1562, cited in Potter, p. 63.

51. *Register of the Great Seal of Scotland* (*Registrum Magni Sigilli Regum Scotorum*) (RMS), IV, p. 299, and *Register of the Secret Seal of Scotland* (*Registrum Secreti Sigilli Regum Scotorum*) (RSS), cited in Forbes, 'Notes', I, Appendix II.

52. *Register of the Privy Council of Scotland*, IV, p. 299; cited in Forbes, 'Notes', I, p. 12.

53. *CSPS*, I, p. 655.

54. Knox, *Works*, II, p. 355.

55. *RPCS*, I, p. 218.

56. *RPCS*, I, pp. 219.

57. Calderwood, *History of the Kirk*, II, p. 196.

58. *CSPS*, I, p. 651; *Diurnal*, p. 73, Calderwood, *History of the Kirk*, II, p. 196.

59. *CSPS*, I, p. 651.

60. Ibid., p. 653.

61. Ibid., p. 651.

62. Arquebusiers are soldiers armed with an early type of portable trigger-operated firearm, weighing about 10 pounds and firing a half-ounce lead ball. It was fired resting on a tripod. See Harry Potter *Blood Feud*, p. 278.

63. Calderwood, *History of the Kirk*, II, p. 196.

64. *CSPS*, I, p. 653.

65. *CSPS*, I, p. 651.

66. Chalmers, *Life of Mary Queen of Scots*, p. 86.

67. Knox, *Works*, II, p. 352.

68. *CSPS*, I, p. 653; Fraser, *Mary Queen of Scots*, p. 241; Chalmers, *Life of Mary Queen of Scots*, p. 88.

69. Ibid., p. 88.

70. *CSPS*, I, p. 653.

71. Ibid., p. 654.

72. Fraser, *Mary Queen of Scots*, p. 241.

73. John Knox, *History of the Reformation in Scotland*, translated and edited by W. Croft Dickinson, 2 vols (London, 1949), II, p. 54.

74. *CSPS*, I, p. 654–6.

75. Ibid., p. 662.

76. Ibid., p. 656.

77. Ibid., pp. 657–8.

78. Calderwood, *History of the Kirk*, II, p. 197; Knox, *History of the Reformation*, II, p. 58; Potter, *Blood Feud*, p. 66.

79. Fraser, *Mary Queen of Scots*, p. 242.

80. Potter, *Blood Feud*, p. 66.

81. *CSPS*, I, p. 657.

82. Calderwood, *History of the Kirk*, II, p. 197.

83. Potter, *Blood Feud*, p. 67.

84. *RPCS*, I, pp. 219–20.

85. *RPCS*, I, p. 219 (Aberdeen, 12 October 1562); *CSPS*, I, p. 660.

86. *CSPS*, I, p. 661.

87. Thomas Duncan, 'Mary Stuart and the House of Huntly', *Scottish Historical Review*, vol. IV, 1906–1907 (July 1907), p. 369.
88. Peter Marren, *Grampian Battlefields* (Aberdeen, 1990), p. 109.
89. Calderwood, *History of the Kirk*, II, p. 197.
90. *RPCS*, I, p. 222–3.
91. Donaldson, *Scotland, James V–James VII*, III, p. 112.
92. *CSPS*, I, p. 665; *Knox History of the Reformation*, II, p. 54.
93. *CSPS*, I, p. 665.
94. Marren, *Grampian Battlefields*, p. 110.
95. Knox, *Works*, II, p. 355.
96. Calderwood, *History of the Kirk*, II, p. 198.
97. Knox, *History of the Reformation*, II, p. 59.
98. *CSPS*, I, p. 662.
99. Calderwood, *History of the Kirk*, II, p. 197.
100. Marren, *Grampian Battlefields*, p. 111.
101. Calderwood, *History of the Kirk*, **II, p. 198**.
102. Ibid., p. 117.
103. *CSPS*, I, p. 662.
104. Calderwood, *History of the Kirk*, II, p. 199.
105. Potter, *Blood Feud*, p. 71.
106. Calderwood, *History of the Kirk*, II, p. 199.
107. Ibid., p. 199.
108. *CSPS*, I, p. 662; *CSP* (Foreign), Randolph to Cecil, p. 399. Refers to 'late' not '11 o'clock'.
109. *CSPS*, I, p. 668.
110. Knox, *Works*, II, p. 352.
111. Fraser, *Mary Queen of Scots*, p. 128n.
112. W. Douglas Simpson, *Castle Findlater* (Banffshire, 1931).
113. Marren, *Grampian Battlefields*, p. 117.
114. *RMS*, IV, 1500, cited in Forbes, 'Notes', III, p. 2.
115. Forbes, 'Notes', III, p. 1.
116. Jenny Wormald, 'Bloodfeud, Kindred and Government in Early Modern Scotland', *Past and Present* (1980), p. 69.
117. Ibid.
118. Margaret H.B. Sanderson, *A Kindly Place?* (Scotland 2002) p. 49.
119. Russell, *Maitland of Lethington*, p. 152.
120. Chalmers, *Life of Mary Queen of Scots*, p. 82.
121. Duncan, 'Mary Stuart', p. 373.
122. Russell, *Maitland of Lethington*, p. 265n.
123. Patricia Wilson, 'Father and Son Relationships' (PhD Thesis, University of Aberdeen, 1997), p. 110.
124. Ibid., 111.
125. Sanderson, *Kindly Place*, p. 49.
126. Wormald, 'Bloodfeud', 69.
127. Ibid.
128. Duncan, 'Mary Stuart', p. 369.

Chapter 2 George Gordon

1. Gordon, *History of the House of Gordon.*
2. Keith, *History of the Affairs of Church and State,* II, p. 23.
3. Chalmers, *Life of Mary Queen of Scots,* I, p. 98.
4. Keith, *History of the Affairs of Church and State,* II, p. 180n.
5. Chalmers, *Life of Mary Queen of Scots,* II, p. 460.
6. Ibid., p. 182.
7. *Diurnal,* p. 74.
8. Gordon, *Genealogical History of the Earldom of Sutherland,* p. 143.
9. Charles Burnett, Ross Herald Extraordinary.
10. *Acts of the Parliament of Scotland (APS),* 12 vols (1814–75), II: 1424–1567, edited by Thomas Thomson and Cosmo Innes (London, 1833), p. 573.
11. Chalmers, *Life of Mary Queen of Scots,* I, p. 98.
12. Keith, *History of the Affairs of Church and State,* II, p. 174, n.1.
13. Chalmers, *Life of Mary Queen of Scots,* I, p. 169.
14. Gordon Donaldson, *All the Queen's Men* (London, 1983), p. 119.
15. *Diurnal,* p. 81.
16. Keith, *History of the Affairs of Church and State,* II, p. 380.
17. Chalmers, *Life of Mary Queen of Scots,* I, p. 171.
18. Keith, *History of the Affairs of Church and State,* II, p. 372.
19. Donaldson, *Scotland, James V to James VII,* III, p. 120.
20. Potter, *Blood Feud,* p. 249.
21. Fraser, *Mary Queen of Scots,* p. 200.
22. Calderwood, *History of the Kirk,* II, pp. 572–3.
23. Donaldson, *Scotland, James V to James VII,* III, p. 120.
24. Keith, *History of the Affairs of Church and State,* II, p. 411.
25. Fraser, *Mary Queen of Scots,* p. 306.
26. Knox, *History of the Reformation,* II, p. 520; *Diurnal,* p. 90.
27. John Spottiswoode, *History of the Church of Scotland to 1625,* 3 vols (Spottiswoode Society, 1851), II, p. 417.
28. Donaldson, *Scotland, James V to James VII,* III, p. 122.
29. Ibid., p. 125.
30. Sanderson, *Mary Stewart's People.*
31. Sir James Melville of Halhill, *Memoirs of His Own Life (1549–1593),* edited by A. Francis Steuart (London, 1929), p. 154.
32. *Diurnal,* p. 99.
33. Donaldson, *Scotland, James V to James VII,* III, p. 122.
34. Keith, *History of the Affairs of Church and State,* II, p. 810n.
35. Fraser, *Mary Queen of Scots,* p. 320.
36. 'Nether' means 'Lower'.
37. Knox, *History of the Reformation,* II, p. 512.
38. Ibid., p. 514.
39. Keith, *History of the Affairs of Church and State,* II, Appendix XVI, p. 138 (from documents in Anderson's Collection, IV, Cotton Library, now in British

Library Manuscripts).

40. Keith, *History of the Affairs of Church and State*, III, Appendix XVI, p. 293.

41. Potter, *Blood Feud*, p. 84.

42. *Diurnal*, 104.

43. Donaldson, *Scotland, James V to James VII*, III, p. 124.

44. *A Complete Collection of State Trials and Proceedings for High Treason and Other Crimes and Misdemeanors*, compiled by T.B. Powell, 21 vols (London, 1816), I, No. 54: Depositions of William Powrie, p. 1504 ff. (from documents in the Cotton Library).

45. *Diurnal*, 107.

46. Keith, *History of the Affairs of Church and State*, II, p. 537n.

47. *Diurnal*, p. 107.

48. *Diurnal*, p. 108.

49. Donaldson, *Scotland, James V to James VII*, III, p. 128.

50. Keith, *History of the Affairs of Church and State*, II, p. 561 ns 1–3.

51. *APS*, II, pp. 576–86.

52. *Diurnal*, p. 109.

53. Ibid., p. 110.

54. Fraser, *Mary Queen of Scots*, p. 317; *Diurnal*, p. 110.

55. *Dictionary of National Biography*, quoting *CSPS*, Drury to Cecil on 6 May, with information from Maitland of Lethington.

56. Donaldson, *Scotland, James V to James VII*, III, p. 130.

57. *Diurnal*, p. 111.

58. Melville, *Memoirs*, p. 180; *CSPS*, I, p. 563, cited in Donaldson, *Scotland, James V to James VII*, III, p. 130.

59. Donaldson, *Scotland, James V to James VIII*, III, p. 130.

60. J.A. Guy, *My Heart is My Own: The Life of Mary Queen of Scots* (London, 2004) p. 331.

61. *Diurnal*, p. 113.

62. Guy, *My Heart is My Own*, p. 331.

63. Fraser, *Mary Queen of Scots*, p. 394.

64. Donaldson, *Scotland, James V to James VII*, III, p. 157.

65. *Diurnal*, p. 121.

66. Donaldson, *Scotland, James V to James VII*, III, p. 159.

67. *Diurnal*, pp. 127–8.

68. Donaldson, *Scotland, James V to James VII*, III, p. 116.

69. *Diurnal*, p. 134.

70. Ibid., p. 134.

71. Ibid., p. 136.

72. Guy, *My Heart is My Own*, p. 436.

73. Donaldson, *Scotland, James V to James VII*, III, p. 161.

74. *CSP* (Foreign), Drury to Cecil, 3 Aug. 1568.

75. Wormald, *Mary Queen of Scots*, p. 178.

76. Keith, *History of the Affairs of Church and State*, II, p. 379–80, n.7.

77. Donaldson, *Scotland, James V to James VII*, III, p. 161.

78. *Diurnal*, p. 143.
79. Donaldson, *All the Queen's Men*, p. 117.
80. Wormald, *Mary Queen of Scots*, p. 179.
81. William Fraser, *The Sutherland Book*, 3 vols (Edinburgh, 1892) p. 134.
82. *RPCS*, II: AD 1569–1578, pp. 8–9.
83. Donaldson, *Scotland, James V to James VII*, III, p. 163.
84. Wormald, *Mary Queen of Scots*, pp. 179–80.
85. Donaldson, *Scotland, James V to James VII*, III, p. 163.
86. Richard Bannatyne, *Memorials of Transactions in Scotland AD 1549–1573*, edited by R. Pitcairn (Edinburgh, 1836), pp. 23, 24.
87. *Diurnal*, p. 171.
88. Donaldson, *Scotland, James V to James VII*, III, p. 163.
89. Edin. Burgh Records, III, p. 271, cited in Donaldson, *Scotland, James V to James VII*, III, p. 164.
90. Raphael Holinshed, *The Historie of Scotland unto the Yeare 1571* (London, 1577), p. 513.
91. Wormald, *Mary Queen of Scots*, p. 119.
92. Ibid., p. 180.
93. Potter, *Blood Feud*, p. 97.
94. Donaldson, *Scotland, James V to James VII*, III, p. 164.
95. *CSPS*, III, pp. 295–7, Letter from Lennox to Sussex received from Randolph and sent by Sussex to Cecil, 7 Aug. 1570, cited in Potter, *Blood Feud*, 97.
96. Holinshed, *Historie of Scotland*, p. 513.
97. Gordon, *Genealogical History of the Earldom of Sutherland*, pp. 158–60.
98. Holinshed, *Historie of Scotland*, p. 514.
99. *Diurnal*, p. 203.
100. Holinshed, *Historie of Scotland*, p. 515.
101. Ibid., p. 516.
102. Donaldson, *Scotland, James V to James VII*, III, p. 165.
103. *Diurnal*, p. 222.
104. Wormald, *Mary Queen of Scots*, p. 180.
105. Donaldson, *Scotland, James V to James VII*, III, p. 165.
106. *Diurnal*, p. 223.
107. Potter, *Blood Feud*, p. 98.
108. Melville, *Memoirs*, p. 113.
109. Gordon, *Genealogical History of the Earldom of Sutherland*, pp. 162–3.
110. Donaldson, *All the Queen's Men*, p. 123.
111. Melville, *Memoirs*, p. 213.
112. Ibid., p. 215.
113. *Diurnal*, p. 253.
114. Athaliah was the daughter of Ahab & Jezebel, who secured the throne for herself. She supported Baal worship. An insurrection headed by the priests had her son Joash made king and she was put to death.
115. Guy, *My Heart is My Own*, pp. 467–9.
116. Donaldson, *All the Queen's Men*, p. 123.
117. Ibid., p. 166.

118. Melville, *Memoirs*, p. 215–16.
119. Potter, *Blood Feud*, p. 101.
120. Wormald, *Mary Queen of Scots*, p. 180.
121. Donaldson, *Scotland, James V to James VII*, III, p. 166.
122. The quotes in this and the following paragraph are from the *RCPS*.
123. Remission here means forgiveness for past sins.
124. Melville, *Memoirs*, pp. 218–21.
125. Ibid., pp. 222–4.
126. Ibid., p. 257.
127. *Dictionary of National Biography* (Oxford, 1917 edn): George Gordon, 5th Earl of Huntly.
128. *RPCS*, II, pp. 338–9, cited in Alastair and Henrietta Tayler (eds), *The House of Forbes* (Aberdeen, 1937), p. 119.
129. National Archives/Records of Scotland, Register of Deeds, RD1/14, folio 269.
130. Donaldson, *All the Queen's Men*, p. 127.
131. Potter, *Blood Feud*, p. 103.

Chapter 3 Adam Gordon

1. Forbes, 'Notes', V, p. 1 (3): 'Lethington's wife' referred to in *Scots Peerage*, IV, p. 537, may have been his second wife, not yet his wife.
2. Gordon, *Genealogical History of the Earldom of Sutherland*, p. 142.
3. Forbes, 'Notes', III, p. 2, 'by decreet arbitral'.
4. *RMS*, V, p. 251. cited in Forbes II, p. 3.
5. *Aberdeen Sheriff Court Book*, I, p. 428, cited in Forbes, 'Notes', II, p. 3.
6. John Maxwell (Lord Herries), *The Historical Memoirs of the Reign of Mary, Queen of Scots* (Abbotsford Club, Edinburgh, 1836), p. 105.
7. Donaldson, *All the Queen's Men*, p. 151.
8. Beauly Priory Charters, p. 50, cited in Tayler (eds), *House of Forbes*, says 'at Aberdeen'.
9. *CSPS*, III, p. 669; *RMS*, V, p. 594, cited in Forbes, 'Notes', II, p. 5.
10. Bannatyne, *Memorials*, p. 194, cited in Forbes, 'Notes', II, p. 5.
11. Bannatyne, *Memorials*, p. 194.
12. W. Douglas Simpson, 'Corgarff Castle, Aberdeenshire', *Proceedings of the Society of Antiquaries of Scotland* (Dec. 1926) p. 89.
13. Forbes, 'Notes', I, p. 8.
14. RMS, VII, p. 1107.
15. Forbes, 'Notes', II, p. 7 (3).
16. Bannatyne, *Memorials*, p. 212. 'Marischal' means officer with high military function, so maybe he thought he should be in overall command.
17. Ibid., p. 197.
18. Ibid., p. 212.
19. Ibid., p. 212.
20. Marren, *Grampian Battlefields*, p. 125.
21. *RPCS*, VII, p. 1024.
22. Raphael Holinshed, *Holinshed's Chronicles of England, Scotland, and*

Ireland, 6 vols (London, 1807–8 edn), II, p. 360, cited in Tayler (eds), *House of Forbes*, p. 91.

23. Holinshed, *Holinshed's Chronicles*, II, p. 380.
24. Robert Lindsay of Pitscottie, *The Historie and Chronicles of Scotland from the Slauchter of King James the First . . .* , edited by A.J.G. Mackay, 3 vols (Scottish Text Society, 1899–1911), II, pp. 270–1.
25. Holinshed, *Holinshed's Chronicles*, II, p. 380.
26. Marren, *Grampian Battlefields*, p. 127. The site of the Craibstane battle has long been built over, and the stone incorporated into a nearby wall at the top of Hardgate commemorates this battle and another on the same site in the civil war in 1644. The Gordon probably occupied the open rise where the Hardgate is crossed by Bon Accord Terrace, the fighting being in the vicinity of Union Glen.
27. Tayler (eds), *House of Forbes*, p. 90.
28. Bannatyne, *Memorials*, pp. 212–13.
29. Robert Lindsay of Pitscottie, *The Historie and Cronicles of Scotland from the Slauchter of King James the First . . .* , edited by A.J.G. Mackay, 3 vols (Scottish Text Society, 1899–1911), p. 272.
30. Ibid., p. 289.
31. *RPCS*, II, cited in Forbes, 'Notes', III, p. 12.
32. *RPCS*, II, cited in Ibid., p. 13.
33. *CSPS*, V, p. 23, Killigrew to Walsingham, cited in Potter, *Blood Feud*, p. 23.
34. Aberdeen Sheriff Court Book (ASCB), I, cited in Forbes, 'Notes', III, p. 13.
35. Gordon, *History of the House of Gordon* cited in Tayler (eds), *House of Forbes*, p. 92.
36. Ibid.
37. *Illustrations of the Topography and Antiquities of the Shires of Aberdeen and Banff*, 4 vols (Spalding Club, Aberdeen 1847–1869), I, p. 457; *Scots Peerage*, IV, p. 538, Huntly.
38. ASCB, I, p. 457, cited in Forbes, 'Notes', III p. 17.
39. *RSS*, VII, p. 1107, cited in Forbes, 'Notes', III, p. 17.
40. ASCB, IV, p. 763–7, cited in Forbes, 'Notes', III, p. 18.
41. ASCB, III, pp. 112–4; *Illustrations of the Topography and Antiquities*, IV, pp. 763–6, cited in Forbes, 'Notes', III, p. 19.
42. Tayler (eds), *House of Forbes*, pp. 105.
43. *RPCS*, III, pp. 260–1.
44. Ibid.
45. *RPCS*, II, pp. 278–9.
46. Ibid., pp. 178–80.
47. *RPCS*, III, p. 280.
48. Simpson, 'Corgarff Castle', p. 87.
49. James Melville, *Memoirs*, p. 209.
50. Donaldson, *All the Queen's Men*, p. 7.
51. Keith Brown, *Blood Feuds in Scotland* (Edinburgh, 1986) p. 145.
52. Donaldson, *All the Queen's Men*, p. 121.
53. Ibid., p. 8.
54. Jenny Wormald, *Court, Kirk and Community 1470–1625* (Edinburgh, 1991) p. 167.

55. Wormald, *Failure*, p. 179.
56. Bannatyne, *Memorials*, p. 23.
57. Holinshed, *Holinshed's Chronicles*, II, p. 379.
58. Forbes, 'Notes', I, p. 6.
59. Tayler (eds), *House of Forbes*, p. 88.
60. Simpson, 'Corgarff Castle', p. 74.
61. Marren, *Grampian Battlefields*, p. 119.
62. Forbes, 'Notes', I, p. 8.
63. Tayler (eds), *House of Forbes*, p. 93.

Chapter 4 Margaret Gordon

1. Tayler (eds), *House of Forbes*, p. 111.
2. Donaldson, *All the Queen's Men* p. 33.
3. Ibid., p. 108.
4. Ibid., p. 112.
5. Rosalind K. Marshall, *Virgins and Viragos: A History of Women in Scotland from 1080–1980* (London, 1983), p. 87.
6. Forbes, 'Notes', I, p. 11.
7. *CSP*(F), pp. 328–30, 30 Sept. 1562, Randolph to Cecil.
8. Forbes. 'Notes', I, p. 11.
9. Tayler (eds), *House of Forbes*, p. 83.
10. Forbes, 'Notes', III, p. 2.
11. *CSPS*, II, p. 466
12. Forbes, 'Notes', I, Appendix IV, p. 15.
13. *CSPS*, III, p. 166; *RPCS*, III, p. 116 n.1.
14. Bannatyne, *Memorials*, p. 26.
15. Forbes, 'Notes', III, p. 4.
16. Tayler (eds), *House of Forbes*, p. 118.
17. Ibid.
18. [Walter Cullen's], 'The Chronicle of Aberdeen', in *Miscellany of the Spalding Club*, Vol. II, Issue 6 (Aberdeen, 1842), cited in Forbes, 'Notes', III, p. 8.
19. Forbes, 'Notes', I, p. 10.
20. Bannatynes, *Memorials*, pp. 212–3, cited in Forbes, 'Notes', III, p. 9.
21. Forbes, 'Notes', II, p. 3.
22. Forbes, 'Notes', III, p. 2.
23. Tayler (eds), *House of Forbes*, Letter from Morton to Laird of Gowrie (Fotheringham) Family Papers, p. 118.
24. Marshall, *Virgins and Viragos*, p. 96.
25. Ibid.
26. Tayler (eds), *House of Forbes*, p. 112.
27. Forbes, 'Notes', III, p. 2.
28. Ibid., p. 5.
29. Tayler (eds), *House of Forbes*, p. 112.
30. Marshall, *Virgins and Viragos*, p. 97.
31. *Scots Peerage*, IV, p. 58.

32. Marshall, *Virgins and Viragos*, p. 103.
33. Tayler (eds), *House of Forbes*, p. 119.
34. Ibid., p. 114.
35. *The Life of the Reverend Fa. Angel of Ioyeuse, Capuchin Preacher, Together with the Lives of the Reverend Fathers, Father Bennet Englishman, and Father Archangell Scotchman, of the Same Order* (Douai, 1623), p. 27.
36. Forbes, 'Notes', I, p. 10.
37. Tayler (eds), *House of Forbes*, p. 115.
38. Convent from the Latin word conventus, which in ecclesiastical usage can refer either to the buildings in which a body of religious live together or to the religious community itself. Historically it has been applied to the domicile of religious of either sex, though in English it tends now to be restricted to the houses of women religious. Source: *Oxford Dictionary of the Christian Church*, p. 412.
39. Tayler (eds), *House of Forbes*, p. 115.
40. *Life of the Reverend Fa. Angel*, p. 27
41. Ibid.
42. Ibid., p. 32.
43. Ibid., p. 35.
44. Ibid., p. 35.
45. Ibid., p. 40.
46. *Scots Peerage*, IV, p. 60.
47. Ibid., p. 53.
48. Tayler (eds), *House of Forbes*, p. 147.
49. Ibid., p. 143.
50. *Life of the Reverend Fa. Angel*, p. 53.
51. Forbes, 'Notes', I, p. 8.
52. Tayler (eds), *House of Forbes*, p. 116.
53. *Scots Peerage*, IV, p. 60.
54. Forbes, 'Notes', I, p. 10.
55. *Life of the Reverend Fa. Angel*, p. 93.
56. Tayler (eds), *House of Forbes*, p. 147.
57. *Life of the Reverend Fa. Angel*, p. 103.
58. Ibid., p. 101.
59. Ibid., p. 112.
60. *Life of the Reverend Fa. Angel*, p. 112.
61. *Scots Peerage*, IV, p. 58.
62. Tayler (eds), *House of Forbes*, p. 147.
63. *Scots Peerage*, IV, pp. 60, 114.

Chapter 5 Jean Gordon

1. See Rosalind K. Marshall, 'Hepburn, James, Fourth Earl of Bothwell and Duke of Orkney (1534/5–1578)', *Oxford Dictionary of National Biography* (Oxford, 2004). Available online [subscription database] at: <http://www.oxforddnb.com/view/article/13001>, accessed March 2012.

2. Sanderson, *Mary Stewart's People*, p. 38.

3. Fraser, *Mary Queen of Scots*, p. 299.

4. Ibid., p. 306.

5. Guy, *My Heart is My Own*, p. 285.

6. John Knox, cited in Sanderson, *Mary Stewart's People*, p. 39.

7. Quoted in Sanderson, *Mary Stewart's People*, p. 45, but the original source is unacknowledged.

8. Guy, *My Heart is My Own*, p. 381.

9. Guy, *My Heart is my Own*, p. 330.

10. Ibid., p. 427.

11. The original dispensation is now at Dunrobin.

12. Guy, *My Heart is My Own*, p. 332.

13. Ibid., p. 338.

14. John Stuart, *A Lost Chapter in the History of Mary Queen of Scots Recovered* (1874), p. 22, cited in Sanderson, *Mary Stewart's People*, p. 41.

15. Gilbert T. Bell, *A Prospect of Sutherland*, p. 26.

16. Gordon, *Genealogical History of the Earldom of Sutherland*, p. 147.

17. Ibid., p. 147.

18. Ibid., p. 149.

19. Fraser, *Sutherland Book*, p. 134.

20. Sanderson, *Mary Stewart's People*, pp. 42–3.

21. Gordon, *Genealogical History of the Earldom of Sutherland*, p. 168.

22. National Archives/Records of Scotland, Register of Deeds, RD1/14, folio 269.

23. Fraser, *Sutherland Book*, I, p. 168.

24. Sanderson, *Mary Stewart's People*, p. 44.

25. Some sources call him 11th Earl of Sutherland, especially early ones, thus ignoring Adam Gordon of Aboyne's being made 'jure uxoris' earl by right of his wife, Elizabeth, who was 'suo jure' Countess of Sutherland. He died in 1537/8.

26. Sanderson, *Mary Stewart's People*, p. 45.

27. Gordon, *Genealogical History of the Earldom of Sutherland*, p. 236.

28. Quoted in Sanderson, *Mary Stewart's People*, p. 52; the primary source is unacknowledged.

29. Gordon, *Genealogical History of the Earldom of Sutherland*, p. 237.

30. Ibid., p. 43.

31. Mrs. Dugeon, Craikaig, personal communication.

32. Fraser, *Sutherland Book*, I, p. 174.

33. Gordon, *Genealogical History of the Earldom of Sutherland*, p. 237.

34. Donaldson, *Scotland, James V to James VII*, III, p. 193.

35. Douglas W. Simpson and Christopher J. Tabraham, *Huntly Castle* (Edinburgh, 1954), pp. 24, 27.

36. Gordon, *Genealogical History of the Earldom of Sutherland*, p. 240.

37. Sanderson, *Mary Stewart's People*, p. 49.

38. Gordon, *Genealogical History of the Earldom of Sutherland*, p. 249.

39. Ibid., p. 255.

40. Ibid., p. 239.

41.   Marshall, *Virgins and Viragos*, p. 131.
42.   Quoted in Sanderson, *Mary Stewart's People*, p. 52.
43.   Gordon, *Genealogical History of the Earldom of Sutherland*, p. 345.
44.   Ibid., p. 409.
45.   Marshall, *Virgins and Viragos*, p. 160.
46.   Quoted in Sanderson, *Mary Stewart's People*, p. 54.
47.   Quoted in Ibid., p. 47.
48.   Gordon, *Genealogical History of the Earldom of Sutherland*, p. 409.

Chapter 6 James Gordon

1.   Peter F. Anson, *The Catholic Church in Modern Scotland* (London, 1937).
2.   Michael Barrett, *Sidelights on Scottish History* (Edinburgh, 1918), p. 133.
3.   Anson, *Catholic Church in Modern Scotland*, p. 4.
4.   *Narratives of Scottish Catholics under Mary Stuart and James VI*, edited by William Forbes-Leith, SJ (Edinburgh, 1885) pp. 71–4.
5.   John Hungerford Pollen, *The Counter-Reformation in Scotland* (London and Edinburgh, 1921), p. 18.
6.   H.A.L. Fisher, *A History of Europe*, 3 vols (London, 1966), II, pp. 556–7.
7.   J. D. Mackie, 'Scotland and the Spanish Armada', *Scottish Historical Review*, No. 45 (1914), pp. 4–5.
8.   Pollen, *Counter-Reformation*, p. 25.
9.   Fisher, *History of Europe*, p. 587.
10.   Ibid., p. 584.
11.   Anson, *Catholic Church in Modern Scotland*, p. 2.
12.   Pollen, *Counter-Reformation*, p. 31.
13.   In the Bible (2 Chronicles 22) Joas was saved by his aunt from being put to death by Athaliah, along with the King's other sons.
14.   Bruce McLennan, 'Presbyterianism Challenged: A Study of Catholicism and Episcopacy in the North East of Scotland 1560–1650' (PhD Thesis, University of Aberdeen, 1977), p. 102.
15.   *Chambers Biographical Dictionary*, edited by Magnus Magnusson (Edinburgh, 1990), p. 1000.
16.   Compton Mackenzie, *Catholicism in Scotland* (London, 1936), p. 94. The Halifax Maiden was an earlier form of a guillotine, introduced to Scotland from Halifax, West Yorkshire, by James Douglas, 4th Earl of Morton. It was called the 'maiden' because it was so rarely used.
17.   Ibid.
18.   Fisher, *History of Europe*, p. 563.
19.   James Quinn, SJ, 'The Jesuits in Scotland', *Tablet*, 30 Jan. 1960, p. 106.
20.   Donaldson, *Scotland, James V to James VII*, III, p. 173.
21.   Calderwood, *History of the Kirk*, III, p. 192.
22.   Fisher, *History of Europe*, II, p. 563.
23.   Pollen, *Counter-Reformation*, p. 87.
24.   Anson, *Catholic Church in Modern Scotland*, p. 2.
25.   Donaldson, *Scotland, James V to James VII*, III, p. 175.

26.   McLennan, 'Presbyterianism Challenged', p. 108.
27.   Machie, 'Scotland and the Spanish Armada', p. 7.
28.   CSP (Foreign, Spanish, Eliza.), III, p. 371; see also Mackie, 'Scotland and the Spanish Armada', p. 6.
29.   Pollen, *Counter-Reformation*, p. 42.
30.   Anson, *Catholic Church in Modern Scotland*, pp. 5–6.
31.   Donaldson, *Scotland, James V to James VII*, III, p. 178.
32.   Pollen, *Counter-Reformation*, p. 55.
33.   *CSPS*, VI, p. 523.
34.   Donaldson, *Scotland, James V to James VII*, III, p. 181.
35.   Pollen, *Counter-Reformation*, p. 47.
36.   Ibid., p. 45.
37.   Ibid., p. 51.
38.   *Narratives of Scottish Catholics*, ed. Forbes-Leith, p. 196.
39.   Donaldson, *Scotland, James V to James VII*, III, p. 181.
40.   Pollen, *Counter-Reformation*, p. 51
41.   Ibid.
42.   Anson, *Catholic Church in Modern Scotland*, p. 2.
43.   Barrett, *Sidelights on Scottish History*, p. 141.
44.   Pollen, *Counter-Reformation*, p. 58.
45.   Ibid., p. 45.
46.   Donaldson, *Scotland, James V to James VII*, III, p. 182.
47.   Anson, *Catholic Church in Modern Scotland*, p. 6.
48.   Pollen, *Counter-Reformation*, p. 55.
49.   Donaldson, *Scotland, James V to James VII*, III, p. 187.
50.   Pollen, *Counter-Reformation*, p. 60.
51.   Barrett, *Sidelights on Scottish History*, p. 142.
52.   Donaldson, *Scotland, James V to James VII*, III, p. 187.
53.   *CSP*, Eliza., III, p. 541.
54.   *CSP*, Spanish, Elizabeth, IV, pp. 42, 43, 101 (*Calendar of Letters and State Papers Relating to English Affairs Preserved in or Originally Belonging to the Archives of Sinancas IV. Eliz. 1587–1603*, edited by Martin A.S. Hume (London 1899).
55.   Mackie, 'Scotland and the Spanish Armada', p. 12.
56.   Donaldson, *Scotland, James V to James VII*, III, p. 183.
57.   *CSPS*, IX, p. 589.
58.   *CSPS*, IX, p. 171.
59.   *CSPS*, IX, p. 229–30.
60.   Mackenzie, *Catholicism in Scotland*, pp. 18–19.
61.   Ibid., p. 95.
62.   Pollen, *Counter-Reformation*, p. 62.
63.   Barrett, *Sidelights on Scottish History*, p. 140.
64.   Anson, *Catholic Church in Modern Scotland*, p. 7.
65.   Pollen, *Counter-Reformation*, p. 61.
66.   Donaldson, *Scotland, James V to James VII*, III, p. 187.
67.   *CSPS*, IX, p. 590.
68.   Donaldson, *Scotland, James V to James VII*, III, p. 185.

69. *RPCS*, IV, p. 103.
70. Calderwood, *History of the Kirk*, IV, p. 686.
71. *RPCS*, IV, Introduction, p. xxxix.
72. *CSPS*, X, p. 301.
73. Mackenzie, *Catholicism in Scotland*, pp. 21–2.
74. McLennan, 'Presbyterianism Challenged', p. 112.
75. Fisher, *History of Europe*, p. 576.
76. Pollen, *Counter-Reformation*, p. 70.
77. Mackenzie, *Catholicism in Scotland*, pp. 22–3.
78. Spottiswoode, *History of the Church of Scotland*, II , p. 391.
79. *RPCS*, IV, p. xxxix.
80. Caroline Bingham, *James VI of Scotland* (London, 1979), p. 112.
81. *RPCS*, IV, 1585–1592, p. 351 (27 Feb. 1589).
82. Spottiswoode, *History of the Church of Scotland*, II, p. 392.
83. *RPCS*, IV, Introduction, p. xl.
84. McLellan, 'Presbyterianism Challenged', p. 114.
85. *RPCS*, IV, p. 372.
86. Spottiswoode, *History of the Church of Scotland*, II, p. 398.
87. Bingham, *James VI of Scotland*, p. 113.
88. *CSPS*, X, p. 3.
89. Spottiswoode, *History of the Church of Scotland*, II, pp. 398–9.
90. George Buchanan, *History of Scotland*, translated from the Latin by James Aikman (London, 1827–9), III, p. 167, cited in McLennan, 'Presbyterianism Challenged', p. 116.
91. *RPCS*, IV, p. 412–3, n.1.
92. *Dictionary of National Biography*, p. 186.
93. *RPCS*, IV, pp. 782–7.
94. *CSPS*, X, p. 301.
95. Ibid., p. 331.
96. Ibid., p. 335.
97. Ibid., p. 332, Bowes to Burghley.
98. Ibid., p. 371
99. Ibid., p. 392.
100. Ibid., p. 409.
101. Ibid., p. 412.
102. *CSPS*, X, p. 424.
103. Ibid., p. 442.
104. Barrett, *Sidelights on Scottish History*, p. 143.
105. *CSPS*, X, p. 266.
106. Ibid., p. 446.
107. Ibid., p. 625.
108. Wormald, *Lords and Men*, p. 118.
109. McLennan, 'Presbyterianism Challenged', p. 117.
110. Donaldson, *Scotland, James V to James VII*, III, p. 191.
111. Mackenzie, *Catholicism in Scotland*, p. 99.
112. *CSPS*, X, p. 740.

113. Ibid.
114. Ibid., p. 748.
115. Ibid., pp. 792–3.
116. *CSPS*, X, p. 810.
117. Francis Shearman, 'The Spanish Blanks', *Innes Review*, III, No. 2 (1950–2), p. 89.
118. *CSPS*, X, p. 812.
119. Ibid., p. 824.
120. David Calderwood, The True *History of the Church of Scotland*, from the beginning of the Reformation, unto the end of the reigne of King James VI (1678 edn), pp. 271–2.
121. Melville, *Memoirs*, p. 201.
122. *RPCS*, pp. 35–6; see also Spottiswoode, *History of the Church of Scotland*, II, pp. 390–1, and Calderwood, *History of the Kirk*, V, pp. 192, 214.
123. John Colville, *Historie and Life of James the Sext* (Bannatyne Club, Edinburgh, 1825 edn), p. 256.
124. James Melville, *The Diary of Mr. James Melvill, 1556–1601* (Bannatyne Club Edinburgh, 1829), p. 205.
125. Colville, *Historie and Life of James the Sext*, pp. 256–8.
126. *CSPS*, XI, p. 10.
127. Spottiswoode, *History of the Church of Scotland*, II, pp. 425–6.
128. *CSPS*, X, p. 828.
129. Colville, *Historie and Life of James the Sext*, p. 261.
130. Calderwood, *History of the Kirk*, V, p. 231; Spottiswoode, *History of the Church of Scotland*, II, pp. 390, 391; *RPCS*, V, p. 35, cited in McLennan, 'Presbyterianism Challenged', p. 119.
131. Calderwood, *History of the Kirk*, V, pp. 192–3, cited in McLennan, 'Presbyterianism Challenged', p. 118.
132. Spottiswoode, *History of the Church of Scotland*, II, pp. 427.
133. *CSPS*, X, p. 830.
134. *RPCS*, V, p. 33.
135. Melville, *Diary*, p. 206.
136. Calderwood, *History of the Kirk*, V, p. 240; *RPCS*, V, pp. 53–4.
137. Melville, *Diary*, p. 214, cited in Gordon, *History of the House of Gordon*, pp. 56–60.
138. *RPCS*, V, p. 38.
139. Ibid., p. 38.
140. *RPCS*, V, p. 42.
141. Keith, *History*, p. 268.
142. Ibid., p. 268.
143. Shearman, 'Spanish Blanks', p. 91.
144. *RPCS*, V, p. 43.
145. *CSPS*, XI, pp. 71, 72, 74, 77, cited in Shearman, 'Spanish Blanks', p. 95.
146. *RPCS*, V, p. 44.
147. *CSPS*, XI, p. 53.
148. Calderwood, *History of the Kirk*, V, p. 249.

149. *CSPS*, XI, cited in Shearman, 'Spanish Blanks', p. 96.
150. W.L. Mathieson, *Politics and Religion: A Study in Scottish History from the Reformation to the Revolution*, 2 vols (Glasgow, 1902), I, p. 360.
151. *RPCS*, IV, p. 163.
152. Potter, *Blood Feud*, p. 210.
153. *CSPS*, XI, Bowes to Burleigh, p. 199.
154. *CSPS*, XI, p. 103.
155. Ibid., p. 204.
156. 'The Gordon Letters: V, James VI to the Earl of Huntly, in *Miscellany of the Spalding Club* (Aberdeen, 1846), III, p. 213.
157. *CSPS*, XI, Bowes to Burghley, pp. 200–1.
158. *CSPS*, XI, p. 108.
159. *APS*, IV, pp. 52–3.
160. Potter, *Blood Feud*, p. 210.
161. *CSPS*, XI, p. 451, cited in Potter, *Blood Feud*, p. 211.
162. *CSPS*, XI, p. 53.
163. 'Documents Illustrating Catholic Policy of the Reign of James VI', edited by Thomas Graves Law, in *Miscellany of the Scottish History Society* (Edinburgh, 1893), I, pp. 59–60.
164. MS by Fr William Crichton, SJ, in Latin, cited in *Narratives of Scottish Catholics*, ed. Forbes-Leith, p. 220.
165. *CSPS*, X, p. 232.
166. *RPCS*, IV, p. 157.
167. Donaldson, *Scotland, James V to James VII*, III, p. 193.
168. Melville, *Diary*, p. 207.
169. Ibid., p. 208.
170. Ibid.
171. *RPCS*, IV p. 146.
172. *CSPS*, XI, p. 52.
173. Potter, *Blood Feud*, pp. 213–4.
174. Spottiswoode, *History of the Church of Scotland*, II, p. 261.
175. *CSPS*, XI, p. 449; Patrick Fraser Tytler, *History of Scotland*, III, p. 277, cited in Potter, *Blood Feud*, p. 214.
176. Ian B.D. Bryce and Alasdair Roberts, 'Post-Reformation Catholic Houses of North-East Scotland', *Proceedings of the Society of Antiquaries of Scotland*, No. 123 (1993), pp. 363–72.
177. Potter, *Blood Feud*, p. 215.
178. Ibid., p. 215.
179. Mackenzie, *Catholicism in Scotland*, p. 97.
180. *DNB*, eds Stephen and Lee, p. 187.
181. Calderwood, *History of the Kirk*, V, pp. 360–1.
182. *The Spottiswoode Miscellany: A Collection of Original Papers and Tracts* (Edinburgh, 1844), I, p. 263.
183. Hagbutters are troops with rifles. A hagbut is another name for an arquebus.
184. *Spottiswoode Miscellany*, I, p. 265.
185. Potter, *Blood Feud*, p. 217.

186. 'A long, narrow triangular or swallow-tailed flag, usually atached to the head of a lance or helmet, originally the ensign of a knight under the rank of banneret, and later the military ensign of lancer regiments' (*Oxford English Dictionary*).

187. Melville, *Diary*, p. 213.

188. Potter, *Blood Feud*, p. 219.

189. Shearman, 'Spanish Blanks', p. 98.

190. *Dictionary of National Biography (DNB)*, edited by Leslie Stephen and Sidney Lee (London, 1890), XXII, p. 188.

191. Melville, *Diary*, p. 214.

192. Letters of John Colville, p. 116 cited in McLennan, 'Presbyterianism Challenged', p. 123.

193. Potter, *Blood Feud*, p. 221.

194. *CSPS*, X (Bowes to Cecil, 29 Oct. 1594) cited in *Dictionary*, p. 188.

195. W.D. Simpson, 'The Architectural History of Huntly', *Proceedings of the Society of Antiquities of Scotland* (1921–2), cited in Bryce and Roberts, 'Post-Reformation Catholic Houses', pp. 363–72.

196. *CSPS*, XI, pp. 472, 474.

197. Potter, *Blood Feud*, p. 221.

198. McLennan, 'Presbyterianism Challenged', p. 123.

199. *CSPS*, XI, p. 469, cited in McLennan, 'Presbyterianism Challenged' p. 122.

200. Bingham, *James VI of Scotland*, p. 136.

201. *CSPS*, XI, pp. 47, 522; *CSP* (Spain, V, Eliza), p. 614, cited in McLennan, 'Presbyterianism Challenged', p. 122.

202. Mackenzie, *Catholicism in Scotland*, p. 97.

203. Potter, *Blood Feud*, p. 222.

204. Calderwood, *History of the Kirk*, V, p. 357, cited in McLennan, 'Presbyterianism Challenged', p. 122.

205. *Narratives of Scottish Catholics*, ed. Forbes-Leith, p. 228.

206. *Letters of John Colville*, pp. 150–1, cited in McLennan, 'Presbyterianism Challenged', p. 123.

207. Pollen, *Counter-Reformation*, p. 72.

208. Mackenzie, *Catholicism in Scotland*, p. 102.

209. *Letters and State Papers during the Reign of King James the Sixth*, edited by James Maidment (Abotsford Club, Edinburgh, 1838), pp. 29–30, cited in McLennan, 'Presbyterianism Challenged', p. 124.

210. Spottiswoode, *History of the Church of Scotland*, II, p. 438, cited in McLennan, 'Presbyterianism Challenged', p. 125. JVI's attitude grew colder as English throne grew nearer.

211. *DNB*, eds Stephen and Lee, p. 188.

212. *CSPS*, XII, pp. 466, 454.

213. Potter, *Blood Feud*, p. 223.

214. Mackenzie, *Catholicism in Scotland*, p. 97.

215. Pollen, *Counter-Reformation*, p. 78.

216. Mackenzie, *Catholicism in Scotland*, p. 97.

217. Shearman, 'Spanish Blanks', p. 83.

218. *Narratives of Scottish Catholics*, ed. Forbes-Leith, pp. 232–61.
219. 'The Earl of Huntly's Answer to the Articles 655', in Calderwood, *History of the Kirk*, V, pp. 616–18, cited in *DNB*, eds Stephen and Lee, p. 188.
220. Bingham, *James VI of Scotland*, p. 136.
221. Barrett, *Sidelights on Scottish History*, p. 143.
222. *Narratives of Scottish Catholics*, ed. Forbes-Leith, p. 167.
223. Shearman, 'Spanish Blanks', p. 84.
224. Anson, *Catholic Church in Modern Scotland*, p. 8.
225. Ruth Grant, 'Henrietta, Wife of the 6th Earl of Huntly' (Lecture at Gordon 2000 event).
226. *Narratives of Scottish Catholics*, ed. Forbes-Leith, p. 265.
227. R.O. Memorial of the Present State of Scotland 1598, quoted by Tytler, *History of Scotland*, IX, p. 258; see also *Narratives of Scottish Catholics*, ed. Forbes-Leith, p. 266.
228. *Narratives of Scottish Catholics*, ed. Forbes-Leith, p. 268.
229. Ibid., p. 267.
230. Ibid., p. 270.
231. Shearman, 'Spanish Blanks', p. 84
232. Mackenzie, *Catholicism in Scotland*, pp. 98–9.
233. *CSPS*, XIII, Part 1, p. 489.
234. Potter, *Blood Feud*, p. 231.
235. Calderwood, *History of the Kirk*, VI, p. 100, cited in *DNB*, eds Stephen and Lee, p. 188.
236. *RPCS*, VI, p. 8, cited in *DNB*, eds Stephen and Lee, p. 188.
237. *RPCS*, VII, pp. 19–20, 460, cited in McLennan, 'Presbyterianism Challenged', p. 126
238. See Julian Goodare, *The Government of Scotland 1560–1625* (Oxford, 2004).
239. G.F. Warner, 'James VI and Rome', *English Historical Review*, XX (1905), pp. 124–7.
240. *Narratives of Scottish Catholics*, ed. Forbes-Leith, p. 281.
241. *Correspondence of King James VI. of Scotland with Sir Robert Cecil and Others in England during the Reign of Queen Elizabeth*, edited by John Bruce (Campden Society, 1861) pp. 36–8.
242. Bryce and Roberts, 'Post-Reformation Catholic Houses', pp. 363–72.
243. Gilbert Blackhall, *A Breiffe Narration of the Services Done to Three Noble Ladyes*, ed. John Stuart (Aberdeen, 1844), p. xxi.

Postscript

1. For more on the last years of the life of the 1st Marquis, see Barry Robertson's *Lordship and Power in the North of Scotland* (Edinburgh, 2011).
2. John Spalding, *History of the Troubles and Memorable Transactions in Scotland* (Aberdeen, 1829 edn), p. 39.

Bibliography

Record Sources

Acts of the Parliament of Scotland 1124–1770, edited by Thomas Thomson and Cosmo Innes (London, 1814–75), Vol. IV.

Antiquities of the Slures of Aberdeen and Banff, 4 vols (Spalding Club, Aberdeen, 1847–69).

Calendar of State Papers Foreign Series of the Reign of Elizabeth preserved in the State Department of her Majesty's Public Record Office, edited by Joseph Stevenson (London, 1867).

Calendar of State Papers Relating to Scotland and Mary Queen of Scots 1547–1603, 14 vols (1898–1969).

Commissariat of Edinburgh, Register of Acts and Decreets, National Archives/Records of Scotland, CC8/2.

Register of Deeds, National Archives/Records of Scotland, RD1/14, folio 269.

Register of the Privy Council of Scotland, edited by David Masson (Edinburgh, 1877–98), Vols 1–14 (1545–1625).

Register of the Great Seal of Scotland AD 1306–1668 (Registrum Magni Sigilli Regum Scotorum), 11 vols (Edinburgh General Register House, 1882–1914).

Contemporary Narratives

Aberdeen Sheriff Court Book.

Bannatyne, Richard, *Memorials of Transactions in Scotland AD 1549–1573*, edited by R. Pitcairn (Edinburgh, 1836).

Buchanan, George, *The History of Scotland*, 2 vols, translated from the Latin by James Aikman (London, 1827–9).

Calderwood, David, *History of the Kirk of Scotland (1524–1625)*, 8 vols (Woodrow Society, Edinburgh, 1842–9).

Colville, John, *Historie and Life of James the Sext*, edited by Thomas Thompson (Bannatyne Club, Edinburgh, 1825).

Diurnal of Remarkable Occurents in Scotland since the Death of King James IV till the Year 1587, from a Manuscript of the Sixteenth Century, edited by T. Thompson (Bannatyne Club, Edinburgh, 1833).

Gordon, Sir Robert of Gordonstoun, *A Genealogical History of the Earldom of Sutherland from its origin to 1603; with a Continuation to the Year 1651* (Edinburgh, 1813).

Holinshed, Raphael, *Holinshed's Chronicles of England, Scotland, and Ireland*, 6 vols (London, 1807–8 edn; first compiled 1577), Vol. II, containing 'The Historie of Scotland . . . unto the Year 1571'.

Holinshed, Raphael, *The Historie of Scotland unto the yeare 1571, 1 vol.* (London, 1577).

Knox, John, *History of the Reformation in Scotland*, translated and edited by W. Croft Dickinson, 2 vols (London, 1949).

Melville, James, *The Diary of James Melvill, 1556–1601*, edited by George Ritchie Kinloch, (Bannatyne Club, Edinburgh, 1829).

Melville, James, *Autobiography and Diary of Mr. James Melvill, 1556–1601*, edited by Robert Pitcairn (Wodrow Society, Edinburgh, 1842).

Melville, Sir James of Halhill, *Memoirs of his Own Life (1549–1593)*, edited by A. Francis Steuart (Bannatyne Club, London, 1929).

Narratives of Scottish Catholics under Mary Stuart and James VI, edited by William Forbes-Leith, SJ (Edinburgh, 1885).

Spottiswood, John, *History of the Church of Scotland, to 1625*, 3 vols (Spottiswoode Society, Edinburgh, 1851), Vol. II.

The Life of the Reverend Fa. Angel of Ioyeuse, Capuchin Preacher, Together with the Lives of the Reverend Fathers, Father Bennet Englishman, and Father Archangell Scotchman, of the Same Order, translated from the French (Douai, 1623).

Various Collections

'Documents Illustrating Catholic Policy of the Reign of James VI', edited by Thomas Graves Law, in *Miscellany of the Scottish History Society* (Edinburgh, 1893), Vol. I.

'Letters of James VI to the Earl of Huntly', in *Miscellany of the Spalding Club* (Aberdeen, 1846), Vol. III.

Letters of King James VI and I, edited by G.P.V. Arigg (Berkeley, 1984).

Early Historical Works

Chalmers, George, *The Life of Mary Queen of Scots – Drawn from State Papers* (London, 1818), Vol. I.

Crawford, George, *Lives of the Chancellors and Characters of the Crown and of the State in Scotland* (Edinburgh, 1726), Vol. I.

History of the Feuds and Conflicts Among the Clans (Glasgow, 1818).

Keith, Robert, Rt Rev., *History of the Affairs of Church and State in Scotland to 1567*, 3 vols (Spottiswood Society, Edinburgh, 1845).

Lindsay, Robert, of Pitscottie, *The Historie and Cronicles of Scotland from the Slauchter of King James the First . . .* , edited by A.J.G. Mackay, 3 vols (Scottish Text Society, 1899–1911).

Tytler, Patrick Fraser, *History of Scotland*, Vol. VII: Mary Queen of Scots (Edinburgh, 1840).

Secondary Works

Anson, Peter F., *Underground Catholicism in Scotland 1628–1878* (Montrose, 1870).

Anson, Peter F., *The Catholic Church in Modern Scotland* (London, 1937).

Barrett, Michael, *Sidelights on Scottish History* (Edinburgh, 1918).

Bell, Gilbert T., *A Prospect of Sutherland* (1995).

Bingham, Caroline, *James VI of Scotland* (London, 1979).

Brown, K.M., *Blood Feuds in Scotland* (Edinburgh, 1986).

Bryce, Ian B.D. and Roberts, Alasdair, 'Post-Reformation Catholic Houses of North-East Scotland', *Proceedings of the Society of Antiquaries of Scotland*, No. 123 (1993), pp. 363–72.

Bulloch, John Malcolm, *The House of Gordon* (Aberdeen, 1937).

Burke, John and Burke, J. Bernard, *Burke's Peerage and Baronetage of the British Empire* (London, 1847 edn).

Burke, Sir Bernard, *Burke's Peerage and Baronetage of the British Empire* (London, 1860 edn.)

Burton, J. H., *The History of Scotland*, 8 vols (1905), Vol. IV.

Chalmers, David. *The Life of Mary Queen of Scots, Drawn from State Papers* (London, 1918).

Chambers Biographical Dictionary, edited by Magnus Magnusson (Edinburgh, 1990).

Dawson, Aeneas McDonnell, *The Catholics of Scotland* (Ontario and London, 1890).

Dictionary of National Biography (Oxford, 1917 edn).

Dictionary of Scottish History, edited by Gordon Donaldson and Robert S. Morpeth (Edinburgh, 1977).

Donaldson, Gordon, *The Scottish Reformation* (Edinburgh, 1960).

Donaldson, Gordon, *Scotland's Conservative North in the Sixteenth and Seventeenth Centuries* (Transactions of the Royal Historical Society, 5th Series, Vol. 16; London, 1966).

Donaldson, Gordon, *A Dictionary of Scottish History* (Edinburgh, 1977).

Donaldson, Gordon, *All the Queen's Men* (London, 1983).

Donaldson, Gordon, *Scotland, James V to James VII*, 4 vols (Edinburgh, 1990), Vol. III.

Fisher, H.A.L., *A History of Europe*, 3 vols (London, 1935), Vol. II.

Fraser, Antonia, *Mary Queen of Scots* (London, 1970).

Fraser, Antonia, *King James VI of Scotland, I of England* (London, 1974).

Fraser, William, *The Sutherland Book* (Edinburgh, 1892).

Gordon, C.A., *History of the House of Gordon* (Aberdeen, 1890 edn).

Gordon, C.A., *History of the House of Gordon*, edited by J.M. Bulloch, 3 vols (Spalding Club, Aberdeen, 1924), Vol. II.

Guy, J.A., *My Heart is My Own: The Life of Mary Queen of Scots* (London, 2004).

Knox, John, *The Works of John Knox*, collected and edited by David Laing, 6 vols (Woodrow Society, Edinburgh 1846–64).

Law, William, *Politics and Religion in Scotland* (Glasgow, 1902).

Lee, Maurice Jr, *John Maitland of Thirlestane and the Foundation of the Stewart Despotism in Scotland* (Princeton, 1959).

Lynch, Michael (ed.), *Mary Stewart, Queen in Three Kingdoms* (Oxford, 1988).

Mackenzie, Compton, *Catholicism in Scotland* (London, 1936).

Mackie, J.D., 'Scotland and the Spanish Armada', *Scottish Historical Review*, Vol. XII, no. 45 (Oct. 1914).

Mackie, J.D., *A History of Scotland* (London, 1969 edn).

Mackintosh, John, *History of the Earls and Earldoms of Scotland* (Aberdeen, 1898).

McRoberts, David (ed.) *Essays on the Scottish Reformation 1513–1625* (Glasgow, 1962).

Marren, Peter, *Grampian Battlefields* (Aberdeen, 1990).

Marshall, Rosalind K. *Virgins and Viragos: A History of Women in Scotland, 1080–1980* (London, 1983).

Mathieson, W.L., *Politics and Religion: A Study in Scottish History from the Reformation to the Revolution*, 2 vols (Glasgow, 1902).

Patton, G.C.H. (ed.), *An Introduction to Scottish Legal History* (Edinburgh, 1958).

Pitcairn, R. (ed.) *Ancient Criminal Trials in Scotland* (Maitland Club, Glasgow, 1829–33).

Pollen, John Hungerford, *The Counter-Reformation in Scotland* (London and Edinburgh, 1921).

Potter, Harry, *Blood Feud: The Stewarts and Gordons at War in the Age of Mary Queen of Scots* (Stroud, 2002).

Quin, James, 'The Jesuits in Scotland', *The Tablet* (January 1960).

Russell, E., *Maitland of Lethington* (London, 1912).

Sanderson, Margaret H.B., *Mary Stewart's People* (Alabama, 1987).

Sanderson, Margaret H.B., *A Kindly Place? Living in Sixteenth Century Scotland* (Scotland, 2002).

Shearman, Francis, 'The Spanish Blanks', *Innes Review*, Vol. III, No. 2 (1950–2).

Simpson, W. Douglas, 'Corgarff Castle, Aberdeenshire' *Proceedings of the Society of Antiquaries of Scotland*, LXI, 6th Series, Vol. I (13 Dec. 1926).

Simpson, W. Douglas, *Castle Findlater* (Banffshire, 1931).

Simpson, W. Douglas and Tabraham, Christopher J., *Huntly Castle* (Edinburgh, 1954).

Smout, T.C., *A History of the Scottish People: 1560–1830* (Glasgow, 1969).

Tayler, Alastair and Henrietta, *The Ogilvies of Boyne* (Aberdeen, 1933).

Tayler, Alastair and Henrietta (eds), *The House of Forbes* (Aberdeen, 1937).

The Scots Peerage: Founded on Wood's Edition of Sir Robert Douglas's Peerage of Scotland, edited by Sir James Balfour Paul, 9 vols (Edinburgh, 1909–14).

Warner, G.F., 'James VI and Rome', *English Historical Review*, Vol. XX (1905).

Wormald, Jenny, 'Bloodfeud, Kindred and Government in Early Modern Scotland', *Past and Present* Vol. LXXXVII, Issue 1 (May 1980).

Wormald, Jenny, 'James VI and I: Two Kings or One?' *History*, Vol. LXVIII, Issue 223 (June 1983).

Wormald, Jenny, 'Gunpowder, Treason and Scots', *Journal of British Studies*, Vol. XXIV, No. 2 (April 1985).

Wormald, Jenny, *Lords and Men in Scotland: Bonds of Manrent 1445–1603* (Edinburgh, 1985).

Wormald, Jenny, *Mary Queen of Scots: A Study in Failure* (London, 1988).
Wormald, Jenny, *Court, Kirk and Community in Scotland, 1470–1625* (Edinburgh, 1991).
Yellowlees, M.J., 'Dunkeld and Nicholas de Gouda', *Innes Review* (Spring, 1993).

Unpublished Works

Forbes, Alexander, 'Notes', Parts I–V (unpublished manuscript, 2005–10).
Forbes, Alexander, 'The Rise of the House of Huntly' (unpublished manuscript, 2010).
McLennan, Bruce, 'Presbyterianism Challenged: A Study of Catholicism and Episcopacy in the North East of Scotland 1560–1650' (PhD Thesis, University of Aberdeen, 1977).
Simpson, Grant, 'The Earliest Gordons' (Lecture at the Gordon 2000 event, Huntly).
Wilson, Patricia, 'Father and Son Relationships' (PhD Thesis, University of Aberdeen, 1997).
Conference Papers
Goodare, Julian, 'James VI's English Subsidy' (Edinburgh, 1994).
Grant, Ruth, 'The Politics of the Counter-Reformation' (Edinburgh, 1994).
Grant, Ruth, 'Henrietta, Wife of the 6th Earl of Huntly' (Lecture at Gordon 2000 event, Huntly).
Grant, Ruth, 'Underground Catholicism' (Lecture at Gordon 2000 event, Huntly).

Biographical Who's Who

Abercrombie, Robert (1536–1613), one of the six taken by de Gouda to the Continent (1562); worked in Braniewi, Eastern Prussia, in Polish Jesuit college; returned to Scotland as Jesuit missionary; recommended by Fr James Gordon to instruct Queen Anne of Denmark; took a post as Keeper of the King's falcons in order to do so, resulting in her conversion; returned to Braniewi.

Abernethy, Alexander (1537–1587), 5th Baron Saltoun (1545)

Alba (or Alva), Duke of, Ferdinand Alvarez de Toledo (1508–1582), Spanish general and statesman; a brilliant soldier and tactician; as Lieutenant General was sent to enforce control of Spanish Netherlands; his 'bloody council' drove thousands of Huguenot artisans to emigrate to England; commanded successful invasion of Portugal (1581).

Albany, Duke of (see **Stewart**)

Alva (see **Alba**)

Angus, Earl of (see **Douglas**)

Anne of Denmark (1574–1619), **Queen of Scotland** (1590), **Queen of England** (1603) daughter of King Frederick II of Denmark; raised by her maternal grandparents, Duke and Duchess of Mecklenburg in Germany; converted to Catholicism by Fr Robert Abercrombie.

Argyll, earls of (see **Campbell**)

Athol, earls of (see **Strathbogie** and **Stewart**)

Arran, earls of (see **Hamilton** and **Stewart**)

Asheby, William, English Ambassador to Scotland (1588–1590), argued for generosity to James VI to counteract Spanish influence.

Bannatyne, Richard (d.1605), secretary to John Knox; author of *Memorials and Transactions in Scotland, AD 1549–1573*.

Barclay, David of Ladyland, with Mary Queen of Scots at Hamilton (1568) and probably Langside; arrested on boat carrying 'the Spanish Blanks'; imprisoned in Edinburgh with Graham of Fintray and George Kerr.

Beaton, David (c.1494–1546), **Cardinal** (1538), Commendator of Arbroath (1524), Archbishop of St Andrews (1539), Chancellor of St Andrews University, Ambassador to France (1519, 1533, 1538), Chancellor (1543), Bishop of Mirepoix in France (1537); leader of French and papal party in Scotland; murdered.

Beaton, James (II) (c.1523–1603), nephew of Cardinal David Beaton, whom he succeeded as Commendator of Arbroath (1543); Archbishop of Glasgow (1551); on success of Reformers, exiled himself to France in 1560; acted for Queen Mary in France and successive administrations under James VI; forfeited partially in 1587 and wholly in 1598.

Beaton, Mary (c.1543–c.1597), one of the Queen's 'Four Marys'; niece of Cardinal Beaton; married Alexander Ogilvie of Boyne (1566).

Bothwell, 4th Earl of (see Hepburn)

Bothwell, Francis, 5th Earl of (c.1563–1612), son of John Stewart, natural son of James V and Jean, sister of 4th Earl of Bothwell; accused of dealing with witches for destruction of James VI; several times attacked royal residences and terrorised James; mainly associated with ultra-Protestants, but sometimes connected with 6th Earl of Huntly; forfeited (1595); died in Naples.

Bowes, Robert (d.1597), **English Ambassador to Scotland** (1580, 1583, 1590–1597)

Boyd, Robert (c.1517–1590), **4th Baron Boyd** (c.1557), a Lord of the Congregation; supporter of Moray and latterly of Mary; killed by 6th Earl of Huntly.

Bruce, Father, messenger from exiled Archbishop Beaton of Glasgow to James VI (1588); drew up plan using unloading Baltic wheat ships to collect Spanish soldiers from Dunkirk to invade England; communicated with Parma and Spanish agents; 10,000 crowns delivered to him by Chisholm for Huntly; became convinced James VI a Protestant at heart.

Bruce, Robert (1554–1631), principal minister in Edinburgh (1587); anointed Queen Anne at her coronation; associated with unyielding Presbyterians against James VI's polices; persuaded Argyll to lead King's force against Huntly with money and promises of Huntly land; banished to Inverness (1605); wrote *Sermons on the Sacraments*.

Buchanan, George (1506–1582), scholar, historian, Reformer, tutor of James VI (1570–1578).

Caithness, Earls of (see Sinclair)

Calderwood, David (1575–1650/1), historian; banished to Holland by James VI for refusal to comply with Episcopal administration; wrote a massive defence of Protestantism (1619) and *A History of the Church of Scotland 1524–1625* (1578).

Calvin, John (1509–1564), French theologian and Reformer based in Geneva; systematised Protestant doctrine and organised ecclesiastical discipline; influenced John Knox.

Campbell, Archibald (1530–1573), **5th Earl of Argyll** (1558), backed Mary.

Campbell, Archibald (1575–1638), **7th Earl of Argyll** (1584), led forces of James VI against Catholic earls at Glenlivet (1594) as King's Lieutenant of the North.

Campbell, Margaret (d.1571), daughter of John Campbell of Cawdor; married John Forbes of Towie (or Tollie); died in burning of Corgarff Castle with sixteen others.

Cassilis, Earl of (see Kennedy)

Catherine de Medici (1519–1589), **Queen of France** (1547–1559), daughter of Lorenzo de Medici; married Henri, Duke of Orleons, the future Henri II of France, 2nd son of Francis I; mother of three kings of France; acted as Queen Regent during brief reign of Francis II, first husband of Mary Queen of Scots (1544–1560) and during minority of 2nd son, Charles IX (1550–1574); at first supported Huguenots against the Guises, then supported Guises, and traditionally implicated in Massacre of St Bartholemew's Day (1572).

Cecil, William (1520–1598), **1st Baron Burleigh** (1571), English ambassador to Scotland (1560), Chief Secretary of State for Elizabeth I.

Chalmers, George (1742–1825), author of *Life of Mary Queen of Scots* (1818); educated in Aberdeen; studied law in Edinburgh; published biographies of Defoe and Paine and wrote an unfinished monumental history of Scotland (1807–24).

Chisholm, Sir James, one of the Masters of James VI's household; excommunicated by minister of Haddington; arrested on boat with letters for Spain – 'the Spanish Blanks' signed by Huntly, Errol and Angus, Fr James under a pseudonym, and others.

Chisholm, William (d.1593), **Bishop of Dunblane,** nephew of previous Bishop of Dunblane, also William (d.1564); was Bishop of Vaison (1570–1585); resigned in favour of his nephew, also William.

Confederates, twelve earls and fourteen lords who signed a bond (6 June 1567) to rescue Mary from Bothwell

Craig, John (1512–1600), Dominican friar who came under suspicion of heresy; narrowly escaped execution in Rome; returned to Scotland (1560); Scottish Reformer; became minister of Canongate (1561); colleague of John Knox (1564); drew up *Second Book of Discipline* with Andrew Melville and drew up the catechism 'The Confession of Faith'.

Crawford, Bessie, daughter of a Haddington smith; Jean Gordon's serving maid; cited in her case for divorce against Bothwell.

Crawford, earls of (see Lindsay)

Crichton, William, one of the six men taken to Continent with de Gouda (1562), who returned as Jesuit missionaries (1581); superior of Scots College of Douai; lived in Spain; attempted to convince Philip II to attempt another invasion; very active in attempts to bring 'Enterprise of England' to fruition.

Cunningham, James (d. c.1631), **6th Earl of Glencairn** (c.1580)

Darnley, Henry Stewart (1546–1567), son of Matthew, 4th Earl of Lennox by Margaret, daughter of Margaret Tudor by 6th Earl of Angus; born in England; returned to Scotland (1565); married Mary Queen of Scots (1565); murdered Riccio; was himself murdered.

De Gouda, Nicholas, Jesuit Papal Legal, came to Scotland 1562 to invite Mary Queen of Scots to Council of Trent; took James Gordon, Edmund Hay, William Crichton, James Tyrie, Robert Abercrombie and William Murdoch back to Continent; all returned later as Jesuit missionaries.

Douglas, Archibald (c.1555–1588), **8th Earl of Angus** (1557), son of 7th Earl; ward of James, 4th Earl of Morton; on latter's fall was forfeited and fled to England; returned to Scotland after Ruthven Raid, but banished (1584), returning again (1585); patron of ultra-Protestant and Presbyterian party.

Douglas, James (c.1516–1581), **4th Earl of Morton,** joined Lords of the Congregation; Chancellor (1562); made Lieutenant General of the King's Forces by Regent Mar; 3rd Regent for James VI (1572–1577/8); executed for involvement in murder of Darnley.

Douglas, William (1532–1591), **9th Earl of Angus,** zealous supporter of Mary Queen of Scots.

Drury, Sir William, Marshall of Berwick, English Ambassador to Scotland (1567), commanded English army accompanying Lennox's return to Scotland (1570); attempted to intercede between Queen's and King's parties.

Du Croc, French Ambassador to Scotland, spoke for Confederates at Carberry begging Mary to abandon Bothwell.

Durie, John (c.1544–1588), one of the six taken by de Gouda to the Continent (1562) who returned as Jesuit missionaries; he converted Lord Maxwell, governor of Dumfries.

Eglinton, Earl of (see Montgomerie)

Elizabeth I (1533–1603), **Queen of England** (1558), daughter of Henry VIII and Anne Boleyn.

Elphinstone, James (1553–1612), **Master of Elphinstone**

Errol, Earl of (see Hay)

Erskine, John (c.1510–1572), **6th Baron Erskine** (1555), **1st Earl of Mar** (1565), official guardian of the young James VI in Stirling Castle; the 3rd Regent for James VI (1571–2).

Farnese, Alessandro (1546–1592), **3rd Duke of Parma**, nephew of Philip II of Spain, one of the great land-force commanders of his era; diplomat; joined his uncle in Spanish Netherlands; as governor-general, captured Antwerp (1585).

Fleming, John (c.1536–1572), **5th Lord** (1558), younger brother of 4th Lord, chamberlain for Mary Queen of Scots (1565); fought in Queen's Party; governor of Dumbarton Castle.

Fleming, Mary (1542–1600), daughter of 3rd Lord Fleming and an illegitimate daughter of James IV; one of the Queen's 'Four Marys'; married i) William Maitland of Lethington (1567), ii) George Meldrum of Fyvie.

Forbes, Arthur (d.1571) of Putachie (1559), known as 'Black Arthur,' son of 6th Lord Forbes by his 3rd wife, Elizabeth Barlow, brother of 7th Lord Forbes; married widow of 1st Lord Elphinstone; Baillie of Kildrummy on behalf of infant nephew, 3rd Lord Elphinstone; led Forbeses against the Gordons at Tillyangus, during which he was killed.

Forbes, Arthur (1550–1574) of Logie, 4th son of 7th Baron Forbes; killed in Paris attempting to assassinate Adam Gordon.

Forbes, John (1542–1606), **Master of Forbes, 8th Baron Forbes** (1594), 1st son of William, 7th Baron Forbes; married i) Margaret Forbes, 2nd daughter of 4th Earl of Huntly (1558, divorced 1574), ii) Janet Seton (1588); at Tillyangus, Craibstone; imprisoned in Spynie Palace (1571–3).

Forbes, John (d.1580) of Towie (or Tollie), held Corgarff Castle as tenant of Earl of Mar; married i) Daughter of John Grant of Ballindalloch, ii) Margaret Campbell, daughter of John Campbell of Cawdor, who died in burning of Corgarff Castle (1571).

Forbes, John (1570–1606), **9th Baron Forbes** (1594, **but since** rescinded), 2nd son of John, Master of Forbes (8th Baron Forbes) and Margaret Gordon; fled to Antwerp (1587); a Capuchin monk in Flanders (1593/4); for five weeks was the 9th Baron Forbes (later dismissed); studied philosophy and theology in Bruges; transferred to Lille to avoid being kidnapped by his family; his mother Margaret joined him there; later they both went to Antwerp; took his deceased brother's name of Brother Archangelus.

Forbes, William (1513–1594), 7th Baron Forbes (1547), 2nd son of 6th Baron Forbes; married Elizabeth Keith of Inverugie (1538); was a gentleman of James V's bedchamber (1539).

Forbes, William (1563–1592), eldest son of John, Master of Forbes, 8th Baron Forbes, and Margaret Gordon; went to fight in Low Countries, changing from Protestant to Catholic side under Duke of Parma; became a Capuchin monk (1589) and renamed Brother Archangelus.

Francis II (1544–1560), King of France (1559–1560), eldest son of Henri II and Catherine de Medici; betrothed in 1548 to five-year-old Mary Queen of Scots; married (1558).

Fraser, Sir Robert, Lord Lion Herald of Scotland, speared to death at Glenlivet and his royal ensign taken to Huntly Castle.

Fraser, Simon (c.1570–1633), 6th Baron Lovat (1576/7)

Glencairn, Earl of (see Cunningham)

Gordon, Sir Adam (d. c.1329) of Berwickshire; pledged homage to Edward I (1296); joined Wallace (1297); Warden of the Marches (1300); fined three years rent for previous opposition to Edward I; sent by Edward II to make peace with Scotland; backed Bruce against Balliol, then Comyn in his struggle for the throne; changed sides to support Scotland on eve of Bannockburn (1314); took Declaration of Arbroath to Rome for Robert I (1320), who granted him barony of Strathbogie (1320).

Gordon, Sir Adam, Baron Gordon (1400) (d.1402), succeeded his brother, Sir John Gordon; married Elizabeth Keith, 4th daughter of William Keith, Earl Marischal of Scotland and Margaret Fraser, only child and heiress of Sir Alexander Fraser, who held the territory of Aboyne and other lands in the shires of Aberdeen, Kincardine and Forfar; killed at Homildon Hill.

Gordon, Adam, Dean of Caithness (d.1528), 3rd son of Alexander, 1st Earl of Huntly, and Elizabeth Crichton, daughter of Lord Crichton, High Chancellor of Scotland.

Gordon, Adam, Lord Aboyne (b. before 1474–1537/8), later jure uxoris Earl of Sutherland, 2nd son of 2nd Earl of Huntly and his second wife Princess Anabella, 6th daughter of James I; married (1500) Lady Elizabeth Sutherland, suo jure Countess of Sutherland, on death of her brother John, 9th Earl(1509).

Gordon, Adam (1545–1580), laird of Auchindoun; 'Edom o'Gordon', 5th son of the 4th Earl of Huntly; escaped execution (1562); had charter from James Ogilvy of Find-later of lands of Auchindoun, Keithmore and others (1567); led Gordons at Tillyangus and Craibstone; burning of Corgarff; sold lands to brother, Patrick (1573).

Gordon, Sir Alexander (d.1348), son of Sir Adam Gordon of Berwickshire; assisted Robert the Bruce at Bannockburn (1314)

Gordon, Alexander (1501–1524), 3rd Earl of Huntly, Chancellor; married i) Jean Stewart (d.1510), daughter of John, Earl of Athol, ii) Elizabeth, daughter of Andrew, Lord Gray; put down disturbances in the Isles (1505); in great favour with James IV; gained grants of many lands; Lieutenant North of the Forth; Lieutenant of all Scotland except Argyll's bounds (1517–18); hereditary Sheriff of Inverness and Aberdeen; escaped Flodden.

Gordon, Alexander (c.1516–1575), younger brother of 4th Earl of Huntly; Bishop of Galloway (1559); titular Archbishop of Athens; the only consecrated bishop to join the Lords of the Congregation; later joined the Queen's party; had to make a public satisfaction to the assembly in 1575.

Gordon, Alexander (d.1553), eldest son of 4th Earl of Huntly; betrothed to Barbara, eldest daughter of Duke of Chatelherault.

Gordon, Alexander (1552–1594), 12th Earl of Sutherland, son of John, 11th Earl of Sutherland and Princess Annabella, daughter of James I of Scotland; just escaped being poisoned by Isabel Sinclair, wife of George Gordon of Garty, on instigation of her cousin, George, Earl of Caithness; married i) Barbara Sinclair, ii)Jean/Jane Gordon, 3rd daughter of 4th Earl of Huntly (1573).

Gordon, Alexander of Bothrom (d.1562), warden of Inverness Castle; executed by Mary Queen of Scotland because he refused her access to the castle.

Gordon, Catherine, known as 'The White Rose of Scotland'; daughter of 2nd Earl of Huntly; married in Huntly Castle to Perkin Warbeck, pretender to the English throne, supported by James IV.

Gordon, Elizabeth (d.1438/9), heiress of Strathbogie and Huntly, Berwickshire, daughter of Sir Adam Gordon and Elizabeth Keith; married Sir Alexander Seton, 2nd son of Lord Seton.

Gordon, Elizabeth, eldest daughter of 4th Earl of Huntly; married 4th Earl of Athol of Balvenie Castle; died shortly after marriage.

Gordon, Elizabeth (d.1606) of Findlater and Deskford, natural daughter of Adam Gordon, Dean of Caithness, son of Alexander, 1st Earl of Huntly; married i) Alexander Ogilvie of Deskford (1535), ii) John Gordon, 3rd son of 4th Earl of Huntly (1554).

Gordon, George of Seton (d.1502), 2nd Earl of Huntly (1470), son of Alexander Seton Gordon, 1st Earl of Huntly, and Margaret (or Elizabeth) Crichton; changed his name from Seton to Gordon; married i) Elizabeth Dunbar, daughter of James Dunbar, Earl of Moray and widow of Archibald Douglas, Earl of Moray (divorced 1471), ii) Princess Annabella Stewart, sister of James II (divorced), iii) Elizabeth Hay, daughter of 1st Earl of Errol; Keeper of the castles of Kildrummy, Kindrochat and Inverness; Judiciar North of the Forth (1479); Chancellor of Scotland (c.1498).

Gordon, George (1514–1562), 4th Earl of Huntly (1524), son of John, Master of Huntly and Margaret Stewart, natural daughter of James IV; married Elizabeth Keith (1530), daughter of Lord Robert Keith, sister of Earl Marischal; Privy Councillor (1535); gained lands and administration of earldoms of Mar and Moray (1548–9); Warden of the Marches, Vice Regent, Lieutenant of the North, Lieutenant General (1557); Chancellor (1546); Knight of the French order of St Michael (1550); Hereditary Baillie of the Bishopric of Aberdeen lands; at Hadden Rig (1542) and Pinkie (1547); Lieutenant General of Scotland (1557); died at Corrichie; corpse tried for treason (1563).

Gordon, George (1535–1576), 5th Earl of Huntly (1565), married Lady Anne Hamilton (1559); condemned for treason and imprisoned (1562); restored to favour (1565); Chancellor (1566–7); supported Mary against regents for James VI.

Gordon, George of Beldorney (d.1575), natural son of Adam Gordon, Dean of Caithness, who was son of 1st Earl of Huntly; brother of Elizabeth Gordon of Findlater and Deskford.

Gordon, George of Gight (d. c.1580), 3rd laird of Gight.

Gordon, George (1562–1636), **6th Earl of Huntly** (1576), **1st Marquis of Huntly, Earl of Enzie, Lord Gordon of Badenoch** (1599), son of 5th Earl of Huntly; married Henrietta Stewart, daughter of Esmé Stewart, Duke of d'Aubigny, Earl of Lennox; was a favourite of James VI; High Chamberlain and Lieutenant of the North; suspected of involvement in Catholic plots with Spain (Brig o' Dee and 'Spanish Blanks'); murdered 2nd Earl of Moray 'The Bonnie Earl of' (1592); fought against forces of the King at Glenlivet (1594); exiled until he submitted to Kirk; made Marquis; restored and embellished Huntly Castle (1602).

Gordon, James (c.1541–1620), 5th son of 4th Earl of Huntly; Jesuit priest; one of the six taken to Continent by de Gouda to train as Jesuits (1562); worked as professor of Hebrew and Divinity at Paris, Bordeaux, Rome, etc; returned to Scotland as a missionary priest; attempted to convert James VI; head of Scottish mission until after Glenlivet; imprisoned at least twice, lastly in Edinburgh Castle; close to nephew George, 6th Earl of Huntly.

Gordon, Jean (or Jane) (1545–1629), 3rd daughter of 4th Earl of Huntly; married i) James, Earl of Bothwell (1566; divorced 1567), ii) John, 12th Earl of Sutherland (1573), iii) Alexander Ogilvie of Boyne (1599).

Gordon, 'Jock' or John styled of Essie or Scurdargue, son of Sir John Gordon and Elizabeth Cruikshank of Aswanley (styled a natural son, but may be offspring of a 'handfasting' union, not considered illegitimate in the Highlands); married Elizabeth Maitland, daughter of Robert Maitland of Netherdale.

Gordon, Sir John (died 1395), re-granted the lands of Strathbogie by Robert II (1376); established Strathbogie as the main Gordon power base; not killed at Otterburn (as supposed), as witness to a charter in 1391; had two sons by Elizabeth Cruikshank of Aswanley, 'Jock' and 'Tam,' styled natural sons but may be offspring of a 'handfasting' union, therefore not considered illegitimate in the Highlands.

Gordon, John (d.1517) **Master of Huntly,** 1st son of 3rd Earl of Huntly and Jean Stewart; married Margaret Stewart, natural daughter of James IV (1510) and Margaret Drummond, with whom had a charter of Badenoch and other lands; predeceased his father.

Gordon, John (1525–1567), **11th Earl of Sutherland** (1537/8) by right of grandmother; married i) Elizabeth Campbell (1546), only daughter of Colin, 3rd Earl of Argyll, relict of James, Earl of Moray, ii) Helen Stewart, daughter of John, Earl of Lennox, widow of William Hay, 6th Earl of Errol, iii) Marion Seton, daughter of George, 4th Lord Seton, widow of John of Menteith. He and his last wife were poisoned by Isabel Sinclair.

Gordon, Sir John (Ogilvie) of Deskford (c.1538–1562), 3rd son of 4th Earl of Huntly; married Elizabeth Gordon, natural daughter of Adam Gordon, Dean of Caithness and widow of Alexander Ogilvie of Deskford (c.1554); executed in Aberdeen.

Gordon, John (1576–1615), **13th Earl of Sutherland**(1537/8), son of 12th Earl and Jean Gordon, daughter of 4th Earl of Huntly; married (1599/1600) Agnes Elphinstone, 1st daughter of Alexander, 4th Lord Elphinstone of Kildrummy, Lord

High Treasurer of Scotland (1600) and Jean Livingston, daughter of William, 6th Lord Livingston.

Gordon, John of Buckie (d. c.1640), master of James VI's household; involved in murder of 2nd Earl of Moray (slashed his face).

Gordon, Margaret, known as 'the White Rose of Scotland', daughter of the 2nd Earl of Huntly and Elizabeth Hay; married in Huntly Castle to Perkin Warbeck, pretender to the English throne, supported by James IV.

Gordon, Margaret (1544–1606), 2nd daughter of 4th Earl of Huntly; married John, Master of Forbes (1558); divorced (1574); cited in divorce of Sir John Gordon of Pitlurg and Isabel Forbes, her ex-sister-in-law; died in Flanders.

Gordon, Sir Patrick (d.1594) of Auchindoun (1590), 7th son of 4th Earl of Huntly; knighted about 1582; married Agnes, natural daughter of exiled Archbishop Beaton and widow of George Gordon of Gight; gained a charter of lands of Auchindoun and Keithmore (1590); sold them to Walter Ogilvy of Findlater (1592), who got a grant of them when Sir Patrick was forfeited and denounced a rebel for complicity with 6th Earl of Huntly in burning of Donibristle and murder of Earl of Moray (1592), Spanish Blanks and Glenlivet; married i) Agnes Betoun, ii)Mariota Ogilvy, widow of George Gordon of Gight; killed at Glenlivet.

Gordon, Sir Robert (1580–1656), of Gordonstoun (1609), 3rd son of 11th Earl of Sutherland and Jean Gordon, daughter of 4th Earl of Huntly; historian: *The Genealogical History of Earldom of Sutherland to 1603* (1813); Vice-Chamberlain of Scotland; Sheriff-Principal of county of Inverness; Lord of the Privy Council; Baronet of Nova Scotia (1625); tutor/guardian of his nephew, 13th Earl of Sutherland; went to London with James VI/I.

Gordon, Thomas, styled 'Tam o'Riven' or Ruthven (now in parish of Cairnie), son of Sir John Gordon and Elizabeth Cruitshank of Aswanley; married i) sister of Sir Thomas Hay of Enzie, ii) daughter of Sir Walter Innes of that Ilk, iii) daughter of Chisholm of Strathglass; said to have had sixteen sons.

Gordon, William (d.1577), 3rd son of 3rd Earl of Huntly, Bishop of Aberdeen (1545); remained un-Reformed.

Gowrie, earls of (see Ruthven)

Graham, David (d.1593), 6th of Fintray, son of Sir David Graham 5th of Fintry and Margaret Ogilvie of Airlie; nephew of Archbishop Beaton; hosted English Jesuit William Holt and Fr James Gordon; warded in Dundee; involved in the 'Spanish Blanks' incident; imprisoned in Edinburgh with George Kerr and Barclay of Ladyland; admitted Abercrombie had revealed Spanish plot to him; executed.

Graham, William (c.1500–1571), 2nd Earl of Montrose (1513)

Gray, Patrick (d.1612), Master of Gray, 6th Baron Gray (1609), in service of Mary Queen of Scots in France; spoke against Archbishop Beaton and Jesuits to James VI; plotted against Chancellor Arran.

Guise, Charles (1525–1574), prelate and Archbishop of Reims, Cardinal of Guise (1547), brother of Mary of Lorraine/Guise and Francis, 2nd Duke of Guise, with whom became all-powerful in reign of young Francis II; introduced the Inquisition to France; exerted great influence at the Council of Trent.

Guise, Francis, 2nd Duke (1519–1563), son of Claude, 1st Duke of Guise; brother of Cardinal Charles de Guise; shared the chief power in the state during reign of the young Francis II; headed Roman Catholic party which repressed Protestantism; brother of Mary of Guise, Queen Regent of Scotland.

Guise, Henri, 3rd Duke (1550–1588), French soldier and statesman; fought against Protestants; was one of the contrivers of the massacre of St Bartholomew's Day (1572); head of Holy League against Bourbons; assassinated.

Hamilton, Anna, 3rd daughter of Duke of Chatelherault; married George Gordon, 2nd son of 4th Earl of Huntly (1558), later the 5th Earl of Huntly (1565).

Hamilton, Claud (1543–1622), 4th son of Duke of Chatelherault, Commendator of Paisley, then Baron Paisley; ancestor of dukes of Abercorn.

Hamilton, James (c.1516–1575), 2nd Earl of Arran (1529), Duke of Chatelherault (1548), as heir presumptive, governor in Queen Mary's minority to 1554; figurehead of revolution (1559–60); rebelled against Mary on marriage to Darnley (1566); in exile to 1561; a leader of Queen's party until 1573.

Hamilton, James (1530–1609), eldest son of Duke of Chatelherault; styled 3rd Earl of Arran (after 1553).

Hamilton, James (1540–1580) of Bothwellhaugh, assassin of Regent Moray; escaped to France and worked in Mary's cause.

Hamilton, John (c.1511–1571), Archbishop of St Andrews, natural son of James Hamilton, 1st Earl of Arran.

Hamilton, John (1540–1604), 2nd son of Chatelherault, Commendator of Arbroath, 1st Marquis of Hamilton (1599)

Hay, Captain, Mary Queen of Scot's messenger; sent to Huntly Castle to demand 4th Earl of Huntly deliver it and Auchindoun, and also his cannon.

Hay, Edmund (c.1534–1591), came with de Gouda from the Continent and returned there with five others (1562) who all came back later as Jesuit missionaries; completed novitiate in Rome; returned to Scotland with Bishop of Dunblane as a papal envoy (1566); active with Esmé Stewart in 'Enterprise of England' plot.

Hay, Francis (1564–1631), 9th Earl of Errol (1585), active with 6th Earl of Huntly and Earl of Angus on behalf of RC and Spanish cause; incident of the 'Spanish Blanks'; in arms against force of James VI at Glenlivet.

Hay, Elizabeth (d.1510), daughter of 2nd Earl of Errol, third wife of 2nd Earl of Huntly.

Hay, George (d.1573/4), 7th Earl of Errol (1541)

Henri II (1519–1559), King of France (1547–1559), son of Francis I; aged fourteen, married Catherine de Medici, by whom had seven surviving children, three of whom became kings of France (Francis II, Charles IX and Henri III).

Hepburn, Adam (c.1530–1593) Bishop of Orkney (1559), joined Reformers and reformed his diocese; Lord of Session (1564); conducted marriage of Mary to Bothwell (1567); annointed James VI at his coronation; surrendered bishopric in favour of abbey of Holyrood (1568).

Hepburn, James (1536–1578), 4th Earl of Bothwell (1556), Duke of Orkney (1567); married i) Jean Gordon (1566), ii) Mary Queen of Scots (1567).

Hepburn, Patrick (d.1573), Bishop of Moray (1538)

Hepburn, Patrick, parson of Kinnoir, natural son of Bishop of Moray; great-nephew of 4th Earl of Bothwell; lover of Margaret Gordon, wife of John, Master of Forbes.

Holt, William, English Jesuit; sent to Scotland in 1574 to investigate the possibility of mission and several other times, reporting back to Spanish ambassador,

Mendoza, who liaised with Philip II; kidnapped to be sent back to England, but freed by James VI.

Home (or Hume), Alexander (1566–1619), 6th Baron (1578) and 1st Earl of Home (1604/5)

Howard, Thomas (1536–1572), 4th Duke of Norfolk (1554), son of Henry Howard, Earl of Surrey; imprisoned (1569–70) for attempting to marry Mary; executed for plot with Philip II to free and then marry her.

James I (1394–1437), 2nd son of Robert III; detained in England (1406–24); murdered at Perth (1437).

James IV (1473–1513), King of Scotland (1488–1513), married Margaret Tudor, sister of Henry VIII; killed at Flodden.

James V (1512–1542), son of James IV and Margaret Tudor; imprisoned by step-father, 6th Earl of Angus (1526–8); married i) Madeleine (1537). ii) Mary of Guise (1538); died three weeks after Solway Moss.

James VI (1566–1625), King of Scotland (1567–1625), King of England (1603–1625), son of Mary Queen of Scots and Darnley; on enforced abdication of his mother, reigned with four regencies (Moray, Lennox, Mar and Morton); married Anne of Denmark (1574–1619); began to direct policy in 1585.

Keith, Agnes (d.1588), eldest daughter of William, 4th Earl Marischal; married James Stewart, Earl of Moray (1562).

Keith, Elizabeth of Aboyne, daughter of William Keith, Marischal of Scotland; niece and heritrix of Lord Fraser of Touch (Stirlingshire); married Sir Adam Gordon.

Keith, Elizabeth, of Inverugie, Lady Forbes, married William, 7th Baron Forbes (1538).

Keith, Elizabeth (d.1568), Countess of Huntly (1524), eldest daughter of Lord Robert Keith; sister of William, 4th Earl Marischal; married 4th Earl of Huntly (1530).

Keith, William (1507–1581), 4th Earl Marischal (c.1527–1581), brother of Elizabeth Keith, Countess of Huntly; was a recluse living in Dunnotar Castle.

Kennedy, John (1574–1615), 5th Earl of Cassilis (1576)

Kerr, George, a Catholic emissary to the court of Spain; arrested with a bundle of letters, the 'Spanish Blanks', bound for Spain.

Kerr, Sir Thomas (d.1586), laird of Ferniehurst (1562), 4th Earl of Huntly's chief counsellor; supported Queen's party; was provost of Edinburgh (1570) when it was ascendant; after a period in France with Adam Gordon, returned to join administration of James Stewart, Earl of Arran.

Kerr, Walter (d. c.1582) of Ferniehurst, Warden of the Marches; active against Mary Queen of Scots 1568–72.

Killigrew, Sir Henry, English Ambassador; mediated between Queen's party and King's party and brought about the Pacification of Perth (1573).

Kirkcaldy, Sir William of Grange (c.1520–1573), Fifeshire laird and soldier; assassin of Cardinal Beaton; at Corrichie; joined rebellion against Mary and Bothwell (1567); pursued Bothwell to Shetland; Keeper of Edinburgh Castle; changed sides to hold it for Mary (1571–3); hanged after its fall.

Lennox (see Stewart)

Leslie, Andrew (1530–1611), 5th Earl of Rothes (1558)

Leslie, John (1531–1569/70)

Leslie, John (c.1527–1596), son of a priest who was an ecclesiastical judge; parson of Oyne, Bishop of Ross (1566); historian; trained in Toulouse, Poitiers and Paris; Lord of Session (1564); emissary of Mary; acted for her at York and Westminster (1568–9); wrote 'A Defence of the Honour of Mary'; involved in a plot against Elizabeth I and imprisoned for a time; went to France where he was made Vicar General of the Archdiocese of Rouen and was raised to the See of Coutances, in Normandy (1592); his *History of Scotland* (1578) was a standard authority for many years.

Lindsay, David (1524–1574), 10th Earl of Crawford (1558)

Lindsay, David (c.1547–1607), 11th Earl of Crawford (1574)

Lindsay, Patrick, 6th Lord Lindsay of the Byres (d.1589); supported Reformation; in plot to murder Riccio; active in compelling Mary to abdicate; took part in Ruthven Raid.

Lindsay, Robert (c.1532–1580) **of Pitscottie**, historian; author of *History and Chronicles of Scotland* (1436–1575), which reflects his Protestant outlook.

Livingstone, William (1528–1592), 5th Lord, father of Mary Livingstone, one of the Queen's 'Four Marys'.

Lords of the Congregation, dates from the First Bond of December 1557; the term is generally applied to the leaders of the Protestant revolution of 1559–60.

MacLean, Lachlan of Duart, 14th chief of MacLean, at Glenlivet in Argyll's force of Highlanders; captured Errol's Pennant and then the Gordon standard, having spiked the horse and sliced the bearer in two.

Maitland, Sir John (1543–1595) **of Thirlestane**, younger brother of Maitland of Lethington; Secretary of State (1584); Chancellor (1587–92, 1594–5); made 1st Baron Thirlestane (1591); introduced the 'Golden Acts', which legally established Presbyterianism (1592).

Maitland, William (c.1525–1573) **of Lethington**, Secretary of State for Mary Queen of Scots (1558–73); joined Reformers because of devotion to Anglo-Scottish amity; married Mary Fleming, one of the Queen's 'Four Marys'; sided with Moray after Mary's abdication, but later joined the Queen's Party; captured when Edinburgh Castle fell and possibly hastened death by poison.

Malcolm III (c.1031–1093), called 'Canmore', son of Duncan I; overthrew Macbeth (1057) and Lulach at Essie, Strathbogie (1058), creating kingdom of Scotland; submitted to William the Conqueror (1072).

Mary of Guise and Lorraine (1515–1560), daughter of Claude of Lorraine, 1st Duke of Guise; married i) Louise of Orleans, Duke of Longueville (1534) who died (1537), ii) James V (1538) at whose death (1542) she was left with one child, Mary Queen of Scots; Queen Regent/Governor (1554); lenient to Reformers until 1559; influenced by the Guises; pursued policy of French domination of Scotland; Protestant nobles rose in rebellion (1559), which continued up to her death in Edinburgh Castle.

Mary Queen of Scots (1542–1587), daughter of James V and Mary of Guise; married i) the Dauphin Francis (1558) who became King Francis II (1559) but who died young (1560); returned to Scotland (1561); married Lord Darnley (1565); son James born (1566); Darnley murdered (1567); married James, Earl of Bothwell (1567); surrendered to rebels; abdicated while imprisoned in Lochleven Castle; escaped (1568); defeated at Langside (1568); fled to England, where imprisoned until executed (1587).

Maxwell, Sir John of Terregles (1512–1583), 2nd son of 5th Lord Maxwell and in right of wife became 4th Baron Herries, Warden of West Marches (1552); rallied to Mary after murder of Riccio; commanded her cavalry at Langside.

Maxwell, John (or James), 8th Lord (1553–1593), created Earl of Morton (1581) (Governor of Dumfries); Warden of West Marches; warded for allowing forbidden Catholic activities in his domains; brought gold from Philip II; imprisoned after a premature rising in Galloway.

Melville, Andrew (1545–1622), educational reformer; professor at Geneva and Glasgow; principal of St Mary's; uncle of James Melville the diarist; Moderator of General Assembly (1578); with others compiled Second Book of Discipline; summoned but escaped to England (1584).

Melville, Sir James of Halhill (1535–1617), employed on diplomatic missions to England 1564 and later; wrote *Memoirs of his Own Time* with vivid but sometimes misleading narrative.

Melville, James (1556–1614), Scottish Reformer and diarist; nephew of Andrew Melville; was in England 1584–5 and again from 1606; was sent by James VI to inform English ambassador Bowes and Edinburgh ministers of measures he was taking against Huntly after Glenlivet; was rightly cynical that they would be carried out; Moderator of the General Assembly (1589); best known for *Autobiography and Diary, 1556–1601*.

Melville, Sir Robert (1527–1621), brother of Sir James of Halhill; in Queen Mary's army at Langside; Treasurer Deputy (1581); Lord of Session (1594).

Montgomerie, Hugh (c.1531–1585), 3rd Earl of Eglinton (1546)

Montrose (see Graham)

Moray (see Stewart)

Morton (see Douglas)

Murdoch, William (1539–1616), one of the six taken to the Continent by de Gouda and returned later as Jesuit missionaries to Scotland; took over from Fr James Gordon as head of mission after Glenlivet; put on trial for saying mass at Dunrobin and other Catholic houses.

Norfolk, Duke of (see Howard)

Ogilvie, Alexander of Boyne (1530–1602?), married i) Mary Beaton, one of the Queen's 'Four Marys' (1566), ii) Jean Gordon, daughter of 4th Earl of Huntly (1599).

Ogilvie, Alexander of Deskford and Findlater (d.1554), gained a charter of Auchindoun and other lands in Banffshire from grandfather; married i) Janet Abernethy, daughter of James, 3rd Lord Saltoun, ii) Elizabeth Gordon (1535), natural daughter Adam Gordon, Dean of Caithness, natural son of 1st Earl of Huntly; disinherited his son, James Ogilvie of Cardell by Janet Abernethy in favour of John Gordon, 3rd son of 4th Earl of Huntly.

Ogilvie, Lord James of Airlie, Ogilvie clan chief; Master of Queen Mary's household; lost an arm in fracas with Sir John Gordon of Findlater (1562).

Ogilvie, James of Cardell and Findlater (d. c.1574), 1st son of Alexander Ogilvie of Findlater and Janet Abernethy; Master of the Queen's Household for Mary of Guise and then Mary Queen of Scots (1562–7).

Parma (see Farnese)

Parsons, Robert (1546–1610), English Jesuit who accompanied Edmund Campion (later canonised) in mission to aid English Catholics; supported Philip II's claim to English throne; rector of the English college in Rome.

Philip II (1527–1598), **King of Spain** (1556) on his father Emperor Charles V's abdication; married i) Infanta Mary of Portugal, who died giving birth to Don Carlos (1546), ii) Mary I of England; remained in Flanders until his father's death (1558); was a champion of religious orthodoxy through the Inquisition; war against France and the papacy (1557–9) and against the Turks in the Mediterranean (1560).

Preston, Sir Simon of Craigmillar (d.1570), Provost of Edinburgh 1538–43, 1544–5 and 1560); Ggovernor of Dunbar Castle, where he had charge of George Gordon, 2nd son of 4th Earl of Huntly; Mary Queen of Scots lodged in his house after Carberry.

Randolph, Thomas (1523–1590), English ambassador to Scotland 1559–66, 1570–2, 1581, 1586.

Riccio, David (c.1533–1566), came to Scotland with Savoy ambassador; employed by Mary Queen of Scots (1561) as musician and then foreign secretary (1564); murdered in Palace of Holyrood.

Robert I (the Bruce) (1274–1329), **King of Scotland** (1306–1329), on the English side against Balliol, but joined Wallace's rising; married i) Isabell, daughter of Earl of Mar, ii) Elizabeth, daughter of Earl of Ulster, who bore David II; submitted to Edward I (1302) but renewed resistance after murder of John Comyn; defeated Edward II at Bannockburn (1514).

Robert II (1316–1390), Son of Walter, 6th High Stewart of Scotland and Margery, daughter of Robert I; succeeded David II (1371).

Rothes, Earl of (see Leslie)

Ruthven, John (c.1577–1600) 3rd Earl of Gowrie, succeeded elder brother; killed as a result of the Gowrie Conspiracy.

Ruthven, Patrick (1520–1566), 3rd Baron Ruthven (1552), took part in murder of Riccio; died in England.

Ruthven, William (c.1541–1584), 4th Baron Ruthven (1566) 1st Earl of (1581), associated with father, 3rd Lord Ruthven, in Riccio murder; Treasurer 1571; instigated Ruthven Raid, holding James VI captive for ten months (1582); executed after attempt to regain ascendancy.

Saltoun, Baron of (see Abernethy)

Semphill, Robert (d.1572), 3rd Baron, supported Mary of Guise against Lords of Congregation; later supported Mary Queen of Scots after her marriage to Darnley, but joined Confederate Lords (1567).

Seton, Sir Alexander, Lord of Gordon (d.1440/1), younger son of Sir William Seton of Lothian; married Elizabeth Gordon, daughter of Sir Adam Gordon and Elizabeth Keith; confirmed in the Gordon lands in both Berwickshire and Strathbogie by Regent Albany; fought at Harlaw (1411) and wars in France (1421), assisting Dauphin with Scottish forces; was one of ten commissioners sent to treat with Henry V for release of James I; became a hostage for his ransom (1424).

Seton, Sir Alexander (II) (d.1470), 1st Earl of Huntly (1445), 1st son of Sir Alexander de Seton and Elizabeth Gordon; built Strathbogie Castle; married i) Jean, granddaughter and heiress of Sir William de Keith, Marishal of Scotland, ii) Egidia Hay (1444) daughter and heiress of Sir John Hay of Tullibody, who bore him one son, ancestor of the Setons of Touch, iii) Margaret Crichton, daughter of 1st Lord

Crichton, Chancellor of Scotland (and therefore de facto ruler) for much of James II's minority; obliged to take name and bear arms of Gordon; charter to himself and his wife of the lordship of Gordon in Berwickshire, Strathbogie, and (from his mother's estates) the lands of Aboyne, Glentanner and Glenmuick in Aberdeenshire, with Panbride in Forfar life rent; lent money to the King and received charter for lordship of Badenoch and castle of Ruthven (1451); overcame Douglas faction on behalf of the King.

Seton, Alexander (III), son of 1st Earl of Huntly and Egidia Hay; inherited Fraser lands of Touch in Stirlingshire, founding family of the Setons of Touch; also inherited his mother's baronies of Tullybothwell (Perthshire), Kinmundy (Buchan) and Panbride (Angus).

Seton, George (c.1530–1585) 5th Baron Seton, provost of Edinburgh (1557–9); strongly supported Mary; captured at Langside.

Seton, Janet, 2nd wife of John, Master of Forbes, 8th Baron Forbes.

Sinclair, Barbara (d. c.1573), daughter of 4th Earl of Caithness; forcibly married aged 32 by her father to Alexander Gordon, 12th Earl of Sutherland, aged 15; he divorced her 1572 on grounds of adultery with Mackay of Far.

Sinclair, George (c.1520–1582), 4th Earl of Caithness (1529), made Alexander Gordon his ward and forced him to marry his 32-year-old daughter Barbara.

Sinclair, George (c.1566–1643), 5th Earl of Caithness (1582)

Sinclair, Isabel, poisoned her nephew John, 11th Earl of Sutherland and his countess in an attempt to gain the earldom and estates for her own son, who was 2nd heir; by mistake, her son took and died from the poison meant for the earl's son, Alexander, who escaped and succeeded as 12th Earl and married Jean Gordon, daughter of 4th Earl of Huntly.

Stewart, Esmé (c.1542–1583), Seigneur d'Aubigny, 7th Earl (1579/80) and 1st Duke (1581) of Lennox, came to Scotland in 1579; became a favourite of James VI; Commendator of Arbroath Abbey and Keeper of Dumbarton Castle; became a focus for foreign intrigue with 'the Enterprise of England'.

Stewart, Francis (1563–1612) 5th Earl of Bothwell (1581), son of John Stewart, illegitimate son of James V and Jean, sister of 4th Earl of Bothwell; accused of dealing with witches for destruction of King; several times attacked royal residencies.

Stewart, James (1531–1570) 1st Earl of Moray (1563), natural son of James V by Margaret Erskine; Commendator of St Andrews Priory (1538); joined insurgents (1559); prominent in government of Queen Mary until her marriage to Darnley; created Earl of Mar (1662); married Agnes Keith, daughter of Earl Marischal (1562); Regent of Scotland (1567); assassinated by James Hamilton of Bothwellhaugh.

Stewart, James (c.1545–1596) Earl of Arran (1581), 'the Bonnie Earl', 2nd son of 2nd Baron Ochiltree; soldier on the Continent; rose to prominence as Earl of Arran on grounds of insanity of Hamilton 3rd Earl and his wife's descent from 1st Earl; Chancellor and head of administration (1584–5); overthrown (1585); murdered.

Stewart, James (c.1560–1592), 2nd Earl of Moray ('the Bonnie Earl'), 2nd son of Sir James Stewart of Doune; married daughter of Regent Moray and Agnes Keith (1580) and styled Earl of Moray; became a favourite of ultra-Protestant faction; murdered by 6th Earl of Huntly and Gordon of Buckie at Donibristle.

Stewart, John (1518–1579), 4th Earl of Athol (1542)

Stewart, John (1563–1595), 5th Earl of Athol

Stewart, Ludovic (1574–1624), 2nd Duke of Lennox (1583), 1st Duke of Richmond (1623), son of Esme Stewart; brother of Henrietta Stewart, Marquess of Huntly (1599).

Stewart, Matthew (1516–1571), **4th Earl of Lennox** (1526), **Regent of Scotland** (1570), forfeited and exiled in England for being an English agent (1545); married Margaret Douglas, daughter of Margaret Tudor by 6th Earl of Angus (1544), making their son, Lord Darnley, next in line to English throne after Mary; returned to Scotland 1564, but returned to England after murder of Darnley; returned with English army under Drury when Elizabeth chose him as Regent after murder of Moray; shot in an affray at Stirling.

Stewart, Robert (1339–1420) **1st Duke of Albany** (1398), 3rd son of Robert II; Earl of Fife and Menteith by marriage and inheritance; Chamberlain (1382–1408); governor of Scotland on behalf of aged father (1388); dominant during reign of Robert II and suspected of causing death of the heir, David, Duke of Rothesay; governor during captivity of James I (from 1406).

Strathbogie, David of, 10th Earl of Athol, hereditary Constable of Scotland; turned against Bruce on eve of Bannockburn; as a result lost lands of Strathbogie to Adam Gordon of Berwickshire.

Sussex, Earl of, mediated truce (1570) between Queen's party and King's party.

Sutherland, Lady Elizabeth suo jure Countess of Sutherland (1515) (d.1535), daughter of John, 8th Earl of Sutherland; married 2nd cousin, Adam Gordon of Aboyne, later jure uxoris Earl of Sutherland, 2nd son of George Gordon, 2nd Earl of Huntly by 3rd wife, Elizabeth Hay; her father (d.1508) and brother John, 9th Earl (d.1514) considered insane; her illegitimate half-brother, Alexander, challenged the decision to pass him over and twice took over Dunrobin Castle.

Throgmorton, Sir Nicholas (1515–1576), **English Ambassador to Scotland** (1565–1567)

Tudor, Margaret (1489–1541), **Queen of Scots** (1501–1524), daughter of Henry VII of England; married i) James IV (1503), ii) Archibald Douglas, 6th Earl of Angus (1514; divorced 1526), iii) Henry Stewart (1526); tutrix of James V; warded George Gordon, 4th Earl of Huntly.

Tyrie, James (1543–1597), one of the six who went to the Continent with de Gouda (1562) and returned later as Jesuit missionaries; tried to get James VI freed from Ruthven Raiders; imprisoned in Tower of London for two years; put in charge of Scottish Jesuit missionaries.

Walsingham, Sir Francis (c.1530–1590), English statesman, ambassador to Scotland (1583); one of the principal secretaries of state to Queen Elizabeth I; efficient spymaster; trapped Queen Mary, resulting in her execution in 1587.

William I (1143–1214), known, without satisfactory evidence, as 'The Lion'; 2nd son of Earl Henry, son of David I; succeeded Malcolm IV (1165).

Wishart, George (c1513–1546), Protestant martyr; burnt at St Andrews by order of Cardinal Beaton.

Index